WITHDRAWN

WITHDRAWN

WITHDRAWN

D0874642

The End of Parliamentary Socialism

The End of Parliamentary Socialism

From New Left to New Labour

LEO PANITCH and COLIN LEYS

SECOND EDITION

including an epilogue co-written with David Coates

VERSO

London • New York

First published by Verso 1997
© Leo Panitch and Colin Leys 1997
This second edition published by Verso 2001
© Leo Panitch and Colin Leys 2001
All rights reserved

The moral rights of the authors have been asserted

Verso
UK: 6 Meard Street, London W1F 0EG
USA: 180 Varick Street, New York NY 10014–4606

Verso is the imprint of New Left Books
www.versobooks.com

ISBN 1–85984–338–7

British Library Cataloguing in Publication Data
A catalogue record for this book is available from the British Library

Library of Congress Cataloging-in-Publication Data
A catalog record for this book is available from the Library of Congress

Typeset in 10pt Stemple Garamond by
SetSystems Ltd, Saffron Walden, Essex
Printed by Biddles Ltd, Guildford and King's Lynn

To the memory of Ralph Miliband

Contents

Abbreviations

AES	Alternative Economic Strategy
ASLEF	Associated Society of Locomotive Engineers and Firemen
ASTMS	Association of Scientific, Technical and Managerial Staffs
AUEW	Amalgamated Union of Engineering Workers
BFAWU	Bakers, Food and Allied Workers Union
CAC	Conference Arrangements Committee
CBI	Confederation of British Industry
CCD	Campaigns and Communications Directorate
CDP	Community Development Project
CDS	Campaign for Democratic Socialism
CLP	Constituency Labour Party
CLPD	Campaign for Labour Party Democracy
CLV	Campaign for Labour Victory
CND	Campaign for Nuclear Disarmament
CSE	Conference of Socialist Economists
CSEU	Confederation of Shipbuilding and Engineering Unions
DATA	Draughtsmen and Allied Technicians Association
DFEE	Department of Education and Employment
DTI	Department of Trade and Industry
EEC	European Economic Community
EEPTU	Electrical, Electronic, Telecommunications and Plumbing Union
EU	European Union
FBU	Fire Brigades Union
GDP	Gross Domestic Product
GLC	Greater London Council
GMC	General Management Committee
GMWU (or GMB)	General and Municipal Workers Union
GNP	Gross National Product
ILP	Independent Labour Publications
IMF	International Monetary Fund

IMG	International Marxist Group
IPPR	Institute for Public Policy Research
IS	International Socialists
IWC	Institute for Workers' Control
JPC	Joint Policy Committee
LCC	Labour Coordinating Committee
MI5	British Security Service
NATO	North Atlantic Treaty Organisation
NEB	National Enterprise Board
NEC	National Executive Committee
NEDC	National Economic Development Council
NHS	National Health Service
NPF	National Policy Forum
NUM	National Union of Mineworkers
NUPE	National Union of Public Employees
OECD	Organisation for Economic Cooperation and Development
OMOV	One Member One Vote
OPEC	Organisation of Petroleum Exporting Countries
PASOK	Greek Socialist Party
PLP	Parliamentary Labour Party
PMO	Prime Minister's Office
PPS	Parliamentary Private Secretary
PR	Proportional Representation
PS	French Socialist Party (Parti socialiste)
PSBR	Public Sector Borrowing Requirement
RFMC	Rank and File Mobilising Committee
RMT	National Union of Rail, Maritime and Transport Workers
SAP	Swedish Social Democratic Workers Party
SCA	Shadow Communications Agency
SDP	Social Democratic Party (UK)
SPD	German Social Democratic Party
TASS	Technical, Administrative and Supervisory Section (AUEW)
TGWU (or T&G)	Transport and General Workers Union
TUC	Trades Union Congress
TULV	Trade Unions for a Labour Victory
UCATT	Union of Construction, Allied Trades and Technicians
UCS	Upper Clyde Shipbuilders
UNISON	Public Service Union
USDAW	Union of Shop, Distributive and Allied Workers

Preface to the Second Edition

The preface to the first edition of this book was written one month after Labour's election victory on 1 May 1997. In it we wondered aloud whether New Labour in office would prove our analysis wrong, and its promise of national renewal via a 'third way' justified. Three years later, it seems to us that the central argument of the book has been rather strongly vindicated, especially its crucial conclusion on the issue of democracy: 'the eventual defeat of the new left in the party removed the issue of a genuine democratisation of the state and the economy from the agenda of British politics ... The Labour new left saw that democratising the state was a precondition for overcoming the injustices of capitalism, and that democratising the party ... was a precondition for democratising the state.' Despite New Labour's rhetoric of pluralism and participation, the thrust of its policies has clearly been in the opposite direction, and after two decades of Conservative rule there has not been any reversal of the shift in class power that took place during the long winter of Thatcherism. We review the evidence for this in an Epilogue to this new edition written in collaboration with David Coates, to whom we are greatly indebted for contributing his expertise on Labour government policy.

24 October 2000

Preface to the First Edition

This book has been a long time in the making. As originally conceived over a decade ago, it aimed to offer a critical analysis of the conflicts produced in the Labour Party by disappointment with the performance of the Labour Governments of the 1960s and 1970s; and especially to understand the significance of the defeat of the 'Bennite' left's attempt to shake the party out of its 'dogmatic adherence' to a conventionally narrow brand of parliamentarism which, as Ralph Miliband pointed out, had always severely constrained the possibility of socialist advance in Britain. The work bore fruit in a long essay in the *Socialist Register of 1988*, but other pressing tasks intervened, new events outpaced the research, and the draft book manuscript – already rather long and still only two-thirds finished – was left to the 'gnawing criticism of the mice'.

When, however, Tony Blair's election as Labour leader in July 1994 opened the way to the full realisation of the 'modernisers" project, it soon became clear that the story of the end of parliamentary socialism, covering the whole span of the transition from 'new left' to 'New Labour', still needed to be told. The modernisers' claim to be doing no more than applying socialist values to changed circumstances could not be properly assessed in the absence of a systematic analysis of what they were replacing – including, especially, the earlier 'Bennite' project, to which the modernisers particularly liked to contrast their own.

Our aim in this book, then, is to analyse what has happened to the Labour Party as a chapter in the history of socialism. We do not believe that that history is over; and there are, we think, some important lessons to be learned from the way the party confronted the choice between socialism and capitalism when the crunch came. We have tried to indicate with as much objectivity as possible what we think some of these lessons are.

The book was completed on May Day 1997, on the occasion of Labour's landslide election victory; if any mainstream commentators noted the irony of the fact that this was the day chosen by the European socialist parties a hundred years earlier to symbolise the coming self-empowerment of the working class, they forbore to say so. Labour's stunning electoral triumph nevertheless provides a fitting dénouement to the events recorded in this book. For although the big swing in votes owed a good deal to the Conservatives' complacency, corruption and errors of judgement (especially over Europe), it owed at least as much to the Labour modernisers' ruthless redesign of party policy to win back former Conservative voters in the marginal seats of 'middle England'. In these terms, New Labour's success was spectacular; the Conservative Party stood revealed as a parliamentary rump, unrepresented outside England, lacking a credible organisational base, and increasingly isolated from traditional sources of support in the City, the press and the intelligentsia. New Labour had definitively ended the Thatcherite era – or had it?

Writing in *The Guardian* on 4 February 1997, three months before the election, Victor Keegan reviewed New Labour's economic policy stance and concluded that 'in all essentials the Conservatives [had] set the parameters for the incoming [Labour] administration in a way that no other outgoing government in recent memory has been able even to dream about'. It was, he said, 'as if the Conservatives were contracting out the business of government while they set about resolving their own power struggles and self-destructing attitudes to Europe'. Only time will show how far this judgement was correct, and how far the Labour Party is now anything more than an alternative manager of the market-driven, inequality-riven society inherited from the Thatcher era, rather than the instrument of 'national renewal' promised in New Labour rhetoric.

Events were propitious for the New Labour Government to show what its promised 'radicalism of the centre' really meant. With a majority of 187 seats it faced no serious parliamentary obstacles. The financial markets smiled on it; unemployment continued to fall; and the difficult choice presented by the impending European common currency seemed likely to be at least postponed, or modified, thanks to the French Socialists' election victory on 1 June and the German Government's growing difficulties in meeting the Maastricht convergence criteria. In fact there seemed to be hardly any rocks on the new Government's chosen path; the question was only, how far was it really a different trail from the one blazed by Mrs Thatcher?

As the answer becomes clearer, the importance of the events recorded in this book will, we believe, become clearer too. For almost a century the Labour Party was committed to 'parliamentary socialism', with all its limitations; with the 1997 election, that commitment was finally abandoned. We need to reckon with this: to consider what 'parliamentary socialism' was, and why it failed; and to understand what the Bennite new left's attempt to transcend it amounted to, and what lessons may be learned from its defeat for the construction of a new socialist project.

A word on the nature of our co-authorship may be in order, especially in light of the various stages through which this book has passed. Although we have worked over every chapter together, Chapters 2 through 9 were written by Panitch, Chapters 10 and 11 were written by Leys, and Chapters 1 and 12 were written jointly. Many people have helped us generously with their time and expertise. If we don't try to name here all the Labour Party officials, politicians and activists who have done so, it is not only because we don't want to leave anyone out inadvertently, but also because it seems possible that being publicly thanked for having provided us with help might risk damaging some people's careers – which, if true, itself says something significant about the passage from new left to New Labour. The people who have helped us know who they are; we hereby very sincerely thank them anonymously and collectively.

We hope, however, that we will cause no embarrassment by thanking the following individuals for the help and insights they provided at various stages during the course of this study: Neil Belton, Caroline Benn, Robin Blackburn, Alan Cave, David Coates, Ken Coates, Vladimir and Vera Derer, Roy Greene, Richard Heffernan, Mike Hobday, Jon Lansman, Neal Lawson, David Marquand, Mike Marqusee, Lewis Minkin, Jim Mortimer, Geoff Mulgan, Colin Robinson, Geoff Sheridan, Ruth Winstone and Barry Winter. We also want to thank Sebastian Budgen, Alan Clarke, Donald Swartz and Ian Taylor for the valuable comments they provided on various drafts. York and Queen's Universities, the Social Science and Humanities Research Council of Canada and the Canada Council's Killam Program provided financial support and in particular made it possible for us to secure the research assistance of Chris Boyle, Bob Marshall, Alan Zuege and, above all, Cara Macdonald, whose tireless and outstanding research and editorial contribution were crucial to the completion of the book.

We are deeply grateful, as well, to Marion Kozak, to Sam Gindin and John Saul, to Adam Leys and Nancy Leys Stepan, and to Melanie, Maxim and Vida Panitch; we could not have done without their affection, support and encouragement. And last but not least, for what they too gave us in these respects, but also for their great material help and profound insights, we are especially indebted to Tony Benn and Hilary Wainwright, and to the late Ralph Miliband, to whose memory the book is respectfully and affectionately dedicated.

3 June 1997

1

From New Left to New Labour

The collapse of the post-war settlement in the late 1960s was a critical turning point in the history of the capitalist countries of the west. The response of the 'new right' was to call for the removal of restrictions on private capital accumulation and capitalist culture, and as far as possible to replace collective decision-making by the operation of markets. The new right soon gained the ascendancy within the conservative parties of the west, which allowed it to reach outwards as a coherent political force, gain office and embark on the market-oriented reconstruction of social, economic and political life that has characterised the past two decades. The response of the 'new left', on the other hand, was to call for 'socialising' capital and democratising the economy and the state. Its fate was to be comprehensively resisted and ultimately defeated.

An important version of the new left project arose within the British Labour Party. Unlike the Conservative Party, which succumbed relatively quickly to 'Thatcherism', the Labour Party was extremely resistant to change. Most of its leaders were wedded to a conception of the state in which ordinary people were passive 'clients of a state over which [they] have no real . . . control', as Stuart Hall noted in a famous essay shortly before the 1979 election. The Labour new left not only proposed to change this: they also saw the need, as a prerequisite of changing the state, to change the party – to give it too 'a more broadly mass and democratic character', to make it capable of shaping a progressive solution to the crisis, winning support for it, and carrying it through in office.[1] These objectives were bound to be bitterly opposed; and the defenders of the status quo proved, as Hall predicted, too deeply entrenched, and the struggle too traumatic, for the project to succeed. The Labour new left's energies were exhausted by it; what they had to offer to the wider society was submerged in the intra-party conflict.

This book is about this project – how it emerged, what it stood for, why it was defeated and what succeeded it: the 'New Labour' Party elected in May 1997 (imitating the American Democrats' use of 'new' to signify a 'new improved' brand of conventional electoralism). Part of our aim in reviewing this story now is historical restitution. The Labour new left's social base, the characteristic backgrounds of its activists, their diagnosis of the crisis and their ideas for solving it were not only caricatured and vilified at the time, but have been deliberately and further misrepresented since. It is not surprising that people with a political interest in writing the Labour new left out of history should do this, but they should not be treated as serious and objective thinkers when doing so.

But a more important reason for writing this book is that free market capitalism has once again begun to show itself to be an unstable and, for growing numbers of people, an intolerable response to the crisis of the post-war system. Inequality has been restored to Victorian levels.[2] By 1996, 32 per cent of all children were living in poverty (i.e., in households with less than half average income). More and more work is part-time and/or casual, and relative wages for young people have fallen. Long-term unemployment has risen sharply, and youth unemployment has risen to twice the national average, feeding an alienated culture of marginalisation and crime. Working hours have become the longest in the OECD. Insecurity has risen while state-provided social services are being cut back. In face of these developments popular acceptance of the idea that free market capitalism is 'natural' and inevitable has begun to falter. In various ways, and however hesitantly, people have begun to return to the view that markets must again be made to serve social purposes, not the other way round.

Constructing a new project on these lines is hampered, however, by the belief that no viable alternative to 'market society' now exists. Of course, theoretical alternatives to global free market capitalism have been proposed, but they have various shortcomings. For instance, models of 'market socialism' and 'participatory democracy' tend to be rather abstract, and generally fail to suggest how they could be realised.[3] Ideas based on 'networking' between the multiple types of new social movement identify important needs and aspirations and have the great merit of building on real social forces; but they tend to lack organisational integration and programmatic breadth.[4] If we are to find workable and persuasive alternatives to late-twentieth-century global capitalism we need at least to examine objectively the most recent democratic socialist project to have emerged in practice, and to learn what we can from it. That the project was imperfect goes without saying – its limitations and defects contributed heavily to its defeat – but it remains important to identify and reclaim what was original and valid in it, as well as its real flaws.

What came to be called the 'new left' in Britain emerged in 1956.[5] It sought to launch a new socialist alternative to democratic-centralist communism and parliamentary social democracy. It never succeeded in spawning a political party to act as the vehicle for this project, yet its leading figures were and remained highly sceptical of any possibility of turning the Labour Party into such a vehicle. Ralph Miliband, whose 1961 study of the history of the Labour Party, *Parliamentary Socialism*, helped define the British new left's politics, went so far as to say: 'the belief in the effective transformation of the Labour Party into an instrument of socialist policies ... is the most crippling of illusions to which socialists in Britain have been prone'.[6]

Nevertheless, a significant current developed within the Labour Party in the 1970s which shared the new left's outlook, but took the view that there was no alternative but to attempt precisely such a transformation. Despite the fact that their attempt to change the party went farther than the sceptics had thought possible, it did ultimately fail after a protracted and exhausting struggle. The seriousness of their attempt generated a bitter and often far from scrupulous resistance, which meant that unlike the new right, the new left was unable to reach out beyond the party to the country, to define the crisis in its own terms, or present a comprehensive alternative – very much as some of the original new left had foreseen.[7] And the electoral costs were severe. Divided parties do not win elections; the result was eighteen years in the political wilderness.

According to the received version of this story the 1981 split, when the 'Gang of Four' broke away from Labour to form the Social Democratic Party, was caused by the attempt of a mendacious and undemocratic left-wing faction in the Labour Party, out of touch with public opinion, to capture control of the party and impose an impracticable extension of 'old-style socialism', or 'centralised state socialism', on a profoundly unwilling electorate. These formulations, by Tony Blair and Peter Mandelson respectively, are typical.[8] Blair rightly insists that the story began in the late 1950s and early 1960s. But whereas he sees these years as the time when 'old-style socialism' became irrelevant, giving rise to the need for the kind of radical rapprochement with capitalism which he and his colleagues call 'modernisation', it was in fact the new left in the Labour Party which grasped the need for a break with 'old-style socialism' – and a break, too, with the old-style practices of the British state and of the Labour Party itself. In their much-discussed book, *The Blair Revolution*, Mandelson and Liddle describe Blair's 'revolution' as a 'reinvention' of the Labour Party, and write that 'the last time Labour reinvented itself was in the 1930s' (i.e., after the electoral disaster of 1931).[9] What this occludes, deliberately or not, is the fact that a far more radical 'reinvention' of the party was proposed by the Labour new left in the 1970s, and that it was to prevent this that a right-wing faction in the leadership pushed matters to a split.

What is at stake here is the rationale and justification for the Labour 'modernisers'' project. If, as they intend, the legacy of Thatcherism is to be accepted as a kind of 'settlement' (akin to the Conservatives' accommodation to the legacy of the Attlee governments in the 1950s), the Labour new left project of the 1970s and 1980s must be made historically meaningless. Its significance must also be forgotten if people are to learn to be content with the extremely limited version of democracy which is all that such an accommodation with 'global market forces' permits. For the special importance of the Labour new left is that it envisaged a much more far-reaching, active and inclusive kind of democracy than anything currently known to the British state or the British Labour Party; it is this vision that is their most important legacy, their potential 'communication with the future' that most disturbs New Labour's 'modernisers'.[10]

The Labour new left saw that 'parliamentary socialism', after reaching its apogee in the post-war settlement, had come to an end. They wanted to replace it with democratic socialism; New Labour would replace it with parliamentary capitalism.

The modernisers claim that the Labour new left of the 1970s, in Blair's words, 'pushed reforms through the party, supposedly making MPs and the leadership more accountable. But nobody asked how to make the party accountable and in touch with the people.'[11] This, however, is the opposite of the truth. The prime strategic concern of the Labour new left in the 1970s was to create a new popular base for democratic socialism. The fact that struggling to overcome resistance within the Labour Party consumed so much of its energy showed how difficult the project was; but there was no lack of concern with the need to bring 'the people' into the process of developing a new democratic socialist alternative. The whole point of trying to democratise the party was to give ordinary people's sentiments and interests a real presence in the institutions of government. The project of the Labour new left was far more radical in this respect – indeed one might say, far more modernising – than that of 'New Labour'. Tony Benn argued that it was necessary to democratise the party in order to 'extend Labour's representative function so as to bring ourselves into a more creative relationship with many organis-ations that stand outside ... to reconstruct the Labour Party so that a Labour government will never *rule* again but will try to act as a natural partner of a people, who really mean something more than we thought they did, when they ask for self-government'.[12]

Also concealed by 'New Labour' is the fact that the Labour new left was ahead of its opponents in grasping the seriousness of the crisis of the post-war order. Even as sophisticated a thinker as Tony Crosland, for instance, believed in 1970 that 'no fundamental rethinking' needed to be made of the analysis of capitalism he had made in the 1950s, and as late as 1974 he could write that there were no 'signs of a new and fundamental crisis' in the western economies.[13] Tony Benn, by contrast, saw as early as 1970 that a fundamental democratic reform of both the party and the state was needed in order to prevent the ascendancy of 'an alternative philosophy of government, now emerging everywhere on the right', dedicated to freeing business and controlling the citizen.[14] This perception was amply confirmed with the publication in 1975 of the Trilateral Commission's famous report on the 'governability of demo-cracies' in which a group of American, European and Japanese capitalists, former bureaucrats and right-wing intellectuals argued that governments in capitalist societies had become 'overloaded' by claims to social justice and participation; governability and democracy were 'warring concepts', the Commission declared, and the balance should now be 'tilted' back in favour of governments.[15]

New Labour ideologists also present a distorted view of 'Bennism' by treating it as a purely national phenomenon, as if the Labour new left was something peculiar to Britain. This deflects attention from the world-wide nature of the crisis to which the Labour new left were responding. As productivity growth faltered in the late 1960s, and international competition intensified, the post-war compromise between capital and labour began to break down. Governments began shifting the burden of taxation from capital to labour in order to sustain after-tax profits, while labour began to seek compensation through higher wages and improved social services. This led to a crisis in social-democratic Keynesian regimes everywhere.

In 1976 even the Swedish Social Democrats were defeated for the first time in forty years; on the other hand the Swedish labour movement simultaneously adopted the Meidner project for democratising the whole economy through 'wage-earners' funds', and quite sober academic analysts expected this to lead to a 'transition to socialism' in Sweden when the Social Democrats eventually returned to power. In Germany, the Social Democratic government of Helmut Schmidt, faced with the collapse of 'Concerted Action' (roughly equivalent to Labour's 'Social Contract'), explicitly abandoned Keynesianism after 1973; the German trade unions tried but failed to get the SPD to adopt an industrial strategy involving investment controls similar to those being proposed by Labour's new left in Britain. In the process the SPD's Young Socialists, whose ideas about radically redrawing the balance between parliamentary and extra-parliamentary activity had many parallels with those of the Labour new left, were stifled; but this in turn contributed strongly to the subsequent emergence of the German Greens. In the Netherlands in the early 1970s a movement very similar to the Labour new left emerged in the Dutch Labour Party and made extensive gains, calling for greater control by activists over the process of candidate selection, and for limits on the power of the party leadership to compromise on the party's declared policies when in office.[16] In Canada, a new left (colloquially known as the 'Waffle' group) emerged in the Canadian New Democratic Party in the late 1960s; by 1971 it was able to make a strong bid for the party leadership before it was expelled in 1972. Meanwhile France's Socialist Party, the PS, which had been out of office for a generation, revived strongly and adopted an economic programme much more radical than the one then being advocated by the new left in the Labour Party. By the end of the decade the PS was poised to achieve a stunning electoral victory under a leader, François Mitterrand, who insisted that his project had 'nothing in common with the corrupt compromises of a Schmidt or a Callaghan'.[17]

The Labour new left was thus part of a much wider response within parliamentary socialist parties to the crisis of the post-war order. What distinguished it from the others, however, was how much farther it went in fighting for a radical reorganisation of the relationship between state and party, and between party and people. For the crisis of the system brought the contradictions within the social democratic movements themselves into focus. The internal life of the social democratic parties had undergone a serious decline as a result of their integration into the institutions of 'managed capitalism'. When the socialist vision gives way to the pragmatic management of capitalism, there is little scope or need for a party-based 'counter-hegemonic' community. Party branches continue to serve an electoral function and play their allotted role at party conferences, but they lose whatever significance they may have had – which of course varied from country to country – as centres of education and mobilisation, oriented to an alternative way of life. In countries where mass socialist newspapers were marginal or non-existent (as in Britain) there no longer appeared any need to develop them, since the leaders' corporatist and pragmatic ideology got sufficient currency (even if not explicit editorial support) through the mainstream media. Where a socialist popular press did exist (as in Scandinavia), it could become increasingly 'catch-all' and ideologically anodyne. Individual membership ceased to be so crucial and in fact tended to decline in all the social democratic parties in Europe in the post-war era, with the single exception of the West German SPD.[18]

The decline of intra-party life did not seem to matter much so long as it did not threaten the social democratic parties' links with the trade unions, while their acceptance as 'parties of government' gave them the legitimacy they needed for periodic election successes. Demographic changes and shifts in the occupational and industrial structure might threaten this situation, but throughout the 1960s the traditional class identification of the older working-class communities, combined with the instrumental, 'catch-all' orientation of the social democratic parties' policies and programmes, seemed capable of sustaining the socialist parties' position (the major exceptions in this decade being France and the Low Countries). Their failure to resume their former active roles in class formation and socialist education, however, meant that they increasingly depended for electoral success on short-term policy programmes and personalities. When the conditions that had made social democratic management of national capitalist economies possible ceased to exist, this 'hollowing out' was suddenly revealed as an acute liability.

The first signs of this crisis of the social democratic parties took the form of popular reactions to international events. As the United States' image as a decoloniser was replaced by that of guarantor of military dictatorships, the 'Atlanticism' of Europe's social democratic governments became a liability; the radicalisation of the student movement in Europe in the 1960s was in large part due to this. But this radicalisation had deeper sources as well. What Ralph Miliband termed 'a state of desubordination' affected an entire generation.[19] The rhetoric of 'social citizenship' that had accompanied the establishment of the welfare state no longer had strong appeal. It was no longer the social justice and political pluralism of social democracy that impressed, but rather the partial character of that justice and the elite nature of that pluralism. Social democratic ministers who had become immersed in the executive structures and parliamentary apparatuses of the state were either uncomprehending or condescending when confronted by the vague cry for 'participation'. When the cry extended to the no less vague, but certainly more militant, 'smash capital', they thought they recognised an old Cold War foe; but they were mistaken. A new generation of socialists had emerged whose politics could not be reduced to those polarities.

Moreover, it was not only students, women, and a variety of newly-activated minorities and causes from gay rights to environmentalism; it was people in almost every segment of the population who were being prompted to new levels of political interest and activism as the contradictions of social democracy and Keynesianism came to a head. A counter-current was also flowing strongly, of course, in the mass consumerism which capitalist markets had generated under the conditions of world-wide economic expansion – 'the joyous ringing of capital's cash-tills'.[20] Which current would prove dominant in the resolution of the crisis was not a foregone conclusion, as the massive ideological effort on the part of the new right clearly showed; throughout the 1970s the issue seemed, and perhaps was, still in doubt.

Meanwhile a generation of workers was also caught in the conflicting currents of consumption and 'desubordination'. Their discontent took apparently more mundane forms, yet it was very evident in factories and offices, and in youth culture, and it may well have posed even deeper problems for social democracy. Young workers did not remember the Depression or have any affinity with Cold War trade unionism. They had been raised in an acquisitive, affluent society in which, they were repeatedly assured, class barriers were being swept away. But the image of the 'high mass consumption society' held up to them by television contrasted painfully with the reality of life on housing estates and the shop floor. To hope to live like the middle class, they had to act like militant workers: to go in for more militant collective bargaining, the one sphere in which they had some real power.

The 'affluent society' thus produced neither an 'end of ideology' nor an end of class conflict. It is true that the two main streams of 'de-subordination' – the 'new social movements' and the militant workers – rarely coalesced, apart from the heady days of May '68, but the socialist parties had lost most of their capacity to appeal successfully to either. The radical students, feminists, ecologists, gay rights activists and others mostly looked elsewhere, while the workers mostly treated politics as instrumentally as the social democratic parties treated them. As a result, when social democratic management of the capitalist economy began to become impossible, the socialist parties had also lost their ability to resume the leadership of the anti-capitalist currents in society. They were compromised by their continuing dependence on private capital accumulation as the engine of economic growth, and by their own absorption into the structures and culture of the state. Their only distinctive governmental device, corporatism, was consistently under-mined by the industrial militancy which the contradictions of capitalism provoked. And when they were in office they found themselves unable to contain the inflationary pressures (and the threat to profits and the balance of payments) which this militancy in turn produced, because capital vetoed what the unions demanded in return for wage restraint – effective price and dividend controls, an effective role for unions in determining investment policy, and a redistributive fiscal policy. Mean-time it became harder and harder to maintain the growth of the 'welfare state', which was in any case administered in a hierarchical and bureau-cratic manner, like the rest of the state, and often resented rather than loved by those most dependent on it.

It was to this increasingly barren prospect that the resurgent left wing in the socialist parties of the west was responding in the 1970s. The extra-parliamentary parties of the Marxist-Leninist left – old and new – had failed to make any significant impression. The problem was seen as one of revitalising the parliamentary socialist parties and redefining their relations with the various social movements and with the state. Even just to preserve the gains of the 'golden age' of the 1950s and 1960s now meant going beyond the compromise which had produced them, and putting socialism back on the agenda. But the socialist or social democratic parties were no longer organisations capable of undertaking this task, if they ever had been. For it to be seriously contemplated, their structure and culture needed to be radically changed.

Here is where the originality of the British new left's initiative particularly lay. In France, Mitterrand's Parti socialiste, in spite of its rhetoric of making a radical break with the 'errors of the past', followed highly traditional lines after it came to power in 1981, both in its relations with the state and in its internal organisation.[21] In Greece the undemocratic nature of Papandreou's PASOK government, also elected in 1981, became a byword, in spite of its democratic pre-election promises.[22] In Sweden, notwithstanding the country's relatively open and democratic culture and state practices, the wage-earners' funds proposal put forward by the trade union movement was not backed by any popular mobilisation; the technocratic and pragmatic wing of the SAP leadership treated the scheme with suspicion and got it referred to a series of commissions which, in the long intervals (three years) between party congresses, diluted its content to the point where it became, in practice, little more than a forced savings scheme to provide employers with a new source of capital.[23] And so on. The Labour new left in Britain was, of course, no more successful than its counterparts elsewhere in winning sufficient public support for a radical new economic agenda. But it did link the drive for its version of such an agenda to an attempt to democratise the party, without which, as all these cases showed, the agenda was doomed anyway.

It was, of course, not the Labour new left but the Social Democrats who in 1981 described their aim as 'breaking the mould' of British party politics. What they meant by this was that Labour and the Conservatives were being pulled by their class bases towards more and more 'extreme' policies, whereas they stood for a new kind of politics transcending class divisions, a new politics of the centre. But the truth was that what the Social Democrats wanted was precisely to *preserve* the old mould of centrist politics, with themselves in charge. It was the new left in the Labour Party, and the new right in the Conservative Party, who were proposing to 'break the mould', and it was the latter, led by Mrs Thatcher, who succeeded in doing so.

Her project, radical though it was by comparison with the post-war regime, was still much less radical than the project of the Labour new left, in at least three respects. First, the post-war settlement had left capitalist social relations substantially intact, and since the mid-1960s even Labour governments had been striving to restore the competitiveness of British capital, and as a means to this, to break the power of trade union militancy and curb state expenditure. It was under a Labour government, during the 'winter of discontent' of 1978–79, that official rhetoric against strikes rose to fever pitch, with Labour ministers demonstratively crossing picket lines and suspending civil servants for refusing to do the work of low-paid public sector strikers; and it was a Labour Chancellor of the Exchequer, Denis Healey, who in 1976 replaced full employment by monetary restraint as the dominant goal of economic policy. In these respects Thatcherism was a continuation of already-established trends.

Second, Mrs Thatcher was able to tap into an already significant degree of public disenchantment with public sector industries that were bureaucratic and unresponsive to consumers, as well as suffering from chronic underinvestment due to repeated government-imposed cuts in their spending programmes. There was also widespread alienation from the similarly pinched and too often patronising agencies of the welfare state, and a significant popular current of racism and national chauvinism to both of which Mrs Thatcher successfully appealed. These were not new values but old ones, tirelessly sustained by the right-wing press and Conservative Party propaganda, and not particularly difficult to exploit.

Third, Thatcherism represented no fundamental break in the mould of the British state. With the emasculation of local government and the enhancement of police powers in the 1980s democratic life became even more exclusively confined to the practice of parliamentary elitism. The dominance of the Prime Minister's office and the Treasury became more pronounced, as the spending ministries were eviscerated through the transfer of staff and functions to quasi-autonomous, business-oriented 'executive agencies'. 'Atlanticism' became even more marked in foreign and military relations. In all this Thatcherism was not breaking the mould, but reinforcing tradition.

The Labour new left project, by contrast, involved breaking with tradition in each of these dimensions, and in order to do this it also involved, as a prerequisite, breaking the mould of intra-party politics as well. In raising this issue the Labour new left was taking on the enormous problem that Robert Michels had identified at the beginning of the century: the tendency to oligarchy in mass socialist parties. Conservative parties were elitist and undemocratic too, Michels noted, but this was not a problem for them, since they existed to defend the existing social order. It was a very different matter for parties nominally committed to radical change, if their leaders were able to insulate themselves from the pressure of socialist activists and the mechanisms of democratic control provided for in the party constitution.[24]

But the issues raised by the Labour new left went further than those raised by Michels, to include the nature of democracy in the state itself. As Max Weber had seen more clearly than his pupil Michels, it was through the embrace of the state, even more than through inner-party oligarchy, that the socialist and democratic thrust of the mass working-class party was neutralised: '. . . in the long run', Weber wrote, 'it is not Social Democracy which conquers the town or the state but it is the state which conquers the party'.[25] In Britain, as observers from R.H.

Tawney to Lewis Minkin have noted, the policy of Labour leaders in office quickly became 'to emulate *in toto* ... the governmental practice of their opponents, playing not only to the existing rules of the game but with the same style as their opponents and, in rapidly increasing measure, for the same ends'.[26]

This assimilation to the routines and perspectives of the British state was the real source of the long-running debate in the Labour Party over the autonomy which the parliamentary party leadership always claimed from the party outside Parliament, whose annual conference was constitutionally invested with the 'direction and control' of the work of the party. The leading student of this debate, Robert McKenzie, advocated changing this provision in the party's constitution because in his view it was inconsistent with the role the party had to play as a party of government under the existing rules of the British constitution.[27] Consistently enough, when the Labour Party's constitution was amended in the opposite direction in 1980, on the initiative of the Labour new left – enhancing the powers of the membership and the conference *vis-à-vis* the parliamentary party – McKenzie condemned the change. What had to be recognised, he said, was 'that political parties are unique among political organisations in that their leaders must *escape* control of their followers if they are to fulfil their broader role as the principal decision-makers in the political community'.[28]

For McKenzie, of course, 'democratic government' meant the efficient management of the existing social order. For the Labour new left, the issue was whether a transition to socialism could be effected through democracy. McKenzie thought that the party leadership must be free 'to take into account all other interest group volitions and demands'.[29] The Labour left thought that the one set of interests that were not being taken into account with the abandonment of the post-war settlement were those of the working-class majority; and that only if the party was democratised could it act as a countervailing force against the 'volitions and demands' of corporations and the international financial institutions. McKenzie was expressing in the British context the general definition of democracy enunciated by Joseph Schumpeter in 1942: for him, democracy was 'that institutional arrangement for arriving at political decisions in which individuals acquire the power to decide by means of a competitive struggle for the people's vote'. On this definition, the people do not decide policies, and so power does not reside with them; they have only 'the opportunity of accepting or refusing the men who are to rule them'.[30]

This conception of democracy clearly does not require, indeed it must exclude, much citizen participation in the state beyond periodically choosing between competing teams of leaders. As Perry Anderson put it in 1977, it is often claimed that the working class has access to the state (elections to parliament), but does not exercise it to achieve socialism because of its indoctrination by the means of communication. In fact, it might be said that the truth is if anything the inverse: the general form of the representative state – bourgeois democracy – is itself the principal linchpin of Western capitalism, whose very existence deprives the working class of the idea of socialism as *a different type of State*, and the means of communication and other mechanisms of cultural control thereafter clinch this central ideological 'effect'.[31]

Anderson's reflections proved prescient. The new right's assault on the welfare state continued throughout the 1980s and 1990s with remarkably little resistance, even though it never enjoyed the support of more than 44 per cent of the votes cast in general elections.

It was thus precisely the Labour new left's focus on the need for 'a different type of state' that was innovative, and that seemed so threatening to the party leadership. For what was at stake was not just whether the leadership would be left free to operate within the rules of the existing state system without having to answer to the extra-parliamentary party. It was also whether, as ministers in office (and even as potential ministers), they should continue to have no responsibility for mobilising popular support for new socialist measures, including measures to change the state – both to broaden its scope and to enlarge the public's role in it. It was, significantly, Tony Benn's experience in office of the contradiction between the need for popular mobilisation, and the restrictions which Harold Wilson sought to impose on him as a minister, that led him to see the need for 'a different type of state'.

The Labour new left's ideas about the changes needed in the state for a transition to socialism were mostly speculative and incomplete. Some things were fairly clear, however. For example, it became evident that public ownership of a good part of the financial sector would be necessary, and that this could not take the form of the mere legal transfer of banks from private to public hands, as in the 1945 nationalisations; both the public and the banking workforce would need to have a different kind of relationship to publicly-owned banks. This in turn required that the party leadership must not only work out new models of public enterprise capable of providing this, but also work actively to win public support for them – the precise opposite of what, following an overwhelming vote in favour of a publicly-owned financial sector at the 1976 Labour conference, the government and the union leadership actually did, which was to do their best to discredit the whole idea and bury it. In general, 'a different type of state', related in a different way to a different type of party as well as to the public at large, called for a leadership with a commitment to a socialist project, and one that did not see a *modus vivendi* with capital – with its corollary of a narrow, elitist conception of parliamentary democracy – as the first principle of government when in office.

What the Labour new left could actually achieve was not only constricted by the need to fight every inch of the way for a few structural reforms in the party – reforms that, far from being very radical, were actually common in many western parties – but also by the inexorable pressure of the crisis on the Labour governments of the 1960s and 1970s. They were so intensely focused on the Labour Party that they often failed to look beyond it to what would be entailed in changing the state. This focus on changing the party also meant that they tended to treat the struggles of the new social movements as secondary. Moreover the Labour new left also contained, inevitably, some sectarian elements which, while never setting its agenda, tended to reduce its effectiveness and limit its appeal.

Nevertheless, it managed to bequeath various practical examples of more democratic and inclusive forms of self-government, and creative ideas about how ordinary people could be involved in, identified with and in control of the public sphere. To say this is already to point to a considerable achievement, and to be reminded once more why the Labour new left project was anathema to the parliamentary leadership in the 1970s – and why 'New Labour' should be so anxious to have it discredited and forgotten in the late 1990s. For what the new left project can still 'communicate to the future' is the fact that many people once refused to take it for granted that the rule of capital is inevitable, and that they cannot organise themselves politically to change their lives. In 1996–97, as 'New Labour' prepared to take office again in yet another *modus vivendi* with capital (this time under the banner of 'realism' in the face of 'global competition'), it was not a message they were anxious to have people recall.

'New Labour' inherited a party still functioning, if somewhat convulsively, according to its traditional logic. Under Neil Kinnock's leadership (1983–92) the Labour new left – the 'Bennites' – were absorbed or marginalised, and key Labour policy commitments – most notably full employment, nationalisation, and unilateral nuclear disarmament – were dropped. Kinnock was able to push through these changes with the support of the trade unions, who were suffering a dramatic loss of members and the progressive dismantling of their legal rights; and with the reluctant but real consent of a significant portion of the activists among the party's individual membership, who were intensely afraid that the scale of Labour's election defeat in 1983 could eventually spell the party's elimination as a party of government. To save the situation the party in effect conceded an unprecedented grant of authority to the leader.

Even so, under Kinnock the party's formal constitution and rules remained largely unchanged. Under John Smith's leadership (1992–94), the principle of 'one member one vote' was introduced for future leadership elections, and the weight of the trade union vote at conferences and in the local selection of parliamentary candidates was reduced; but it was not until Tony Blair's election as leader in 1994 that a radical break with Labour's past was undertaken. The centralisation of power in the hands of the leader was carried forward in a series of *de jure* changes, culminating in the establishment in 1996 of the leader's right to draft a 'pre-manifesto' declaration to be endorsed by the party membership in a nation-wide postal ballot; and there was a further reduction in the weight of trade union votes at conference and in candidate selection, and an end to trade union sponsorship of MPs. The leadership remained theoretically subject to the will of the membership, but Blair's practice of appealing directly to a much expanded membership drastically reduced the only constraint on the leader's freedom that had really mattered in the past – the votes of activists in the party and the trade unions.

Blair also set in hand a much more radical revision of party policies, symbolised by his successful personal campaign early in 1995 to replace 'the common ownership of the means of production, distribution and exchange' with flattering references to 'the market' in a new statement of the party's principles. The resulting package of new policies was widely criticised as lacking any 'big idea' and consisting only of numerous minor reforms. But New Labour's big idea was to accept definitively that global capitalism, and the political power of global capital, was a permanent fact of life, so that socialism, if it still meant anything at all, was a set of values that should guide public policy *under* capitalism, nothing more.

Only time will show whether Blair and his fellow-modernisers were right in claiming that there is no alternative to this position, and that a better life, even one that might justify the name 'socialist', can be achieved on this basis. But the omens are not good. It was difficult to see in the proposals that New Labour put before the public in 1997 a 'package' proportional to the severity of Britain's accumulated economic and social problems, which two decades of neoliberalism had aggravated, not resolved.

Even before the 1997 general election, a sense of the need to go further than New Labour declared possible or even desirable was spreading well beyond the ranks of Labour 'dissidents' (as the media tended to call Labour members with the temerity to disagree with the modernisers). Even significant elements within the Conservative Party – likewise contemptuously dubbed 'Tory grandees', mere 'pragmatists', and the like – were increasingly disaffected. Three Conservative MPs left the party, and an unprecedented number announced their intention to quit politics at the end of the 1992–97 Parliament. Outside the ranks of market fundamentalists there was a growing unease in face of the growing social costs of 'market society', and a dawning realisation that defining a new social order in which the market would be re-subordinated to society, and finding a political route to it, was the new millennium's greatest challenge.

For any serious attempt to meet this challenge, a necessary preliminary will be a sober comparison of New Labour's project with that of the former Labour new left – their different understandings of capitalism, their different attitudes to the political power of capital, and their very different ambitions for, and expectations of, ordinary people. And in Britain the question must be squarely faced whether the energy needed to remake the socialist project should be absorbed, and its creativity stifled, in yet another effort to remake the Labour Party. Given the parallel trajectories of virtually all other social democratic parties in the 1990s, moreover, the answer to this question may have relevance for socialists everywhere.

2

Origins of the Party Crisis

Political memories are short. Who now remembers that 'modernisation' was a central theme of Labour Party discourse in the early 1960s? Or that the effort to radicalise the party in the 1970s was a reaction against the failures of that earlier modernisation? It is also easy to forget that the attempt in the 1970s to radicalise the Labour Party had its roots in a much broader radicalisation that the Wilson governments of the 1960s largely ignored or even sought to suppress. As Eric Hobsbawm wrote in 1981:

> ... even at the peak of the affluent society and the great capitalist boom, in the middle 1960s, there were signs of real recovery of impetus and dynamism: the resumed strength of trade unions, not to mention the great labour struggles, the sharp rise in the Labour vote in 1966, the radicalisation of students, intellectuals, and others in the late 1960s. If we are to explain the stagnation and the crisis, we have to look at the Labour Party and the labour movement itself. The workers, and growing strata outside the manual workers, were looking for a lead and a policy. They did not get it. They got the Wilson years – and many of them lost faith and hope in the mass party of the working people.[1]

The theme of 'modernisation' emerged as the Labour Party attempted to cope with the three election defeats of the 1950s and bring to an end the 'wasted years' of Conservative rule. The famous intra-party controversies over Gaitskell's attempt to excise the commitment to public ownership from Clause IV of the party's constitution, and the unilateralists' attempt to excise the commitment to the nuclear arms race from the Atlantic alliance, were set aside in the years preceding the 1964 election. Left and right in the party leadership combined to seek election by adopting a Kennedyesque technocratic modernism (anticipating Tony Blair's 'Clintonism' by thirty years), as well as by striking a corporatist incomes policy agreement with the unions. The Gaitskellite journal *Socialist Commentary*, previously at the forefront of the campaign to downplay Labour's working-class links, now sought to take advantage of the Tories' conversion to incomes policy by arguing that

Labour's modernist and managerial appeal 'can only prove superior if Labour can show that its close alliance with the unions is an asset, which it alone enjoys, and not a liability'.[2] This in fact defined the core of the Labour Party's political strategy under Wilson. It was a vague and contradictory – but glossily packaged – blend of modernity and traditionalism.

Thanks to Harold Wilson's talent for double-talk, the Labour Party approached the 1964 election seeming to some to promise fundamental social change, to others efficient capitalist management, and for most both at once. There was the celebrated invocation of the 'white heat of technology'; there were virulent denunciations of the Treasury and the City; there was an appeal to corporatism ('We shall ... as a national Party ... be frank in condemning all those who shirk their duty to the nation. The professional fomenters of unofficial strikes ... equally with businessmen who cling to out-of-date methods and out-of-date machinery because it yields them profits ...'[3]); and there was a socialist appeal. Wilson promised to replace 'a system of society where making money by whatever means is lauded as the highest service',[4] and proposed instead, in a famous speech that was actually worked on by Tony Benn, that the 'fundamental inspiration of our social life should be the age-old principle: from each according to his means, to each according to his needs'.[5] Left-wing union leaders like Frank Cousins temporarily accepted the socialist promise in the 'planned growth of incomes' policy on the grounds that 'Harold says this every time he gets the opportunity. He is wanting to be part of a team that is going to change the system, and the trade union function will change along with a change in the political function; it is bound to do so.'[6] Stalwart socialist intellectuals like Michael Barratt Brown, Royden Harrison and John Hughes in the pages of *Tribune* looked forward to an incomes policy serving as the cutting edge of a socialist strategy. They argued that 'to plan to advance real wages in line with production and at the expense of property-derived incomes is to embark upon the transformation of capitalism into socialism'.[7]

Perry Anderson was more sceptical: 'Wilson above all has offered a strategy to the Labour Party – it is this that has enabled him to temporarily cancel the divisions within it and dominate the party. A strategy for the Labour Party as it exists today, however, is one thing; a strategy for socialism is another. It is precisely in this that so much of the difficulty lies.' Yet even he was optimistic, hopeful that the new Labour Government represented a creative new phase in which the liberal and working-class traditions in the party might potentially be brought together to 'touch one of the deepest chords in the British experience ... the simple idea of democracy, understood in its largest and most explosive sense. ... One of the encouraging results of the new phase inside the Labour Party has been the release of the generous, creative potential of each of these traditions – personified perhaps in men like Benn on the one hand, and Cousins on the other, in the present Government.'[8]

And the results of the 1964 and especially the 1966 elections did appear to give the lie to those who had earlier insisted that Labour's electoral base had withered beyond repair.[9] They seemed to confirm Goldthorpe's and Lockwood's central thesis in their famous 'affluent worker' study, i.e., that there was no evidence for an irreversible 'embourgeoisement' of the working class, with ineluctably negative electoral consequences for Labour.[10] Rather, they argued, the 'instrumental collectivism' of the new working-class communities allowed for a new, and potentially more radical, working-class identification with Labour. A new generation of working-class voters had come on to the electoral roll in the 1960s who were more class-conscious than voters who had first entered the electorate before 1929, and they did largely opt for Labour in the mid-1960s. But these new voters were also less class-conscious than those who had joined the electorate in the intervening thirty years, and it was primarily these same new working-class voters who, in great numbers, deserted the Labour Party in the 1970 election.

The critical years for understanding the electoral shifts that gripped the attention of 'psephologists' (and British Eurocommunists) during the rise of Thatcherism were 1966 to 1970. It was only in 1970 that a substantial portion of the working-class vote deserted Labour for the first time, with manual workers' support falling from 69 per cent in 1966 to 58 per cent in 1970 (where it stayed through 1974, falling still further to 50 per cent in 1979 after a second experience of Labour Government). Mark Franklin has plausibly argued:

> The Parliament elected in 1966 provided the first Labour majority in fifteen years that was large enough to have a chance to build upon the achievements of 1945–50. The Parliament of 1966 thus provided the first opportunity for young voters to become disillusioned with the prospects for a socialist Britain. The same election will also have provided the first opportunity in fifteen years for the party to prove to potential supporters from middle-class backgrounds that it was content to govern a mixed society. The latter objective was the one Harold Wilson espoused. Paradoxically, his very success in achieving this objective may have been what cost the party so much support among members of the working class. Young voters may have ceased to see any class difference between the parties during this period, and so become responsive to appeals that were not class-based.[11]

Of course the Wilson Government had little success in actually governing a 'mixed society'. Indeed, the fact that it was content to do no more than try to do so, and that it failed so miserably, was no doubt its

– and Labour's – undoing. When the overwhelming majority of 1966 gave Harold Wilson the opportunity of turning his ambiguous phrases into practical policies, the shallowness of his strategy was revealed. Despite all its modernist pretensions, this Labour Government displayed 'an almost pathological preoccupation with respectability'.[12] A foreign relations orthodoxy grounded in Atlanticism and anti-communism was symbolised by the Government's support for American policy in Vietnam and by its readiness to blame strikes on communist influence ('a tightly knit group of politically motivated men', as Wilson called them in the Seamen's Union strike). A fiscal orthodoxy inherited from the British Treasury (and policed by the American Treasury) ruled out devaluation until 1967, by which time the defence of sterling had already led to the replacement of the 'planned growth of incomes' by a draconian deflation and a statutory wage freeze. This in turn nullified the corporatist promise that the trade union leadership would participate in running the economy. Instead, maintaining wage restraint and limiting strikes became the Government's most visible concern, with dire long-term consequences. Indeed a plausible case can be made that the seeds of Thatcherism were planted here. As Trevor Blackwell and Jeremy Seabrook put it, '[t]he public admission by a Labour Government that the only thing wrong with Britain was its irresponsible working class set the tone for the 1970s, and indeed furnished them with their *leitmotif*'.[13]

As the meaning of Wilson's phrases became less obscure, those elements of the working class whose consciousness was 'instrumentally collectivist' drew harsh and cynical conclusions. This was inevitable when real earnings before tax fell in four of the six half-yearly periods between the 1966 election and the summer of 1969, when the much-vaunted price controls proved laughably ineffective, and when increases in social benefits did not nearly compensate for the effects of wage controls, inflation and higher taxation on working-class incomes. For the first time in decades, the party's opinion poll ratings fell to well below 40 per cent and local elections proved nothing short of disastrous. Local councils that had traditionally gone together with Labour 'like fish and chips' slipped from the party's control.[14] In Labour's worst local election results in the post-war period, the Conservatives in 1967 took control of the Greater London Council, Bradford, Cardiff, Leeds, Leicester, Liverpool, Manchester, and Newcastle among other cities. In the following year, Labour obtained only 17 per cent of the seats in the London and provincial borough councils and urban districts, and the Tories not only consolidated their gains of the previous year but took Sheffield for the first time since 1932; Labour was left with only four of the twenty London boroughs it had once controlled. Moreover, there was a veritable explosion of 'action group' protest and community-based politics explicitly divorced from mainstream party politics; and an industrial militancy of proportions unprecedented since the early 1920s swept through the working class, most notably among previously quiescent low-paid public sector workers. Although party loyalty, and fear of the sharp right-ward shift that was beginning to occur in the Conservative Party, combined to effect a brief recovery in Labour's electoral standing, so that in the 1970 election the party still retained 43.1 per cent of the vote, this only temporarily concealed the electoral rot that had set in under the Wilson Government.

It was not surprising that a great many of the activists who stayed with the party through this debacle (and even more who subsequently joined it in the 1970s) thought that Labour could only recover if it adopted policies of direct and manifest benefit to working people, and also provided a definition and vision of socialism that would distinguish it from other parties and make it possible for people to identify with. Some of these activists arrived at this conclusion from rethinking (and romanticising) the history of the Labour Party, such as the origins of Clause IV of the Party Constitution in 1918, or the victory of 1945. Others read the *Communist Manifesto* (which by 1968 had acquired a new popularity), where the immediate aim of all working-class parties was defined as 'the formation of the proletariat into a class' through socialist education and agitation. Probably most of them, like Ken Livingstone (who was nineteen in 1964), drew their conclusions from the best teacher of all – personal experience:

> I trembled with excitement on the night of the '64 election. No one need get involved with politics; poverty and bad housing would be abolished in five years. And you would have believed that if you had grown up and never known what a Labour government was like ... People like myself have shifted to the left not on any theoretical basis but because we have seen two Labour Governments in the 1960s and 1970s fail to deliver ... [The] social democrats ... believe that because they have been educated in middle-class homes, gone to university with some sort of academic success, that they have some inalienable right and talent to run the country. And they have run it appallingly badly.[15]

The feeling was mutual. As Labour's new left gained strength through the 1970s and put forward an alternative economic policy and, more fundamentally, an alternative conception of politics and political leadership, they were seen by the social democrats at the top of the parliamentary party, as Dennis Healey delicately put it in 1976, as 'out of their tiny Chinese minds'.[16]

Various elements converged to initiate the attempt to change the Labour Party after the 1970 defeat – none of them Chinese. In the amalgam of old and new left activists who had stayed with the party, or joined it, in the early 1970s, very few were Maoists (as in Italy or France), or even middle-class 'poly-Trots' or organised 'entrists', and many of them were as 'organically' linked to the working class as any Labour Party 'intellectuals' had ever been. Their social origins often were working class; they often were active members of, or at least had close ties with, a trade union (albeit increasingly a white collar or public sector trade union); their political base lay in the working-class communities in which they had grown up or in which they participated as local Labour Party activists. Moreover, in their lack of deference to established party authority, they were often encouraged by left parliamentarians and trade union leaders. Indeed, to appreciate why so much space opened up for a new left to emerge within the Labour Party after 1970, as well as the constraints faced by that new left in its attempt to change the party, we have to take into account the impact on the party of changes that were already taking place in the trade unions.

'Watch the Unions: That's My Tip'

As early as the 1965 Labour Party Conference a seasoned veteran of the left like Ian Mikardo could sense a new political radicalism among the union delegations at party conferences and appreciate what this might mean for the party: 'Watch the Unions: That's My Tip', he told his readers in *Tribune*.[17] Hidden beneath the government's control of the Conference through its ministerial domination of the party's National Executive, an important shift was occurring in the attitudes of the union delegates, which Mikardo had discerned by taking part in the Conference's 'extra-curricular sessions' in the bars. This shift led to the party leadership being defeated on many of the government's policies at subsequent party conferences in the late 1960s. During the Attlee governments the right-wing trade union leaders that dominated the movement had often shared the sentiments of resolutions criticising government economic policy, but had always successfully instructed their delegations to vote against them. On this basis the government had been able to treat Conference resolutions as votes of confidence and present themselves as treating them seriously. Now, with union discipline seriously attenuated, Labour ministers had to repudiate the authority of the Conference, since they had no intention of 'taking instructions' from the extra-parliamentary party, even though it was the organisation that had put their 'team' before the electorate. 'The government must govern' became Harold Wilson's stock phrase as he suffered a series of defeats at party conferences of a kind Attlee had never known.

Significantly, in light of the ideological prison the Cold War had fashioned, the first major defeat concerned Labour's foreign policy. When the 1966 Conference voted against the war in Vietnam and against military commitments in West Germany and East of Suez, this was the 'first time in the history of the Party [that] a Labour Government suffered defeat on major questions of foreign and defence policy'.[18] This was followed at subsequent conferences by defeats on economic policy, above all on the incomes policy (an event heralded by Frank Cousins's resignation from the Cabinet over the statutory wage freeze in July 1966).

But it was not only the government's policies that were being challenged. Also brought into question was the authoritarian manipulation of the unions' block votes by their leaders; appeals to an old mechanical 'loyalty' to the parliamentary leadership; and the notion that the only 'good conference' was one that was well under the control of 'the platform' – which, surprising at it may seem in the late 1990s, was in the 1960s still deeply ingrained in the trade union movement. The shift of much of the leadership of the British trade union movement, from the defensiveness of the post-General Strike era (subsequently reinforced by the Cold War) to the militancy of the 1960s and 1970s, had many facets. Not least important was the challenge to centralised discipline and deference towards the leadership as constituting the primary meaning of solidarity.

This change gradually found expression at the level of the unions' national leaderships. Left-wing union leaders were elected in the late 1960s in four of the six largest unions (Jack Jones, Cousins's successor in the TGWU, Lawrence Daly of the Mineworkers, Richard Seabrook of the Shopworkers and Hugh Scanlon of the Engineers), and all four were noted for their respect for shop stewards' autonomy, as well as for having broad sympathy with notions of independent working-class power. This also coloured their political orientations: at conferences of the Nottingham-based Institute for Workers' Control they were critical of 'top-down' models of public ownership, and open advocates of industrial democracy. Faced with the disappointments of the Labour Government, strong alliances had emerged in some unions between the Labour left and the Communists (most notably in Scanlon's victory in 1967 over the right wing of the Engineering union); and this development of the 'broad left' in the union movement laid the political basis for the 'discontinuation' in 1973 of the party's 'List of Proscribed Organisations', indicating a partial opening to both old and new socialist currents. Eventually – albeit not until the mid-1970s, as the new left-wing union leaders were careful not to upset traditional voting arrangements among the various unions – it produced a left-wing majority on the party's National Executive Committee.[19] But even before this, the emergence of 'a new breed of capable left-wing Labour union leaders ... had an immediate impact on the political atmosphere' and weakened the intolerant and tightly-disciplined power structure – what Eric Shaw has aptly called 'social democratic centralism' – that had prevailed in the Labour Party throughout the post-war period to the benefit of the right-wing parliamentary leadership.[20]

Another immediate effect of the union delegations' new pattern of behaviour at Labour Party Conferences was to give a greater political salience to resolutions in favour of public ownership which, as Minkin has shown, union conferences had kept on passing throughout the 1950s and 1960s, albeit somewhat mechanically and with little passion, despite the domination of the party by the Croslandite 'revisionists'.[21] Now, suddenly, during the 1968 Conference debate on incomes policy, a resolution was nearly passed which declared 'that the policies of this Government have been and are being dictated by the monopolies and the big financial interests to the detriment of the needs and desires of the working class', and called for 'taking into public ownership the 300 monopolies, private banks, finance houses and insurance companies' and for a 'socialist plan for production, democratically administered, involving the trade union and Co-operative movement, shop stewards and housewives' committees, scientists, teachers, technicians, doctors and the whole spectrum of working people of Britain . . .'. So little was this resolution taken seriously by the leadership that Barbara Castle, responding for the NEC (and the Government) to the debate on incomes policy, did not even bother to instruct the delegates to vote against it.[22] Yet trade union support for radical socialist resolutions now became common at party conferences.

But as the 1960 debate on Clause IV had already indicated, this said little about the union leaderships' – or activists' – industrial and political priorities. Industrially the unofficial strike wave of the late 1960s was an instance of the broader wave of 'direct action' protest demonstrations that marked this political conjuncture quite generally. It expressed a popular mood of being 'fed up'; union militants were concerned about a lot less than the nationalisation of the 'commanding heights' of the economy – and yet, in a certain way, they were also concerned about a lot more. As real wages fell and unemployment doubled from 300,000 to 600,000 during the late 1960s, and then as mass redundancies loomed large under Heath's initial determination to let 'lame-duck' industries go to the wall and to establish legal controls over worker militancy in the early 1970s, direct action escalated beyond strikes over wages. It became political, but primarily in the anarchic sense of 'bugger your laws'. It was not so much the massive TUC-staged demonstrations against the Industrial Relations Act that reflected this, as the determined illegality of the 'Pentonville Five' Dockers in 1972 and the sympathy they got from activists throughout the labour movement. Even more telling about the mood was the famous work-in over the threatened closure at Upper Clyde Shipbuilders in 1971, the massive support this got, and the fact that it was followed by no fewer than 102 similar occupations between July 1971 and February 1974.[23]

All this was far from being a coherent movement for political change, as was evident in the way both ordinary members and leaders in the unions related to the Labour Party immediately before and after the 1970 election. There certainly was considerable disaffection from the Labour Government, but this did not lead automatically to political radicalisation. Whether it would have such an effect depended very much on the outcome of the attempt to change the Labour Party which had at this point barely begun. The political significance of the Labour Party's vast trade union membership had always been questionable. The number of union members indirectly affiliated to the party had doubled from 2,500,000 to almost 5 million when the 1945 Attlee Government reintroduced the law requiring individual trade unionists specifically to 'contract out' of paying a political levy as part of their union dues if they did not wish to pay it. The number then stayed virtually constant until the mid-1970s, hovering around 5.5 million (thereafter rising to nearly 6 million as union membership grew apace in the late 1970s). But this only reflected the steadiness of the unions' official organisational link with the party and concealed any trends in the level of individual trade union members' support for, or activity in, the party. Throughout the late 1960s, it was common to see reports of branches voting to disaffiliate from the party because of the actions of the Labour Government.[24]

Union journals and conferences were replete with appeals from leaders to their members and branches not to show their displeasure in this negative fashion. Writing in *Tribune* as part of a campaign initiated in May 1968, Jack Jones argued: 'If we were to allow Government policies to destroy the assumption of working people that Labour is *their* party, the result would be ... to put the clock back one hundred years ...'. Instead, the unions should rely on their industrial bargaining power so as to 'associate Labour with high wages and high efficiency in industry, not low wages and stagnation'.[25] And this was the course the union leaders took, as they increasingly made what had previously been unofficial strikes official. They tried to protect the Labour Party by calling on workers to vote for it and above all by continuing to finance it – but they also entered into open conflict with the Labour Government through 'direct action' industrial militancy.

It was a mark of their political desperation – and one of the deepest roots of their growing preoccupation with the accountability of trade union-sponsored MPs who supported the Government's policies.[26] Yet, while the unions' renewed concern with the behaviour of these MPs was a portent, it was never at the forefront of their approach to resolving their difficulties with the party leadership. Even during the controversy over the government's 'In Place of Strife' proposals in 1969 for legisla-tion to curb unofficial strikes, the union leadership were concerned to contain the conflict and not raise broader issues regarding the leadership and the independence of the parliamentary party. The 'solemn and binding agreement' they struck with Wilson and Castle over 'In Place of Strife' was specifically designed to avoid a 'civil war' in the party.

What the union leaders really came to insist on after 1970 was that the corporatist 'partnership' that Wilson had promised in 1963–64 should really be adhered to next time. Cousins had enunciated this in his last speech to the House of Commons in October 1966: 'I am a representa-tive of a very large union and of a large number of workers who want to help this country out of its economic difficulties ... They are willing to be partners, but partners whose voice is heard, understood and respected and a voice to which regard is given.'[27] The union leadership did not see themselves as rivals for political leadership of the labour movement, even when they had sharp strategic as well as policy disagreements with the leaders of the PLP. And although many union delegations would eventually come to support constitutional reforms to make MPs more accountable, even left-led unions still respected the autonomy of the party leadership and saw the way forward in terms of a more effective 'elite accommodation' between the industrial and the political leadership.

This is not to say that the unions were not concerned with the substance of policy, although public ownership was nowhere near the top of their list of concerns. From 1968 onwards the TUC had begun to produce its own comprehensive annual Economic Review, in which it set out the rationale of a Keynesian reflationary policy and insisted that government economic planning must extend to external trade and financial flows and must embody detailed forecasts and specific require-ments for the investment decisions of large firms. On this basis the TUC was prepared to cooperate in a voluntary incomes policy. This was an important source of the celebrated 'Social Contract' of the mid-1970s, and of a significant part of 'Labour's Programme 1972' and the 'alterna-tive economic strategy' which grew out of both of these later in the 1970s. And it was Jack Jones's insistence on not being sold a pig in a poke, as in 1963–64, together with his spirited commitment to the closing of wage differentials and to strengthened shop floor bargaining arrangements, that made the parliamentary leadership's independence from the extra-parliamentary party and the broader labour movement look more contingent than ever before.

This insistence came to be institutionalised in the creation in January 1972 of the TUC–PLP–NEC Liaison Committee which was to become from then on the effective final arbiter of party policy. It was also this insistence that gave Michael Foot his prominence in the next Labour

Government. As the leading Bevanite left out of Wilson's 'team' in the 1960s, Foot's opposition to the incomes policy from 1966 onward had been based not on opposition to the principle of statutory wage restraint but on concern over the breach it created with the left union leadership.[28] Foot became in the 1970s what Benn accurately called the parliamentary leadership's 'link and buckle with the industrial wing of the trade union movement',[29] and Foot's retention of this politically crucial role into the 1980s proved, as we shall see, crucial in the ultimate defeat of the Labour new left's attempt to change the party.

The priority which even the left trade union leadership still attached to securing a 'real' partnership with the parliamentary leadership placed limits on how far change in the party could go in the 1970s. Nevertheless, their pursuit of this goal and their general ideological outlook encouraged both rank-and-file activists and the left in the PLP to make their own mark on the party. The ties between the left trade union leaders and the left-wing Tribune Group of MPs were close. The unions' refusal to allow a pre-election incomes policy agreement to be offered as an electoral reassurance to 'received opinion', as most of the party leadership would have liked, meant that a more comprehensive economic programme had to be fashioned instead, and this helped to undermine the policy hegemony of the parliamentary leadership. Perhaps most important, however, was the new union leaders' greater tolerance for dissent, their view that radical socialist activists were part of the labour movement's 'family' rather than its enemies, as the revisionists and right-wing leaders in their own unions had for so long insisted.

The New Activists

By the end of the 1966–70 Labour Government it was obvious that the Labour Party was in the throes of a severe membership crisis.[30] Until then, it was by no means clear that the Labour Party was in worse membership trouble than other European social democratic parties. Only the Swedish and Austrian parties managed to maintain a significantly higher ratio of party membership to the total electorate throughout the post-war era.[31] To be sure, it was a sign of the bankruptcy of Labour's revisionist leadership that the staggering membership growth between 1945 and 1952 (when individual membership more than doubled to 500,000) was not used to establish anything like the social democratic hegemony achieved by these two sister parties in the political life of their respective countries. The Labour leadership's view that the membership was an increasingly bothersome and antiquated device for electing its team of parliamentary leaders was barely concealed. Crosland had said as early as 1960 that: '. . . the elan of the rank and file is less and less essential to winning elections. With the growing penetration of the mass media, political campaigning has become increasingly centralised; and the traditional local activities, the door-to-door canvassing and the rest, are now largely a ritual.'[32] By the 1990s such a view would become widespread, yet the scale and speed of the collapse of membership that occurred in the mid- to late 1960s could not be treated so lightly.[33] There is no reason not to accept Seyd and Minkin's account: '... the greatest depletion took place in 1966–70, during the Wilson government ... A combination of social change, neglect and political disillusionment almost destroyed the Labour Party as a mass party. In terms of ward and committee attendance – and electoral work – activity was the lowest in individual memory.'[34]

But – and this is the important point – this decline in Labour Party membership and activism did not mean a decline in political activism. On the contrary, there was a virtual explosion of activity at both national and local level.[35] From squatters to tenants associations and Shelter, from community action groups to the Community Development Projects, from the Vietnam Solidarity Campaign to the Irish Civil Rights Solidarity Campaign, from local student activism in the schools and universities to the Radical Students' Alliance and the Revolutionary Socialists Students' Federation, from the sixty local women's groups federated in the Women's Liberation Workshop to the National Joint Action Campaign for Women's Equal Rights, from AgitProp to Cinema-Action, from Black Voice to the Gay Liberation Front, from Black Dwarf to Poster Workshop, and not least, from IS to IMG and Big Flame – the new politics was everywhere to be seen. Marjorie Mayo's retrospective view of this frenetic period of radical politics is apt:

> Amongst the new left radical intelligentsia there was at the time a mood of often totally unrealistic optimism about the possibilities of radical change ... coupled with a pervasive scepticism, not only about the nature of the state and officialdom, but also about traditional organisations and political parties of the left ... Simultaneously, there was a tendency to romanticise and over-idealise the 'poor' and their possibilities for radical action ... Student politics and then the women's movement were seen, along with community action ... as short cuts to creating a new radical movement whilst by-passing the struggles of the traditional parties and the organisations of the working class and the labour movement.[36]

Their by-passing of the Labour Party was partly a matter of not wanting to join a club that traditionally was not receptive to them anyway. Studies of constituency parties through the 1950s and 1960s invariably show a markedly exclusionary practice, particularly *vis-a-vis* left-wing activists. Barry Hindess captured some of this in his study of the party in Liverpool in the 1960s: 'Normally, in solid Labour areas, the Labour Party hardly exists except at election times. Between elections the Party organisation tends to wither away ... anyone who tries to stir up political activity must be a trouble-maker however much he or she may claim to represent the local membership or the working class.'[37] The party's full-time agents often saw their role less as organisers than as security guards against leftist activists. One of them told the American political scientist Austin Ranney that 'the main reason why so few anti-leadership candidates were adopted by C.L.P.s in his region was that he made it his business to see that they were kept off short-lists if at all possible. Any regional organiser who does not do the same, he felt, is not doing his job properly.'[38] This was, indeed, a central aspect of the National Executive's practice of 'social democratic centralism', summarised by Eric Shaw:

> The outstretched arm of the Party centre was felt over the whole range of internal Party activities. Local Party organisations (and individual members) were discouraged from engaging in activities (like holding conferences) unless they were expressly authorised. The Proscribed List was employed to limit the rights of members to associate with aims (like friendship with the Soviet Bloc) which the NEC found objectionable. Further, where politically charged disputes occurred at local level, the Executive almost invariably interceded on behalf of the right. Finally, in the crucial field of parliamentary selection, the NEC exerted a significant measure of control ... Social-democratic centralism fell considerably short of democratic centralism in that it did not curtail criticism of the leadership. But it did look askance at sustained and organised efforts by dissidents to challenge a whole range of official policies ...[39]

A continuing stream of expulsions (the most infamous case being that of Bertrand Russell in 1962) ran through the 1950s to the mid-1960s, reflecting, as Shaw shows, 'a deep-seated authoritarianism within the dominant right' and often displaying 'scant regard for the rights of members and for natural justice'.[40] John Palmer (who had stood as a Labour candidate in 1964 but was barred by the NEC from running in 1966) told a fringe meeting at the 1969 Party Conference: 'Whether you're in or out – that's largely a question of whether you're allowed to be in or out.'[41]

Many local parties were already in an appalling state long before the electoral set-backs of the late 1960s. During Jack Braddock's dictatorial rule as leader of the Liverpool City Council from 1955 to 1963 his party 'stalwarts' were in the main unskilled workers whose

> chief motive for public service ... was not to 'do something' but to 'be someone' ... For such people, policy is unimportant compared to the trappings of civic pomp ... membership in the Parks and Gardens Committee, with its official dinners and tours of inspection, and well paid senior officials of the city being polite and helpful to working men who may well get no respect or satisfaction in their everyday lives. Obtaining and retaining the Leader's approval was the way to obtain such offices, and having done so a

member would be reluctant to challenge the Leader, since if the Leader was displaced he would stand a good chance of losing his offices too.[42]

The system of patronage that governed Liverpool in this period may have been quantitatively extreme but it was not qualitatively unique. The NEC had helped in this since the 1930s by trying to enforce the same principle of independence of councillors from their local parties that the PLP sought to maintain at the national level.[43] A 1966 study of the Borough of Islington described a local party which had become 'exclusionary, feared local activists, and had a council leadership made up exclusively of older members . . .'[44] Another in West Ham showed that the Labour group dominated by Sam Boyce for thirty years 'largely avoided political principles as a topic of debate and concentrated on enjoying patronage, power and prestige'; while in Newcastle, 'the chief beneficiaries of the old leader's powers of patronage were friends and loyal retainers'.[45] As some new activists told Cynthia Cockburn in the course of her study of Lambeth in the early 1970s, the local parties were in the main 'caucus parties, cliques after their own self-perpetuation. They contribute nothing to the Labour movement as a whole. They have a very low membership and are run by a few people who don't encourage new membership because they want power to themselves. They would be threatened by a large active membership. It happens in areas where there is a large majority.'[46]

But the control of these cliques was by now precarious. The massive defeats of local Labour parties in 1967 and 1968 had severely undermined the domination of the old right wing in these parties since their power had been based on the ability of the local machine to keep producing electoral majorities.[47] Tony Benn noted in his diaries at the time that there 'was a school of thought, of which Gerald Kaufman was one of the leading exponents, that the Labour Party doing badly had the great effect of sweeping out the most ghastly reactionary old Labour councils and bringing in new leadership.' Benn thought this 'a very cynical view', but it proved correct.[48] As David Blunkett, who was elected to the Sheffield City Council while still a student in 1970, later said: 'Sheffield was more towards the traditional right while I was growing up – Roy Hattersley was on the council – but gradually in the late 1960s began to swing left. Labour lost power in the council in 1968, just for a year, but that year was traumatic. It began a shift in attitudes as well as in politics.'[49] A similar development had occurred in other local parties when councils swung back to Labour in the early 1970s. Illtyd Harrington, who had been refused endorsement by the NEC in the early 1960s after having been selected as a parliamentary candidate in Dover, and who in the early 1980s would play a key role in swinging the leadership of the London Labour Group to Ken Livingstone, wrote a remarkably prescient article in the *New Statesman* in 1971, entitled 'Young Turks of the Town Halls', to mark Labour's return to office in Islington and Lambeth that year. He pointed out that the majority of new councillors

> were political virgins, with an appropriately virginal combination of inno-
> cence and ambition. And they were very young, especially for politicians:
> average age around 30 ... [Few] seem to hunger for the hidden ecstasies of
> the mayor's parlour. The slogan is 'Do it now!' Rents have been frozen;
> Lambeth worked out within days a copybook agreement with the powerful
> South London squatters group; Islington declared war on the private town-
> house developer; Lambeth moved quickly at the London Borough Associa-
> tion to speed up the introduction of concessionary fares for the old and sick
> ... the youthful meritocracy who have seized power in parts of London may
> well have long political lives ahead of them.[50]

By no means were all these new councillors radical socialists. Many of them were indeed meritocrats from the 'new middle classes' who exhibited a distinctly technocratic orientation to politics, tinged with a vaguely participationist flavour. A few of them, such as Gerald South-gate, a management expert who became Islington's deputy leader in 1971, later ended up in the SDP; many more were eventually to join Kinnock's 'team' in the realignments of the 1980s. But what was crucial for the politics of the Labour Party in the 1970s was that they differed from the old guard not only in their technocracy; they also, at least at this time, were far more tolerant of debate and dissenting opinion. They simply did not share the old right's Cold War outlook, and this gave a new fluidity to local Labour politics, and an opening to people who had been more profoundly touched by the radicalism of the late 1960s. A discernible drift towards joining the Labour Party began in the early 1970s, especially among young community activists who started to take a more pragmatic view of alliances with trade unions in anti-cuts campaigns, and to develop a more sophisticated view of the state than the term 'cooptation' allowed for. As the limits of 'direct action' or sectarian Trotskyist politics became clearer on the one hand, and as the technocratic planning and limited participation of local Labour admin-istrations in the early 1970s quickly produced disappointments on the other, a more radical and more determined set of activists joined the Labour Party.

It is true that most of these new activists were also 'new middle class', although they tended to be teachers or social workers (or studying to be such) rather than management or public relations types. But like the two-thirds of Labour's middle-class voters who had working-class origins,[51] so did most of the new activists. And like Lockwood's 'Black Coated Worker' radicals of the 1950s, the new radicals of the early 1970s (who, of course, preferred denim) were distinctly marginal members of the middle class, who did not internalise the norms that traditionally went with professional status.[52] Indeed many of the young activists who joined the party in the 1970s had been educated in the 1960s by school teachers who reflected this marginal status and the iconoclastic norms that went with it.[53]

The experience of the twelve Community Development Project (CDP) teams set up under Home Office auspices in 1969 is often cited as indicative of the political trajectory of many activists who joined the party in the 1970s. Their 'inter-project' report in 1974 indicated that they had moved from the 'social pathology' approach that had led the Labour Government to establish them in 1969, towards an 'assumption that social problems arise from a fundamental conflict of interests between groups or classes in society. The problems are defined mainly in terms of inequalities in the distribution of power and the focus of change is thus on the centres of organised power (both private and public). The main tactic is organisation and raising levels of conscious-ness.'[54] Most of them came to share Cynthia Cockburn's view that ' "Community" belongs to capital': that participatory democracy, if conceived 'apart from the arena of conflict between the dominant and the exploited class', would become

> a tournament between small groups more closely related to each other: within the working class and its near neighbours ... they shake out as tenants, mothers, ratepayers, teenage youth, house owners, swimming enthusiasts and squatters. All are asked to compete and defend their special interests against each other, while the class with real power remains untouched...[55]

This did not mean that they gave up on the local state; on the contrary they saw it increasingly in terms of 'class struggles in the field of reproduction' and attempted to connect their local activities with the struggle to transform the Labour Party and through it the state at the national level. Many of these activists came to see Labour's new 'young turks' elected to local councils in 1970–71 as part of the 'management team' of the local state, but as the conflict inside the party heated up through the 1970s, many more joined the battle to change this.

There was thus a very important change through the 1970s on the part of the '1968 generation' in their attitude to working within the Labour Party and the broader labour movement. One activist in the Notting Hill Summer Project of 1967, which is often portrayed as the 'birthplace' of British community action, had clearly stated their initial position: 'To the Labour Party people were ticks on a canvass register – here they were to be central to the solution to their own problem. For me, from then on, the Labour Party was dead as a possible political organisation. The same was true of the hundreds of other young, and not so young, people who turned to the ideas of community action as a basis for their political life.' But by the mid-1970s, partly as a result of their own experience in community action and partly as a result of the challenge led by the left wing of the parliamentary party, and especially by Tony Benn, they began to face 'the old intractable problem of the political left' (as the same Notting Hill activist put it), i.e. whether to work within the Labour Party.[56] This was generally cast in terms of 'a major shift in focus in community work . . . [to] the whole issue of alliances with the mainstream of the Labour movement'.[57] As the Coventry CDP put it in 1975: 'the greatest potential for change may lie in new initiatives which create alliances across the neighbourhood, the factory floor and local political parties'.[58] Left-wing MPs and councillors were sought out to legitimise CDP campaigns, and on the other hand the ideas of community activists began to surface in the local election manifestos. This was especially notable in Sheffield, Nottingham and London by 1973, and was reflected not only in policies such as concessionary fares on local transport but also in pledges to make councillors more independent of local authority officers and more responsive to local party activists. Tensions between the Labour Groups and the new activists remained high in this period, as the promise of the local manifestos often went unfulfilled, but the increasing tension had the effect of lessening the discipline in the Labour Groups in the councils, especially when many of the new activists themselves became councillors and did not always adjust their politics to fit their new hats.[59]

If there was one theme that constantly resurfaced among the new activists once they joined the party, it was their strong opposition to what Blunkett called 'legislative paternalism':

> . . . [T]he belief in paternalistic, parliamentary change is . . . strong within the Party . . . We have to persuade those who are still living in the 1950s and 1960s that the way forward is to commit people from the bottom up in a jigsaw – a jigsaw that doesn't ignore national and international parameters, but relates to them . . . This can only be done from the local level, because you do have to fire people's imagination and commitment. They do have to have an alternative vision of the world, if you are going to overcome the obstacles. The idea that legislative paternalism is going to be successful has been discredited so many times that it is amazing that anyone in Parliament still believes it.[60]

Cynthia Cockburn found a similar attitude among the radical new activists in the Norwood local party in Lambeth in the early 1970s. They differed from traditional Labour practice in having 'a more purposeful and intrusive relationship with local popular organisations than other Labour parties' and they were active in recruiting and fund-raising for propaganda. The agent told her that 'We get our councillors active quickly in new street groups and tenant associations as they emerge.' Cockburn concluded that 'a relatively dynamic party . . . could afford to "use" local activists with a support base in tenant associations, etc., to curb the strength of the councillors'.[61] It was a mark of the way they differed from the previous norm that a great many of these university-educated, articulate, 'new middle-class' activists, the stuff of which the Parliamentary Labour Party had been increasingly made for decades, did not seek to become parliamentary candidates as soon as possible.[62] Ken Livingstone put it this way: 'I thought I could achieve far more as a full-time local government politician than I could ever achieve as a backbench MP. All through the period from 1968 to 1975 I never tried to get selected as a Parliamentary candidate. I stayed fully active in local government . . . it seemed in local government that you had a chance to actually involve people in the running of their lives, to break up the concentrations of power . . .'[63] But they combined their local level work with a struggle at the national level to make parliamentarians as well as councillors accountable to their parties.

Livingstone had joined the Norwood party in 1968 because he thought 'that you weren't going to achieve social change other than through the Labour Party. No outside group was going to replace it . . .' In the context of a 'totally debilitated' party, he, like other new activists who joined over the next decade, found that you didn't need to be part of an organised 'entrist' tendency to have an influence. After attending his second branch meeting he became chairman and secretary of the Young Socialists and was put on the local government committee. By the third meeting he was membership secretary of the party and on the executive committee. 'There was simply no one else around to do those sorts of things. Everybody else had left. It was incredible. At general management committee meetings in Norwood there were only about twenty-five people present . . .'[64] Yet by 1973 the Norwood ward party had around 1,000 members (as compared with well over 500 constituency parties which had fewer). What invariably came up over a decade later in discussions with people who were active in Norwood in the early 1970s was the breakthrough they felt they had made with their weekly Sunday canvass. They would pick an issue relevant to the community and knock on doors to discuss it. Persisted in week after week, rain or shine, it proved an immensely successful way for party activists to get to know the community and to become known to many people within it.

What is particularly noteworthy about this orientation to local politics is that it did not reflect a class difference between new middle-class and new working-class activists, nor between northern and southern constituencies. The councillors who propelled Clay Cross to prominence by refusing to implement the rent increases required by the 1971 Housing Finance Act were all working class and they had already transformed their local party in the 1960s even more radically than others were to do in the 1970s. One of the sons of Tony Skinner, a member of the Communist Party in the early 1950s, set to work on a local Labour

Party which in 1959 had fifteen members and only two councillors. In this project Dennis Skinner, who had previously only been active in his NUM branch, was joined by other young miners, and later by his two brothers who became members of the Labour Party Young Socialists when they were still at school. They took the view

> that if they, the Labour Party, were to win the confidence of the people, they needed to embark on a course of political education for everybody. There was nothing patronising about their attitude; they wanted people to know what was going on ... [N]ight after night, doors were knocked [on], leaflets distributed, public meetings organised and attended ... That was always stressed: you talked to people, and you listened; you heard what they wanted to say and you told them what the Labour Party was proposing. And you talked to them in their own language; they knew that you were one of them. Practical politics they called it.[65]

Even allowing for a touch of exaggeration, this kind of politics was clearly not primarily about sectarian infighting within the party. By 1963 they had swept the municipal council and begun to implement a policy and style of administration that was rather revolutionary. They cleared the slums and built new council housing at a rate more than twice the national average. They bent the rules, scattering Compulsory Purchase Orders 'like confetti' and transferring money from the general rate fund to avoid paying high interest rates on government loans which only 'lined the bankers' pockets'. They insisted that the whole community should pay for this ambitious project and charged the lowest rents in the country.[66]

Although Clay Cross was exceptional, the attitudes its policies reflected were becoming widely held by Labour councillors. A 1975 study of the political attitudes of seventy-one Labour councillors from five local authorities in England, in very different areas, provided some interesting insights to a radicalism that stood in sharp contrast with the attitudes of the parliamentary leadership on national issues. A very large majority of them agreed with the following propositions: 'the central question of British politics is the class struggle between labour and capital' (71 per cent); 'Labour ameliorates rather than attacks inequality' (74 per cent); 'Labour should nationalise profitable industries' and 'should implement Clause IV of the party constitution' (both 78 per cent); 'hived off industries should be renationalised without compensation' (84 per cent); 'Britain should reduce defence spending by one billion pounds' (71 per cent); 'there are not enough working-class MPs' (68 per cent).[67]

The orientations of the new activists produced varying reactions at the top. In 1969 Ron Hayward had been appointed National Agent, following Sara Barker's twenty-seven years of authoritarian rule in this key position at the head of party organisation. It was an appointment which signalled a shift to the left on the National Executive Committee and a more open and tolerant intra-party regime, which was further strengthened when Hayward was appointed General Secretary of the Party in 1972. In January 1971 Hayward wrote a fascinating editorial in *Labour Organiser*. It began by relating a conversation he had with 'Old Bill', chairman of a ward party, who had complained about a new member in his party. 'The first time I set eyes on him I knew he was up to no good,' said Old Bill ... 'you can't trust him, never ought to be in the Party, he's a ruddy Left-winger ... First time he came to the ward meeting, he questioned my ruling on selecting our local government candidate and he's been throwing questions at me ever since.' Hayward, with his long experience as a party organiser, recognised a general syndrome:

> We all pay lip service to recruit new members into the Party ... But, if we are going to 'tie labels' around their necks at first sight or after hearing their first views, then we ought not to pretend that we believe in 'democracy', 'communication' and 'liaison'.... We should encourage the cut, thrust and parry of debate. We should talk more politics at our meetings and not spend so much time on Minutes, Matters Arising, jumble sales and Any Other Business ... The clobbering of a member usually new to our ranks, is the only bit of life this type of party shows from year to year.[68]

Hayward called on the party to spend its time working to defeat 'our political opponents who are *outside the ranks of our Party*'. It was to become a familiar refrain on the centre and right of the party. But if we are to understand the history of the attempt to change the Labour Party we should remember that the call was first issued in support of new left-wing activists in the face of the resistance offered by the old guard at national and local levels.

The case that became most visible at the national level in the early 1970s (and that incidentally set a new pattern for media bias against left-wing constituency activists) was the conflict between the Lincoln CLP and its MP, Dick Taverne. The immediate issue was Taverne's stand in favour of Common Market entry and his having voted with the Conservatives for it in the Commons in 1971, along with sixty-eight other Labour MPs, in defiance of both Conference and PLP policy. But what was involved here was far more than an isolated case of 'individual conscience' for an MP. The way Taverne had first been adopted as Lincoln's parliamentary candidate in 1961 itself spoke volumes about the hypocrisy of the Gaitskellites in their attacks on the left's allegedly undemocratic factionalism. Taverne had been a prominent member of the Campaign for Democratic Socialism. The CDS had originally been organised to reverse the 1960 Conference decision in favour of unilateral nuclear disarmament, but, as Peter Paterson disclosed in 1967, it continued to organise, under the aegis of a secret committee meeting in the House of Commons, 'a much more high-powered effort to secure the selection of loyal and steadfast Gaitskellite candidates ... with the object of allocating available candidacies to "reliable" individuals and ensuring that sufficient votes would be available inside each local Labour Party concerned to make the success of the committee's nominee as certain as possible'.[69]

The number of right-wing candidates actually selected as a direct result of this activity was not great, and more vacancies left by retiring MPs in 1964 were filled by people publicly identified with CND or *Tribune* than by Gaitskellites. But Taverne was selected at Lincoln in this manner for a by-election in 1961, with the three nominees on the short-list before the selection conference offering, as Taverne himself said, 'politically a choice between Tweedledum, Tweedledee, and their triplet brother'. The temporary Gaitskellite majority for this selection on the Executive Committee and the General Management Committee of the Lincoln party did not even last as long as the run-up to the by-election. New elections to the GMC swung the balance to the left where it stayed thereafter. Taverne described the ensuing situation: 'I was a Gaitskellite and Social Democrat MP who had been introduced to Lincoln because of the part I played in fighting the left-wing in the CDS. I faced a GMC that was not just left-wing, but dominated by a small group of very determined left-wingers who knew what they were doing – fighting for power in the Party, locally and nationally, against people like myself.' Still, they were not nearly as clear or determined as they might have been: Taverne himself admitted that from his perspective as a junior minister in the Wilson Governments 'it was amazing how much active Labour Party members tolerated'.[70]

During the intra-party debate on the Common Market in 1970–71, Taverne played the role he had adopted since 1959, along with Bill Rodgers, as a key organiser for the Gaitskellite faction in the party. No observer at the Party Conferences, and especially at the Special Conference on the question of entry to the Common Market in July 1971, could fail to notice Taverne's constant activity in organising the pro-market vote and the cheer-leading, heckling and arm-twisting that went with it. In passionate commitment to his intra-party faction and in mobilising discipline within it and support for it, he could have taught not only the Campaign for Labour Party Democracy but even Militant a thing or two. Indeed, two decades later, Bryan Gould saw the remarkable cohesion of the right wing in the Shadow Cabinet in terms of a factional allegiance that stretched all the way back to that moment in 1971 when they had voted against the Labour whip in order to carry the Heath Government's European legislation: 'This common experience of shared tribulations and of being bloodied in the same battle gave members of the group ... a sort of confidence which endured and did not need to be constantly reaffirmed. It also explained their almost religious conviction on the European issue and their resistance to anyone who did not share the True Faith.'[71]

Nobody on the left was proposing that Taverne should be drummed out of the Labour Party for his role as a factional organiser, but his constituency party had enough of him as their MP. After the 1970 election fierce arguments between Taverne and his local party had already broken out over the Conservative Government's new Industrial Relations Bill, and after he voted against the Labour Whip on the Common Market his GMC finally voted in June 1972 to ask him to retire at the next general election. Taverne was in fact the only one of the sixty-nine MPs who had voted with the Tories to be dismissed by his local party, although many other CLPs were extremely upset by their MPs' behaviour. But the media as well as the social democrats in the PLP played up the Taverne case as proof of the Labour Party's 'intolerance', and this was already a strong indication that the subsequent attempt to subject all sitting Labour MPs to reselection would be treated as 'undemocratic', and that this would prove a major barrier to any attempt to change the Labour Party.

Nevertheless, the Taverne case set an important precedent. Taverne's resignation as MP in October 1972, forcing a by-election, in which he successfully stood against the Labour candidate, revealed to many activists and trade unionists that the party loyalty of right-wing MPs was highly conditional, to say the least. Perhaps most important, however, the Taverne case showed that it was by no means 'entrists' or even new party activists alone who were going to challenge their MPs. The Lincoln constituency was led by long-standing activists in the party, many of them with impeccable trade union credentials. They had experienced at first hand the 'social-democratic centralism' that had governed the party through the post-war era. 'Not surprisingly,' Shaw remarks, 'the sudden fervour with which disciplinarians from this period embraced "tolerance", "the rights of minorities" and "the rights of dissent" when *they* found themselves in the minority was treated with cold scepticism by left-wing veterans of the Bevanite wars.'[72]

As they made common cause with political activists of all kinds outside the party through the 1970s, it was increasingly clear that the new left inside the party were a force to be reckoned with. To be sure, the process of building a challenge to 'parliamentary paternalism' was a painfully slow one. During the course of the Wilson governments of 1964–70 the only serious attempt to provide organisational cohesion for such a challenge at the national level was the establishment in 1968 of Socialist Charter. This quickly gained the formal support of 188 party and union organisations, but it had few active members and made little impact.[73] But even without the kind of organisational coherence that was later provided by the Campaign for Labour Party Democracy, by 1970 no one could mistake the very broad sweep of opinion in the constituencies and the unions which not only saw Labour as a working-class party that ought to pursue more socialist policies, but was also ready to question, challenge, and try to limit the autonomy of the parliamentary leadership.

When Wilson published his own retrospective version of his time in office, its tone and attitude – its notorious celebration of his government's accumulated failures as 'the art of the possible' – was exactly what the Labour new left had been so opposed to, and so frustrated by. E.P. Thompson caught the mood when he asserted instead that: 'The art of the possible can only be restrained from engrossing the whole universe if the impossible can find ways of breaking back into politics, again and again.'[74] The attempt to change the Labour Party in the 1970s was motivated by a determination to accomplish this by building on the radicalism of the period, focusing not only on socialist policies but also on the need to overcome the limitations of British democracy.

3

Tony Benn: Articulating a New Socialist Politics

In the early 1970s the new left activists in the Labour Party had only barely begun to make themselves felt. Their politics were still relatively inchoate, and they had not thrown up any nationally recognised leaders of their own, or developed any independent organisational focus. But one national leader heard what they were saying and expressed it in a way that gave it a clearer shape and purpose. What enabled Tony Benn to do this – to become the pre-eminent spokesperson and interpreter of Labour's new left – was his remarkably early perception of the political forces that would eventuate in Thatcherism, his understanding of the limits of parliamentary socialism as practised by the Labour Party, and his articulation of an alternative conception of socialist practice.

It is a mistake to put too much emphasis on the role of any individual, but it is also a mistake to deny it when an individual's significance is exceptional – and not least when that individual has been so systematically misrepresented. Even sympathisers with the Labour new left have tended to misrepresent it in retrospect as merely 'clinging to the old formulae'.[1] They have failed to recognise and acknowledge the extent to which their own critique of the limits of Labourism were articulated by Benn as early as the beginning of the 1970s.

On the other hand, although Benn played the leading role in articulating the Labour new left's politics and getting its agenda debated in the Cabinet and Shadow Cabinet, and in the party executive and its committees, the main organisations that composed the Labour new left were not built around him.[2] Even in Parliament, no 'Bennite' faction of MPs emerged, as the 'Bevanites' had in the 1950s. Benn's role was not as the Labour new left's organiser but as its tribune, its 'prominent voice'.[3]

Benn had always been an iconoclast in relation to both the traditional left and the traditional right of the parliamentary party, but he had hardly been seen previously as a dissident, much less as a radical socialist. He had stayed in the 1964–70 Labour Governments throughout, first as Minister for the Post Office and then in the more senior office of Minister of Technology. But by 1968, in a series of speeches, he had already begun to show clear signs of his passage from radical liberalism to radical socialism by an unusual route – experience of the limitations and frustrations of high governmental office. As he began articulating with great clarity – and, as it soon turned out, with great commitment – what was at stake in changing the Labour Party, and through it the British state, it was not his espousal of more state intervention (or of Clause IV) that made an impression on the new activists. If this was all there had been to it, he would have appeared indistinguishable from the old Tribune left or from the Communist Party. Perhaps only someone who had precisely *not* been integrated into the traditional Labour left could have understood so clearly not just that socialism was the necessary extension of democracy, but also that *if* democracy was to fulfil its radical promise, then '. . . our long campaign to democratise power in Britain has, first, to begin in our own movement'.[4]

Benn before 'Bennism'

Thanks to his early mastery of television, and the leading role he played in adapting the party to it, Benn was seen in the 1950s and early 1960s as the archetypal 'moderniser' in the Labour Party. As early as the 1955 election he took the view that 'the old days of petitioning, indoor meetings, 100 per cent canvasses and the rest, are probably dead and gone forever'; and from his perspective as media guru at the centre of the 1959 election campaign team, he was impressed at 'how efficient the Party can be' when the electoral technocrats and media spin doctors were left to run the show: 'Without the NEC and the Publicity Committee and the Shadow Cabinet everything works fine. I am sure there are lessons in this for the future.'[5] Nye Bevan, so far from seeing Benn as a left-wing figure, did nothing to conceal his dislike for someone who symbolised to him the young middle-class professional career politician responsible for turning politics into TV campaigns and surveys of public opinion. Benn was acutely aware, as he felt Bevan's sting, of personally being at the receiving end of 'the inverted class feeling which is so strong in the Labour Party'; but he also saw this as an obstacle to bringing the young middle-class professional strata into the party, which he believed was necessary.[6]

Although Benn voted for Bevan in the 1955 deputy leadership contest he was most certainly never a 'Bevanite'. Asked to join the Tribune Group shortly after he had been elected at the age of twenty-five to succeed Sir Stafford Cripps as MP for Bristol South East in 1950, he refused because he 'didn't want to be tied to a whipping system, which they had quite rigidly, on a scale smaller than the party itself'.[7] He was impatient at being lectured about 'sacred socialist principles' by leading

Bevanites on the one hand, and he was critical of the simplistic views of 'the rank and file left winger' on the other. Most notably, in view of his own later role, he was 'depressed beyond words' at 'the obvious relish' the Bevanites seemed to show when 'trouble was brewing' inside the party; and was 'disquieted' when he saw that youth had a 'dislike of Party or intra-party squabbles except as entertainment'.[8] He eventually came to appraise Bevan in terms of his 'total failure ... to offer constructive thought or generous political leadership'.[9] The challenge that would confront Benn himself two decades later would precisely be to offer such thought and leadership as would make the inevitable conflicts associated with trying to change the Labour Party from the left into something more constructive than 'troubles' or 'squabbles', both to those inside the party who participated in them and to those who observed them from the outside.

But Benn was also uncomfortable with Gaitskell's leadership (above all, with what he regarded as 'his pedestrian mind'),[10] as well as with the politics of 'revisionism' as the way to modernise the Labour Party. Although throughout the 1950s he accepted a more or less Croslandite understanding of the nature of the modern capitalist economy, and was not an enthusiast for more nationalisation, after the 1959 election Benn found himself on the left in the argument over abandoning the party's commitment to public ownership as embodied in Clause IV of the party constitution. He saw Gaitskell's speech on this to the 1959 Conference as:

> a ghastly failure because it was constructed in quite the wrong way and without regard to the needs of the Party. In effect he asked, 'How much of what we once believed will the electorate now stomach?' The answer he produced was not surprisingly, 'Very little'. But that is not the question you should ask. If he had said, 'Here is the modern world full of causes for us to take up. Here is what we must do. Here are the changes we must make in ourselves to do them' the Party would have risen to him like a man. But he is quite incapable of inspiring people.[11]

Benn was thus certainly not part of the traditional left, but in contrast to the Labour right and centre, he was already reaching for a less cautiously 'respectable' and more positively radical approach to modernising the party. This could be seen in the way he sought to approach issues by constantly trying to broaden the range of political controversy rather than narrowing it, and by refusing to allow conventional or establishment opinion to dictate the terrain of debate. For example, on the crucial problem of the party's relationship to the trade unions, Benn wanted to 'focus on the need for the unions to modernise themselves and extend the limits of their support. This is in contrast to the Jenkins–Crosland school who believe it must all be done by weakening the traditional links.'[12] In his view, the key shortcoming of the politics of Gaitskell and the centre-right was that they followed the media instead of leading them in the definition of issues. Benn reacted against Gaitskell's apparent subservience to conventional opinion and was revolted at how, when he was under attack for an anti-establishment or unconventional position taken by a left-wing Labour MP, Gaitskell 'concentrated on the object of the press hunt ... and thus encouraged it [by] repudiating a colleague who was in difficulty'. This kind of behaviour was a 'demonstration of the Gallup poll mentality defeating the ordinary instincts of personal loyalty and leadership'.[13] A similar mentality led the party leadership to run for cover to avoid controversial issues it needed to confront. Thus, at the time of the race riots in London in 1958, Benn urged Gaitskell to do a party broadcast on them and to visit Notting Hill personally, but he was told that this couldn't be done without Butler's (the Conservative Government's Home Secretary at the time) permission. 'I came away very dejected,' Benn confided to his diary. 'What is wrong with the Party is that it is inactive. We ought to be offering a constructive daily alternative on a wide range of issues. We are just not doing it.'[14] It turned out, in fact, that the speech he made in 1950 at the Bristol South-East constituency meeting that first selected him as a parliamentary candidate was actually quite an accurate indication of his political orientation. He had insisted that:

> socialism is not just a question of material progress ... It is a faith and a way of life and a way of thinking that can find its expression in every city and every community and every home ... We cannot, as a movement, live forever on the black memories of the thirties or on the wisdom of the socialist pioneers. We must inspire people afresh and especially young people with faith. That is our job. Make, teach and keep socialists.[15]

There can be no doubt that Benn's long and tenacious struggle to avoid being 'elevated' to the House of Lords was a major factor in sustaining the radicalism that otherwise ebbs so naturally away from even left-wing Labour MPs once they become schooled in 'parliamentary paternalism'. His father, a minister in the 1929 and 1945 Labour Governments, had been made a peer and Benn had been acutely aware that this typical example of Labour's embrace of the archaic British constitutional order would mean, by virtue of his automatic inheritance of this peerage upon his father's death, that he would be required to give up his seat in the House of Commons. In the course of his fight to avoid this, he had to become a constitutional expert, but he also learned forever to distrust the clap-trap that goes with the defence of 'tradition' in British constitutional discourse. When he was indeed excluded from the House of Commons after his father died in 1961, he secured the full involvement of his local party in two successful by-election campaigns and in raising a petition, signed by 10,000 constituents, aimed at mobilising the people of Bristol 'to wrench the Parliamentary system away from its feudal origins and pitchfork it into the twentieth century'.[16] As the best biography of Benn has put it: 'The successful outcome of his ten-year campaign to remain a commoner ... showed that reform only came about through the public bringing unceasing pressure to bear on Parliament. It drove Benn to the conclusion that parliamentary democracy and the rule of law were empty phrases unless rooted in popular democracy, and that Parliament was either an instrument of the people or nothing.'[17]

Benn was, therefore, in several ways well prepared for the explosion of popular politics in the late 1960s. The by-election campaigns in Bristol had stimulated an interest in community politics in the local party and, together with the constituency agent, Herbert Rogers, and a number of local Labour leaders, Benn founded the New Bristol Group which, with over a hundred active members, from 1962 to 1966 published broadsheets and held seminars and meetings on a broad range of local issues from transport to race relations, all aimed at encouraging greater local democracy and a more innovative and active role for local government. The Labour-led Bristol City Council denounced it, but the group saw themselves primarily as a centre for socialist education which would serve as a model for other cities in mobilising 'the new generation'. To some extent Benn explicitly saw himself following in this respect the example of the anti-colonial African leaders he had got to know in the 1950s when he was a member of a loose grouping of internationalist MPs (including Fenner Brockway, Geoffrey Bing and Ian Mikardo) who saw their role as speaking up for the African independence movements in Parliament and the labour movement. It was characteristic of him that he should have later seen the radicalism of the new activists of the late 1960s and early 1970s in anti-colonial terms, and compared the charges of extremism that were made against them with those that had earlier been levelled at Nehru and Nkrumah. 'Extremist is the first compliment the Establishment pays you,' he said in 1973. 'We are the last of the colonies and the Establishment is trying to stop us breaking away.'[18]

Benn's much publicised defense of various people who were victims of the anti-communism of the early 1950s also led him to be accused of pro-communist sympathies. He found this hurtful but it did not dissuade him. His initial opposition to the Common Market in the 1950s was largely based on what he saw as 'the strong anti-Russian cold war bias that lay behind it'.[19] In opposing a 1956 bill to tighten the security vetting of civil servants he told the House that 'far from dismissing any member of the Foreign Office who had read Karl Marx, my inclination would be to dismiss anyone who had not read Karl Marx'.[20] Benn's civil libertarianism was determining here, but he distinguished himself from most Labour parliamentarians not only by having the courage (and sense of the ridiculous) to make such a statement in the middle of the Cold War, but also by the fact that he never shared the sneering attitude to Marxism or the McCarthyite impulses of so many of his colleagues. He was being perfectly consistent when, in a speech to the Young Fabians in 1968, while Minister of Technology, he stressed the need for renewed study of Marx: 'Some of what Marx said was wrong, is unacceptable, or out of date. He has however been unfairly held responsible for the horrors perpetrated by Stalin and others, in his name, long after his death. But it is high time that Marx and others were studied again within the democratic socialist movement. They still have something important to say to us, about the nature of society.'[21] Whereas Wilson seemed proud to assert that he had never read Marx, Benn was ashamed that he had not done so to any significant extent and he would try to remedy this in the 1970s, even while a minister, reflecting the view he came to by 1973 that a socialist party without Marxism 'really lacks a basic analytic core'.[22] Two decades later, in reaction to a 'New Labour' leader in the 1990s who peppered his speeches with sneers at Marx, Benn commented: '. . . when Labour leaders have said that Marx is dead, it's a bit like saying Galileo is old hat, or Darwin got it wrong, or Freud muddled things up'.[23]

But Benn's experience as minister in the first Wilson Governments did not make him a Marxist. What it did was to make him increasingly uncomfortable with the contradictions between his radical liberal and democratic populist orientations and the technocratic strategy which he had helped construct as part of Wilson's team. At first these differences emerged only under the cover of night. Faced with what Benn judged to be 'an apparent loss of impetus by the government' only a few months after Labour's triumph at the 1966 election, Wilson summoned a group of those he saw as his old political friends to Chequers where a discussion that 'ranged over the whole field of politics' went on until 3 a.m. According to Benn's account:

> [Wilson] began with his now famous theme that the British public was bored with politics and wanted him to be the doctor who looked after the difficulties so that it could go on playing tennis. I challenged that fundamentally and said I thought it was an elitist view of politics and was incompatible with a radical Government. Maybe the public didn't understand economics and was sick of the abuse of party politics, but it was interested in real politics and it was our duty to pick those issues which related to matters we thought important and actually make them controversial. I cited education as an example and said I thought the status of women in society might be another.[24]

Afterwards Benn recorded his worry that Wilson was 'going to preside over a period of decline just as serious as occurred under Macmillan under the same basic philosophy of "never had it so good" affluence. . . . Consensus is no substitute for putting key issues and institutions deliberately into the crucible of controversy. If we don't change things fundamentally we shall have failed in our job even if we survive as a Government.'[25]

It was only a month later that Benn succeeded Frank Cousins at the Ministry of Technology and became not only a member of the Cabinet but also the minister most directly responsible for policy to overcome Britain's industrial decline – the centrepiece of Labour's 'modernisation' project. That he already had an analysis of the roots of the problem, and a capacity to communicate it effectively, was made clear only weeks after his move to 'Mintech' at a lunch with the leaders of the major machine tool manufacturing and engineering companies.

> [W]hat has gone wrong with Britain in the industrial field is not due to two years of Labour Government, thirteen wasted Tory years, six years of socialist misrule, the War, the depression, the First World War. The origins of our difficulties go back much further. Germany overtook this country in the 1880s and indeed we began losing our lead in about the fifties or sixties of the last century ... [when] we opted to become an imperial country instead of continuing as an industrial one. . . . In my childhood I had been taught a great deal about the engineers of the late eighteenth and early nineteenth centuries ... after that the school books concentrated on viceroys and generals, civil servants and diplomats ... Thus all the schools had geared themselves to producing the sort of people the empire needed ... The truth is that Britain must now give up being an imperial country and become an industrial country again and only in this way can we reshape our society . . .[26]

The problem Benn faced as a new Cabinet minister with this type of analysis, however, was that the Labour Government had already reverted to the traditional practice of trying to manage the crisis of the old order. This had already been made abundantly clear by Government's wage freeze and the abandonment of the National Plan (its five-year corporatist blueprint for economic growth, painstakingly negotiated with the TUC and the CBI) as the cost of avoiding devaluation – itself a choice made in deference to the City of London. Benn, having entered the Cabinet through the very door by which Cousins had left in protest at the wage freeze, was acutely aware of the contradiction in which he was caught. He confided to his diary: 'I am so out of sympathy with the continuation of our banking and world roles that I don't know that there is any advice I can give within the orbit of existing policy.'[27] Benn had spoken in Cabinet in favour of devaluation rather than deflation, but he knew that this was just a symptom of a deeper set of problems.

He was finding it increasingly hard to escape the conclusion 'that parliamentary democracy, which is our proudest boast, is not working in this country'. As Minister at the Post Office, Benn had encountered strong opposition (on even as minor if imaginative a proposal as 'establishing a Fellowship to study the way the Post Office might provide a link between the social services and those in the community who need their help') not just from officials in his own department, but from an alliance of officials across several departments. Coordination among Labour ministers could overcome such networks of bureaucratic reaction, he was convinced. But this involved first having 'a really dynamic political party that is elected knowing the difficulties that will face it and determined to get control of the Whitehall machine and really use it to carry through fundamental changes. I just don't believe that this impetus exists within the Labour Party or within the Labour Cabinet ... we are going to go on floating, governed by civil servants with Ministers from the two parties coming in and out by a curious quirk known as the electoral cycle.'[28]

There was still a further problem, beyond the absence of policy direction in the Cabinet and bureaucratic resistance in Whitehall, and this was the actual incapacity of the state in relation to the structure of the economy, including not only the City of London but also manufacturing industry itself. This had already been recognised by Cousins, who shortly after he resigned expressed his frustration to the House of Commons that as a minister he had very little power *vis-à-vis* private corporations, not least because he depended on them for the information that determined state policy: 'I saw the type of planning we did ... I could get better facts related to the growth prospects of some of the major companies through my position as General Secretary of the Transport and General Workers Union.'[29] Benn eventually came to the same conclusion. He had understood that problems of management, not poor labour discipline, were the most important sources of British industry's notoriously low productivity, and he tried to work closely with private industrial firms to address this; indeed he even was prepared to agree with those industrialists, such as Sir Denning Pearson of Rolls Royce, who told him that the productivity situation might be improved if the Government's own research and development efforts would take direction from businessmen, rather than research scientists.[30] In light of the enormous resources that Mintech made available to Rolls Royce while Benn was minister, he eventually had a lot of explaining to do as to why he had not foreseen the collapse of Rolls Royce in 1971. The explanation he offered in the House the Commons was, in fact, remarkably similar to what Cousins had said five years earlier: 'The Government did not have the expertise to check the figures of the most experienced air engineering company in Britain.'[31]

It was for these reasons, and not because of any dogma, that Benn also followed Cousins in becoming much clearer and more determined about the necessity of public ownership of the 'commanding heights' of the economy. Yet there was a still deeper lesson that each of these two men learned from their experience at the top of the state: namely that their role in managing the economy precluded them from continuing to act as political leaders of the class that had put them in office. To attempt to defend that class in its struggles ran fundamentally against their function as ministers. It was when he saw this clearly on the issue of wage controls that Cousins had resigned. Benn felt he was forced to face up to it when he was required to deal with the obstreperous employees of the firms he was so 'hooked' (as he put it) on merging in order to produce the internationally competitive corporate giants which the Government saw as the salvation to Britain's export and productivity ills.

> I have never forgotten the day I was sent by the Cabinet up to UCS . . . I got up at four in the morning and I got there before light and went to the shipyard and it was a foggy day and I climbed on one of the cranes and addressed the people because I always liked to do it direct. I said 'look we're pouring money in and you've got 18 per cent absenteeism', and some guy shouted at me 'if you had to stand in an open yard with cold metal on a foggy morning like this you'd be absent most of the time'.[32]

This was in March of 1969, at the time of the open confrontation with the unions over the Government's proposals for legislation to contain strikes. Benn did not take a stand against the policy, but he was coming to the conclusion that the Government's main weakness lay in its being unable to offer its own supporters any overall sense of 'where we are going and what we want to do. This is the great weakness of pragmatism. It isn't that people want ideology, but they want analysis and explanation and at the moment they are simply not getting it.'[33]

Benn had begun to express this publicly in speeches in 1968. His main theme was the contrast between the unpopularity of Labour as a government and a party, and the flowering of extra-parliamentary political radicalism and activism. He saw the community action groups, the student protests, the industrial unrest, Black Power, and Welsh and Scottish nationalism, all as evidence of one central issue: 'Much of the present wave of anxiety, disenchantment and discontent is actually directed at the present Parliamentary structure . . . It would be foolish to assume that people will be satisfied, for much longer, with a system which confines their national political role to the marking of a ballot paper with a single cross every five years.' Just as popular pressures had transformed the parliamentary system in earlier centuries, there now was the need for

> . . . equally radical changes in our system of government to meet the requirements of a new generation. I am not dealing here with the demand for the ownership and control of growing sections of the economy. I am thinking

of the demand for more political responsibility and power for the individual than the present system of Parliamentary democracy provides ... The widening gulf between the Labour Party and those who supported it last time could well be an index of the Party's own obsolescence. Party reform now is just as important as the evolution of the parliamentary system ... It will be a tremendous task. Indeed the whole function and role and character of the party will inevitably have to change ... Beyond parliamentary democracy as we know it we shall have to find a new popular democracy to replace it.[34]

The kinds of solutions that Benn offered at that time involved an end to secrecy in government; decentralisation, devolution and self-regulation for regions, unions, community, and professional groups; referenda; and the allocation of press space and broadcasting time to the broadest range of community and political groups (this last proposal landed him in the most trouble with his Cabinet colleagues as well as with the press). But at the same time, he usually presented these solutions as extensions of the Government's practice and they often had a distinctly corporatist ring – more consultation, with a view to greater managerial efficiency. Even as he asked the most challenging question – 'what special characteristic would a popular democracy have that is now lacking in parliamentary democracy?' – his own answers revealed both the constraints of his role in the Cabinet and his own still rather technocratic orientation. Nevertheless he was immediately attacked both in the PLP and the Cabinet for breaching 'Cabinet responsibility', a doctrine which he increasingly came to see as a 'major weapon of repression.'[35] Yet Benn would not resign from the Cabinet. He had once previously used resignation from office as a political tactic when in 1960, reflecting his own highly ambivalent position on unilateral nuclear disarmament, he had carried out his threat to resign from the NEC if Gaitskell and Cousins did not try to arrive at compromise which would reflect the range of membership positions on the issue. This was a reckless act for a young and ambitious Labour MP and, when he failed to get re-elected to the NEC until 1962, '... he learned what he felt to be an important lesson: that influence was of greater value than isolation, and that resignations, on the whole, achieve nothing'.[36]

These were some of the often contradictory currents in Benn's thinking as he went through his process of political re-evaluation in the late 1960s. If he was determined not to resign, he was gradually becoming no less determined to attempt a radical reconstruction of the leadership's function in a mass socialist party. In 1968, he seriously considered standing for the General Secretaryship of the Labour Party, for while he was enjoying being at Mintech, he thought 'the reconstruction of the Party is the most important task. ... The student power movement, the Black Power movement and the discontent among trade unionists are very powerful and important new forces in society, and I believe the

Labour Party has got to enter into a creative relationship with them.'[37] At a Cabinet meeting in the dying days of the Government, he insisted that the real issue in the forthcoming election ought to be 'the people versus the elite' and that the key task was to encourage people to have confidence in themselves. He even offered them a quotation attributed to Lao-Tzu: 'As for the best leaders, the people do not notice their existence; the next best, the people honour and praise; the next the people fear; and the next they hate. But when the best leaders' work is done, the people say "we did it ourselves".'[38] As the Labour Party went back into opposition after the June 1970 election it was on this question of what was the proper role of political leaders that Benn made his break with Labour Party tradition, left and right.

The Emergence of 'Bennism'

Benn set out his thinking in a Fabian Society pamphlet entitled *The New Politics: A Socialist Reconnaissance* in 1970. Unlike the Tribune MPs who focused on Clause IV, Benn preferred to leave the question of economic policy aside for the moment. For him, the real issues had to do with democracy – not only how to fashion intra-party democracy so as to ensure that leaders once elected still played the role of party leaders while they were in government, but also how leaders both inside and outside the state could help to build the kind of mass popular support for, and involvement in, radical social change. Benn's starting point in these speeches was the extra-parliamentary militancy of so many new activists, and the meaning this had for democracy. He thought it had been triggered not only by the heightened expectations produced by the rising incomes and collective bargaining strength of the post-war boom, but also by higher levels of education and training which had improved people's analytical capacities, and by the media revolution which gave people an unprecedented mass of information about current affairs and exposure to alternative analyses of events. He repeatedly pointed to 'the thousands of ... pressure groups or action groups [that] have come into existence: community associations, amenity groups, shop stewards' movements, consumer societies, educational campaigns, organisations to help the old, the homeless, the sick, the poor or under-developed societies, militant communal organisations, student power, noise abatement societies ...' He saw in them 'a most important expression of human activity based on issues rather than traditional political loyalties, and [they] are often seen as more attractive, relevant and effective by new citizens than working through the party system'.[39]

But he recognised at the same time that was only one side of the story. He took very seriously what Heath's 'Selsdon Man' presaged, and did not make the mistake of seeing it as a throwback to an earlier type of conservatism, as did most Labour Party spokespeople on the left as well as the right. Far in advance of later commentators Benn recognised as early as 1970

> [an] alternative philosophy of government, now emerging everywhere on the right, [taking] as the starting point of its analysis that modern society depends on good management and that the cost of breakdowns in the system is so great that they really cannot be tolerated and that legislation to enforce greater and more effective discipline must now take priority over other issues. The new citizen is to be won over to an acceptance of this by promising him greater freedom from government, just as big business is to be promised lower taxes and less intervention and thus to be retained as a rich and powerful ally. But this new freedom to be enjoyed by big business means that it can then control the new citizen at the very same time as Government reduces its protection for him.[40]

This was a most serious reaction, Benn contended, to a situation where people were showing that by banding together collectively in a myriad of new organisations with clear objectives they could win surprising victories on given issues against large and centralised corporations and governments which were increasingly vulnerable to dislocation. The locus of decision-making power still remained in place in these 'lumbering monoliths', however, and the perpetuation of their power, now intimately bound up with a philosophy of less state regulation of the economy but more discipline over an obstreperous citizenry, was intimately bound up with the claim to legitimacy of traditional structures of democratic government:

> If the people have so much potential power why do those who enjoy privileges seem to be able to hold on to them so easily? The awful truth is this: that it is outdated concepts of parliamentary democracy accepted by too many political leaders in Parliament and on Local Authorities, which have been a major obstacle ... [P]olitical leaders often seem to be telling us two things: *first* – 'there is nothing you have to do except vote for us'; and *second* – 'If you do vote for us, we can solve your problems.' Both these statements are absolutely and demonstrably false. ... the historic role of democracy is to allow the people to have their way. A real leader will actually welcome the chance to give way to the forces that he has encouraged and mobilised by a process of education and persuasion. *Legislation is thus the last process in a campaign for change* ... The people must be helped to understand that they will make little progress unless they are more politically self-reliant and are prepared to organise with others, nearest to them where they work and where they live, to achieve what they want. An individualist philosophy tenuously linked to an aristocratic political leadership will get them nowhere. This is not a wishy-washy appeal for 'participation' as a moral duty or 'job enrichment' as a management technique, or 'involvement' as a Dale Carnegie philosophy of life. It means telling people the truth: if you don't organise

with others to change your life situation, the only change we can guarantee you is the 'ins' and 'outs' of alternative parties in power. Democratic change starts with a struggle at the bottom and ends with a peaceful parliamentary victory at the top. That is what I want to call Popular Democracy.[41]

Benn argued that if Labour reacted defensively or with hostility to the new structures of issue politics that had emerged outside the party, rather than recognising that each had a role to play in the process of socialist construction, with many people working both in the party and in the new groups, the party would become obsolescent. 'We have to extend our representative function so as to bring ourselves into a more creative relationship with many organisations that stand outside our membership ... so that a Labour government will never *rule* again but will try to create the conditions under which it is able to act as the natural partner of a people, who really mean something more than we thought they did, when they ask for self-government.'[42]

It is important to remember that throughout the struggle that ensued, Benn continued to insist that he 'passionately' believed in parliamentary democracy, and that all the great achievements of the left had come about by pressures from below which made 'the parliamentary system serve the people rather than the vanity of the Parliamentarians'.[43] While he showed through the 1970s and 1980s that he was prepared to support direct action against laws which restricted democratic or egalitarian pressures, he insisted that this did not entail a break with parliamentarism: 'No man should tell another to break the law to by-pass Parliament ... But the person who is punished for breaking the law, may if he is sincere and his cause wins public sympathy, create a public demand to have the unjust law changed through Parliament.'[44] He was convinced that 'the debate between extra-parliamentary violence versus parliamentarism ... is highly diversionary'. Where there was no democratic route to change there was a moral right to revolt, but where democratic popular organisation and parliamentary change were not prohibited, socialist strategists could not pretend these means were ineffectual; to do so was to adopt 'the pessimism of the ultra-left', which he refused to share.

> My criticism of those who call themselves revolutionaries is that they speak as though reform had been tried and failed. Reform hasn't been tried ... I don't think there are any real revolutionaries in Britain. There may be dreamers, but there is nobody on the left who is actually planning and preparing themselves on the assumption that the transfer of power will come by revolution.[45]

Benn's parliamentary colleagues on both the left and right (and many of the new activists as well) doubted the genuineness of his rhetoric. This was scarcely surprising. Benn had after all not just stayed in the

Government throughout, but had actually accepted promotion by taking on the Ministry of Technology after Frank Cousins had resigned. On the most divisive issues, especially on incomes policy and the 1968 White Paper on industrial relations, *In Place of Strife*, he did not take a distinctively dissenting position in public. When Roy Jenkins, whose distaste for Benn's populist rhetoric knew no bounds, made a speech in 1972 accusing populists of 'talking left and acting right', no one could have any doubt to whom he was specifically referring.[46] But, as Benn gradually began to match his deeds more and more closely to his radical thinking and speaking, the social democrats' attitude to him – later matched by the attitudes of others like Foot, for whom parliamentarism plus the unity of the Labour Party formed the bedrock of politics – so far from improving, grew from distaste to hatred.

The gradual development of such an attitude towards Benn on the part of an old Bevanite like Foot stemmed from no little sense of self-righteousness. From the mid- to late 1960s it had been the Tribune Group of MPs who had shouldered the main responsibility for leading the intra-party opposition. In Parliament they had conducted a series of what they invariably termed 'regretful revolts' on economic and defence policy, and had led the trade union group of MPs in opposition to *In Place of Strife*.[47] In policy terms, after some initial confusion over the allegedly socialist potential of the incomes policy, they advocated a programme by no means dissimilar to what became the alternative economic strategy of the mid-1970s. As *Tribune* put it in 1968: 'To close the balance of payments gap, by rapid expansion of the economy ... requires measures to protect us from the pressures of the speculators, the capital exporters and the bankers in the meantime. And that means exchange controls, export directives, extended public ownership, maybe import controls and the mobilisation of some of the country's immense financial reserves.'[48] Although they faced fierce attacks for their disloyalty by Wilson at PLP meetings, their opposition was somewhat emboldened by the rather more liberal whipping system introduced by Richard Crossman as Leader of the House and John Silkin as Chief Whip in 1966. In any case, the fact that the Tribunites now increasingly had Conference votes on their side made it impossible to maintain the kind of repressive discipline exercised by the leadership in the 1950s.[49]

After the 1970 election defeat the main thrust of the Tribune Group of MPs, and particularly Michael Foot, was to raise the issue of public ownership again. They returned, in other words, to reviving the old debate of 1959–60 over more or less nationalisation, which Wilson had by-passed through attaching the Labour Party to his vision of the 'scientific revolution'. Ian Mikardo produced a document for the NEC setting out the case for greater public ownership, and his position was echoed in *Tribune* by Stan Orme and others with statements to the effect that 'it is time for a basic shift in control and ownership'. Foot went further, writing that 'what is needed is a strong shift leftwards ... the Party in Parliament ought to start that process, but if it won't the Party Conference will have to do it for them'.[50] The chances of the parliamentary party doing it were indicated when Foot, who was elected by the PLP to the Shadow Cabinet in 1970, was nevertheless twice defeated when he stood against Roy Jenkins for the deputy leadership in July 1970 and November 1971, and yet again (this time by Ted Short) in April 1972.

The Conference was indeed another matter, and when Foot decided to stand again for the NEC in 1972 (he had not stood since 1950) he immediately replaced Benn at the top of the poll. As we shall see in the next chapter, Conference agendas from 1970 to 1973 were replete with resolutions on public ownership, and many of them passed. But in so far as the Tribune MPs were determined to make a call for more public ownership in the next manifesto the key issue, the question was not about the number of firms to be targeted for public ownership, but about how to realise Foot's promise that the Conference would force the PLP to 'do it'. Mikardo, Frank Allaun and Jim Sillars wrote a Tribune Group pamphlet in July 1972 which took up the issue of the accountability of Labour representatives at all levels, including as its 'most important proposal' the election of the leader by the whole party at conference, not just by the PLP.[51] This broad line of argument was endorsed by thirty-eight other Tribune MPs, but Foot's name was conspicuous by its absence from the list; this was because he was already in the process of trying to mend the left's fences with the parliamentary leadership. He strongly opposed an inquest after 1970 into the mistakes of the Labour Government.[52] As he explained in 1972: 'It was a dangerous moment. The Left within the Labour Party could have demanded a grand inquest on all the delinquencies of 1964–70, could have mounted a furious attack on the leadership.'[53] From the moment when he became Shadow Leader of the House in 1972, his crucial role became that of repairing the frayed bonds of trust among the parliamentary and trade union elites – to avoid dissension within the party so as to present a united parliamentary front against Heath's Government, which he saw as the 'most hard-faced Conservative Government since Neville Chamberlain'. This overarching concern with party unity led him to oppose, not encourage, the forces that now began to try to change the Labour Party.

Benn, as we have seen, took the opposite tack. He had come to the view that it was necessary to reconceptualise the role of the Labour Party in relation both to the explosion of organisational activism in the country at large, and to the new conservatism which he believed heralded something more profound and more dangerous than a throwback to the Tory Party of the 1930s, let alone than what Heath represented. And in so far as most of the new progressive forces had developed outside the Labour Party this had much to do with the fact that the party's 'internal democracy is also riddled with the same aristocratic ideas as deface our national democracy'. He therefore saw the problem of achieving greater party democracy as crucial. Most of the reforms proposed in the 1972 Tribune Group pamphlet he had already raised in his October 1971 Fabian Society lecture. All the sensitive constitutional issues were there: the process for selecting parliamentary candidates; who should elect the leader and deputy leader; the accountability of Cabinet members, MPs, local Labour groups, councillors, and trade union delegations ('those who exercise this massive voting power should be accountable to their own members for the use they make of it').

Benn was concerned at this stage that the debate should 'not get bogged down in detail' and thought that 'it would be a great mistake to start this debate by looking for precise solutions to problems of democratic responsibility that have not been properly analysed and considered'. It was not on 'narrow and legalistic constitutional grounds' that these issues had to be taken up, but in terms of their contribution to fostering democratic socialist objectives. Even in terms of the primacy of Party Conference it had to be recognised that there were 'serious defects in the system of debate and decision which lie behind conference decisions. We should see them not as pieces of party legislation precise enough for enactment . . .' Nevertheless the real issue could not be avoided, and this was that if the new activists were going to be induced to make their presence felt in the party, 'conference decisions, however imperfectly they may be drafted, and however impracticable some of their specific proposals may be, are at present the only means by which the instincts and aspirations of the movement as a whole can be expressed'. The real problem was that even if conference decisions were universally accepted in the party as only laying down broad political objectives, Labour Governments were likely to continue to treat them with disdain. There was not only something close to a denial that the movement might ever exhibit greater wisdom or have a surer political instinct than the Cabinet or Shadow Cabinet, but even a tendency to see mass pressures as in some sense *less* democratic than pressures emanating from the Establishment.

> The problem of achieving greater party democracy is now the central internal problem facing the Movement. It is not just a question of considering constitutional amendments – though constitutional amendments might well follow from the debate at a later stage. It is not a question of re-opening old arguments about the relationship of conference decisions to the Parliamentary Labour Party . . . It is not just about the merits or demerits of the block vote

... It is not just about organisation, although the vitality of our party ultimately depends upon the morale and motivation of those who have to make it work. It involves all these things and it does so by making Party democracy a major *political* theme ... which we must come to see as just as important as what policies a future Labour Government may one day pursue. Some people ... almost imply that democratic pressures are by definition improper, and divert elected representatives from performing their duty as laid down by Edmund Burke two hundred years ago ... A conference resolution is seen as a threat to the independence of Parliament ... This idea is so deeply rooted in the aristocratic philosophy of politics that it is time we examined it more critically ... The strength of undemocratic pressures [is] enormous. Cabinets are subject to foreign pressures on major questions of economic policy, industrial pressures from large corporations, pressures from the mass media which are accountable to no-one – to name but a few. The case for positively stimulating democratic pressures is in part to act as a countervailing power to prevent representatives from being dominated by other sources.[54]

As we have seen, in the 1950s Benn had been quite sensitive to the danger that people outside the party, and especially young people, would dislike intra-party 'squabbles' except as entertainment. But now he insisted that 'the public will become very interested if they think we are ready to criticise ourselves and really want to make ourselves and British politics more democratic', and urged 'a period of intense public discussion about the nature of Parliamentary democracy and the nature of Party democracy ... If it is thought ... too difficult, or too dangerous or too divisive to embark on this debate I fear we shall miss a great opportunity.' If the party just devoted itself to 'more research to produce detailed policies which will win back public confidence in our capacity to run a modified capitalism', or if it treated with hostility the direct action of the new activists and their criticisms of the party system, it would entirely mistake the reasons it lost the 1970 election. For this defeat was very largely bound up with the party's concentration 'on the role of Government to the exclusion of the part that the people themselves could play in solving their own problems'. The solution therefore lay in a fundamental change of direction:

People who want change in the community in which they live, the conditions under which they work, and the world in which their children will grow up, are now everywhere engaged in a struggle to get the power that will allow them to do all these things. It must be the prime objective of socialists to work for the redistribution of political power ... in which more people exercise more responsibility than those in authority anywhere yet seem ready to yield to them.[55]

When in 1972 Benn coined the phrase 'a fundamental shift in the balance of wealth and power in favour of working people and their families', he was in his own mind putting the stress on the word 'power', and meant by this much more than a shift in ownership and control from capital to the state.

The speeches Benn now embarked on making to as many groups as possible, inside the party and out, were to become a hallmark of his style of political leadership. He kept an annual tally of the hundreds of meetings at which he spoke, and it seemed that he partly judged his success as a politician in these terms. This was consistent with the role of motivator and educator, rather than legislator and decision-maker, that he now ascribed to political leadership. His leitmotif was giving people a sense of their own power and encouraging them to use it. It is important to stress that Benn's speeches did not always get a favourable reception from the new activists or the trade unions in this period, nor were they always calculated to. Many of the new activists were suspicious of his 'conversion', given his association with the previous Government. He was given a particularly rough ride when he spoke at a Yorkshire Labour Women's rally in June 1971 and embraced the feminist movement.[56] And, despite his strong support for the occupations and strikes at the time, he still felt the sting of his association with the Labour Government and *In Place of Strife* when he spoke for the first time at an Institute for Workers' Control Conference in April 1973. And in June 1973 he faced an even more hostile National Community Action Conference ('... this sense of betrayal was very evident', Benn wrote in his diary. 'These people had absolutely no confidence in me or in the Labour Party.') Nor was Benn merely seeking to curry favour. 'You think you've discovered pressure groups and community action,' he told the Conference. 'The trade union movement began community action 150 years ago and you have separated yourself from it. That is why you are ineffective ...'[57]

Similarly, when Benn spoke at trade union conferences in this period, his insistence on applying the democratisation theme to their own structures produced some discomfort among his audiences. At the 1972 Trades Union Congress, Benn made the following argument, hardly one the union delegates were accustomed to hearing from a Chairman of the Labour Party bearing the party's fraternal greetings to their annual congress:

> It is simply not good enough to blame the Labour Government or the Parliamentary Labour Party entirely for our defeat in 1970. The Trade Union Movement, with all its virtues, must also accept its share of responsibility. Until very recently, the unions have hardly made any serious effort to explain their work to those who are not union members, even to the wives and families of those who are. You have allowed yourselves to be presented to the public as if you actively favoured the conservative philosophy of acquisitiveness. The fact that the Trade Union Movement came into being to fight for

social justice, as well as higher wages, has just not got across. If the public opinion polls prove nothing else, they certainly prove that. Finally, neither the Party nor the TUC has given sufficient support to other movements of legitimate protest and reform. . . . The lower paid, the unemployed, the poor, the old, the sick and the disabled, *expect* the Labour and Trade Union Movement to use its industrial and political strength to compensate for their weakness . . .[58]

'I am hoping to start a great new debate within our movement,' he told the AUEW Foundry Section annual delegate meeting in May 1971. And a critical aspect of this had to be the role the unions could play in turning their collective bargaining power towards securing control over management: 'I have always thought it was a great pity that working people set their sights so low. A wage claim to offset rising prices and improve real living standards is very important for workers and their families . . . [but] it doesn't alter the power relationship between the worker and his employer at all. Indeed if the higher prices led to higher profits and dividends it can actually widen the gap between rich and poor and thus prop up the very system that we ought to be trying to replace.' The system of ballots that Heath's Industrial Relations Act had introduced to thwart trade union militancy should be turned about by a Labour Government to require that boards of directors and managers presently nominated by shareholders be subject to workers' ballots; the general level of their salaries as well as their recall or replacement should operate on the same procedure. He did not believe this would be impossible to secure in the private sector, but in any case if industrial democracy were really applied there it certainly would change the character of the argument both for the extension of public ownership and an egalitarian incomes policy. The union movement 'ought now to develop a conscious long-term policy of negotiating itself into a position of real power in industry', and be prepared to use prolonged strikes to do so. A Labour Government would 'have to legislate to make it possible to finish the job by giving the workers the explicit right to do this. . . . This is not a particularly revolutionary suggestion in all con- science. No one is suggesting – at least I am not – that you do it by throwing petrol bombs or starting a guerilla war in Morecambe. You could do it just as easily by peaceful collective bargaining and by removing the obstacles through legislation.'[59]

This was not as modest a proposal as Benn claimed. The trade unions' reluctance to raise their bargaining aims to this level has never been purely a matter of economism, but also reflects their implicit awareness that capital would never bargain away its control over its own plant. Nationalisation with generous compensation would be a preferable alternative to this for capitalists – at least then they could take their money and invest it on their own terms elsewhere. For this reason even trade union leaders as open to the idea of industrial democracy as Jack Jones understood by it primarily increasing the scope of shop stewards to engage in something more akin to guerilla warfare over managerial prerogatives at plant level. But there is no question that by raising the issue in the open and challenging way he did, Benn was not endearing himself to all of his trade union audiences, and perhaps least of all to those close to the Communist Party who were apt to be the most suspicious of such 'naive' ideas. The fact that he also raised the possibility of changing the character of the incomes policy debate by connecting it to industrial democracy can only have increased their discomfort.

But Benn went even further in challenging the unions. In his 1971 Fabian lecture he had explicitly connected the issue of union democracy to that of party democracy. The 'same thread of accountability' applied to the unions as to party representatives and the 'same question should be asked about the representative system within the trade union movement in respect of the big political decisions in which they participate in annual conference'.[60] For a Labour politician to tread on to the sensitive ground of the defects in the unions' internal organisational structure, let alone their economism, was dangerous indeed. Yet in doing this he was to some extent taking his cue from key union leaders. Jack Jones, in particular, was a very vocal advocate of democratisation in the party in the late 1960s and early 1970s, and did not dissent when Benn pressed him on the question of the block vote.[61]

The workers' occupation at Upper Clyde Shipbuilders (UCS) in June 1971 was a formative political as well as industrial event of this period. Benn's immediate support for it not only upset the parliamentary leadership ('Wilson nearly murdered me,' he said later) but also the TUC hierarchy ('Feather was furious, absolutely wild with anger that I was talking to shop stewards when he was trying to get the whole thing stopped. It made you wonder . . .')[62] But his contacts with the stewards had already been extensive by virtue of his responsibility for shipbuilding in the Labour Government, and soon after UCS was put into receivership he had led a march of 30,000 through the streets of Glasgow. A month before the work-in Benn had secured the PLP's support for a resolution on nationalising the industry and had introduced a private member's bill in the House using the wording of Clause IV to frame a demand for the public ownership of UCS 'under the best obtainable system of popular administration and control', whereby 'the workers by hand and by brain' would develop their own economic plan for the company. It took political courage for Benn to face the charge from senior Labour colleagues as well as the Tories that he was engaging in unparliamentary behaviour. His portrayal of the occupation as 'an historic moment' in which the 'power of the workers has gone from the negative to the positive' no doubt encouraged the workers, but it cut little ice in the House of Commons. When Wilson went to the Clyde he expressed his sympathy for the workers' plight and urged the Government to assume responsibility for the shipyard, but he specifically refused to endorse the work-in because it was illegal.

As the party leadership squirmed in palpable discomfort at its inability to escape association with the many industrial confrontations with the Heath Government, Benn prepared a long paper for a Shadow Cabinet discussion in October 1972 on law and order. In the end it was never submitted but it is a remarkable document that reveals much about the strategic positions he articulated then and later, and he subsequently published it in 1974 while Minister of Industry. In it he predicted with remarkable accuracy that the corporatist honeymoon between the TUC and the Government that followed Heath's U-turn to a voluntary incomes policy would not last, that a statutory pay policy would follow, and that in the face of further strikes the Tories would switch at once to a 'Who Governs Britain?' campaign since they had nothing else they could still try:

> [T]he theme of anarchy, deliberately raising public anxiety and putting the blame on the trade unions is undoubtedly the best bet as they see it. It is, therefore, a political campaign directed against them that the trade union movement now has to face, and we are deeply involved. If we are to respond effectively we shall have to re-examine some of the fundamentals of our political faith. Democracy and socialism in Britain are built on three principles ... the supremacy of conscience over the law ... the accountability of power to the people ... the sovereignty of the people over Parliament. These three principles are now under direct attack. The Tory campaign on Law and Order is designed to get us to accept the idea that all laws made by the State must be blindly obeyed.[63]

To confront this effectively, Labour leaders would have to undertake their own campaign to remind people 'of the long history that lies behind our political and democratic traditions. In the end it is these values that make us what we are, and shape our future, and protect us from totalitarianism of the extreme right or the extreme left.'

In this context, Benn raised a further critical issue – the relation of the media to democratisation: 'The bias of the media against working people' could no longer be ignored as a long-term strategic issue. Benn insisted that it was important that the Shadow Cabinet see this issue 'correctly'. The main point was not that the media's treatment of the party hurt its electoral prospects. Media overkill against Labour leaders was often counterproductive and Labour leaders had enough access to the media that they 'are able to look after themselves'. The real problem was that the media closed off the possibility of revealing what broad popular support might exist or be developed for the social forces that underlay radical change. 'The greatest complaint against the media is that its [sic] power is used to dominate the community, that it excludes ordinary people and that it is not accountable in any way, save the crude test of market success. The main victims are the trade unions whose motives are regularly distorted, whose members are insulted and ignored, and who are presented in a way that denies them the opportunity to describe their work and interests properly.'

Government censorship would be 'totally wrong and unacceptable'; and so would industrial action 'arbitrarily exercised by anyone in the production chain who took exception to something that was being printed and transmitted'. But the unions obviously had to address the issue: they should demand that a Code of Conduct be agreed with the broadcasting media for equality of treatment in the handling of industrial disputes and they should demand that the TUC be allocated a certain number of hours per year, like the parties, to present their policies and explain the position of member unions. More fundamentally, unions in the media, who concentrated too narrowly on the traditional issues of collective bargaining, ought to be encouraged to form a federation and bargain for the establishment in each newspaper or broadcasting unit of a council, elected by the whole labour force, which would be responsible for receiving, discussing and issuing published reports on complaints against bias or victimisation of journalists for what they had said or written. This would not encumber the daily process of producing news, but 'accountability *afterwards* is perfectly practicable and would influence future action'. It was a typical 'Bennite' proposal. Even in a paper with the Shadow Cabinet in mind, he concentrated not on a legislative programme but on strategic perspective, and even in relation to media policy he thought less about what a Labour Government could do than about how it might encourage those directly involved to act creatively for themselves.

As the predictions he had made in October 1972 came to pass with chilling accuracy, and the Heath Government drew to an end in a direct political confrontation with the unions over 'Who Governs Britain?', Benn again revealed the sharp divergence between his strategic approach and that of the rest of the Labour leadership, now including Foot. The Shadow Cabinet scrambled to get a last-minute form of words from the unions that would promise a clear commitment to voluntary wage restraint. This would have made it easier for them once again to run an election campaign that deflected attention from the underlying issues by merely claiming that Labour would secure industrial harmony and price stability where the Tories could not. Benn's own approach was very different. As we shall see in the next chapter, he had played a large role in framing the 'Social Contract', but he sided with the unions in insisting that wage restraint should have binding conditions attached, to the effect that the government really would prosecute socialist policies. This was the very thing that made the rest of the senior Labour leadership most defensive in face of the press and Tory charges that they were beholden to the unions. Benn simply refused to adopt this defensive posture; even if it succeeded electorally in the short run, he thought it would only aggravate Labour's crisis in the longer term.

What Benn had come to see was that on the ideological terrain of politics conducted through the mass media, the party simply could not pretend, in the context of the industrial militancy of the 1970s, that it was not a working-class party. An apologetic and defensive approach to the attack on the unions might work in the short run but was bound to make it even more difficult to evolve an adequate long-term political strategy. In a speech to a joint conference of the London Cooperative Party and the London Federation of Trades Councils, just a month before the February 1974 election, Benn addressed the issue of class discourse and the media even more squarely than he had in his paper for the Shadow Cabinet a year and a half before. He argued that the Heath Government's confrontations with the unions had once again made class the central issue of British politics. 'Questions of class have not been properly discussed for over a generation. Yet the reality of class privilege, and class deprivation, remained and was understood and accepted by all classes even if only as an undiscussed and undiscussable fact of life.' The Conservative Government's clashes with the unions had 'awakened people, who had never thought about class before, to what class means, and how it relates to their own experience', and this could redound to the advantage of the unions and the Labour Party if two critical blockages were overcome. The first was the corporatist illusion that pervaded British political culture:

> [a] version of national unity [which] rests upon the creation of the illusion that the rich are kind and that if only working people would be restrained we could all raise our living standards together in an unending bonanza of capitalist growth fuelled by some 'necessary' inequalities to provide the profits, mainly needed for investment. That is the master illusion of British politics. If we cling to that illusion we shall condemn ourselves to a continuation of the present sterile stalemate in British politics.[64]

The second blockage, however, was the 'denial of the existence of class as a factor in British politics' which was one of the fundamental 'acid tests by which all political leaders are to be judged, before they can be supported by editors, and television and radio commentators'.

Labour had to confront both these blockages directly. In a major speech on the three-day week in the House of Commons in early January 1974 Benn tried to show how this was possible:

> I have a word to say here to those commentators and editors who look through every speech and every manifesto for a sentence containing a

reference to a tough incomes policy as somehow a test of credibility and statesmanship ... When we are told this is the time for straight talking, for plain speaking, for doses of reality and for moments of truth, let us perform our representative function and say to those who put that to us that they must now learn the hard truth, listen to some straight talking and have a dose of reality. For tight wage control will not work, and by consent will never be achieved unless we are able to make a change in our whole approach to the sort of society we have. [Hon. Members: 'Ah'.] Obviously, what those Hon. members who shouted 'Ah' meant was that this House is inextricably linked in its existence and its democratic practice with one form of distribution of wealth and income, and that the people cannot use Parliament democratically to change the distribution of wealth and income. But it is of course just that change we must have. Unless and until there is a major social reform to make our society fairer and more equal, workers will not co-operate in wage control where they have bargaining power and if they have the strength to resist. And they are right ... The paradox that confronts the House is that in this country today moderate people want radical change. ... They want justice in areas where injustice had been preserved. They want more democracy and not less democracy. They want a sharing of power and an enfranchisement of the community, of industrial workers, of tenants, and of the regions, and not the corporate ideas which are being put forward by this Government.[65]

It was a kind of rhetoric more common at Labour Party Conferences, where it invariably got a better reception. Peter Walker, replying for the Tories in the debate, immediately contrasted Benn's speech with the appeal Harold Wilson and Reg Prentice from Labour's Front Bench had made to the miners for moderation. They had urged the Government to propose a solution that would secure a compromise with the moderates in the miners' union. Benn had tried to present the militants as moderates and tried to point their economic demands in the direction of radical political change. It was indeed a crucial distinction. The 1974 election manifesto incorporated Benn's phrase 'a fundamental and irreversible shift in the balance of wealth and power in favour of working people and their families' and admitted that 'only deeds can persuade ... that an incomes policy is not some kind of trick to force [workers] ... to bear the brunt of the national burden'. In light of the record of the new Labour Government that barely managed to scrape back into office in February 1974, such words would produce an even more widespread and dangerous cynicism than the record of the 1964–70 Government had done.

But an ideological innovation cannot get far without a corresponding organisational one – and here we encounter the limits of Benn's self-assigned role as a 'tribune'. Some of the activists who became personally associated with him, including some of those closest to him in his Bristol constituency, were not uncritical of this role, feeling that he should spend less time delivering speeches around the country and more time organising. And while he certainly felt much freer in opposition to take on the role of educator and motivator than when he had been under the constraints of Cabinet responsibility, the contradictions of being at once within and against the broader system of parliamentary paternalism were still inescapable. Some of the new intake of MPs were attracted by his ideas (Neil Kinnock wrote to him in September 1970 expressing 'wholehearted endorsement' of Benn's *New Politics* pamphlet).[66] When Benn stood for election to the deputy leadership in 1971 (in which at that time only MPs could vote), he received 46 votes to Foot's 96 and Jenkins's 140. But his decision to run was very much a personal one; in sharp contrast, for instance, to Mitterrand or Rocard at this time in the French Socialist Party, Benn did not seek to establish around himself a disciplined intra-party faction. And he still did not join the Tribune Group throughout the 1970s (although they put him on their slate for the PLP's Shadow Cabinet elections from 1972 onwards). He had no connection with the Campaign for Labour Party Democracy when it was formed in 1973.

In so far as a tight parliamentary faction existed, it was that of the Europeanist social democrats who, despite their defiance of both PLP and Conference policy, nevertheless managed to get Jenkins elected as deputy leader. Benn's diary entry shows that he well understood the implications of this: 'It means that Bill Rodgers's CDS group have got a majority in the PLP and that is something one will have to accept. But politically as well as personally, I am most depressed.' It was in this context that his PPS, Frank McElhone, urged him to drop 'this forward-looking stuff which is damaging you with MPs who think you are an extremist' and concentrate instead on getting a good press and building up support in the PLP.[67] Benn resisted this; indeed he tended more and more to the view that 'there would have to be a showdown in the Parliamentary Party and I might have to say what I thought about party democracy, even though it would be very unpopular. It might be that I might have to be thrown out of the Shadow Cabinet in order to establish that there really was a real argument going on about Party democracy.'[68] He nevertheless continued to resist building his own organised faction to advance his cause, or attempting to use Tribune as one, as some on the extra-parliamentary left of the party were constantly urging him to do (especially Ken Coates);[69] and he continued to resist this even in the face of evidence that the right-wing faction were acting in a concerted fashion to undermine him not only within the PLP, but in the extra-parliamentary party and the media.

Given that he was burning his bridges with most of the PLP by the positions he was taking, and that Foot was emerging as the trade union voice in the party hierarchy, it is ironic that many MPs grew cynical about Benn's motives, ascribing his actions to personal ambition alone and seeing them as a transparent bid for the party leadership. There can be no doubt that Benn thought he had a chance at this (as did some of those who levelled the accusation against him). But it is clear that he was little prepared to trim his sails so as to increase his acceptability to the majority of MPs (in whose hands the choice of the leader resided until 1981), or even to the majority of union leaders who, together with the MPs, were sure to dominate any electoral college for leadership election of the kind he had called for as early as 1971. On the other hand, to have become leader on the basis of the kind of principles he was espousing and the new forces he was encouraging would indeed have given him a mandate for radical transformation of the party. As attached to this goal, his leadership ambitions were hardly discreditable; indeed realising them probably would have been a necessary condition of success in any attempt to change the party at that time. The fact that many of his parliamentary colleagues sought to denigrate what he was saying and doing, by constantly pointing to his leadership aspirations, says more about their own narrow conception of Labour Party politics as a personality contest than about Benn's politics.[70] This especially applies to Foot, who increasingly insisted on treating 'Bennism' almost exclusively in this light, although he had always been scathingly dismissive of the same charge when it was made against Bevan.

It is true that Benn was highly media-conscious – he has always seemed to believe that the most dangerous thing for his style of political leadership was to be ignored by the press. This may have been a fatal error, since by the early 1970s the media already began treating 'Bennism' as a metaphor not only for a mendacious ultra-leftism, but for a 'loony' brand of it. 'Benn', Hatfield noted, became a four-letter word which fitted comfortably into a single column in the largest type-face and symbolised the leftward shift in the party. ' "Bennery" was coined and assumed to be synonymous with demagoguery, populism, public ownership, syndicalism and workers' control. Yet the prejudicial approach toward his often tentative, exploratory, restless views blinded many to what he was seeking.'[71] In this respect, the British press demonstrated its partisan guardianship of the Burkean interpretation of parliamentary democracy and its extreme defensiveness against Benn's criticisms of the systemic bias of the media.[72] It also showed that when it came to discrediting a prominent political dissident – and especially one who was a 'traitor to his class' – by labelling him as psychologically unstable, many editors and journalists were capable of extreme unscrupulousness. Holding the 'fool' up to public ridicule has always also been an effective means of exclusion – and it was used liberally in alternation with the 'most dangerous man in Britain' approach.

The social democrats in the parliamentary party exploited the media's willingness to do this to Benn, as every morning they opened their copies of *The Times* or even *The Guardian*, fearing with trembling hands to find yet another example of what Benn had allegedly said the night before that might have tarnished their precious respectability. 'Was Benn speaking for the Labour Party?' was the question the press was always asking. Their response was increasingly to use the media as a weapon on their side in the intra-party debate.[73] Unless 'Bennery' was defeated, the party would also suffer the fate of not being treated seriously by received opinion.

As is often the case with contradictions, this produced less a resolution of the problem than a vicious circle. 'Bennism' *did* have a strong base in the party – and a growing one. The Labour new left was not called into being by Benn, nor would he play much role in its actual organisation through the course of the 1970s as the strongest extra-parliamentary force in the Labour Party's history. The leadership role he played lay in his clear articulation of the new left's understanding that 'our long campaign to democratise power in Britain has, first, to begin in our own movement'. Yet during the critical years of Labour's period in opposition between 1970 and 1974 very little had changed in the Labour Party. The implications of this – which were already clearly visible even before Labour was re-elected in February 1974 – are the subject of the next three chapters. Only by understanding the frustrations and the costs associated with advancing radical democratic socialist goals while parliamentary paternalism remained dominant in the party can we appreciate why by the late 1970s the Labour new left pursued constitutional change with such determination and tenacity. It will also help us see the broader configuration of forces that ensured why it was that, despite the left's eventual victories, the outcome was ultimately futile.

It was also tragic, because the eventual defeat of the new left in the party removed the issue of a genuine democratisation of the state and the economy from the agenda of British politics. When today's 'modernisers' and the media belittle and denigrate the new left that emerged in the party in the 1970s, they conceal the fact that democratisation was its central theme. The Labour new left saw that democratising the state was a precondition for overcoming the injustices of capitalism, and that democratising the party – and enhancing its 'educational' role so as develop popular capacities to rule – was a precondition for democratising the state.

4

The Search for an Alternative Strategy: The Limits of Policy

According to conventional wisdom, the shift to the left in the Labour Party after the 1970 election defeat was primarily about economic policy.[1] The policy-makers in the eighty-odd committees and study groups that toiled at Transport House between 1970 and 1974 were indeed mainly preoccupied with the hitherto under-appreciated power of multinational corporations; and this question did eventually play a key role in defining the thrust of the 'Alternative Economic Strategy', which was an important part of the Labour new left's programme. But what was most original in the Labour new left's thinking was that however hesitantly, and initially in an uncoordinated manner, it began to address the structure of power in the party.

The economic programme that the NEC brought to the 1972 and 1973 Conferences was not in fact as novel as it seemed. Its proposals for planning agreements as a means of governing the investment and pricing behaviour of the leading corporations, and for a national enterprise board to act as a state holding company and a channel for public investment in profitable industries, were similar to, and to some extent inspired by, the practices of countries such as France and Italy which had put less stock in Keynesian macroeconomic fiscal policy than the British, and more in what the Germans called 'strukturpolitik', direct planning at the level of the firm. They certainly were conceived with a determination to go well beyond the tepid industrial policy of the first Wilson Governments, but they tended to ignore the specific historical context which had made these particular forms of state intervention possible in these other countries, in which new liberal democratic regimes had sought to reconstruct war-torn economies, and capitalist classes discredited by collaboration with the fascists had been obliged to accept state leadership as the necessary price of their own restoration.

To assert such a degree of state management of the British economy, in the context of the 1970s and against the opposition of British capital, was a political venture of a different order. This was what made the programme seem far more radical than French planning or Italian 'state venture capitalism'. And this was what made old revisionists wary of even the idea of a state holding company, although they had themselves advanced this in the 1950s as an alternative to nationalising the 'commanding heights'. For in Britain an industrial strategy such as the Labour left conceived in the early 1970s could only have been carried through with very tight exchange controls, the nationalisation of much of the financial system, and a radical transformation of the nature and role of the Treasury and Bank of England. The real question, in other words, was whether a Labour Government would have the will to go ahead with the policy once it became clear what else it would involve, and whether it could transform its own approach from one of managing the existing system to one of mobilising popular support, so as to retain its mandate (such as it was in 1974) if it did go ahead.

The left, through the Party Conference, were trying to get the leadership to develop a radical strategy, not only in terms of an economic programme but in terms of an outward-looking campaign to mobilise support for it. Such a campaign would also entail a radical change in the party's internal practices, and in the ideological orientation of its leaders. In response to Roy Jenkins's claim that 'Socialism is just a slogan,'[2] Brian Sedgemore (then a councillor in Wandsworth, elected as an MP in 1974), captured the orientation of the extra-parliamentary party when he told the 1971 Conference that there was indeed 'a crying need in this party for someone to translate the abstractions of economic control into concepts that people can understand – growth, leisure, participation, responsibility, the environment – and to translate them in such a way that makes them not just moonshine, but something which is eminently and imminently practical'. But how could this be done when the party's own leadership were not interested in a socialist strategy and considered it irrelevant or actually harmful? How could public ownership possibly become popular with the electorate, Sedgemore asked, 'when our own leadership steadfastly refuses to discuss, still less to support ... such ownership'?[3] It was not fetishisation of Conference, but an attempt to provide an answer to this dilemma, that led to a new struggle to assert the sovereignty of Conference over the PLP. This is why the most important issues brought on to the Labour Party's agenda in the early 1970s pertained to the adequacy of the vehicle, not just the adequacy of the policy. One could say that it was in the difference between the politics of Tony Benn and the policy of Stuart Holland (the main theorist of the party's new economic programme) that the radical potential for changing the Labour Party lay.

Setting the Agenda

The preliminary agenda for the 1970 Labour Party Conference contained no fewer than thirty resolutions (over one-tenth of the total submitted) on 'Party Administration'. Most of these expressed a feeling that the election defeat was a product of disillusion and dismay at the base of the party.[4] Of course, the Wilson Government's consistent flaunting of Conference decisions could not but be a central issue. But it was remarkable how many of the speeches at the Conference went beyond mere recrimination and raised more strategic concerns, and this was reflected in many more of the Conference debates than the brief one that was allowed on a resolution which 'deplored the Parliamentary Labour Party's refusal to act on Conference decisions'. In speaking to the anodyne economic policy document presented to the Conference for the NEC by Callaghan, Jack Jones argued that if the party's view of socialism were to be made relevant to 'the things that were worrying ordinary people today', this involved going back to the social ownership of the means of production, distribution and exchange as 'the essential base – and I mean Clause IV'. But, he went on, 'in order to achieve that we have got to start to build genuine democracy in Britain instead of the sham democracy which exists at the present time ... we have a great barrier of custom and practice in our Parliament which acts as a keep out notice to the man in the street'. The issue, he insisted, was not only that of eliminating the House of Lords and making MPs account-able to CLPs: to meet the demands that dozens of citizens' groups were now making it would be necessary to set up such things as 'representa-tive conferences' through which MPs would be required continually to consult with community organisations.[5]

In the one contribution from the floor which was permitted in the debate on the resolution on Conference decisions, the key point was made by a CLP delegate, Margaret McCarthy: 'Our Executive says we should wrest the leadership of the pressure groups, and bring them into the Party ... How can we go to the pressure groups and say, "If you join us perhaps we can say to you that your policies will be accepted and implemented"? We cannot.' Unless the participation that had been strangled in the party was renewed, the party itself was no more than another pressure group. She insisted that the leadership should not insult the delegates by going back to the old argument about 'day-to-day' decisions having to be made by representatives. The delegates from the constituency parties and the trade unions operated and well understood the relationship between them and their Labour Groups, GMCs and union executives. 'They operate those systems every day of their lives. So we are not asking that we should cross every "t" and dot every "i" for the Parliamentary Labour Party ... I do not think we are asking for very much. We are asking that the broad outlines of party policy should be determined here.' Yet it was just this argument about 'day-to-day decisions' to which Harold Wilson returned in replying to the debate and in asking that the resolution be remitted to the Executive. 'A Prime Minister is responsible to the House of Commons and acts on the basis of the Cabinet's judgement of what is necessary in the public interest in so far as and as long as he commands the confidence of the House of Commons, and he cannot be from day to day instructed by any authority from day to day other than Parliament. That is the constitutional position.'[6] His repetition of the cant phrase 'from day to day' betrayed perfectly clearly that his position really had nothing to do with day-to-day decisions but with fundamental political direction. The mover and seconder refused to remit and the Conference passed the resolution by 3,085,000 to 2,801,000. The question at the time was whether this outcome merely reflected pent-up frustration following the 1970 defeat, or foretold something new.

Whatever the preponderance of radical sentiment in the constituencies, the left-wing majorities at Conference were inevitably dependent on the unions' block votes. The TGWU and AUEW delegations together consistently cast almost 2 million of the Conference's 6 million total votes in favour of left-wing resolutions. Even the more moderate union leaderships, such as those of the General and Municipal Workers and the Miners, were becoming preoccupied with how to cope with the industrial militancy of their members in this period, and with the challenge of a broad left now appearing in their unions. But there was little coherence in the union vote. The unity among the unions on policy – even between the left-wing leaderships of the TGWU and AUEW – 'was fragile and typically lacking in planning'.[7] The left made no attempt to secure control of the Conference Arrangements Committee (traditionally dominated by right-wing union officials). Above all, no union seemed to have a policy of trying to ensure that the resolutions they voted for at Conference would see their way through the intra-party policy-making process into the party programme. The programme the NEC produced in 1972, which was by no means as radical as the Conference resolutions passed the previous year, did become the basis of the 'Social Contract' alongside established TUC policy; but this was secured by intra-elite bargaining on the TUC–PLP–NEC Liaison Committee, not as a result of any open reassertion of the principle of Conference control over the parliamentary party.

Although Benn, as we have seen, was himself wary of 'precise solutions' at this stage, he did not seek to keep the issue bottled up and it was indeed the first theme he raised in his Chairman's address to the 1972 Conference: 'The Party sees Conference as its own representative assembly, and even those who are not members of the Party understand that this is the main political forum in Britain through which working people can influence major political decisions ... Conference never has and never will want to dictate to a Labour Government, but they do expect Labour Governments to take conference decisions seriously and not deliberately to reverse or ignore them.'[8]

Benn played a more active role as Party Chairman in 1972 than was customary. He was a key player in Ron Hayward's selection as General Secretary in January 1972. The choice was a highly politicised one, made all the more so by a speech that Hayward had made to the NEC saying that adherence to Clause IV and the power of the Conference would be his dominant considerations. But it was above all in relation to Conference itself that Benn really was innovative as Chairman. He ensured that the NEC's 1972 programme went out to delegates in advance so they could frame resolutions in light of it. (That this was an innovation itself said a great deal about the traditional centralist workings of the party.) He introduced a new system for selecting speakers at the Conference whereby they were all issued with 'request to speak' cards so that he could maintain a balance of speakers from the various sections as well as by age and gender, removing the advantage normally enjoyed by those who had had a personal word with the Chairman. (Benn told the Conference on the first day that he had just been handed a note from an MP condemning his innovation 'very violently, saying "It is quite wrong that people should put in notes to the Chairman," and he signed it "P.S., I want to be called on Monday afternoon."') A crucial ruling Benn made at the Conference also severely limited the time-honoured manoeuvre of the NEC whereby they accepted radical resolutions but added qualifications and reservations in the course of their acceptance so that it was no longer clear what exactly the Conference had passed, and the result could be easily shrugged off by the leadership. Many of the union leaders were unhappy with this. In his closing address, Benn told the delegates that 'one very senior organiser ... was heard to remark as I sat down today that a notice would be put on the rostrum: "Do not adjust your sets; normal conference will be resumed next year." I very much hope that is not true.'[9]

But the senior organiser was right, a reason being that, on the whole, the NEC were far less ready at this stage to be moved on intra-party democracy than on resolutions on public ownership. Although the NEC's composition shifted towards the left from 1967 onwards,[10] it did so only marginally and gradually as left-wing unions continued their long-standing practice of voting for right-wing 'sitting tenants' on the union and women's sections of the executive, where their block votes predominated. Lewis Minkin found little evidence of political bias on the part of the Conference Arrangements Committee in this period and discerned a greater balance and fairness in its procedure in 'compositing' resolutions (combining many different resolutions on the same subject into one or a few for debate) than previously.[11] But it is significant that after the initial resolution in 1970 that Conference decisions should be binding, no further resolution on this was accepted in 1971 and 1972. Delegates complained of this, but were not well organised enough – and left-led unions were not committed enough – to secure a 'reference back' of the agenda on this critical issue.

Subsequently, as part of an enquiry into changes in party structure made necessary by local government reorganisation (the enquiry involved consultations with 2,700 activists from 570 constituency parties), the NEC did invite the raising of issues relating to the selection of parliamentary candidates as well as other constitutional matters. Because the area-level consultations were held from June to December 1973, this provided grounds for the NEC to secure remission of resolutions submitted to the 1973 Conference on the reselection of MPs, the election of the leader by Conference, and the PLP's right of veto over the election manifesto. (As one of the resolutions put it: '. . . the relationship and responsibility of the Parliamentary Labour Party to the Labour Party and of individual MP's to their constituencies is becoming increasingly confused to the average Labour Party member.')[12] All of the central constitutional issues which divided the party so severely by the late 1970s and early 1980s thus arose *before* the election of the 1974 Labour Government; but the NEC was able to defer their discussion until after the 1974 election, at which point it produced a 'stand-pat' report.[13] In the interests of party unity, the left on the NEC went along with keeping the lid on demands for specific constitutional reforms.

It is important to stress that, at this time, 'the preliminary agenda of the Party Conference with its approximately 500 resolutions and amendments was remarkable for its spontaneous character.'[14] Few groups attempted to stimulate resolutions from the constituencies in this period. This may not have been an entirely unmixed blessing. For without an organised means of monitoring and publicising what happened to the resolutions passed, or of keeping the pressure on with further resolutions and intra-party mobilisation in support of them, successful radical resolutions, even if they had apparent NEC endorsement, could be watered down in NEC policy-making, if not simply ignored. The 'miraculous majorities' for the left at Party Conferences in this period were in a sense all too spontaneous, lacking the organisational coherence needed for an effective transformation of party policy. Thus it was left to the closed meetings of the NEC and its committees, and the particular balance of left and right within them (where the 'left' was in any case not necessarily the same sort of 'left' that had produced the Conference resolutions in question), really to determine party policy. A motion at the NEC by Benn, which would have entailed NEC motions and votes being published as minutes in the Party's Annual Report, was set aside – after being attacked particularly vehemently by Michael Foot.[15]

One group that did organise to ensure that certain resolutions reached the conference agenda at this time was the Militant Tendency. It was smaller than rival Trotskyist organisations on the British left; between the launch of its paper, *Militant*, as a fortnightly in 1971 and its conversion to a weekly a year later, it recruited 137 new supporters, but this still raised the total number of Militant supporters to only 354.[16] Nevertheless, its steadfastly 'entrist' determination to work within the Labour Party (the 'mass party of the working class') had given it a presence in a few CLPs (for example, this was the reason for Brighton Kemptown's constant visibility in moving Conference resolutions), and in the leadership of the Labour Party Young Socialists.

The immediate context for Militant's success in the LPYS was the decision of the NEC in 1969 to restore to the party's young members the right to elect their own leaders. And when the NEC finally dropped its List of Proscribed Organisations in 1973, formally ending the Cold War regime in the Labour Party, this gave Militant a wider berth within the party. As we shall see later, however, this did not mean that many national and regional party agents stopped being primarily ideological policeman rather than organisers, nor that a great many right-wing MPs, especially those around Callaghan, were content with the relaxation of social democratic centralism.

In any case, the right wing of the Labour Party had difficulty in seeing, or perhaps deliberately chose not to see, that Militant had a purpose and practice which was very different from that of Labour new left. Militant saw the industrial strategy of Holland and Benn as the merest reformism, in contrast with the revolutionary intent of its own resolutions, calling for the nationalisation of the top 250 corporations, which it consistently managed to get on the Conference agenda. The cynicism with which Militant leaders regarded Benn was indicated by their frequent designation of him as 'Kerensky'. Unlike most of the Labour new left (but rather like Arthur Scargill and Ted Knight), Militant's leader, Ted Grant, had no time for notions of industrial democracy or for seeking links with pressure groups and social movements. Indeed, Militant's doctrine (what Wainwright termed its 'Marxism pickled in Labourism')[17] contradicted almost everything that defined Benn's 'new socialist politics'. When Benn met Grant for the first time (one of the very few times they ever met), at a debate staged between them by the LPYS in 1973, Benn came away 'feeling that he is really a theological leader. . . . he is absolutely rational, logical and analytical up to a point and then he just goes over the top and keeps talking about "the bloody settlement that the capitalists are preparing for the workers"'. Benn directly criticised this revolutionary posturing in the debate: 'If I believed it, we wouldn't be here passing resolutions, we would be planning guerilla warfare. If the young people, with all their passion and idealism, were diverted to thinking in civil war terms, it would weaken rather than strengthen their influence.'[18]

The Debate on Economic Policy

The primary strategic concern of the left on the NEC, led by Benn and Mikardo, was to use the resolutions on socialist policy passed by the Conference to strengthen their hand *vis-à-vis* the parliamentary leadership in the preparation of the party's programme. It is important to stress that the resolutions on public ownership and industrial democracy were not, for the most part, put forward in terms of returning the party to its tradition, but, as with the constitutional reforms, were concerned to pull the party out of the failed patterns of its past behaviour. The emphasis on industrial democracy was very much propelled by a critical attitude towards the statism of Labour's public ownership tradition. The tone of the debate at the 1971 Conference was set by Brian Sedgemore, who addressed not only the problems of the 1964–70 Governments but also

> the mistakes of 1945 when, almost by accident, Clement Attlee's Government modelled the nationalised industries on Herbert Morrison's water boards. Was it any wonder that what we got was not what people wanted or expected, but centralised bureaucracies run by broken-down generals, bankrupt private industries bailed out by the taxpayer, and managements responsible neither to workers, consumers or Parliament? Public ownership suffered a blow from which it has never recovered and, worse, the Party ran scared and has continued to run scared ever since.[19]

Given the historic importance of finance in British capitalism, as well as the enormous subsequent growth in the scope and power of financial capital globally, the most important resolution which appeared at this time was one moved in 1971 by Jo Richardson, calling for the next manifesto to include proposals to nationalise all banks and insurance companies and for the NEC to set up a working party to put forward proposals on this to the next Conference. Similar resolutions in the previous few years had been excised from the final agenda. The resolution went too far for the NEC, but it was carried against the NEC's recommendation by 3,316,000 to 2,316,000 votes – just over a two-thirds majority, which according to the party constitution should have guaranteed it a place in the next manifesto (but of course, in the event, it didn't).

The success of the left in pushing forward radical economic strategy resolutions at Conference, and the hopes of Benn and Mikardo that the NEC could shift the locus of effective policy-making away from the Shadow Cabinet, reflected the enormous vacuum in economic policy that then existed at the top of the parliamentary party. What the majority of the PLP and the Shadow Cabinet had to offer by way of alternatives was woefully weak. The former Gaitskellites (now increasingly reincarnated as 'Jenkinsites') seemed to have only two policy pillars: entry to the Common Market, and reflation plus incomes policy, neither of which, after the middle of 1972 at least, clearly distinguished their economic policy from Heath's. Even Crosland's thinking in this period lacked both perspicacity and substance. In a Fabian lecture in November 1970 he drew an explicit contrast between 'the position today' and that of the 1950s, when in light of full employment and the welfare state 'a fundamental rethinking was required'. In the 1970s there was no need for another such departure from the 'agreed ideals' of the 1950s, he claimed, 'and the evidence is the lack of any furious ideological ferment within the party'. This astonishing lack of awareness, let alone comprehension, of the ideological ferment that was already taking place within the party, was matched by his blindness to the deep contradictions that were just then on the verge of ushering in the severest and longest recession since the thirties. Even by 1974, Crosland was still convinced that 'if we examine the Western World as a whole we cannot detect signs of a new and fundamental crisis ... full employment is maintained; economic growth continues; world trade expands ... growth may be slower in the future, [but] no long-term crisis comparable to that of the 1930s seems imminent'. The 'one possible exception' to this, he acknowledged in 1974, was Britain.[20]

This also explains the obsession of the Jenkinsites (though not of Crosland himself) with Common Market entry. To ride on the coattails of an ever-expanding European capitalism was a political as well as an economic panacea – the last hope for consensus politics in Britain. But the Jenkinsites were unable to carry even the majority of the PLP with them, let alone the Party Conference, on the issue of Common Market entry. They therefore suddenly began to employ on their own behalf the Tribunites' old demand for tolerance of minority opinion in the PLP, especially after their vote with the Conservatives on the Common Market in October 1971. The Jenkinsites' self-image, almost invariably accepted by the media, in which they cast themselves as the voice of moderation and tolerance standing up against the gang mentality of a dictatorial left, was actually the reverse of the truth. Even Crosland, who did not share their degree of emotional involvement on the Common Market, suffered at the hands of the Jenkinsites' tight discipline and intolerance when he abstained on the 1971 vote. 'Tony is indecisive again' was the view expressed by Roy Hattersley and Bill Rodgers, with the latter characteristically intoning: 'He's behaved like a shit and we must punish him.'[21] This they proceeded to do in the Shadow Cabinet elections.[22] Crosland, who had reciprocal doubts about the degree of emotional commitment Roy Jenkins now had even to the 'agreed ideals' of the 1950s, saw the Jenkinsites' attacks on him as 'the gang mentality. They are a bullying little clique.'[23] But Crosland did not air publicly this criticism of his friends, and in the 1975 referendum he joined with them as a strong supporter of the pro-Market campaign.

Benn, like Crosland, was not passionately pro- or anti-Market in the way the Jenkinsites were on the one side, and Michael Foot and Peter Shore were on the other. Although he had earlier been opposed, Benn had moved through the 1960s towards being broadly in favour, regarding himself by the early 1970s as a 'long-term federalist'. Yet his grounds for supporting entry in the early 1970s were very different from those of the social democrats, and very much like those of the Italian Communists: what interested him was the opportunity the Common Market provided to develop the necessary machinery and strength to deal with multinational corporations. This made him very sensitive to the actual terms of entry. What Benn was passionate about was getting the process right, given that he saw it as an historic and irreversible decision which would fundamentally affect British sovereignty. This meant ensuring that the decision was made in as democratic a way as possible and one which did as little damage as possible to the Labour Party and the forces for change within it. In January 1971, he made his case for a referendum to the Shadow Cabinet:

> I drew attention to the fact that we simply could not have a free vote in Parliament, with the Shadow Cabinet voting different ways, after the Conference had given its collective view. You couldn't have senior members of the Shadow Cabinet saving Heath on a vote of confidence. I thought it would produce a major crisis in the Party and maybe break the party system ... So I outlined the alternative – the Conference would come out for a General Election and after the Election we would have a Referendum on entry. This would mean that if you voted Tory you were voting for entry and if you voted Labour you would have the opportunity to choose for yourself. I said if the three Party Leaders couldn't persuade the British public, then it was most unlikely we should go in ... .[24]

Benn advanced his Referendum proposal not only in terms of democratic principle, but also because it had 'the great tactical advantage of keeping the Party united'. Even in this respect, however, Benn immediately ran up against the tendency of most of the Shadow Cabinet and the media to take all his actions and utterances as an attack on the leadership. Only Callaghan on the Shadow Cabinet initially recognised that Benn has launched 'a life-raft that both sides in the Party would one day be happy to scramble aboard'.[25] When the Labour Shadow Cabinet resisted his Referendum proposal, Benn 'felt for the first time like resigning . . . I thought if the Party is going to make an issue of not permitting the public to be consulted, one does wonder if this is the right Party to be in. But I resolved a long time ago that I would never resign again, but just go on campaigning in favour of what I believed from whatever position of power I occupied.'[26]

Benn was also worried by the 'authoritarian flavour' in the left's thinking that led it to fear that a Referendum would undermine the leadership of the trade unions; and, more broadly, he was concerned at the left's tendency to feel 'that if the public were consulted it would never go along with what you wanted to do, and you would never get socialism'. Yet he increasingly discerned that the opposition from the other side of the PLP was not only related to the fact that his Referendum idea 'went absolutely against the elitist thinking of the right-wing of the party', but that the Jenkinsites' determination to take a stand on the Common Market issue was part of a broader strategy. As he wrote in his diary in May 1971, ten years ahead of the defection of the 'gang of four' and their formation of the SDP:

> There is a small group of highly dedicated Marketeers led by Roy Jenkins, with Bill Rodgers as their campaign manager, and including the old Campaign for Democratic Socialism types. They are genuinely pro-Europe (I give them credit for that), but they also see a last opportunity to do to the Labour Party what they failed to do over disarmament and Clause IV, namely to purge it of its trade union wing and of its Left. This group, working with the conservative Europeans, really represents a new political party under the surface in Britain.[27]

In this context, Benn's own attitude towards entry slowly began to shift. He began to revert to the position he had held in the 1950s that the Common Market was in practice more likely to enhance the power of the multinational companies than provide a framework to control them. What underlay this reassessment was a growing awareness that European social democrats, like the Jenkinsites at home, were not likely to be allies in a socialist strategy for Europe. He was 'absolutely horrified' when he attended the June 1971 Socialist International in Vienna: 'It is entirely without roots in the working-class movement and is just an international Fabian Society, with people like those in the Campaign for Democratic Socialism: intelligent, agreeable people, some of whom, of course, do have a long record of struggle behind them; but they have more or less eliminated the ideology of socialism from their vocabulary . . .'[28]

The fact that most members of the PLP opposed entry in 1971 obscured the actual line-up of Labour MPs on the fundamental issues of economic strategy. Many MPs opposed entry only on the short-sighted and opportunist grounds of 'sticking it to the Tories'. Neil Kinnock, elected as an MP in 1970 and making his first speech to a Party Conference, made their case quite explicit: '. . . we cannot with one tongue be the enemies of this class-ridden Government and with the other tongue embrace them and their policies'.[29] In fact most of those who opposed entry, including some of the most vociferous in this regard on the Front Bench, did not significantly differ from the revisionists in economic analysis or prescription. This left them with only one weak reed in economic policy – Keynesian reflation plus an incomes policy agreement with the unions.

This was the policy vacuum that presented an opportunity to those who were trying to push a radical economic strategy through the NEC. Benn warned in 1970 that just concentrating 'more research to produce detailed policies' on public ownership might lead to the avoidance of the fundamental issue of the nature of parliamentary and party democracy. As head of the NEC's Publicity Committee after the 1970 election he first concentrated on political education, and on trying to work with the TUC to get the unions presented 'in a more favourable light'. But by 1972 he threw himself into the intra-NEC struggle over economic strategy. It was his goal, as he later explained just before the February 1974 election, to confound 'one of the great arguments of the Right . . . that you can't win an election with a left-wing programme. If you have a left-wing programme and you win the election, then the Right will have lost that argument, and that will be a historic moment in the history of the British Labour movement.'[30] He had been impressed by the arguments in the flood of papers on a new, more radical economic strategy that Judith Hart and Stuart Holland had put forward through their Public Sector Working Group; and he came to think that he had short-changed 'the socialist argument' in his 1970 Fabian pamphlet.[31]

The strategy that Hart and Holland were articulating was not really as radical as Benn thought; it did not go as far as Conference resolutions passed at the time. Yet even this strategy was simply not taken at all seriously by the overwhelming majority of the parliamentary leadership. They saw their role in the NEC struggle exclusively in terms of trying to limit the electoral damage they thought a radical economic pro-gramme would do to their chances of returning to office; and once back in office they had no intention of paying the slightest heed to a socialist strategy. With total accuracy, Benn was later to describe the process to the 1980 Conference: 'I have seen policies develop in the sub-com-mittees, come to the executive, go to the unions for consultation, be discussed in the Liaison Committee with the unions, come to the Conference, be endorsed; then I have seen them cast aside in secret by those who are not accountable to this movement.'[32]

Immediately after the 1970 election, Ian Mikardo and Terry Pitt initiated attempts to upgrade the importance of the party's own research and policy-making role and capacity.[33] This was strongly opposed by most of the parliamentary leadership (most vociferously by Crosland), despite the failures of 1964–70. Wilson himself took the defeatist, if not purely cynical view that 'the party could have all the policy committees it liked in Opposition, but it was still liable to be overtaken by events which prevented the party from doing what it intended'.[34] In the interim, the principle that guided most of the Shadow Cabinet after 1970 (and this increasingly was the case with Foot as well) was to have as little awkwardness with the extra-parliamentary party as possible. And this governed their behaviour in relation to the policy committees of the party perhaps even more than to the Conference. For while no self-respecting journalist would be naive enough to believe that the Shadow Cabinet could be associated with the 'impossible' resolutions passed by the 'mindless' militants and 'bolshy' trade union delegates at Conference, policies that emerged from the NEC would be more likely to be taken by 'received opinion' as representing what a Labour Government might actually do. To control the Conference was now probably too much for those who, like Wilson, practised 'the art of the possible', to hope for. To control party policy was not. Once it became clear that a majority on the NEC supported a radically enhanced research programme, it was inevitable that there was going to be some awkwardness between the NEC and the Shadow Cabinet.

During 1970–73 there were two important sub-committees charged by the Home Policy Committee of the NEC (which oversaw the work of the research department) with formulating economic strategy. One was the Finance and Economic Affairs Committee, on which right-wing MPs were overwhelmingly dominant. The other was the Industrial Policy Committee, where the balance between left and right was much more even. As Chairmen of the former committee, first Jenkins and then Healey, closeted with their Keynesian economic advisers, were determinedly 'cautious and conservative' in the face of almost every proposal emanating from the research department.[35] Whether it was a question of acquiring some of Britain's overseas assets to prevent speculation against the pound, or making Labour's long-standing commitment to a wealth tax more firm and specific, this committee proved tenaciously obstructionist.

Above all, they wanted to avoid the issue of bringing the financial institutions into the public sector. Jo Richardson's resolution to the 1971 Conference, calling for a special working group to work out the means of effecting this, was designed to take the issue away from the committee. The new working group was set up, but most of the people appointed to it could be counted on to resist the bank nationalisation that the Conference, by a two-thirds majority, had called for.[36] When a report was finally produced, very much bearing Mikardo's imprint and setting out three models for public ownership of building societies, insurance companies and the banks, only John Hughes was prepared to sign it, the others refusing because of the section on bank nationalisation. It was published unsigned, with the lowly status of a 'discussion document', before the 1973 Party Conference; the NEC promised to draw conclusions after public discussion on the document and a debate at Conference. No such debate was held, and the issue was carefully set aside until after the election.

Round one to the right. But things appeared to be proceeding in a very different direction in the Industrial Policy Committee. It spent most of its time examining price control, which was acceptable to the right as a means of getting the unions back to the incomes policy issue, and to the left as a means of effecting an anti-inflation policy without a statutory incomes policy. After the 1971 Conference, however, the Industrial Policy Committee created a Public Sector Working Group which became the locus of policy development for a general extension of public ownership and planning. Judith Hart was the driving force behind it among the left parliamentarians, and she largely succeeded in forging it into a relatively homogeneous small left-wing 'think tank', centred around the economists Richard Pryke and Stuart Holland.[37]

Anticipating almost all of the debate of the 1990s about under-investment, 'stakeholding' and Rhineland capitalism, Holland and Pryke's basic position was that Labour had hitherto advanced no means of overcoming Britain's chronic under-investment in manufacturing industry. Even if grants and tax subsidies covered the whole of an investment project, private management would only undertake the investment if it was convinced that there was a ready-made demand for increased capacity. Joint state–industry ventures in manufacturing industry were useless if all the government had to offer was money. Control of key firms was required, and this could only be had by selective nationalisations of profitable manufacturing firms and by transferring to a state holding company the control over manufacturing assets that went with the institutional investments of the insurance companies and pension funds. On similar grounds they advocated state planning agreements with private firms. These agreements would enable the government to get from firms the information on investment plans and pricing policy, the lack of which both Cousins and Benn had pointed to as a prime source of the weakness of the 1964–70 Labour Governments.

The ambiguity of the NEC's 1972 'Programme for Britain' on all these points, despite the breadth of its interventionist proposals and its radical tone, led Eric Heffer to complain that its state holding company proposal began 'to take the right road' but drew back at the decisive moment; while Jenkins, on the other hand, saw the Green Paper on a

National Enterprise Board that the Public Sector Group produced for the NEC as 'dogmatic' and not 'remotely sensible'.[38] But since the unions were demanding radical economic measures in exchange for renewed cooperation in wage restraint, it appeared that the Shadow Cabinet were going to have to live with a policy programme which they regarded as excessively radical. When a joint TUC–Labour Party policy document was finally published in February 1973,[39] it promised an extensive and permanent system of price controls, food subsidies and 'large-scale' redistribution of income and wealth; and in order to solve the 'fundamental . . . problem of the control and disposition of capital', it offered 'effective' public supervision of the investment policy of large corporations, the development of new public enterprises and the control of capital movements overseas, as well as the extension of collective bargaining to include joint control over investment and closure decisions. The document's promise of a wide-ranging agreement between the next Labour Government and the TUC, to deal not only with inflation but with 'all these aspects of economic life', did indeed give the appearance of portending a fundamental shift in direction compared with the last Labour Government. The left on the Industrial Policy Subcommittee meanwhile continued further to concretise the party programme after the 1972 Conference, not least by means of a proposal that twenty leading manufacturing companies, one of the major banks, and two or three of the leading insurance companies should be brought into the state sector under the aegis of the NEB.

Here was born the famous 'twenty-five companies' issue. The proposal was endorsed by the Industrial Policy Subcommittee in October 1972, over Crosland's vociferous objections. Benn, who took on the committee's chairmanship in December, added the idea of an 'industrial powers enabling act' to be shepherded through Parliament and administered by a powerful Trade and Industry Department, and an 'industrial commissioner' who might be put in to assume control of a company which sought to frustrate the objectives of the Government, along the lines of the Housing Commissioners used by the Tories to enforce the Housing Finance Act. These proposals, along with the twenty-five companies proposal, were incorporated into the draft of 'Labour's Programme 1973' which passed the Home Policy Committee and went to the NEC in May of that year.

It is important to understand clearly what impelled the left to specify the twenty-five companies as a minimum figure for new public ownership. There was no magic in the number, although rationalisations could be found in the notion of one company in each sector, as well as in the proportion of total assets, sales or investment involved. Most important, which firms would be targeted might reflect the degree of support expressed in discussions among workers themselves.[40] In a party in which there was no fundamental ideological divide between socialists and non-socialists, or at least in one where the predominant part of the leadership were socialists, the specification of the number of firms to be brought into public ownership would have made little sense. The way in which a socialist programme was presented would be governed by tactical and ideological considerations at the time, the aim being to maximise the potential for broad popular support – before and after a successful election campaign – for a challenge to capital's power. The reason for specifying numbers was the knowledge that the social democrats were opposed to pursuing an electoral or governmental strategy that even remotely reflected the spirit of the Party Conference in this period. The aim was to try to tie down the leadership and oblige them to comply with the general direction of policy established by Conference. As Mikardo explained at a Tribune rally at the 1973 Conference: 'The fact is that those who wanted twenty-five companies written into the policy were not really advocating the nationalisation of just twenty-five companies. In normal circumstances one would have said that the proposed National Enterprise Board has got to take a big slice of the economy and continue to add to it. Why did anyone seek to quantify it at all? It was there because there was a lack of confidence in the leadership.'[41]

And with good reason. The predominant feeling in the Shadow Cabinet was not only that the programme would ensure an electoral disaster, but that by rejecting Keynesianism in favour of direct impositions on capital, it represented an 'ideological' throwback to a bygone era. In the Shadow Cabinet Benn alone offered a strong defence of the document. Given that he, along with Mikardo and Hart on the NEC, made his case not in terms of a specific number of companies, but in terms of the need for a commitment to a strategy of quick and broad-scale intervention, the majority on the Shadow Cabinet thought the NEC would drop the twenty-five companies from the programme. Such a calculation may well have been partly based on the fact that, in a very important indication of what was to happen under the next Labour Government, left-wing union leaders put no pressure on the party leadership on this issue. Indeed, Jack Jones told Benn that he ought to concentrate on pensions rather than this 'airy-fairy stuff' of nationalisation, and that it was too late to try to convert the Labour Party into a socialist party. This was a remarkable *volte face*, given the positions he had taken and supported at both Party Conference and the TUC. It led Benn to conclude that Jones had 'settled down into a central position which could best be described at the moment as the Healey stance'.[42] The right on the Shadow Cabinet now also had an ally in Foot; as recently as January he had argued in the Shadow Cabinet that 'investment failure is the failure of the system and socialisation of investment is the only answer', but now he came out very sharply against the specific proposals. Foot's narrow and over-riding economic policy objective was now simply withdrawal from the Common Market. He was prepared to 'sacrifice, as an expedient, some of the left's proposals on state interventionism – on the grounds they could damage Labour's electoral chances – if it would facilitate the return of a Labour Government to take Britain out of the European Community. His earlier demands for a "sharp shift leftwards" had to be trimmed in order to achieve this short-term, over-riding objective.'[43]

Benn challenged the defeatism entailed in this position. In a speech at a *Financial Times* conference on the future of the City of London, days before 'Labour's Programme 1973' was published, he calculated the total assets of the banks and other financial institutions represented at the Conference as amounting to four or five times total Government expenditure, and insisted that the Labour Party was right to ask 'what effect all this power will have on the nature of our democracy'. On this basis he addressed openly the opposition of Wilson and the Shadow Cabinet to the twenty-five companies proposal:

> What is at issue ... is not the precise number of firms ... although it might be noted in passing that if Slater-Walker can acquire twenty-nine companies in a year, 1972, a government target of twenty-five does not sound excessive ... Whatever the merits of these arguments might be, some people automatically assume that if the Labour Party put them forward in a general election we would be heavily defeated. I wonder. Do the British people really want a society in which industrialists and bankers have more power over Britain's economic future than the governments they elect?[44]

In making this case, Benn was taking the position Foot had taken in 1959–60 at the time of the Clause IV debate; but obsessed with the hope (forlorn, as it turned out) that he could win the parliamentary leadership over to withdrawal from the Common Market in exchange for giving up any new commitments to public ownership, Foot now turned on Benn the charge that the revisionists used to level at the Bevanites when Foot was one of them. Did Benn really want to win the next election? This was the 'trump card' Foot now played along with the rest of his Shadow Cabinet colleagues against the 'awkwardness' which Benn's penchant for 'open discussion' of socialist strategy raised for the leadership; indeed when he himself became leader in 1980 Foot was to play it against the left with more tenacity than Wilson had ever done. Hatfield's comment is apt: 'Benn, in fact, was as anxious to win the general election as Foot, and the latter knew this: their real argument was about electoral strategy.'[45]

Searching for a compromise, the majority on the NEC at an eleven-hour-long meeting to finalise 'Labour's Programme' shifted towards watering down the document. There were no fewer than ten critical areas of economic policy where the final printed document that emerged from the NEC diverged from the draft, all designed to obscure and soften the interventionist thrust.[46] It appeared that the 'moderates' had won the day – not least when by a vote of eleven to three the section on renationalisation of privatised firms without compensation was removed from the document. But when, towards the end of the meeting, it came to an amendment moved by Healey on removing the twenty-five companies proposal, it turned out that among the members who had not drifted away from the meeting by this point there was a seven to six majority against the amendment. Although Foot voted with the right, the determining vote which swung the decision to the left's advantage came from John Cartwright, the Co-op representative, who surprisingly and uncharacteristically switched sides in a fit of pique at a disparaging remark Healey had made to the effect that nationalising Marks & Spencer would make it as inefficient as the Co-op.[47] In this heroic way the left won the battle in the NEC on the twenty-five companies. Obviously a socialist strategy could not be forged out of such a fiasco. But what was the Shadow Cabinet to do with the awkwardness this now caused?

Wilson did not hesitate. In a statement he released to the press the next day, he stated that it was 'inconceivable that the party would go into a general election on this proposal, nor that any incoming Labour Government be so committed'. The Shadow Cabinet, responsible with the NEC for the party manifesto, would 'not hesitate to exercise its veto at the appropriate time'. Wilson had asserted the authority of the leader: there would be party unity on his terms or none. This puts in perspective the charge that it was Benn who was fomenting disunity. But how many would see this clearly through a media filter which invariably presented Wilson as the epitome of good sense and Benn as the voice of lunacy? To be sure, if the Party Conference now endorsed the proposal by a two-thirds majority, even more awkwardness would ensue, since the Shadow Cabinet would then have no constitutional authority to excise the proposal from the manifesto. To avoid this, the Conference would have to be manipulated, in the interests of party unity, to turn its back on the resolutions it had passed in the previous few years, as well as defeat the majority of the sixty-four resolutions on public ownership submitted to it in 1973 which endorsed the NEC's decision or called for the party to go further.

Since there was no way of being sure that the trade union block votes would sustain his position, Wilson attempted to get the NEC to agree to meet with the Shadow Cabinet before the Conference to decide what elements from the programme would be included in the manifesto, and to present this to the Conference as a *fait accompli*. He was prepared to horse-trade: the NEB, planning agreements, the Industry Act, public ownership of development land, minerals, ports, shipbuilding, aircraft and some sectors of machine tools and road haulage would be endorsed. Why then divide the party over twenty-five companies? Ostensibly, the NEC seemed to understand why more clearly than it had in May: the lengths to which Wilson had gone over the twenty-five companies had indeed been a symbolic statement about fundamental strategic direction. It refused the joint meeting on the grounds that only the NEC had the authority to present statements to Conference, and it even voted by seventeen to six to reinstate the section of the programme on nationalisation without compensation. But a compromise had to be struck; the party could not go into an election with its leader running against it.

It was saved by the Conference Arrangements Committee which, reflecting a long-standing practice of selecting the most far-reaching and radical resolution in order to minimise the chances of a specific commitment being passed, put together an amalgam of resolutions which specifically endorsed the twenty-five companies proposal but attached it to a Militant-inspired call for also nationalising the 250 major monopolies.[48] The left had been out-manoeuvred. Benn, in the unhappy position of replying to the debate for the NEC, had to endorse the two general resolutions and oppose the Militant one on the grounds that the 250 companies figure 'confuses strategy with tactics', and that if the NEC and PLP had to take Conference decisions seriously so did Conference itself. The Militant resolution was defeated, as Benn recommended, on a card vote of 5,600,000 to 291,000. In his speech Benn tried to use this episode to offer a salutary reminder of what the attempt to change the Labour Party, which was by no means over, was all about:

> [I]f we are only concerned to win the votes we shall never mobilise the strength we need to implement the policy ... We are offering much more than legislation. We are offering a perspective and a vision which will transform the political atmosphere of cynicism which has developed in recent years. Without a vision people will turn to their immediate and narrow self-interests. With some sense that they are part of a change in our society we shall be able to draw much more from them. We must mean what we say and say what we mean and not run for cover when Fleet Street turns upon us. I must say this quite seriously to Conference: if it looks tough now it is as nothing to the roaring attack that will descend on us as we seek to carry through this programme ... We are saying, at this Conference, that the crisis that we inherit when we come to power will be occasion for fundamental change and not the excuse for postponing it ... In light of that, it is not the drafting but the will that matters.

He forbore to add what he very well knew: that as far as the parliamentary leadership was concerned, the will was not there.[49] To be sure, the Conference had endorsed what still appeared to be a very radical-sounding programme. And further radical resolutions were also passed, including one which declared the party's opposition 'to any British defence policy which is based on the use of nuclear weapons either by this country or its allies, [and] demands the removal of all nuclear bases from this country, British and American on British soil or in British waters . . .'[50] Wilson himself offered a shopping list of industries to be nationalised, amid praise for 'Labour's Programme 1973' as deriving 'its idealism from the socialism which created and today inspires our movement'. Reg Prentice attached his call for an incomes policy to the promise of socialist planning, only making the sensible observation that 'socialist planning is not just something we impose on other people'. And Denis Healey himself instructed the Conference on the fundamentals of socialist analysis, saying: 'Inherited wealth is the single strongest buttress of the class system of Britain, and the class system is probably the most dangerous single obstacle to the social and economic changes our country so desperately needs . . . Comrades, the enterprise we are engaged on is of mammoth proportions. It is to unite a nation which has been divided by centuries of class discrimination.'[51]

Neil Kinnock, no doubt like many other delegates, left the Conference 'talking excitedly of all that Labour would do after the election'. Glenys Kinnock brought him down to earth, as they left the hall. 'Don't be stupid, Neil. These are the people who sold us out last time and they'll do just the same next.'[52] The leadership's sudden radicalism was, as David Coates put it, 'visibly only skin deep . . . a set of rhetorical conversions to the prevailing mood and language of Labour Party conferences'.[53] It reflected no inclination to turn this mood outwards, as Benn had insisted would be necessary. The Labour new left had shifted the discourse of the party, including that of its leadership, to a more radical plane than at any time since the 1930s. But it had achieved very little in terms of democratising the party or changing its structure so that socialist mobilisation would replace 'parliamentary paternalism'.

5

The Labour New Left in Government: Containment and Marginalisation

The closest Labour's new left ever came to occupying a position of state power was in the first fifteen months after the February 1974 election. Benn became Minister of Industry, with Eric Heffer as his Minister of State, Michael Meacher as his parliamentary Under-Secretary, and Francis Cripps, Stuart Holland and Frances Morell as political and economic advisers. The way they operated in the Department in some ways also provided a model for later Labour new left policies in local government. But the Labour Government as a whole had a very different complexion. The composition of the new Cabinet reflected that of the Shadow Cabinets that immediately preceded it, with the 'centre-right' in the majority. Although Benn hoped for some support from what were then called 'soft left' ministers like Foot, Shore and Varley, he knew that most of the Cabinet would oppose all his proposals and he soon felt as isolated as he had been in the Shadow Cabinet before the election.[1]

Harold Wilson told the 1974 Party Conference that the two General Election results of that year had confirmed Labour as 'the natural party of Government', but the Labour Party came to office with less than 40 per cent of the vote for the first time since the elections of the twenties; and the 'natural party of Government' was now burdened with governing the country at the onset of capitalism's greatest economic crisis since the slump. The failure of Heath's 1970–74 Government, hard on the heels of the failures of the Labour Governments of the 1960s, reflected what Benn had termed (long before this became a staple term in left-wing intellectual analysis) 'a crisis of consent', which not even the election of October 1974 (giving Labour a bare parliamentary majority of three) could be seen as resolving. '[B]oth parties have failed,' Benn told Harold Evans and Hugo Young of the *Sunday Times* the previous December. 'The crisis is a crisis of confidence shared by the establishment. It is not just a case of crooks governing morons. There is something else wrong. It is a crisis of consent as in the late colonial period.'[2]

It was the new Labour Government's incapacity to address this crisis creatively from the left that allowed Thatcherism to gain strength and achieve power. It was precisely the waning 'naturalness' of Labour's post-war regime that allowed Margaret Thatcher to run her 1979 electoral campaign on the slogan 'Labour isn't Working'. This conveyed a triple message: Labour Governments don't work; more and more workers can't find work; and those lucky enough to still be in work aren't, under Labour's aegis, working hard enough.

To be sure, it was of some significance that Labour should have come to office in 1974 with a more radical programme than any since 1945. It was certainly thought to be significant by considerable sections of establishment opinion within Britain and the United States who not only worried that the Labour Party might no longer be trusted, but that British democracy might no longer be trusted to produce results which would serve the 'national interest'.[3] But from the perspective of the Labour new left, the significance of 1974 elections was that at the very least they confounded the dire predictions of electoral disaster that had accompanied the Labour Party's turn to the left after 1970. Certainly, the centre-right in the parliamentary party, and some of the old left, like Foot, were more than ready to blame the new left in 1974, and Benn in particular, if Labour had lost. These different perceptions of what was electorally feasible were, in fact, fundamental and informed the divisions in the party through the rest of the decade and beyond.

The two election manifestos of 1974 had faced both ways: beckoning towards the Labour new left's policy while at the same time defending the old Keynesian compromise as the way forward. As a result, the victories (such as they were) of 1974 made it possible for both sides to claim electoral plausibility. The Labour new left's view, increasingly strengthened through the 1970s as Thatcher moved up in the opinion polls with her own radical reaction against consensus politics, was that the old policies could not work and that it was on the basis of their failure that Labour would end up being judged electorally. Survey evidence provided support for this, as Whiteley remarked in pointing to the strong correlation between a declining Labour vote and rising levels of unemployment and inflation (especially the former) under Labour administrations:

> Solemn declarations in the party manifesto and resounding declarations during elections may influence some voters, but for most the Labour Party performance is what counts. If radical socialist policies were to bring performance successes, particularly in the economic field, they would become electorally popular. If centrist policies fail, as they have done for the most part during Labour's tenure in office, no amount of moderation will bring electoral success. Butskellism in practice has been tried and found wanting, and it remains to be seen whether the alternative strategy of the left, if given a chance, can bring the success the party needs if it is to survive.[4]

But the bulk of the parliamentary leadership were determined not to give it a chance. They couldn't quite hide the Labour new left's project from view, but neither were they prepared to do more than attach it, as a weak addendum, to the last chance they briefly gave to Keynesianism in 1974, before they abandoned even this. The policy symbols associated with the social contract and the industrial strategy were retained as a minimal index of the Government's ties to the party and the unions, but once in office the Labour leadership framed and administered these policies in a way that emptied them of all radical content.[5]

'Bennism' and the 'Foot–Healey axis'

Yet Benn occupied an important and prominent position in the new Government, and there was some expectation in establishment circles, including the parliamentary elite, that having 'talked left', Benn would now 'act right'. His appointment, like Foot's, would symbolise the new strength of the left in the party, but would also contain it. As *The Times* commented: 'This will not by any means be a government of wild men ... The Labour administration will include people of the highest ability ... even among its more left wing people ... Mr. Benn has proved himself a capable administrator, however little sympathy one may have with the speeches he makes on broad political issues.'[6] Although *The Times* had called for Benn's defeat in Bristol before the election, the faith of the establishment that men of the 'highest ability' could be counted on to settle down to office, and divorce 'capable' administration from socialist mobilisation, had still not been wholly shaken by the events of 1970 to 1973, even with regard to Benn. It would not take long, however, before *The Times* was reporting that 'some of the senior civil servants were horrified' when not only Benn but even Heffer presumed to tell them 'in blunt Liverpudlian terms that the manifesto must be translated into government policy'.[7]

The nature of the relationship between manifesto commitments and the policies of a Labour Government had always been hazy and uncertain. The traditional principle, on which this Labour Government also operated, was that the manifesto went into abeyance as soon as the Labour Government was elected, until such time as parts of it were endorsed specifically by the incoming Cabinet.[8] And what really mattered in this respect was that the key economic policy position was occupied by Healey, whose 'team' at the Treasury drew exclusively on the personnel and attitudes that had led the party's Finance and Economic Policy Committee to oppose the substance of Labour's 1972 and 1973 programmes. Whereas Benn and Cousins had learned from their experience in the 1964–70 Governments that the role they were expected to play when in office precluded them from continuing to act as leaders of the class that had put them into office, for Healey this posed no contradiction. He 'accepted that, notwithstanding his commitments to his "trade union constituency", and notwithstanding all the other political juggling he was involved in . . . he was primarily Chancellor of the Exchequer'.[9] Of course, this did not mean that he divorced himself from the party and the trade unions. Indeed he saw himself as 'the most political Chancellor' Labour ever had.[10] But his political aim was to win support for an

> attempt by the government machine to harness the power of organised labour for a rescue operation for the British economy as a whole. This involved 'educating' the unions in the hard realities of a continued free for all in wages. Education meant making many of the economic forecasting and research resources of the Treasury available to the TUC secretariat and the principal trade union leaders, and many nights in which Chancellor Healey pleaded with, cajoled and bullied the union leaders with dire predictions of the horrors in store if they did not cooperate with the Government.[11]

Healey's pre-eminence in the Cabinet was sustained by what Barbara Castle, in her diaries covering the period 1974–76, called the 'Foot–Healey axis . . . round which the Government revolved'.[12] From the beginning, Michael Foot's crucial role in the Government was as custodian of the 'Social Contract' with the trade union leadership.[13] This involved establishing a legislative framework for extending trade union rights in collective bargaining, which had the important effect of fostering union membership growth through the remainder of the decade despite steadily rising unemployment. Moreover, in the period between the February and October elections of 1974, before restraining public expenditure became the main motif of economic policy, Foot also played a key role in getting the Cabinet briefly to adhere to some of the 'social justice' aspects of the social contract around price controls, food subsidies and pensions. But even more crucial than this, Foot's role was to show that under this Labour Government, unlike the previous one, the union leadership would be treated, as Frank Cousins had asked a decade before, as 'partners whose voice is heard, understood and respected and a voice to which regard is given';[14] and on this basis, to persuade the union leadership to defend the Government by maintaining voluntary wage restraint.

The strong support that the Government secured from Jack Jones and Hugh Scanlon as well as more 'moderate' union leaders such as David Basnett was very largely the product of Foot's promise of such a partnership. What Foot and the TUC got in return was the holding in abeyance of a statutory pay policy (which the Treasury wanted), and the Cabinet's support for progressive (but not costly) industrial relations legislation.

The overall weakness of the partnership was exemplified not only by the Government's continual rejection of the unions' calls for reflation, a wealth tax and import controls, but also by Jack Jones's comment that 'with the exception of Michael Foot, who was always sympathetic, I found it impossible to have a man-to-man discussion with any top Minister'.[15] But Jones followed Foot in attaching overriding primacy to keeping the Labour Government in power as at least a defence against the worst depredations of what Foot told the 1975 Conference was 'a crisis of Capitalism of a most formidable character'.[16] Only in this light can we explain the fact that Foot was to play a key role in removing the teeth from the industrial strategy in the summer of 1974 and that, as Barbara Castle noted as early as April 1975, 'no one was currently more acquiescent about high unemployment' in the Cabinet than Foot.[17]

Inside the Cabinet, this 'Foot–Healey axis' created a common front against 'Bennism'. While Benn's political passage from radical liberal to radical socialist now led him to try to act, even from inside the state, 'to keep the hopes of the Left alive and alight',[18] Foot was constantly involved in 'trying to help solder the Cabinet together again' in the face of actions by Benn 'which defied collective Cabinet responsibility'.[19] This reinforced the alliance which also quickly emerged between senior civil servants in Benn's Department and centre-right Labour ministers and their permanent secretaries, with the Treasury at the hub, to have the industrial strategy aborted by Cabinet before it saw the light of day.[20] Adrian Ham, who was Healey's special assistant, later described a 'Whitehall-wide conspiracy to stop Benn doing anything ... Some civil servants went so far as to brief anti-Benn ministers behind the backs of their own ministers. They had an obsession about defeating "Bennery" – a term coined in Whitehall long before Fleet Street picked it up.'[21] Someone with greater experience in government might have seen this in less sensational terms. After all, only the naive could expect otherwise. Thus Joel Barnett, as the Treasury Minister responsible for carrying through public expenditure cuts, took it as a matter of course that he would be apprised by his officials of differences of view between the Permanent Secretaries of other Departments and 'strong-minded Ministers' such as Benn, Castle, Shore and Crosland. But he appreciated the bureaucracy's power, especially when it was ranged on his side in Labour Party controversies: 'when [senior officials] are united they can be devastating, particularly when arguing against a proposition'.[22]

When this bureaucratic power was joined to the power of the Prime Minister and the Chancellor, no force inside the Government could stop it. This even applied to public expenditure cuts, where there was far less unity among the centre-right ministers in the Cabinet. Barnett (Healey's number two man at the Treasury) stated: 'With the Prime Minister and Chancellor in tandem, there never was much doubt about obtaining

Cabinet approval. But we had to go through the motions and that meant some tough talking.' When it came Benn's insistent advocacy of an alternative strategy, virtually the whole Cabinet saw this as a matter of going through the motions. As Barnett fair-mindedly commented, 'Benn, always the main, and most articulate, advocate of a major switch, was never able to convince a single one of his colleagues … In a way it was surprising, but it was due in some measure to the majority of the Cabinet disapproving of what they saw as Tony Benn's left-wing pose after his comparatively moderate political position up to June 1970, when he was Minister of Technology. This tended to make otherwise perfectly rational colleagues start off biased against his case before he started.'[23] Before long, most of Benn's Cabinet colleagues came to take the cynical view that Benn's continued and enthusiastic arguments in favour of the Labour new left's economic strategy, in a Cabinet obviously determined not to take it seriously, amounted to, as Barnett put it, 'talking to history'. Or as Foot saw it: 'At some stage during the proceedings of that Cabinet, Tony Benn lost interest in the present, in the sense of seeking to influence immediate decisions, and turned his brilliantly agile mind to the future. *It was more, I believe, a psycho-analytical than a political problem.*'[24]

Thus Foot, who attributed this largely to the 'claustrophobia' produced by the 'unconscionable' media assault on Benn, ironically came to share, and even eventually fuel, the media's own favourite weapon for dealing with Britain's leading political dissident. The truly appalling history of this treatment, whereby Benn's politics were almost invariably portrayed as absurd rather than contested on their merits, cannot be gone into here.[25] But it was chillingly captured by the Glasgow Media Group's analysis of a television programme aired during the 1981 deputy leadership campaign which bore directly on Foot's relationship to Benn during the 1974 Government.

> … the treatment of Benn is unique in that of all the political figures discussed only criticism of him is delivered straight to the camera by a journalist. In a section on the history of Benn's campaign and the groups behind it, we are told of a series of meetings held by the left-wing Ministers in the last Labour Government. The reporter tells us that they met over dinner, and in recounting the story he sits at his desk and occupies a position normally used by a newscaster, presenter, or some form of expert. He looks directly at us, and the camera closes on his face to accentuate the punchline:
>
> 'Benn arrived after dinner apparently to say goodbye. He astonished his fellow diners by telling them that he thought that Britain was turning into a police state; that as a Minister his own phone had been tapped and that the country was ruled by the Civil Service. According to one of those present, Michael Foot summed up their reaction when he said: (camera close up)
>
> "Tony, you're going nuts." '[26]

Both Benn's comments and Foot's response have to be taken in the context of an informal gathering among political 'friends'. But if the media's treatment of their exchange was crudely biased, Foot's subsequent statement that he meant what he said in it reveals limitations of a different order. It has, of course, since been extensively documented that by 1974–75, as Dorril and Ramsay's authoritative account puts it, 'the secret state had embarked not just on a campaign against the Labour Government, but against the whole liberal-left of British politics'.[27] The full extent of this could hardly be known at the time, but plenty of signs were there. Benn's suspicion that his telephone was tapped was well founded; and even Lord Gardiner (who as Lord Chancellor was the country's highest legal officer) 'thought it more than likely that MI5 was bugging the telephones in my office ... When I really had to speak to [the Attorney General] in confidence, I took him out on one or more occasions in the car ...'[28]

Far from being a 'psycho-analytical problem', Benn's problem with this Cabinet – and with Foot himself – was quintessentially political. Benn believed that, even if his arguments could not carry the Cabinet, some evidence of popular mobilisation and pressure behind them, such as Benn was determined to encourage, still might. He may indeed have been speaking to history and looking to the future when he continued to make his case in Cabinet, once its course became clearly set. But in so far as he was not giving up on the Labour new left's attempt to change the party, at this still comparatively early stage, his continued advocacy of socialist policies while remaining in the Cabinet helped to show that the behaviour of Labour leaders inside the state was not inevitably so narrowly determined. This helped focus the party's attention on what might be done if Labour had a leadership less deferential in the face of bureaucratic statism, and more committed to mobilising popular support for socialist policies.

In fact when the first public breach between the Government and the party arose within a month of the election, Foot himself had initially joined with Benn in turning to the NEC and to Conference decisions to strengthen the left's voice in Cabinet. This occurred not over economic strategy but over the highly emotive (and, to a Labour Party committed to 'fundamental change', far from irrelevant) issue of Chile. Six months earlier, the Allende Government had been overthrown in an exceptionally brutal military coup. The 1973 Labour Party Conference had passed an emergency resolution which condemned the Heath Government's precipitate recognition of the Pinochet regime and called for withholding all aid to it. Before the vote Allende's former ambassador to Britain was given the floor and received a standing ovation.[29] The Labour front bench had followed this up by calling for the Government to prevent all arms sales to the junta. Yet in March 1974 the new Cabinet's Defence and Overseas Policy Committee decided to honour pre-existing naval contracts with Chile and supply the dictatorship with two frigates and two submarines, and refit a destroyer. Although no new contracts were to be entered into, the revelation in the press of this decision (heretofore unknown to most of the Cabinet, let alone the PLP or NEC) produced an immediate furore.

Upwards of 100 Labour MPs protested to Callaghan, the Foreign Secretary, and a debate ensued in Cabinet on whether to consult the PLP before confirming the decision. Barbara Castle recorded in her diary that Healey raised 'the awful spectre that the party might decide to cancel the contracts and then we stood to lose £70 million'. Fred Peart (the Agriculture Minister, sometimes thought of as 'soft left') wanted an immediate decision, 'otherwise ordinary people will have a veto over Cabinet decisions, which would be absurd'. Castle stressed the irony that while Labour leaders talked a lot about participation they never practised it: 'The speeches made round this Cabinet table this morning could be echoed in every boardroom in industry.'[30] Nevertheless, the PLP was consulted – Wilson was sure the MPs' 'good sense' could be trusted. In reality, they could only be trusted to be divided on the issue, which is what Callaghan reported back to the Cabinet after his consultations. The Cabinet then endorsed Callaghan's decision to supply the ships, with only Benn and Foot still speaking against.[31] At meetings of the NEC – which had not been consulted – Foot and Benn spoke out again, and the NEC passed a resolution that the decision should be reviewed by the Cabinet. A similar scenario would play itself out later in the year over combined naval exercises with the apartheid government of South Africa.

That the initial division between the Government and the party should have taken place over Chile was a script ready-made for Chris Mullin's novel, A Very British Coup. Not that anyone in the Cabinet was drawing lessons from the substance of the Allende experience; that government had been rather more committed to fundamental change. But the incident set the stage for Harold Wilson to interpret 'the doctrine of collective responsibility [as] totally binding on a minister, whatever he is doing or in whatever capacity he is acting' and applying this 'in particular to his membership of party bodies'. In a memo to the offending ministers in May 1974, Wilson declared: '... where any conflict of loyalties arose the principle of the collective responsibility of the Government was absolute and overriding in all circumstances ... if any Minister felt unable to subscribe to this principle without reservation, it was his duty to resign his office forthwith'.[32] The practical implication of Wilson's memorandum was that the price of state office for the most prominent representatives of the Labour left was to give their primary loyalty, neither to the party nor to their socialist convictions, but to their centre-right colleagues in the Cabinet.

The issue thus raised gave Benn the opportunity of formulating clearly – in a memorandum in response to Wilson's which he sent to his two junior ministers in the Department of Industry, and then published two years later – his very different views on the role of socialists who held high state office. It granted that they were, as ministers, 'collectively responsible for all Government decisions and collectively obliged to explain what the Government has decided, and to see that Government policy is understood'. They should not comment on sensitive matters for which other ministers were directly responsible without prior consultation with them ('and we are entitled to expect they will do the same'). In these senses, they were indeed answerable to their Cabinet colleagues and answerable to the public and the party for the Cabinet's decisions. Nevertheless:

> There is a distinction between the broad exercise of our political role and our official Ministerial acts and statements. The movement and the Government has everything to gain by seeing that that difference is widely understood. Our twin role allows us to act as spokesmen, representatives, champions and educators as well as mere managers within a Labour Government machine. This is necessary if we are to mobilise the energy of our movement to work enthusiastically for the policies we have jointly discussed and agreed . . . In short we are still ourselves, Labour Party and Trade Union members, as well as Ministers; and our accountability is to our consciences, to the people, to the party, and to the movement as well as to the Government.[33]

On this basis Benn continued in his errant ways. Wilson did not dismiss him, fearing that Benn was more dangerous outside the Government than in it: Benn leading a revolt from the back benches was 'the last place I wanted to see him'.[34]

On Benn's determination to maintain his freedom to campaign on key issues depended the fate of the Labour new left's industrial strategy. If it was to have the slightest hope of making an impact, it had to be popularised, especially among workers. Benn had explained this to the 1973 Conference, as we have seen, and his argument there was under-scored by the fact that a subsequent poll commissioned by the party just before the election showed that the National Enterprise Board proposal commanded the clear support of only 6 per cent of Labour voters. On the general question of more nationalisation the poll gave more hope (37 per cent in favour), but this paled beside the degree of support for pension increases (74 per cent).[35] It was obvious that the majority of the Cabinet would use such poll figures to confine the interpretation of the Social Contract to the narrowest redistributive terms. It was thus crucial for Benn and his team in the Department of Industry to use the legitimacy and the resources that state office provided to spread the word about the industrial strategy, and to build support among the unions and in popular opinion, if a decision by a Cabinet hostile to its spirit was to be avoided. It might not work, but it had to be tried: why else were they ministers and what else were they in the Department of Industry to do? In any event, the industrial strategy was party policy and in the election manifesto. Benn was Minister of Industry and charged with implementing it. The question was only one of how far he would be able to use his mandate to accomplish any really significant change.

The Fate of the Industrial Strategy

Virtually the first change Benn sought to inaugurate in his Department was to supplement its previously exclusive ties with business by close ties with the unions. He was appalled at the ignorance of his officials even regarding the union bureaucracy, let alone the shop stewards' movement. (One of his favourite stories was of their blank look when he made a reference to consulting the Confederation of Shipbuilding and Engineering Unions – CSEU – perhaps the most powerful union body in industry.) His goal was to make his Department's ties with the unions as comprehensive as those of the Department of Employment, and he immediately appointed a trade union adviser available to all his ministers as well as officials in the Department. He made it clear, in a paper on the industrial strategy submitted to the Labour Party–TUC Liaison Committee in May 1974 ('A Note on the Current Work of the Department of Industry'), that his intention was to cleave very closely to Labour's 1973 programme; and that discussions with the unions on their role in making and administering planning agreements, and on experiments in industrial democracy, would be central to developing the framework for what he clearly intended to be the first really serious effort at economic planning in Britain since the war.

But to leave matters here, however much these measures might have strengthened the British state's previously weak and unstable corporatism, and brought it closer to Sweden's, was inadequate and potentially even counterproductive. For a close association with the union leadership alone would give the appearance of trade union power without necessarily developing enough mobilisation behind it to make the unions an effective force in support of the industrial strategy. So Benn's paper also stressed the need for a national political campaign which had to go well beyond discussions with leaders of the TUC and CBI: 'The policy changes outlined above, when carried through, will represent such an important development of policy that *there is no chance of success without a long period of public explanation, debate, consultation and development.* Apart from highly political comments in the context of the Labour Conference and the General Election, very few people really know what the programme says or what the argument is all about.'[36] Overcoming this would involve meetings throughout the country with representatives of local trade unions and employers' associations with local authorities, and with 'shop stewards and gatherings of working management whose support is essential if our policies are to succeed'. Only in this way would it be possible to 'isolate real opponents from others who might not be opponents'.

At the Liaison Committee meeting, while Jones and Scanlon 'sat silent', Wilson declared that a public campaign based on Benn's paper was 'certainly not a vote winner'. Benn retorted that while he didn't 'for a moment think we shall have the support of our opponents', he had personally fought the election on this.[37] Although they would not say so in front of the union leaders, the legitimacy that Benn sought to derive from quoting the party's election manifesto, or from pre-election speeches by Wilson himself, cut no ice with most of his Cabinet colleagues. According to Benn, Callaghan told him later, in the privacy of the Cabinet Industrial Policy Committee: 'You can't write a manifesto for the party in opposition and expect it to have any relationship to what the party does in Government. We're now entirely free to do what we like.'[38] Indeed, it was now clear that Wilson would sanction the campaign against the radical version of the industrial strategy that was being initiated by the Treasury and by Benn's officials in the Department of Industry.[39] Benn therefore had no alternative but to attempt to fight the battle out in public, and sooner rather than later. In a series of speeches he had already detailed the massive amount of state aid (at least £2 million a day under Heath) that was being poured into privately owned companies to little effect in terms of industrial investment, and stressed the need for contractually-binding planning agreements and a powerful NEB. But now the attack on Benn and the industrial strategy by the CBI, the Tories and the media reached entirely new levels of hysteria.[40]

Benn had predicted this before the election, as we have seen. But the sheer breadth of this attack raised severe questions about the hopes of Holland, Hart and Benn himself, that by framing the industrial strategy along the lines of Italian and French models of planning they might make it ideologically acceptable to substantial sections of bourgeois opinion.[41] The CBI, the City and the financial press, fed by the senior civil service and Labour ministers with 'inside' stories about Benn's 'true' intentions, and in turn feeding international business opinion, treated 'an NEB with a significantly different approach to investment from that of a merchant bank . . . as anathema. So long as Benn was at the Department of Industry and the radical version of the NEB was on the agenda, then the City and private corporate management treated it *as if it was* nationalisation.'[42] Indeed, even the apparently modest goal of just securing disclosure of investment and pricing policy information from private corporations was treated as a struggle over 'management prerogatives' on which capital simply refused to yield. The CBI, perhaps well understanding that the majority of the Cabinet had no intention of allowing extensive acquisitions by the NEB, seemed to treat the disclosure of information issue as the central one all along. Its Director General told Labour MPs on the Industry Bill Standing Committee that if the Government allowed trade unionists to get by law information that companies would not of themselves provide to them, companies would defy the law.[43]

In so far as the leaders of the Labour new left believed that a strong mobilisation of business opinion against the industrial strategy could be avoided, they were clearly wrong. That the British business class should have reacted with such virulence to a strategy inspired in good part by continental capitalist models was indicative of the mood that had already brought Thatcher to power in the Conservative Party. But it is also likely that they were quite aware of their advantage in relation to the balance of forces in the Cabinet. For the opposition to Benn's plans was not only privately but also publicly supported by the leading figures in the Government. Five days before Benn presented his paper to the Liaison Committee, Denis Healey had already told the CBI that the Government had 'no intention of destroying the private sector or encouraging its decay'; it wanted 'a private sector which is vigorous, alert, imaginative and profitable'.[44] The press also revealed that Benn's report to the Liaison Committee had drawn 'bitter comments from senior ministers'.[45] Indeed, Wilson was determined to derail Benn's attempt to initiate a public campaign for his version of the industrial strategy. Although Benn had won the consent of the NEC's Home Policy Committee to publish his 'Note on the Current Work of the Department of Industry', this did not impress Wilson. He was furious that Benn should have counterposed the party's manifesto commitments to Cabinet sentiment in this way, and he played a large role in instigating the tremendous uproar that greeted the publication of the paper. His speeches began vociferously to echo Healey's, and go further: 'Private industry must have the confidence to maintain and increase investment to do their duty to the people. And confidence demands that a clear frontier be established between what is public and what is private.'[46]

Of course, Wilson's concerns were by no means only electoral ones. He was very sympathetic to the substance of the business argument against the Benn's plans, and even to the CBI's view on disclosure of information. As he recalled later:

> The more I thought about it, the more another anxiety plagued me. The Planning Agreements would be a charade unless the firm was going to reveal its

plans, not only for this year's production, but for future developments . . . If the trade union representative, who under the Planning Agreements system was to have access to his firm's innermost secrets, were an employee, e.g. a shop steward, he would have to be tied to the firm for life, by some new statutory form of serfdom, to provide a guarantee against leakage or other abuse.[47]

Significantly enough, Wilson did not apply this logic to managerial mobility between companies, or to interlocking directorships.

Of course, no one could ignore the fact that the industrial strategy was being launched in the midst of the greatest working-class industrial mobilisation and militancy in Britain for fifty years. Benn, perhaps more than any other leading Labour figure over that half-century, understood that the critical strategic task was to channel union militancy into a struggle for greater power in industry and the state. As we have seen, much of this militancy had its roots in an 'instrumental collectivism' that was not inherently radical. But neither did it defer to established patterns of managerial authority; and a significant layer of the leadership of this instrumental working class, as we have seen, *was* politicised, and associated itself with, and even helped define, the project of the Labour new left. And although the shop stewards' combines and the factory occupations of the early 1970s were still mainly defensive, sectional and local struggles, they did signal a pronounced shift towards something more far-reaching than economistic wage demands, reflecting the ability of many shop stewards to engage workers on issues related to the politics of production. Given the inhospitable balance of forces inside the state to a fundamental shift in wealth and power, and the mobilisation of hostile capitalist opinion, it was crucial to try to develop further this source of political power outside the state.

The very election of Labour was bound to encourage militant working-class activity initially, and this happened in ways that went considerably beyond traditional trade union economism. By far the most publicised rank and file action during the Government's first months in office took place in a London hospital, where the 'battling grannie', Esther Brookstone, led a strike of low-paid National Union of Public Employees (NUPE) members against 'pay beds' for the wealthy. This intervention against the prerogatives of the medical establishment within the NHS, and their inegalitarian effects, was indeed not only a sign of the scope of working-class militancy at the time, but of its potential to raise workers' political consciousness and self-confidence. Moreover, since the Labour Government had entered office amidst a profitability and liquidity squeeze in industry, and a growing spate of closures and mass redundancies in the wake of the three-day week, even the mere defence of jobs provided the basis for a strong linkage between the Labour new left's industrial strategy and the interventions of many shop stewards in the politics of production.

Immediately after the election, the Department of Industry became, according to Benn, 'like a field hospital in the Battle of the Somme. Every day the place was crowded with shop stewards.'[48] Benn's support for workers' efforts to take over and run bankrupt companies, like the Meridan and Kirkby coops, along with the more short-lived one at the *Scottish Daily News*, became the most prominent examples of the new regime at the Department of Industry in 1974. The resistance of Benn's own officials as well as the Treasury to giving financial aid to these coops – minuscule in comparison with the vast amounts spent on the bail-out of the City during the secondary banking crisis at the time – was enormous.[49] But Benn persisted, seeing the coops not only in terms of saving jobs, but as pointing the way to a new form of decentralised, worker-controlled social ownership. Similar expectations were raised among workers, in British Leyland and in the shipbuilding and aircraft industries, who, like Benn, favoured a form of nationalisation which broke decisively with the pattern of Herbert Morrison's centralised and hierarchical public corporation.

It was in this context that the famous workers' alternative production plan at Lucas Aerospace was hatched at a meeting with Benn later in 1974. The Shop Stewards' Combine Committee at Lucas, drawn from several unions and representing some 13,000 workers in seventeen factories, white collar as well as manual, grew directly out of the militant atmosphere of the late 1960s. The strike that the committee led in 1972, and subsequent struggles around redundancies, while they represented remarkable successes in forging rank and file organisational cohesion, were still primarily economistic and defensive. Nevertheless, many of the leaders of the Combine Committee were socialists who favoured public ownership but well understood their members' reservations about it. Accordingly in the summer of 1974 they initiated a debate among the membership in which they stressed not only the job security that public ownership might afford, but also the limits of old-style nationalisation where management was not democratically accountable. They offered the vision of a genuine industrial democracy which would allow workers to determine 'the product ranges the industry handles, to engage on socially useful products ... [and] to create an industry where the skill and talent of our members is used to the full, and in a much truer sense, in the interest of the nation as a whole'.[50]

A delegation of thirty-four shop stewards crowded into Benn's office for a two-and-a-half-hour meeting. Benn was impressed by how well organised they were and by the homework they had done on the state of their firm and the industry. He suggested that the Combine Committee should draw up a corporate plan for Lucas, and offered to arrange a meeting between the committee, the company and the Government to discuss an alternative to further layoffs. The committee took up Benn's suggestion, stressing 'a new concept' for nationalisation in the way of an alternative plan. But being more wary than Benn of the corporatist implications of attempting to draw up such a plan in conjunction with management, they would develop the plan themselves and then present it to government and management. Thus was born 'the Lucas Plan', which was to inspire numerous other projects for the conversion of military production to peaceful purposes as well as serve as a model for industrial democracy. The immense amount of favourable comment it secured internationally led it to be nominated for the Nobel Peace Prize. In Britain, it was to become a constant reference point for the Labour new left at both local and national levels.

While such initiatives were important in raising expectations of the radical nature of the NEB and the Industry Act, even while the industrial strategy was being effectively disembowelled by the Cabinet, they did not in themselves amount to the kind of mass campaign at the grassroots level for which Benn and his co-ministers were calling. In this respect surprisingly little initiative came from the labour movement.[51] Indeed, the absence of organised trade union pressure for the industrial strategy was remarkable. Such a mass campaign as there was depended very largely on what Benn and Heffer could manage to conduct from within the Department of Industry itself, over the heads of hostile civil servants and within the increasingly tight constraints of collective Cabinet responsibility. The reasons for this have partly to do with the trade union leadership's continuing search for a stable corporatist relationship as the most effective means of exerting influence on the state; and partly with an even more traditional defence of official trade union authority structures. There was a good deal of concern in the union hierarchies about Benn and his Department going over their heads to their rank and file, or at least encouraging unofficial initiatives. The continually obstructive behaviour of the CSEU *vis-à-vis* the Lucas Combine was the most notorious example of this, although it also reflected the suspicions of some of the union leadership (including not only the right-wing leaders but also Communists) that mobilisations around workers' control indicated little more than the influence of Maoist or Trotskyist shop stewards.[52]

But the bulk of the union leadership were not motivated by such concerns, and Benn had every reason to expect that those left-wing leaders who had been so supportive of the shop stewards' movement and the Institute for Workers' Control would also insist on the need for workers' involvement in a new industrial policy and for radical economic policies generally. Moreover, almost all the elements of the industrial strategy had been articulated in the TUC's own Economic Reviews even before they appeared in Labour's programmes. When push came to shove, however, the union leaders backed off. Given their knowledge that the Cabinet was opposed to a campaign in favour of a radical version of the industrial strategy, the left-wing union leadership turned out to be conventionally pragmatic. 'The ideological thrust of their activities was limited by a trade union perspective. When Labour took office after 1974, it was the turn of the left-wing union leaders to undergo a loss of ideological self-confidence and the beginning of, in some respects, a rapid deradicalisation,' Minkin has observed. 'Certainly [Jones] and Scanlon lacked anything near the amount of confidence required for them to go out on a limb in support of Benn's economic diagnosis and prescriptions.'[53] In June 1974, when Benn asked Scanlon why the unions were not pushing harder in support of his industrial strategy paper, Scanlon told him straightforwardly: 'Why go out on a limb now for a policy to be published which we know can't be implemented?'[54] Nor were they prepared to jeopardise the 'real partnership' that Foot insisted was on offer on the basis of the other elements in the Social Contract.

Yet Jack Jones well understood the effects of the absence of a mass campaign on the industrial strategy. As he later told the Trades Council's inquiry: 'To be honest with you, I don't think there was enough understanding of planning agreements and the NEB. We had not sold the ideas to the membership. The TUC Economic Review, where these policies were spelt out, might be intelligible to you but it's not understood or read by most of the members...' But as Jones looked back on 1974, after he had reluctantly acknowledged that the Government had been 'hijacked off course', he recognised what had held them back from doing something about this: 'Other things were being done at the time, the Employment Protection Act, social policies like better pensions and food subsidies. These were important to us. We could not say "we're not playing", just because of the industrial policies.... Moreover, we were not prepared to do anything which might threaten the Labour government. We were almost more concerned to keep the Labour government in power than was the Labour government itself.'[55]

Wilson's response to Benn's attempt to initiate a public campaign on the industrial policy was to take direct control over the Cabinet Committee which would receive the Green Paper being prepared in Benn's department by Eric Heffer's working group. And when it was submitted, enshrining all the major policies of *Labour's Programme*, and somewhat further radicalised in tone by Benn, it was promptly rewritten, to become the very different document published in August 1974 as a White Paper entitled merely, *The Regeneration of British Industry*.[56] The new hand was Michael Foot's, writing, as Wilson put it, 'within the parameters we laid down', so that it was no longer 'a sloppy and half-baked document, polemical, indeed menacing, in tone, redolent more of an NEC Home Policy Committee document than a Command Paper'.[57]

The new version actually far more deserved to be called 'half-baked', but it was certainly no longer menacing. The planning agreements were to be only voluntary as far as companies were concerned, and in any case they were to play a less prominent role than the NEB, which was itself scaled down in terms of the finances it would command, and above all in terms of having to operate, as Wilson had demanded, within normal 'Stock Exchange procedures', so that it had 'no marauding role' via compulsory acquisition powers. As for its tone, *The Regeneration of British Industry*, whatever else it was, was certainly not a campaigning document for mobilising a working-class assault on the prerogatives of capital.

In this way the battle over industrial strategy was effectively lost in the summer of 1974. From this point on, the role of the new left ministers in the Department of Industry, and of Benn in the Cabinet, was effectively that of 'damage limitation'. They shepherded the subsequent Industry Act through the legislative process on the principle that, while it fell short of what was needed, it was still a useful starting point. Benn and Heffer spoke more openly and critically at party meetings, and were grateful for such belated support as they secured from the labour movement, but they could not publicly expose the fact that Harold Wilson had offered fundamentally contradictory pledges to the TUC and CBI, respectively, on the role of the NEB.[58] Benn and Heffer even surreptitiously encouraged radical amendments from backbench MPs like Audrey Wise and Brian Sedgemore in Standing Committee, but at the same time they were obliged officially to oppose these amendments on the grounds that the Government could not accept them. The effect of Benn and Heffer's continued presence at the helm of the Department of Industry was thus very contradictory. It encouraged those in the labour movement who still wanted to believe in the Government's potential radicalism, but it ensured at the same time British capital's continued and vociferous hostility to even the watered-down legislation.[59] This lasted until Heffer and Benn were removed from the Department of Industry by Wilson in the spring of 1975.

The Common Market Referendum and Labour's New Left

The occasion (or more accurately the pretext) for the sacking of Benn and Heffer was their stand on the Common Market. Although, as we saw earlier, the Referendum idea was Benn's, the tactic of concentrating the Labour left's stand on the issue of the Common Market was characteristically Foot's. We have seen in the previous chapter that Foot was prepared to sacrifice the industrial strategy in the hope of holding the Labour leadership to withdrawal from the EEC, and that his hopes for doing so were based on the extensive support this had within the PLP itself. But the compromise that was struck on this, whereby Labour committed itself to renegotiation of the terms of entry to be followed by a Referendum, had worn thin by the time of the October 1974 election returns. It was clear that Wilson and Callaghan's conception of renegotiation did not extend to challenging any of the provisions of the Treaty of Rome.[60] By the end of November 1974 Benn got Michael Foot and Peter Shore to sign a letter he had drafted to Wilson, asking that collective responsibility be suspended and that ministers should have the right to express their convictions publicly. Any other arrangement would indeed not only have endangered the Foot–Healey axis, but endangered the Government itself, given the balance of opinion in the PLP. In these circumstances, Wilson allowed a limited break with collective responsibility on this issue only. When the renegotiated terms were announced in March 1975, leaving the basis of Britain's membership substantially unaltered, only seven Cabinet members (Foot, Benn, Castle, Shore, Silkin, Varley and Ross) announced that they would publicly dissociate themselves from these terms in the Referendum campaign, while the other sixteen would line up in favour. The junior ministers split evenly, as the PLP very nearly did itself, with 137 Labour MPs voting with the Tories in favour of staying in, and 145 against.

All this spoke volumes about the weakness of the Labour left – old *and* new – *vis-à-vis* this Government. Foot and the 'soft left' had refused to join Benn and Heffer in a campaign on the industrial strategy, but Benn and Heffer were ready to join Foot and the 'soft left' in a campaign against the Common Market. In relation to the struggle for extending democracy that was so much a part of the Labour new left's agenda, it was very much to the point to address critically 'the democratic deficit' that underlay (and still underlies) Europe's political institutions. As Benn put it, when opening his public campaign against Britain's continuing membership on New Year's Day, 1975: '. . . the power of the electors of Britain, through their direct representatives in Parliament, to make laws, vary taxes, change laws which the Courts must uphold, and control the conduct of public affairs, has been substantially ceded to the European Community whose Council of Ministers and Commission are neither collectively elected nor collectively dismissed by the British people, nor even by the peoples of all the Community countries put together'.[61] Nor was the European issue irrelevant to a socialist – or even a Keynesian – economic strategy. As Nicholas (later Lord) Kaldor put it, in explaining the demise of Keynesianism: 'The obligations entailed by membership of the Common Market made it impossible to pursue the post-war policies of demand management on a national basis, while the institutions of the Community were not designed to coordinate such policies on a European basis.'[62] Moreover, as Benn and Heffer in particular stressed during the Referendum campaign, the radical version of the industrial strategy, not to mention the extensive capital and import controls sought in the alternative economic strategy, would have been disallowed by Brussels on the basis of the Treaty of Rome. Benn explicitly told Wilson as early as June 1974 that it was his experience of the limits imposed on his authority as Minister of Industry that had now made him shift his position from 'neutral' to 'bitterly hostile' on the Common Market.[63] This certainly also reflected the extent to which the pro-marketeers themselves saw the Common Market as a prophylactic against the Labour new left. What was at stake, in their view, was the entire Cold War order. 'It isn't only Europe,' Jenkins said. 'It is question of whether this country is going to cut itself off from the Western Alliance or go isolationist.'[64]

The fact that all the opinion polls in 1974 showed a substantial majority against the Market strengthened the case for the left taking their stand on this issue. But it also obscured matters. The anti-marketeers had widely differing views on economic and industrial strategy, as well as on the left's democratisation struggle in relation to the Labour Party, parliamentarism and the British state. They took their collective stand in the Referendum mainly on the issue of defending the sovereignty of the British people through Parliament, and secondarily on the question of whether EEC membership would contribute to unemployment. What this obscured was the fact that the first obstacle that both radical democratic reforms and a socialist economic strategy had to confront lay not in Brussels but in Westminster, Whitehall and Downing Street. Ironically, the suspension of collective Cabinet responsibility that was allowed during the Referendum actually cemented the position of the parliamentary elite as a whole. For pointing to the limits that Brussels would impose on the radical version of the industrial strategy if it were government policy disguised the fact that it was *not* in fact government policy. When the Referendum was over, the Foot–Healey axis was the stronger for this.

The apparent victory the anti-Common Market forces secured when a special Party Conference voted 2–1 in favour of the 'no' campaign, was more than offset by Wilson's successful veto against the party throwing its organisational resources and electoral machine into the campaign. Wilson's insistence that 'the party machine must remain neutral' was challenged by Benn alone; Foot and Jones demurred.[65] With the dissenting ministers left mainly to their own organisational resources, with the 'Britain in Europe' campaign out-spending the anti-EC 'National Referendum Campaign' by more than 10 to 1 (the largest donation to the NRC came from the TGWU, the princely sum of £1,377) and with Labour supporters confused by the division in the party, the outcome was scarcely surprising.[66] Nor was it surprising that the outcome was interpreted inside the Cabinet as legitimating the complete marginalisation of the Labour new left inside the Government, despite the fact that the campaign had obscured rather than clarified differences over economic strategy. Wilson had already sacked Heffer for speaking against the renegotiated terms in the House in advance of the campaign, and immediately after the Referendum Benn was dismissed from the Department of Industry.[67] Both Foot and Jones urged Wilson not to do this. Jones had warned Wilson publicly that this would be 'a grave affront to the trade union movement', but as with so much else that had gone before, in the event neither Foot or Jones did anything to mobilise party or union opposition to it.[68] Still convinced of the futility of resignation, Benn accepted Wilson's switch of Eric Varley to Industry and himself to the Department of Energy.

Yet Benn's demotion had little to do with the Common Market, as the contrary fate of the other dissenting ministers, and notably Varley, clearly showed. It had everything to do with the way the centre-right of the Cabinet, the senior civil service and business circles saw Benn's socialist commitment. With the spectre of another sterling crisis taking shape from the beginning of 1975 onward, as Joe Haines tells it: 'The whispers from the Treasury's contacts grew stronger. Only if Tony Benn was sacked, it was said, would the confidence of British industry be restored. If confidence was restored then industrial investment would begin again...' Haines, no great left-winger himself, added: 'It is astonishing that this sort of naivety is expressed by otherwise intelligent men.'[69] Neil Kinnock angrily warned in *Tribune*: 'The appeasement, like most appeasements, won't work. Those who demand the change will simply ask for more. But we are now in the extraordinary and dangerously undemocratic situation where our foes have a direct influence on the selection of Labour Ministers.'[70]

In March 1976 Wilson resigned. In the PLP leadership ballot for his successor, the right-wing Callaghan emerged victorious over Foot, while Benn obtained only thirty-seven votes before throwing his support to Foot in the second round. This outcome registered several facts. The new left's project had been sustained in the Cabinet only by Benn, whose influence on policy was effectively neutralised by Wilson with the support of the rest of the Cabinet, the civil service, and media and business opinion. Crucial to this outcome was the fact that the union leadership had failed to give serious support to the industrial strategy. It was becoming more and more clear that without a democratisation of the party – and the unions – this was the logic of parliamentary socialism in practice.

But contrary to the judgement of contemporary observers like Peter Jenkins, the defeat of the left inside the parliamentary party did not mean that the Croslandite social democrats had triumphed. On the contrary, what the social democrats inside and outside the Cabinet had yet to grasp was something that both Labour's new left and the Thatcherites, from very different perspectives, had already understood, i.e., that the post-war mode of social democratic regulation had become unsustainable. In the month before Wilson passed the torch to Callaghan, the Government had announced the freezing of public expenditure in a White Paper which detailed the most extensive cuts in planned social spending in modern British history. Not only would this be followed by two further packages of massive cuts in public expenditure by the end of the year, but the new leader would bluntly tell the Labour Party Conference, in what would immediately be seen as a 'defining moment' speech, that public expenditure, once seen as the solution to economic crises, had now become their cause. Burk and Cairncross, in their study of the 1976 IMF crisis, effectively described the illusion under which the social democrats were labouring: 'By March 1976 ... the moderates and right-wingers in the Cabinet ... felt they had made hard decisions and choices and were now on the path to recovery. What they were on the brink of was a major exchange crisis, as a result of which the markets virtually refused to lend money to the Government. This combination of crises would ultimately force the government to make a public recantation of some cherished economic and political beliefs'.[71] In other words, to abandon Keynesianism.

6

The Abandonment of Keynesianism

The abandonment of Keynesianism and the inauguration of monetarism in Britain by a Labour Government was a defining moment in the politics of 'globalisation'. As governments tried to cope with the inflationary effects of industrial militancy in the advanced capitalist world, and of rising prices of resource commodities from the third world (especially the quadrupling of the price of oil in 1973), the world economy had already entered the first of what would prove to be a series of severe recessions over the last quarter of the twentieth century. This was taking place, moreover, in the context of the breakdown of the post-war international monetary order. The rapid development of unregulated Eurodollar banking through the 1960s (much encouraged by Britain), alongside the growth of institutional funds (pensions, insurance, trusts) and the financial activities of multinational corporations, had the effect of setting vast pools of money free to engage in international speculation in currency exchange rates and interest rates on government bonds. The scale of the speculation against sterling that led to the previous Labour Government's devaluation in 1967 had already shown that even when the substantial foreign exchange reserves of a leading capitalist country were bolstered by unprecedented funding by the IMF and other capitalist countries, this could not stabilise a currency against the pressure brought to bear by the financial markets. And it soon turned out that the pound had been only the front line of defence for the dollar. By 1971, speculation against the dollar led the Americans to preserve their policy autonomy by renouncing the dollar's convertibility to gold.

This renewed scope and power of financial markets, unseen since the twenties, was in the process of breaking up not only the Bretton Woods system of stable exchange rates but also the limited controls over the movement of capital that had provided the framework for European and Japanese reconstruction, and then for the Keynesian and social democratic policies of the post-war era.[1] The initial response among some governments in Europe and Japan was not only to tighten their capital control regulations but also to revive Keynes's original proposals for a system of cooperative arrangements among member states to make capital controls really effective in the face of such large and powerful speculative forces. This initiative, as Eric Helleiner has shown, was quickly killed by opposition from the United States, which 'for the first time since 1945–47 had begun to press for a fully liberal financial order', and indeed abolished its own capital controls by the beginning of 1974.[2] Both interest and ideology were at work here. Speculative capital movements would do what negotiations could not: shift the burden of the USA's chronically large current account deficit abroad and preserve Wall Street's and the Eurodollar market's dominance in international finance. Broad opposition to capital controls had emerged in the US business community in the late 1960s and early 1970s, a stance supported within the Nixon administration by a powerful circle of officials who were close to Wall Street and armed with Milton Friedman's monetarist theories, and whose prejudice against social democratic welfare states was almost as strong as their anti-communism.[3]

In his account of his 'ordeal with the IMF', Denis Healey was to describe Bill Simon, the American Treasury Secretary who had made his first million as a bond trader before he was thirty, as 'far to the right of Genghis Khan and totally devoted to the freedom of financial markets'.[4] But the ideas Simon was espousing were hardly foreign to Britain. Under the rubric of monetarism these ideas would come to be expounded far more popularly than anywhere else by Margaret Thatcher, who had taken over as leader of the Conservative Party in 1975. And even before this, monetarist ideas (articulated especially effectively in widely circulated stockbrokers' publications) had already become the prevailing economic philosophy among the people who ran the banks, insurance companies, pension funds and stockbroking houses, and their advisers in the City of London – that is, among all the institutions that represented international financial markets within Britain. The incoming Labour Government did not have to wait to be apprised of the City's monetarist views by the Governor of the Bank of England; through their widespread coverage in the financial press, these views were on the new ministers' breakfast tables every morning.[5]

A Labour Government had once again come to office with the belief that its main contribution to managing the economy lay in being better able *to secure the moderation of the unions through incomes policy*. The monetarists' message was clear – this whole perspective was passé; at best irrelevant, at worst counterproductive, to the real challenge of public policy, which was *to win the confidence of the financial markets through monetary policy*. Monetarism here needs to be understood less in terms of arcane theories about the quantity theory of money, than in terms of a belief that the containment of inflation, not unemployment, is the first priority of economic strategy and the prime measure of its success.[6] Inflation is taken as the effect of deficit financing of excessive public expenditure, with the latter having the further effect of soaking up resources that would otherwise go to private investment and private consumption even under conditions of recession and unemployment. The association between increasing public expenditure and inflation became the symbol of governments foolishly or mendaciously trying to escape the constraints imposed by the operation of free financial markets. In domestic policy terms, monetarism meant rejecting both fiscal (taxation and expenditure) policies and corporatist (prices and incomes) policies as modes of regulating the economy, and instead putting overriding emphasis on getting monetary policy 'right' (limiting the growth of the money supply). On this view, the behaviour of financial markets in buying and selling currency and government bonds should be seen as a positive constraint on the behaviour of governments, subordinating political discretion and state intervention to the confidence of these markets.

A foretaste of the shift towards monetarism in British economic policy had occurred during Roy Jenkins's tenure as Chancellor of the Exchequer after the 1967 devaluation, when the Treasury, encouraged by the IMF, gave priority to tight control of the money supply as the means of making the devaluation effective in restricting consumption and holding down imports. The Heath Government's decision in 1971 to abandon the Bank of England's controls on bank lending (which meant that domestic credit would be rationed only by interest rates), followed by the floating of the pound in 1972 (which meant that the exchange rate would also be determined by relative interest rates), had the effect of handing considerable power to the financial markets and giving more importance to monetary policy than to fiscal policy.

But it was the subsequent failure of Keynesianism in the mid-1970s – the experience of *both* rapidly rising inflation *and* rapidly rising unemployment after the Heath Government's 'U-turn' back to a policy of fiscal reflation and wage controls (policies maintained through the first year of the new Labour Government in 1974–75) – that really marked the turning-point. The sterling crises of 1975 and 1976 revealed the power of the financial markets, in conjunction with the American state, to redefine the terms of debate over economic policy. Before this episode was over, the assertion that 'there is no alternative' to monetarism would come to sound like common sense to many erstwhile Keynesians in the Treasury, the media and – not least – the Labour Cabinet. As Simon Clarke put it: 'Monetarism triumphed not because of its own merits, whether as an economic theory or political ideology, but because of the failures of Keynesianism. The ideological power of monetarism derived from the fact that it could explain and legitimate policies that had been forced on Keynesian governments.'[7]

It is important to distinguish between the Government's rejection of the Labour new left's economic strategy, and its reluctant but definitive abandonment of Keynesianism. The 'hollowing out' of the left-wing policies that successive Party Conferences had endorsed cannot really be attributed to resistance from the opposition parties, senior civil servants, the CBI, the City, the IMF, the American state, the media, the Treaty of Rome and the Brussels bureaucracy, or even the anonymous international financial markets, although such resistance there certainly was. Most of the Labour leadership had always anticipated such resistance and long before incorporated it as part of their justification for persisting in the 'art of the possible'. But when maintaining this accommodation with capital involved them having to renege on their Keynesianism, most of them were not anticipating powerful forces, but yielding to them, and they knew it. Indeed, they found it hard to credit that things had come to such a pass. But in rejecting and even ridiculing radical left alternatives directed at challenging these forces they helped to make credible Mrs Thatcher's claim that 'there is no alternative'. Their acceptance of defeat by the monetarists was also decisive in precipitating a new and far more determined effort by the new left in the Labour Party to tackle the causes of their chronic subordination to the right-wing minority. The abandonment of Keynesianism, even more than the rejection of the new left's policies, was what accounted for the tenacity and increasing sense of urgency with which the Labour new left mobilised right through the 1970s – and even while the Government was in office – to attempt a fundamental redefinition of the relation between leaders and activists.

The 1976 Crisis: The Triumph of Monetarism

Given that sterling crises, even in the post-war era, had been 'a repeated and tedious fact of life',[8] the Labour Government elected in 1974 could hardly have escaped yet another one. The new Government inherited a negative shift in the terms of trade of some 25 per cent since 1972, an inflationary time-bomb sparked by the indexed wage thresholds introduced under Heath's statutory incomes policy, a secondary banking crisis in the City, a growing liquidity crisis in industry and a slump in stock market prices. It initially avoided a deflationary policy, partly because, as Clarke put it, 'in place of the industrial strategy, the government sought to buy votes, and buy off the militancy of its supporters, by introducing expansionary budgets in July and November 1974 which enabled it to fulfil some its promises of income redistribution'.[9] But this budgetary stance was not only a matter of engineering the defeat of the radical industrial strategy in 1974; it also reflected the continuation of Treasury policy under Heath. Since 1972, even before the oil price increases, the Treasury had chosen to finance the balance of payments deficit through courting short-term capital inflows (using the promise of the surpluses that would eventually flow from North Sea oil) rather than deflate. This policy was reinforced in 1973–74 by the concern that during the energy crisis western governments should try to sustain aggregate demand rather than undercut each other's exports through competitive austerity.[10] Yet most other countries did not follow suit, which aggravated Britain's balance of payments crisis; moreover, by the time the Labour Government had secured a majority in the October 1974 election it was facing a rate of inflation of over 20 per cent, as well as a budgetary deficit in November 1974 more than twice as large as had been predicted in March. Although the reserve currency status of sterling, and the role of the City as one of the world's two leading financial centres, meant that OPEC oil revenues poured into Britain throughout 1974 and thus provided a breathing space, this also made the Government all the more vulnerable to a run on the pound.

The budget of November 1974 already signalled a retreat from the price controls and food subsidies promised in the Social Contract, and a concern to give 'priority to investment and the balance of payments over both public expenditure and private consumption'.[11] In December, a memorandum from the Treasury's permanent secretaries, copied to the Governor of the Bank of England, told Healey that 'current policies were unworkable [and] there was no longer support for them at official level in the Treasury'.[12] And by January 1975 Labour ministers were being readied for a 'package' (a dreaded word in Labour Cabinets) that soon had them talking in terms of 1931, let alone 1966. Although Healey made it clear to his officials that he wanted to avoid a 'traditional deflationary package', he later admitted that 1975 was the year in which he 'abandoned Keynesianism'.[13] This did not mean that he or all his officials in the Treasury embraced monetarism as a credo. But they did rule out a reflationary policy, despite the fact that unemployment was growing rapidly month by month. Also ruled out were import controls and capital controls, which were, as we shall see, advanced in the Cabinet by Benn as early as February 1975 as part of his alternative strategy, as well as by Kaldor from within the Treasury as special adviser to the Chancellor.

Initially, the Treasury put greatest emphasis on the need for a real wage reduction through a statutory incomes policy, but this did not exclude public expenditure cuts as well as tighter monetary policy. The proposal for a £1 billion cut in public expenditure which Healey brought to the Cabinet at the end of March sparked the first major confrontation between Healey, supported by Jenkins and Callaghan, and Crosland,

Shore and Benn. The April 1975 budget sought to mollify financial market opinion by limiting growth in the money supply, and although the £1 billion cut in the Public Sector Borrowing Requirement (PSBR) was to be effected through indirect tax increases rather than expenditure cuts, the budget marked 'a clear break with the Keynesian tradition'.[14] By the end of May Healey was telling the Cabinet that he needed to take a further £2–3 billion out of the economy, primarily through expenditure cuts, in addition to statutory wage restraint. But this was for later. Neither Healey nor Wilson was about to risk such unpopular measures before the forthcoming European Referendum in June. Having proved their respectability as a government by having defeated the left on both the industrial strategy and on Europe, and with the long-term promise of North Sea oil, they expected that there would be no difficulty in financing the deficit through continuing capital flows into sterling (as they were constantly assured by Harold Lever, a millionaire member of the Labour Cabinet with extensive personal links to the financial markets).

The fact that there was no such difficulty until just after the left and the unions were defeated on the Referendum on Europe probably tells us something about the political filters through which financial markets actually perceive economic matters. With the Referendum finally out of the way, and Benn shifted from the Department of Industry, the discipline of the financial markets was immediately brought to bear on the negotiations with the unions over wage restraint through severe pressure on the pound in June and July 1975 (in what has been called 'the dry run for the sterling crisis of 1976').[15] In May 1975 Jack Jones had taken the initiative of proposing that unions should voluntarily adhere to a flat-rate wage increase with no increase at all above a certain level of salary – thereby benefiting the less well paid. With Healey warning that 'anything could trigger off a run on sterling',[16] and with Wilson and Foot apparently having convinced Jones that a 1931 situation was imminent, the TUC General Council narrowly endorsed a £6 per week flat wage increase, which meant a real wage reduction.[17] Healey explicitly told the Cabinet at the height of the negotiations with the TUC that 'some of our creditors don't believe in incomes policy – they want cuts in public expenditure'. But he also told them that if he could obtain a form of words that legislation had already been prepared to give statutory backing to the wage restraint controls as soon as ever it was needed, he might 'get away with that'.[18]

The Government's concessions on some of the egalitarian principles (with a freeze to be applied on incomes over £8,500 a year), while holding statutory powers over unions and workers in reserve, fuelled financial market frustrations with incomes policies as giving too much power to the unions. On the other hand, the Government's clear commitment to 'a virtually permanent incomes policy', alongside the guarantee that legislation with penalties would be implemented as soon as the limits were breached, had right-wing social democrats gloating that 'all the opponents of a statutory policy had achieved was a fig leaf to cover their embarrassment'.[19] Jack Jones had told the TGWU Conference in July that it was necessary to accede to the incomes policy because 'the betrayal of 1931 could happen again ... The MacDonalds, the Snowdens, the Jimmy Thomases are lurking around, their names do not need to be spelt out.'[20] But the question was bound to arise whether the unions were really saving the government at the price of acceding to the very policies that MacDonald and Snowden had demanded.

The union leadership and the 'soft left' in the Cabinet had wanted to believe that wage restraint was all about giving the Government space to preserve the social wage. But this was an illusion. The Prime Minister's announcement of the incomes policy agreement with the unions had included notice of a new system of cash limits on departmental budgets, which by limiting indexation at a time of high inflation, would have the effect of beginning 'a sharp change in the trend in public expenditure without parallel in the post-war years'.[21] Of course this wouldn't be proved for some time – at least not to the satisfaction of the financial markets and their media spokesmen whose 'increasingly apocalyptic diagnoses ... about British inflationary trends and the threat they posed for democracy ... were reaching the ultimate guarantor of the British economy – the American Government'.[22] Now that the incomes policy had been secured, Treasury officials were united in demanding public expenditure cuts, even though the Treasury's projections (accurate in this respect) showed unemployment rising to 1.2 million by the winter – double the level of the year before.

Due to the economic recession (Britain showed the greatest swing from expansion to contraction between 1973 and 1975 of any industrial country except Italy) the current account deficit was actually showing significant improvement. Yet by the beginning of August Treasury officials were telling ministers that it would not be possible to finance the current account deficit from private flows of capital and, while still rejecting import controls, were recommending seeking a loan from the IMF within the UK credit tranche.[23] In the context of rates of growth far below the Government's forecasts, and automatic increases in social security and unemployment benefit due to rapidly rising unemployment, the growth of the Public Sector Borrowing Requirement did not abate. But nor was it anything near as bad as Treasury forecasts at the time were suggesting. Predictions that the PSBR for 1975–76 would rise from £9 billion to £12 billion (i.e. to 5 per cent of GDP) proved inaccurate, and the Treasury's figures also exaggerated the rate at which public expenditure was growing, and the proportion of GNP it accounted for.

Even Healey's deputy at the Treasury, Edmund Dell, by far the greatest hawk for public expenditure cuts in the Labour Government, admits:

> Public expenditure was, at the time, presented in a way which exaggerated the proportion of gross domestic product it constituted. The figure of 60 per cent of GDP devoted to public expenditure was one to strike horror in the heart of the most valiant social democrat. . . . When, in 1976, public spending was redefined in the same way as in other countries, UK spending was reduced by £7.7 billion at one stroke. And when GDP was costed, like public expenditure, at market prices, the ratio of public spending to GDP fell from 60 per cent to 46 per cent.[24]

Of course, even at 46 per cent in 1976, the increase from 39 per cent in 1972 was hardly insignificant; but it was barely greater than in Germany (where public expenditure had risen from 40 per cent to 47 per cent of GDP), and only slightly more rapid than in most other European countries. Indeed the rapid increase in public expenditure and fiscal deficits in relation to GDP primarily reflected the effects of the recession rather than policy choices. By 1978, with the massive cuts the Labour Government introduced, public expenditure fell to 43 per cent of GDP – lower than in France, Germany, Italy and Belgium, let alone Sweden and Norway. Notably, in comparison with all these European countries, as well as with Canada and Japan, it was only the US and the UK that would actually go on to cut, rather than increase, their ratio of public expenditure to GDP from 1976 to 1978.[25]

Healey, in retrospect, would accuse the Treasury of deliberately 'misleading the Government, the country and the world for so many years about the true state of public spending in Britain. Indeed I cannot help suspecting that Treasury officials deliberately overstated public spending in order to put pressure on governments which were reluctant to cut it.'[26] But although as early as March 1975 Crosland objected to the Treasury's muddling of the figures, at the time Healey would have none of it. Moreover, as the Treasury pressed the Cabinet harder and harder through October and November 1975 for public expenditure cuts, Healey increasingly made the case for them via the straightforward monetarist argument that, in addition to being directly inflationary, public expenditure was crowding out the resources needed for private consumption and manufacturing investment. Crosland powerfully put forward the Keynesian case that with so much of public expenditure accounted for by transfer payments rather than new claims on resources, and with so much labour unemployed and plant capacity under-utilised, the monetarist position on public expenditure was absurd. But he was unable to rebut Healey's argument that laying out 20 per cent of public expenditure on interest payments on the debt was something that could not be ignored, even if the financial markets would go on supplying the credit – which, given their own monetarist credo, they might not – especially if they anticipated a reduction in the exchange rate.[27]

Paradoxically, it was precisely in the context of the Government taking strong and visible action to target public expenditure that the run on sterling finally took off. By the end of 1975, after the Government had also availed itself of its right to IMF stand-by credits, the exchange rate seemed to have stabilised; indeed the pound was even thought to be perhaps somewhat overvalued – so that when in February 1976 the Government introduced a White Paper on Public Expenditure, freezing all planned increases, this seemed to be a very tough measure in the circumstances. Yet even before thirty-five Labour MPs abstained on the vote on the White Paper on Public Expenditure on March 10 (while sustaining the Government in office in a subsequent vote of confidence), a run on sterling had begun. Indeed, it had started a week earlier, apparently triggered by the coincidence of the Bank of England selling sterling to bring about a slight depreciation in the currency at the same time as a large withdrawal from sterling by the Nigerians.[28]

Whether or not Wilson's announcement of his resignation on March 16 (with the PLP electing Callaghan to succeed him two weeks later) was designed to correct whatever had upset the financial markets, or only had the effect of further upsetting them, the fall in the pound was precipitous and appeared virtually unstoppable. It fell from just over US $2.00 at the beginning of March to almost $1.70 by the beginning of June, and bonds were proving difficult to sell to finance the Public Sector Borrowing Requirement. Under these conditions a second year of wage restraint was obtained from the union leadership in April (with tax decreases as compensation), but this impressed the financial markets even less than it had the previous year. Indeed, it may only have convinced them that the Government – and even too many officials in the Treasury – still hadn't got the message that monetarism, not corporatism, was what was really required. This was now the clear message from the Conservative Opposition under Mrs Thatcher's leadership. But while Mrs Thatcher's power over her party did not extend to the Labour Cabinet and the Treasury, that of the Republican administration in Washington did. The opportunity was provided when the Government, having used up by May, in support of sterling, all the IMF funds made available in December, tried to arrange another stand-by credit to convince the markets that there would be a floor beneath sterling.

'Our role was to persuade the British that the game was over. They had run out of string.'[29] These are the words of Stephen Yeo, a banker from Pittsburgh, who was William Simon's Under-Secretary for Monetary Affairs at the American Treasury. As Scott Pardee, Vice-President of the Federal Reserve Bank of New York responsible for foreign exchange operations, later put it, they 'had decided that Britain had to make some fundamental changes because they were sick of sterling crises'.[30] The view of American financial officials that the Labour Government was 'profligate' was encouraged not only by most of the press in Britain, and Mrs Thatcher, but also by reports from City institutions as well as by what they were told in private meetings with counterparts inside the Treasury and the Bank of England who felt the turn to monetarism had yet to be properly effected.[31] The key disciplinary instrument proved to be a £5 billion loan obtained from the European central banks, the Bank of International Settlements and the US Treasury and Federal Reserve in June. It was provided, on American insistence, only on the unusual condition that it had to be repaid in six months. This severely qualified whatever confidence the loan provided for sterling in the financial markets, thus guaranteeing that the Government would have to be very sensitive to these markets throughout the remainder of 1976. And it also ensured that the Government would be forced to turn to the IMF for a conditional loan (thus effectively making credit from all sources unavailable without an IMF 'seal of approval') before the end of the year. For the US to work this way to get international agencies like the IMF to force countries to adopt certain policies was, as Burk and Cairncross put it, 'traditional rather than innovative; what was more unusual was that the pressure in this case was being put on a rich, industrialised country, and the US made no attempt to dissemble'.

> Simon and Yeo decided to use the British need for the stand-by to force them to change policies. The American government as such could not tell the British what to do, but Simon, Yeo and Burns trusted that the IMF could enforce the financial and political discipline which they believed the British so sorely needed. As Yeo later said, the Americans 'put up the money for the bait' – i.e. to hook the UK economy into IMF control when it had to be repaid.[32]

A massive package of £1 billion in public expenditure cuts and a £1 billion increase in employees' National Insurance contributions, agreed to by the Cabinet through seven agonising meetings over a two-week period in July, failed to restore confidence. It certainly failed to impress the American Treasury, who were determined that 'Britain's economic problems were not going to be solved by higher taxes'.[33] Healey's own explanation for the failure of the package was that although the Government had been framing money supply targets since 1975, the July statement had omitted any explicit reference to them.[34] But behind all this was something much deeper. 'What seems clear in retrospect was that no matter what the government did, short of repudiating both its history and its supporters, the market would continue to demonstrate its total lack of confidence, unless and until an approach was made to the IMF.'[35] Burk and Cairncross's conclusion is only marred by the words 'short of'. It would take *both* an approach to the IMF *and* a public repudiation of its history and supporters.

It was in the context of renewed and widespread selling of sterling that Callaghan was moved to issue a fulsome proclamation of the death of Keynesianism at his own Party Conference in the autumn of 1976. Even at this point Callaghan still used the language of 'fundamental change', but it was a 'fundamental change' of a wholly different kind from that offered in 1973, however ambiguous that may have been:

> For too long, perhaps ever since the war, we postponed facing up to fundamental choices and fundamental changes in our society and in our economy ... We used to think that you could spend your way out of a recession, and increase employment by cutting taxes and boosting Government spending. I tell you in all honesty that that option no longer exists, and that in so far as it ever did exist, it worked on each occasion since the war by injecting bigger doses of inflation into the economy, followed by a higher level of unemployment as the next step ... Now we must get back to fundamentals.[36]

Peter Jay, Callaghan's son-in-law, and as economics editor of *The Times* a leading advocate of monetarism, had a hand in drafting the speech. Ten years later, he noted that this was the speech that Milton Friedman had 'most frequently quoted with approval of any delivered by any politician anywhere'.[37] For the first time since the war, a Labour leader had cast aside, even in rhetoric, the rationale for the expansion of the welfare state and the Keynesian logic that had impelled its growth. And he would go further still: 'Hold on to your seats,' Callaghan warned the delegates as he entered this political minefield for Labour Party politics: 'The willingness of industry to invest in new plant and machinery requires, of course, that we overcome inflation, but also that industry is left with sufficient funds and has sufficient confidence to make the new investments ... I mean they must be able to earn a surplus and that is a euphemism for saying they must be able to make a profit ... the wealth must be created before it is distributed.'[38]

There should be no underestimation of the contribution this Labour Government made, as it sought to justify its policies, to rendering credible Mrs Thatcher's 'there is no alternative' theme both within Britain and internationally. The fact that the message had to be delivered with such fanfare at a Labour Party Conference, with the explicit purpose of demonstrating to Britain's creditors that the Government really meant it (because it was re-educating its own supporters in the new reality), was specially significant. Those within the Cabinet who had resisted the Government's new direction most strongly, above all

Benn and Crosland, had understood that the main battle had to be about how people would understand the crisis of capitalism they were living through. They were well aware that, given the balance of opinion within the Cabinet, let alone the broader balance of forces domestically and internationally, the alternatives they were advancing were unlikely to be adopted, let alone successfully implemented. Their advocacy of alternative policies was a way of putting forward alternative explanations. Their intent was in this sense more political than economic, as both Crosland and Benn independently put it at the time. As revealed in Crosland's notes reflecting on what had transpired over the summer of 1976, he assessed the greatest costs as having been not only the 'Demoralisation of decent rank and file' but the 'breeding of illiterate & reactionary attitudes to public expenditure'. And he saw his advocacy of import controls as 'probably necessary to ease *politics* of situation, tho' doubt it will make much difference to the reality'.[39] Benn would write almost exactly the same thing in his diary while reflecting on the validity of the arguments of Healey and Callaghan that his alternative strategy would involve heavy sacrifices which would be difficult for people, even in the unions and the party, to accept: 'I have now got to argue the case for the alternative strategy politically, not as an economic case, because I recognise the real difficulties.'[40]

The Politics of the Alternative Economic Strategy

It is in these terms that the formulation of the alternative economic strategy during the course of the Government's transition from Keynesianism to monetarism needs to be assessed. Burk's and Cairncross's study of 'the gathering crisis' confirms that Benn had seen earlier and with greater clarity than other ministers its broader economic and political dimensions, and that this was reflected in the paper he put before the Cabinet in July 1976. In fact, it was much earlier, indeed as early as the beginning of 1975, at the very outset of the shift in policy we have outlined above, that Benn put his alternative strategy on the Government's agenda. After organising a large meeting of officials and advisers at the Department of Industry in January 1975, Benn presented to the Cabinet's Ministerial Committee on Economic Strategy on February 25 1975 a paper drafted by Francis Cripps. In this paper, entitled 'A Choice of Economic Policies', Strategy 'A' described all too accurately the path the Government was actually about to follow: it comprised 'tax increases and public spending cuts; some form of enforceable pay restraint; and the further transfer of cash to the company sector' which would lead to 'heavy deflation, rising employment, cuts in real wages and the withdrawal of support from the Government by the

TUC and the Labour Movement'. The famous 'alternative economic strategy' was born with Strategy 'B'. It was set out for the committee by Benn in twelve points, the first of which certainly was, in political terms, the most important: '1. A full explanation by the Government to the nation of the reason for the crisis – that is to say it is a world slump related to a failure to invest, and not just the fault of the unions.'[41]

Among the specific policy proposals that followed the key ones were (a) selective import restrictions and the rationing and allocation of some imported materials and (b) the extension of controls on capital outflows and control over banks and other financial institutions.[42] In light of the need for import and capital controls, Benn invited his colleagues to consider whether the Common Market was, as Roy Jenkins believed, 'a life-raft or whether we were being tossed into the deep in a strait-jacket'. He recognised that strategy B would 'strain international relations, strengthen middle-class opposition and impose some stress on relations between the Labour movement and the Government'. But the course the Government had embarked on would 'merely deepen the existing social divisions'. As he undoubtedly expected, the paper did not get a warm response from Healey and Wilson. Benn wrote in his diary that night: 'I came away exhausted. It is getting awfully tough now.'[43]

The alternative economic strategy also took shape publicly in February 1975 in the form of a *Spokesman* pamphlet by John Eaton, Michael Barratt Brown and Ken Coates, *An Alternative Economic Strategy for the Labour Movement*. It was written by members of the Council of the Institute for Workers' Control who had been 'involved in urgent discussions about the need for, and content of, an alternative strategy for the labour movement to that being pursued by the present government'. While very similar in content to what Benn presented to the Cabinet Committee, the pamphlet made it clear that the strategy was not being presented to the movement as 'a policy statement' but was being proposed as a 'line of march' and as 'a basis for discussion, amendment and urgent appraisal'. The centre-right inside and outside the party alleged that the strategy was a recipe for a statist 'economy'; but its authors actually saw it as an intervention in the crisis that would lay the basis for a 'democratically controlled economy' involving popular participation at all levels through unions as well as 'workers' organisations in production and many other forms of people's organisations in the communities and at the grass roots ... supported by research teams from Universities, Polytechnics and other institutions of higher education and, to a limited extent, schools'. This presumed that the capacity could be developed for a 'new kind of economic management' which would entail extensive institutional change (not least, it was stressed, in the unions) and 'a considerable amount of supporting "educational" activity ... with Government backing'. It did not shy away from insisting that the 'main cost of a democratically controlled economy is active involvement of people themselves everywhere', but it argued that this cost would come to be recognised as a benefit when 'social production is made thereby a much more stimulating activity and much less a drudgery of work'.[44]

Aided by more and more detailed papers drafted by Cripps, Benn continued throughout 1975 and 1976 to make the argument in the Cabinet that the course the Government was following, involving both wage restraint *and* accelerating cuts in public expenditure, would guarantee that there would be no return to full employment within its term of office, and that this 'economic nonsense' would lead to 'political suicide', which could be temporarily staved off only by recourse to a coalition government. Even other left ministers referred to this disparagingly as his 'familiar theme'. Benn, said Foot at a key meeting at Chequers in June, was 'dodging the issue' that the country's main problem was inflation, and the best way to defend the unions was for them to have a policy that worked to stop it.[45] Benn, of course, was not opposed to an egalitarian incomes policy (including wage restraint by those sections of the working class best placed to secure money wage increases in the crisis – he himself had suggested the 'flat rate' increase approach to Foot the year before).[46] And he accepted that 'public expenditure may need to be re-planned in the full employment context and even cut back, especially where high import content may be shown to exist'.[47] But what Benn understood (and what the published versions of the alternative economic strategy at the time also made explicit) was that a policy that was primarily defined in terms of deflation through a fall in real wages and public expenditure cuts, besides being unjust, could not solve 'the deep-rooted and many-sided sickness of the economy'. And he recognised that it would have the long-term political effect of making the unions and public expenditure scapegoats for the economic crisis.

Without endorsing Benn's alternative strategy, Foot, Shore and Crosland would eventually take up the demand within the Cabinet for restrictions on imports. The economic case for this was being strongly advanced at the time by the New Cambridge group of economists associated with Lord Kaldor, Francis Cripps and Wynne Godley. It accepted the need for a reduction in the budget deficit (putting the emphasis on tax increases to effect this), but insisted that import controls were required to prevent unemployment from rapidly rising even further, and to limit what would otherwise have to be a severe deflationary policy which depreciation of the exchange rate on its own would not be sufficient to offset. This was not conceived as a 'beggar-thy-neighbour' strategy. As attached to a policy of expansion, the goal was to secure a reduction in the import to export ratio, but not a fall in the absolute level of imports.[48] Outside the context of the broader alternative economic strategy, however, the case for import controls by themselves was ultimately a weak one, for a number of reasons. They would be likely to damage overall trade unless there were accompanying exchange controls. Indeed, the proposals that Kaldor advanced inside the Treasury from the beginning of 1975 included not only import quotas and deposits but a dual exchange rate system. Setting separate rates for trade and capital transactions was aimed at curbing the power of currency speculators to affect the terms of trade. Although in use by three other industrial countries and twenty-two developing countries at the time, this proposal was rejected by the Bank of England and immediately dropped by the Treasury. The problem was political, not technical, as Kaldor indicated when, after charging Healey with having followed the route taken by Snowden in 1931 and resigning 'dispirited and disillusioned' from the Treasury in August 1976, he leaked the information that the Treasury had a complete plan (known as 'the unmentionable') for exchange as well as import controls 'locked away in a cupboard'.[49]

One could not proceed very far with an alternative strategy, in other words, without confronting the power of the City, the Treasury and the Bank of England over the issue of control over financial markets and banks. Addressing this not only gave greater coherence to the Labour new left's alternative strategy but went to the heart of an alternative *explanation* of the crisis by linking the analysis of Britain's industrial decline, on which the radical industrial strategy rested, to the diminished ability of states to control the burgeoning new financial markets. The argument set out by a more radical group of Cambridge economists (Michael Ellman, Bob Rowthorn, Ron Smith and Frank Wilkinson) in an influential pamphlet, written in June 1974 and published under Ken Coates's *Spokesman* auspices, was particularly important in this respect. Explicitly situating itself in support of Benn's industrial strategy, it linked this to an analysis of the power of financial markets in the context of the breakdown of the international monetary system constructed after World War II. Rejecting 'the chauvinistic excesses and little Englandism that have characterised much of the campaign against the common market', on the one hand, and the view that 'it is no longer possible on a national basis to gain any freedom of action to pursue progressive policies', it soberly set out the necessity for and the limits of both emergency measures and a more fully flexible and comprehensive system of capital controls. Recognising, as had Keynes, that 'without the active cooperation of other states it would never be possible to develop a foolproof or even adequate system of controls on the operation of international capital', it explained why it would be necessary for the Government to take over and directly administer wide sections of the City and wind down much of its international business.[50]

Although Benn spared no effort in trying to put this kind of alternative before the Cabinet, he was under no illusions that he could carry the argument at that level. It was not only a matter of trying to take on the Chancellor, who had the whole technical and statistical apparatus of the Treasury behind him (as well as the key support of the Prime Minister throughout); the whole make-up of the Cabinet was against it. While branding Benn's alternative economic strategy unrealistic because it would not get through the Cabinet, Foot had to admit that even his own limited proposals on import controls were very unlikely to get through either. Benn recalls having told Foot a month before the run on sterling that 'monetarist ideas had embedded themselves in the heart of the government'. Foot lamely disagreed, saying the problem was not having a working majority. Benn replied:

> Look, it isn't because we haven't got a majority, Michael. You know that as well as I do. It's because the Cabinet doesn't believe in the [Keynesian] policy. If we had a majority of a hundred we wouldn't implement it. . . . The position is really this. We can't expose our strategy fully because in fact our strategy is to fight inflation by increasing unemployment, to pretend that we're keeping prices down when we're really trying to get prices and profits up, to pretend we're defending the public sector when we're really trying to cut it back.[51]

The problem was compounded by collective Cabinet responsibility, prohibiting the promotion in public of an alternative explanation of the crisis, which Crosland and Benn understood was so important for the mobilisation of support for alternative policies. As early as February 1975 Wilson forbade any minister from speaking publicly about import controls. Even to write an article that included reference to the 'anarchy of capitalist markets that had developed after 1970' was considered inappropriate for a Government minister.[52] And the problem was made even worse by the fact that the TUC – despite the resemblance of its annual economic reviews to much of the alternative economic strategy, not to mention overwhelming Congress votes for resolutions calling for import and capital controls – did little or nothing to explain or popularise the ideas behind these policies. Indeed, once the Government's rejection of import controls to offset a deflationary policy was made clear in early 1975, it was even dropped 'as a central part of the TUC–Government dialogue'.[53] Healey's deployment of the argument that public expenditure was squeezing out resources for investment in manufacturing industry also had the effect of dividing the labour movement, apparently pitting the interests of public sector workers versus private sector workers. This argument carried enormous weight in finally securing the strong support of the Engineering Union's leader, Hugh Scanlon, for the Government's approach. As Minkin observes:

The transformation of the economic perspectives of the Prime Minister and of the Treasury Ministers towards monetarism appeared to be based on practical exigency – an approach which always appealed to trade union leaders. Lacking any strong economic facilities within their own unions, Jones and Scanlon were dependent on advice from the TUC Economic Department, itself heavily influenced by changing Treasury thinking ... an avalanche of advice was showered on the union leaders, all pointing to the common sense of the Government's general approach.[54]

Although Foot raised the idea of import controls at the Liaison Committee in September 1975, the 'Foot–Healey axis' was actually crucial in muting the TUC as an effective voice for an alternative strategy. For his part, Crosland might come to lament the political effect the Government's monetarist discourse was having in breeding reactionary popular attitudes and demoralisation among the rank and file, but he now, as always, stayed aloof from the mobilising side of politics.[55] Benn, on the other hand, was determined to launch a campaign even from within the Government. After a long discussion with Foot, Castle and Shore on how the Government's course had been clearly set by Healey in the Cabinet meetings of July 1975, Benn reflected in his diary on Ken Coates's advice 'to get out':

> I thought about it. If you come out, you're accused of rocking the boat and the movement doesn't want to endanger the Government; but then you have a vested interest in the failure of the Government because you have left it, and everybody disregards what you are doing on the grounds that you are trying to bring the Government down. If you leave the Cabinet but vote with the Government right through, then you are sustaining a Government you have left. The whole thing is so complicated, and I believe the best strategy is to develop the campaign from inside the Government.[56]

Recognising that while the unions had become 'more powerful and more sophisticated, they have been weakened and frightened by the slump', Benn depended on the National Executive of the Labour Party to present an alternative. By concentrating on convincing the TUC while ignoring the NEC, the Government had allowed the space for this. At a special meeting of the NEC on the economic situation in July 1975 Ian Mikardo had bitterly complained that while the Government was constantly talking to the TUC, it was 'expressing contempt for the party even worse than the 1964–70 Government', treating the party as 'dogs-bodies to go and knock on doors'.[57] For their part, the left-wing union leadership, despite the conflict their accommodation to the Labour ministers' expediency sometimes caused (such as Jack Jones's angry confrontation with Mikardo at a Tribune rally at the 1975 Labour Party Conference), continued to support the left in NEC elections and thus 'legitimised the co-operation of left-wing trade unionists and trade union MPs on the NEC with the alternative left political leadership'.[58] This made it possible for Benn, who had been elected unopposed as Chairman of the NEC's Home Policy Committee in January 1975, to advance the alternative economic strategy under the auspices of the party.

This approach bore fruit in the form of the NEC's 150-page-long *Labour's Programme for Britain*, published in May 1976, which explicitly asserted that the radical version of the industrial strategy articulated in the 1973 programme was 'the right one' by comparison with the one adopted by the Government.[59] It also made a considered case for import controls, both as a way of dealing with the balance of payments crisis without severe deflation, and as providing a 'breathing space for the reconstruction and regeneration which our industrial policies will secure'. At the same time, the Home Policy Committee also took up once again the question of the power of the City of London and Britain's place in the international economic order – which, as we have seen, had been one of the first issues raised in the turn to the left in the early 1970s, but which the centre-right in the leadership had successfully marginalised. After two studies on the subject were completed early in 1976, the NEC endorsed[60] a statement on *Banking and Finance* in August which called for the nationalisation of the big four clearing banks and the top seven insurance companies, in order to establish 'a coherent framework of financial planning'.[61] The degree of divergence between the party's National Executive and the parliamentary leadership was now greater than at any time in the party's history.

The Resolution of the Crisis: The IMF Loan

The production of the NEC's two policy statements may have been an important factor in convincing the Americans that what was at stake in the sterling crisis involved more than reining in a 'profligate' government. As the American Treasury surveyed the 'danger signals of economies in peril' through the winter of 1975–76 (featuring Italy, Portugal, Mexico, France), Britain figured prominently on the map. As Yeo put it, 'To our great dismay, we realised we were going to have a major UK experience ahead. . . . We feared that if a country like Britain blew up, defaulted on its loans, introduced foreign exchange controls and froze convertibility, we could have a real world depression.'[62] It is hard to imagine why he and Simon should have expected such uncharacteristic behaviour from Britain (despite its long experience with sterling crises) unless he was relying on reports of the Labour Party's plans (though default was not among them), and naively believed they might become government policy.

If this was the slender basis of the Americans' judgement, then even the TUC, for all its moderation and loyalty, might have frightened them too. The General Council's Report to the TUC Special Congress in June 1976 on the second phase of wage restraint called for major reforms in the banking system and financial institutions and 'a full inquiry into short-term capital movements in order to assess the reasons for the speculation and the identity of those actively engaged in speculation and to avoid irrational movements which have adverse effects on Britain's economy'. While endorsing the incomes policy, trade union leaders like Clive Jenkins made fiery speeches calling for 'immediate import controls' and condemning 'the unacceptable facelessness' of financial capital. 'I believe it is nonsense to argue that investment in manufacturing industry will miraculously reappear simply by chopping the public sector,' said Allan Fisher, the leader of Britain's largest union of public employees. 'Investment will not be increased in this country and controlled unless we have Government direction of investment and controls on the export of capital.'[63] Even a moderate union leader like David Basnett wrote an article in *The Times* on 25 September, just days before the opening of the 1976 Labour Party Conference, which called for an import deposit scheme and restrictions on the outward flow of capital.

The Government, of course, had no inclination whatsoever to take this route. Yet while Callaghan might treat contemptuously the paper Benn presented to the July 1976 Cabinet meetings ('a complete alternative strategy which is quite unacceptable to us. It can't be discussed. I don't see why you wrote it'),[64] he was aware, given the messages that were now coming from the unions, that the 1976 Party Conference was very likely to endorse just such an alternative strategy. In this context, no matter how much Callaghan's speech to the Conference impressed Milton Friedman and the American administration, the Conference proceedings themselves could hardly be read as an endorsement of the Government's policies. Although Callaghan's speech was accorded the obligatory ovations, the Labour Party was in a very schizophrenic state by this point (hardly surprising, given the experience it was being put through). Since the balance of forces in the party was very different from that inside the Government, the Conference did what the Cabinet refused to do, asserting that there was an alternative explanation for the crisis, which implied alternative strategies for dealing with it. The same delegates to the 1976 Conference who were induced to applaud the Government's accommodation to monetarism, had the day before endorsed the NEC's *Labour's Programme for Britain*. The latter had been introduced by Benn, who contended that, in addition to the economic price that the country was now paying,

> as a party we are also paying a heavy political price for twenty years in which
> ... we have played down our criticism of capitalism and our advocacy of
> socialism.... Comrades, the political vacuum we have left has been filled by

many different voices ... by the monetarists, by the nationalists, by the racialists and by all of those who seek each in their own way to divide working people from each other and to breed despair so we may be driven to lose faith in ourselves and our capacity to control our own destiny. Unless we speak more clearly now we shall be fighting the next election defensively, deep inside our own political territory, instead of being on the offensive on behalf of our own people.[65]

It was in this context that, two days after Callaghan's momentous speech, the Conference also passed, with an overwhelming majority (but with ominous abstentions by unions in the financial sector itself), the document on *Banking and Finance*. One union delegate in the debate, commenting on Callaghan's attempts to derail the document before it saw the light of day, and his pledge not to include the proposals on public ownership in the next election manifesto, expressed appreciation for the role being played by Benn and the NEC: 'In resisting such pressure throughout the year ... the National Executive has shown great political courage.'[66]

Of course, the party's adoption of such a policy could by this point have no effect on the Government, crisis or not. And its immediate effect was inevitably to scare the financial markets further. Healey and Callaghan announced in the middle of the Conference that they were making a formal application to the IMF for a £4 billion conditional loan, the largest ever requested. And just as the Conference ended, the Governor of the Bank of England persuaded Healey of the need to make his commitment to monetarism unambiguously explicit by effecting a drastic reduction in the money supply through an interest rate set at the unprecedented level of 15 per cent.[67] Only after both these actions did the value of sterling somewhat stabilise. In an attempt to secure support in Washington for relatively lenient terms for the IMF loan, Callaghan suggested to President Ford that he might be pushed into adopting import controls along the lines of the 'alternative strategy that is being dangled in front of people' and that 'if the alternative strategy were adopted it would call into question Britain's role as an Alliance partner, which I am anxious to preserve'.[68] The State Department's William Rodgers later told a journalist:

> We all had the feeling it could come apart in a quite serious way ... it was a choice between Britain remaining in the liberal financial system of the West as opposed to a radical change of course, because we were concerned about Tony Benn precipitating a policy decision by Britain to turn its back on the IMF. I think if that had happened the whole system would have begun to fall apart ... so we tended to see it in cosmic terms.[69]

But neither the White House, nor the German SPD Chancellor Schmidt, to whom Callaghan also appealed, did anything to deflect the

US Treasury or the IMF from their purpose.[70] Through the harrowing Cabinet meetings of November and December 1976, Benn continued to present the alternative strategy, while Foot, Shore and Crosland looked for allies to support their case for restrictions on imports. But having left Benn so isolated for so long, the Keynesians and soft left now found they had left themselves few grounds for counter-argument whenever Healey pronounced their own proposals dangerous and inadequate. At one point, an exasperated Crosland virtually went all the way over to Benn's side. Since there was no economic case for the massive cuts that were already being made in public expenditure, whatever was offered the IMF should be mainly cosmetic and have minimal deflationary effects. Beyond this,

> the Government should then say to the IMF, the Americans and the Germans: If you demand any more of us we shall put up the shutters, wind down our defence commitments, introduce a siege economy. As the IMF was even more passionately opposed to protectionism than it was attached to monetarism, this threat would be sufficient to persuade the fund to lend the money without unacceptable conditions. Politically the IMF could not refuse the loan. If the Government kept its nerve, it could insist on its own terms – could limit the cuts to 'window-dressing' to appease the irritating and ignorant currency dealers.[71]

It was very much the argument that Benn had made in Cabinet a year and a half before. Notably, the social democrats in the Cabinet immediately treated Crosland with the same disdain: Crosland, in Dell's words, had 'lost all political judgement',[72] (which was, of course, what Crosland had often said of Benn). By the time the decision was finally made to endorse the onerous terms comprised in the Government's Letter of Intent to the IMF, Crosland had backed down. The more thoughtful Cabinet members must have felt deeply Crosland's reputed despair in the Cabinet room, as he called the whole exercise 'crazy' but nevertheless voted for it.[73]

Although it was probably not obvious to those involved at the time, it is quite clear from all accounts that the main effect of the anguished Cabinet meetings was to delay rather than alter the final outcome. It is worth noting that even so, a social democrat like Dell felt that this *gave the Cabinet too much influence*: 'There are questions too serious for Cabinet Government,' he writes, at the same time heaping praise on Healey's Letter of Intent to the IMF for being the effective constraint on the Government's economic policies 'it was intended to be'.[74] The language of monetarism suffused the letter: 'an essential element of the Government's strategy will be a continuing and substantial reduction over the next few years in the share of the resources required for the public sector ... [and] to create monetary conditions which will encourage investment and support sustained growth and the control of inflation'. And although the actual size of the cuts promised was smaller than what had already been effected in the previous twelve months, this was nevertheless 'the third cut in a single year and brought the total reduction in the 1977–78 programme to £3 billion and in the 1978–79 programme to over £5 billion.' Mrs Thatcher, Burk and Cairncross note, 'when her turn came ... never succeeded in making cuts of that size'.[75]

Most important for the Americans, the IMF and the financial markets, the Letter of Intent confirmed that 'The Government remains firmly opposed to generalised restrictions on trade and does not intend to introduce restrictions for balance of payments purposes.' And it pledged that 'the Government does not intend to introduce any multiple currency practices or impose new or intensify existing restrictions on payments and transfers for current international transactions'. As Helleiner notes, this episode in Britain was the first turning point and one of the 'most significant in [the] political history of the reemergence of global finance. Had controls been introduced ... the globalisation trend would have been set back considerably.'[76] For the IMF and the US Government, as Keegan and Pennant-Rea have explained, the point was not the exact size of the cuts. 'What they achieved was a respect for financial discipline that they did not believe was sufficiently widespread before.' By the autumn of 1977 'the ebullient Healey ... in his new capacity as chairman of the IMF's key policy committee of ministers, was even preaching the virtues of IMF conditionality to other governments, including third world ones'.[77]

The Bankruptcy of Parliamentary Socialism

While they remained in office, Labour's parliamentary elite were left with no Keynesian clothes to cover their political and ideological nakedness. The Government's support for lifting exchange controls in the EEC in order to move towards completing the free movement of capital; its decision to put the main emphasis on cutting taxes rather than increasing the social wage when the pressure on the pound finally abated in 1977–78; the selling off of half the Government's shares in British Petroleum (although justified as offsetting even further public expenditure cuts) – all this pointed in a very different direction from the old social democratic corporatism. The Government still retained the symbols of the social contract and the industrial strategy, but the effects of having attached them to monetarism rather than to the alternative economic strategy were increasingly apparent. Under Eric Varley the Department of Industry established 'a high degree of compatibility' with the Treasury.[78] The NEB was starved of funds, burdened with lame-duck firms rather than profitable ones, and run on conventionally commercial rather than social criteria. The notion of planning agreements had all its teeth drawn from it (the only one signed with a private sector firm was as legitimation for the Government's bail-out of Chrysler). The centrepiece of the industrial strategy once again became the tripartite talking-shop of the NEDC and its sectoral committees, dependent for their information on what firms chose to tell them.

The result of retaining the symbols of the social contract and the industrial strategy while emptying out the substance, proved to be anything but the clever political balancing act so much praised by media pundits at the time. Although the financial markets' confidence in the pound was restored in 1977–78, there could be no positive political attachment to the Government and its policy symbols on the part of capital. Even the CBI abandoned its long-standing enthusiasm for conventional corporatist arrangements. The CBI noted the TUC's formal commitment to the alternative economic strategy, including industrial democracy, and feared that in the context of the growing radicalisation of the Labour Party such policies might yet come, if not from these leaders then from others.[79] As we have seen, both Wilson and Callaghan played on these fears as a means of proving their own 'responsibility' to capital.

The partnership with the union leadership in these conditions yielded such poor returns to their members that it could not sustain mass support. Even those shop stewards who initially accepted the logic of restructuring their firms under the aegis of the NEB came to recoil from its commercial logic.[80] To be sure, the trade union leadership were still assiduously consulted, and continuing rounds of wage restraint were exchanged for marginal reductions in taxation, but this could hardly conceal the fact that the social contract had effectively become a euphemism for a more draconian and longer-lasting incomes policy than ever before.[81] Ignored were the union leadership's highly politically-sensitive warnings in 1978 that a further year of severe wage restraint could not be sustained – signalled most clearly over a year earlier by what Jack Jones himself called his 'momentous defeat' on incomes policy at the 1977 TGWU Conference.[82] Meanwhile, the majority report of the Bullock Inquiry on industrial democracy, which already involved a retreat from the TUC's proposals for parity representation on company boards, was further watered down by the Government's 1978 White Paper, and legislation was postponed until after the election.

The union leadership maintained its loyalty out of a sense of partner-ship, because of the consultations; out of hope that the substance might return to the social contract and the industrial strategy once the economy 'turned around'; above all out of the reasonable fear that a Thatcher government would be worse. Their policing of wage restraint, added to the fear induced among union members themselves by the massive inflation and profit squeeze of 1974–75, had in fact abruptly put an end to the industrial militancy of 1968–74. But its recurrence in the 'winter of discontent' of 1978–79 showed that the central problem was completely unresolved. And this new outbreak of rank and file militancy – especially the strikes involving low-paid public sector workers (which drew more fire from the media and the Government than private sector ones about recovering lost differentials) – was caught in a fatal contradiction. To the extent that it involved, beyond the desperation of the low-paid, trying to defend public services by temporarily withholding access to those services, the rest of the population experienced only its negative effects. Even more than had been the case with the strikes and occupations earlier in the decade, this militancy needed a political resolution of the kind that Benn had offered in the early 1970s.

But instead of trying to build positively on the 'desubordination' that industrial militancy expressed, as the Labour new left had proposed, the Labour leadership could now only follow Thatcher in her call for 'law and order'. The Prime Minister ostentatiously crossed the picket lines of low-paid workers, while still claiming (more and more implausibly, given his acceptance of monetarism) that a corporatist consensus provided a way forward. And his frequent and contemptuous attacks on the NEC's proposals for public ownership of banks combined with Mrs Thatcher's assault on the public sector to create an ideological climate in which public attitudes against nationalisation and privatisation suddenly and dramatically changed. Support for more nationalisation had actually increased among British voters between the elections of 1964 and October 1974 (from 28 per cent to 32 per cent), while the number favouring the status quo declined from 51 per cent to 47 per cent and those in support of privatisation held steady at 21–2 per cent. It was only in between 1974 and 1979 that there occurred a rather sudden change so that for the first time more voters in the May 1979 election preferred privatisation (40 per cent) to more nationalisation (17 per cent), although the most popular option still was the status quo (43 per cent). Among those voters who identified themselves as Labour supporters, over 50 per cent were in favour of more nationalisation in 1974, as they had also been in the mid-1960s, but this suddenly plummeted to only 32 per cent in 1979.[83]

The role of the media was very important in this, as it also was on 'law and order'. For when both party leaders are united on a theme like this, the media feel they have a licence to play the politics of ridicule against the 'extremists'. This had already emerged during the Referendum on Europe, which had revealed, as Alfred Browne of the Press Association put it, 'the power of the press when linked with the big battalions of politics ... [when] the emphasis is in one direction the readers are swayed in that direction'.[84] Again and again, when defending their designations of Benn and others on the Labour left as 'extremists' or 'dictators' or 'loony', journalists would justify themselves by pointing to the fact that leading figures in the Parliamentary Labour Party agreed with them.

The Labour leadership's own arguments thus directly contributed to a shift of attitudes by 1979, even among Labour supporters, against more spending on social services, public ownership and trade unions.[85] Yet the Labour leadership did not adopt the reactionary ideology that was to become known as Thatcherism. Their accommodation to monetarism had been a matter of expediency, not a conversion. Even Healey who, as we have seen, had embraced the monetarist principles of the IMF (all the while deriding the Labour new left's alternative strategy as the work of 'tiny Chinese minds'),[86] stopped defending them after he left office in 1979. In opposition, the parliamentary leadership quickly returned to Keynesian reflation plus incomes policy as the centrepiece of their economic approach – which they also opportunistically labelled an alternative economic strategy.[87]

But although the Labour leadership had yet to understand this, it was no longer possible to win votes by claiming that Labour's special relations with the unions equipped them to be better managers of the economy. High-profile deals with union leaders on wage restraint, coupled with their repeated collapse at the hands of rank-and-file militancy, had fostered the impression that unions had 'too much power'. As the Government, in its dying months in office, negotiated with great fanfare a new 'concordat' with the TUC for a 'national economic assessment' against the backdrop of the strikes of the Winter of Discontent, this impression was further magnified in the public mind. But the reality of the situation was precisely how little power the unions had – as shown, on the one hand, by their consistent inability to influence the Government on the fundamentals of economic policy, and on the other hand by their inability (after a number of years of wage restraint in these conditions) to control their own members' actions or to influence their political understanding of, or response to, the crisis. But the illusion that the unions had too much power now proved to be a very powerful force in ushering in a new era of British politics.

In February 1975 Benn had expressed the hope that the extra-parliamentary party would be able 'to use this crisis to break out of the circle of deception which lies at the heart of parliamentary labourism'.[88] Eighteen months later he told the 1976 Conference that the Labour Government's failure was not just one of policy and administration. It was a failure even to attempt to articulate a socialist discourse which would explain the crisis of capitalism through which working people were living, and identify the forces that were resisting a progressive solution. In saying this, Benn was once again expressing the view of a great many activists who were organising themselves within the party to challenge the autonomy of the parliamentary elite, and also trying to practise the new politics at the municipal level. Encouraged, no doubt, by the actions of Benn and the National Executive during the course of this Government, the mood among party activists was not one of disillusionment and despair, as it had been in the late 1960s. On the contrary, there was a new mood of determination which, for the first time in many years, focused the broader left's attention on the possibility of changing the Labour Party. But with Thatcher having so effectively articulated an 'authoritarian populist' ideology as the counterpoint to monetarism, precious time had been wasted. Many of those working-class voters who, as we saw in Chapter 2, voted for Labour in 1964 and then abstained in 1970, had by 1979 responded positively to Thatcher's definition of the causes of their frustration and alienation. While the Labour new left's attempt to formulate an alternative economic strategy was an achievement, and deserved the attention it got, the political conditions for realising such a strategy were not in place.

As Energy Minister during the final years of the Labour Government[89] Benn certainly tested the doctrine of collective cabinet responsibility to the limit and beyond by using his chairmanship of the NEC's Home Policy Committee so effectively to promote alternative policy proposals. And while he had to be careful not to dissent too openly on economic policy, he defied censure in a great many public speeches calling for freedom of information legislation, and for curbs on the security apparatus, to break through the impenetrable wall of secrecy behind which political and administrative decisions were taken. This increased the hostility of his Cabinet colleagues, and Callaghan, like Wilson, was more than once on the verge of firing him, but held back in view of the political risks entailed in making of him a political martyr on such impeccably democratic issues. Benn's public campaign for 'open government' as the only way of making the state accountable to a democratic public certainly reinforced the lesson that many activists drew from the practice of this Labour Government on the importance of intra-party constitutional reform. But this would not itself prove sufficient to overcome the party's incapacity to act as an effective vehicle for articulating and popularising an alternative strategy.

The lesson many activists learned from the limited turn to the left that had taken place in the early 1970s was thus the necessity of using the crisis to remake the party into such a vehicle before anyone could really expect 'fundamental change' from a future Labour government. Even before the Labour Party went into opposition in 1979 the activists' determination and organisational capacity to bring this about were stronger than they had ever been. But they overestimated the significance of the changes they were able to secure in the party's constitution, and underestimated the strength and determination with which 'parliamentary paternalism' would be defended, and the lengths to which the parliamentary elite was prepared to go to avoid conceding anything to the new left's politics.

7

The Conflict over
Party Democracy

So long as economic conditions sustained the Keynesian welfare-state regime, it was very much the case that, as Weber said, the social democratic parties were progressively 'conquered' by the state. But with the breakdown of that regime, amidst a world-wide capitalist crisis, the relationship between state and the party became more open to challenge; a fact made clear by Thatcherism itself, as Stuart Hall argued in *Marxism Today* five months before the 1979 election.[1] What had distinguished the Conservative Party under Mrs Thatcher's leadership since 1975, Hall pointed out, was precisely 'the radicalism of its commitment to break the mould ... It means, not to tinker with this or that mechanism, but to change the terms of the struggle, to shift the balance of class forces radically to the Right. It is the only parliamentary political force resolutely committed to the view that "things cannot go on in the old way".' But what made Thatcherism effective, Hall argued, was neither the economic crisis nor the appeal of the new right's ideology, taken on their own. What had disorganised the labour movement and the British left, and provided such fertile ground for the new right, was the contradiction within social democracy itself. At the heart of this contradiction was the fact that, in the name of the 'national interest', successive Labour governments had acted 'not to advance but to *discipline* the class and the organisations it represents'. The new right's ideological assault against the state was successful because when it was in office social democracy 'represented the dominated classes as passive recipients, as clients of a state run by experts and professionals over which people have no real or substantive control'. There could be no effective counter to the new right, Hall concluded, unless 'the deeply undemocratic character of most of the major institutions of the Left itself' was confronted: 'The question of the nature, procedures, organisational structures and conceptions of new forms of political representation, of a more, broadly mass and democratic character' was on the agenda: it was not a matter to be attended to 'after the immediate struggle is over' but had to be 'what the "immediate struggle" is about'.[2]

As we have seen, this had been the central and distinctive goal of the Labour new left's thinking from the early 1970s, but the lack of organisational coherence among the activists meant that little progress had been made towards achieving it. This had begun to change, however, even before the 1974 election, with the formation in June 1973 of the Campaign for Labour Party Democracy. And in sharp contrast to the previous decade, when the disappointments with the Labour Governments of the 1960s had caused a flood of activists out of the Labour Party, the response of party activists to the bitter experience of Labour Governments of the 1970s was to start organising themselves within it. This is not to say that there was not once again a considerable number of members who left the party during the 1974–79 Labour Governments, especially, as Whiteley noted, among 'the instrumental members, who are disproportionately working class and [who] are leaving the party as a result of . . . failures of policy outcomes'.[3] But the vast flow of activists out of the party that occurred in the mid- to late 1960s was not repeated in the mid- to late 1970s, as the new activists we examined in Chapter 2 made themselves felt at the local level and were encouraged by the greater openness of the NEC to this activism, and by the promise which Benn and the AES afforded at the national level.[4]

The Strategy of the CLPD

The Campaign for Labour Party Democracy (CLPD) – which for a while became the core organisation of perhaps the most powerful movement for radical intra-party reform ever to arise within western social democracy – was set up in June 1973 in direct response to Harold Wilson's public declaration that the Shadow Cabinet would 'exercise its veto' immediately after the NEC's vote to include a specific commitment to take twenty-five companies into public ownership in Labour's 1973 programme. This proposal, we saw earlier, reflected the widespread distrust among party members of the leadership's commitment to the more radical policies that the Party Conference had adopted in the early 1970s. The activists who founded the CLPD did so because they 'felt the need to counter the moves which would merely ensure the repetition of the sorry tale of 1964–70'.[5]

Their decision to concentrate exclusively on issues of intra-party democracy throughout the 1970s was partly a pragmatic one. By sticking to 'a strictly formal democratic platform' the CLPD hoped that 'party members and trade unionists holding very different views on policy issues could unite in support of this vital democratic reform'.[6] But the CLPD's resolute abstention from campaigning on issues of policy during the 1970s should not obscure (and certainly did not, in the eyes of most observers) the fact that the CLPD's founders and activists were left-wing socialists like so many others in the party, motivated by the turn to the left that produced the party's 1973 programme, and especially by the provisions in it that involved controls over capital and public ownership. When the CLPD did produce its first major pamphlet on policy much later, in 1986, it was entitled 'The Case for Public Ownership' and was aimed at resisting the policy reversals initiated by Neil Kinnock as leader after 1985.[7] In the eyes of its founders, however, what distinguished the CLPD from other left groupings was that the latter 'do not attempt to win the support of the majority, or, if they believe that this is what they are doing, the methods they choose to adopt to pursue their basic aims ensure they are not realised'.[8] This perspective was very clearly outlined in a paper written in 1988 by Vladimir Derer, who became the CLPD's Secretary in 1974 and remained the most important figure in the organisation throughout its existence. 'The basic problem of the Left', Derer argued, was 'its unwillingness and therefore inability to come to terms with the political environment of bourgeois democratic institutions which constitute the framework for political activity'. The institutions of parliamentary democracy, including the established political parties, had 'displayed a degree of stability quite unexpected by those who prophesied their inevitable collapse'. Their survival 'cannot be put down just to the "betrayal" of the leaders of mass working-class parties ... the fact that the great majority of members of these parties as a rule chose to follow reformist leaders rather than "revolutionary" critics was not acciden-tal ...' Derer contrasted the left inside the Labour Party, which assumed that radical change could be initiated through socialist activities within the party, with the left outside the party, which rejected this belief and

> bases its politics on the assumption that political changes will come about as a result of mass movements, springing up spontaneously in places of employment and within working-class communities. Such movements would create [their] own organs of political power, by-pass representative parliamentary institutions, come into conflict with them and ultimately replace them ... [I]n practice both conceptions ... share a failure to gain any significant political influence.

Derer's contention was that the Labour left was not wrong to take parliamentary democracy seriously, but its failure was due to the fact that

> there was never any serious attempt on the part of the Labour Left to make use of the opportunities available to it within the Labour Party in order to gain influence through winning its membership to a socialist programme. Such an effort would, of necessity, involve systematic activity to create a rank and file organisation opposed to the leadership but built on a programme that at any given time is acceptable to the mass of the Party's individual and

affiliated members. In the absence of such activity the politics of the Labour Left parliamentarians is no different from that of the socialist sects outside the Labour Party. Both expect to be rescued from their chronic political impotence by spontaneously arising mass movements. . . .

Derer drew five conclusions from this analysis:

1 In countries with established parliamentary traditions a crisis will only occur when a radically reforming government goes beyond the limits of the capitalist framework.
2 If therefore the Left is serious about a situation in which transition to socialism is a realistic possibility, the election of such a government must become its overriding priority. It follows that everything else must be subordinated to this aim.
3 This means winning majority support within the Labour Party for a programme for a radical reforming government. Consequently not general socialist propaganda, but organisation and mobilisation of Labour Party members behind demands that are potentially acceptable to the majority and meet their needs, must be the Left's primary objective.
4 Majority support can only be won by appealing to the existing Labour Party membership, taking account of its existing level of consciousness. This means that demands are not pursued which go beyond what is acceptable to the majority . . .
5 Any effective campaign on these lines is not possible without a rank and file organisation acting as a pressure group . . .[9]

The CLPD's rank-and-file character did not rule out strategic or tactical cooperation with left-wing Labour MPs. Some MPs and national trade union officials were listed prominently on CLPD circulars as supporters (and even as honorary presidents and vice-presidents), but their role was mainly symbolic.[10] The organisation was run by unpaid activists, headed by an elected executive, and as it grew this increasingly involved newer party members (usually with some higher education) in their twenties and thirties. Like the long-standing party activists who founded CLPD, they showed little desire to become career politicians, and remarkably few of them ever took that path. Operating with a budget that was still less than £5,000 per year in 1978–79 (rising to a high of £10,000–£15,000 in the early 1980s), almost all the expenses went on printing, paper and secretarial assistance to feed the most important weapon in the CLPD arsenal – the gestetner in Vera and Vladimir Derer's house – the CLPD's only 'office'.

The campaign itself involved building support through affiliations by constituency parties and trade union branches as well as through enlisting individual supporters; sending out model resolutions and convincing CLPs (each of which had the right to forward only one resolution to the party's annual conference) to use them; and organising among trade unions to have their delegates mandated to support reforms to the party's constitution. Throughout the year, regional coordinators would be contacted (the priorities usually being set at executive meetings in London) and told they needed this or that resolution to be advanced or supported in CLPs or unions by working through the established structures of these bodies, which the CLPD was always exceedingly careful to respect. All this entailed a lot of work but it proved remarkably easy to get results, thanks to the political vacuum that by then existed at the base of the party. Much additional work was done in the immediate run-up to the Annual Party Conference and at the Conference itself, not only in mobilising support for key resolutions (especially among union delegations), but also in educating delegates at fringe meetings on how the Conference really worked, how the agenda was set and by what procedures it could be challenged. Whereas most fringe meetings at Conference, and especially the mass Tribune meetings, were political rallies addressed by a leading parliamentary or movement figure, the CLPD meetings were more like workshops where strategy was debated (or at least explained), the tactics of challenges to the platform or agenda outlined, and delegates guided on how to vote – all on the basis of detailed information on the Conference timetable and policy agenda. A crucial victory for the CLPD was when one of its most active members, Pete Willsman, was elected to the Labour Party's Conference Arrangements Committee. His reports to the CLPD fringe meetings on how resolutions were composited were like reports by meat inspectors about what went into the sausages.

The key to 'the iron law of oligarchy' in mass socialist parties had always been the leadership's control over the party administration and conference agenda, on the one hand, and disorganisation and deference among the active membership, on the other.[11] It was this pattern that the CLPD was challenging. The central figure in the Labour Party more and more resembled the 'notable' – the MP who had cut his teeth politically in the Oxford Union – rather than the classic labour movement 'organiser'. The number of full-time agents working for the party (who could hardly ever have been designated as central figures in the party, and who, as we saw in Chapter 2, often acted more as gatekeepers rather than organisers) had declined from 296 in 1951 to only 77 by 1978.[12] The CLPD activist, stepping into this vacuum, resembled in some ways the classic 'organiser'. But it was an organising role turned inwards on the party as a collective organisation: the mobilisation of active party members to challenge the policy autonomy of the 'notables'. The assertion by the CLP delegate Margaret McCarthy from the floor of the 1970 Party Conference, that the precondition for any successful externally-oriented organising activity was internal organisational change, expressed precisely what drove Labour new left activists to their exceptional efforts through the 1970s.

The Struggle for Reselection

The CLPD's initial Statement of Aims of June 1973 undertook to ensure that conference decisions were binding on the parliamentary party by focusing mainly on the role of the NEC, calling on it to carry out fully its responsibility as the custodian of Conference decisions, to take 'firm action' to ensure that the election manifesto accurately reflected these, and to be responsive to rank and file opinion between Conferences by making its meetings open to CLP representatives, sending out quarterly written reports, and extending the process of consultation with CLPs.[13] This focus on the NEC was soon dropped, however. The 150–200 constituency activists who attended the CLPD's first public meeting at the 1973 Conference demonstrated an overwhelming interest in automatic reselection conferences in Labour-held parliamentary seats (nine of those in attendance were fresh from the battle to deselect Dick Taverne as their MP in Lincoln). The CLPD responded to this by deciding to concentrate on mandatory reselection as 'the immediately most appropriate means' of realising the CLPD's 'basic aim – the translation of Labour Party programme into Labour Government policies'.[14] (After the PLP elected Callaghan as leader in 1976, the CLPD added the election of leader by the Party Conference as its second objective for constitutional reform.) This shift in focus was partly adopted for the highly pragmatic reason that 'reselection alone ... appeared capable of commanding wide support'. But there was also a good strategic reason for the shift. The fact that rank and file activists were turning to deselection in the early 1970s showed that they recognised the limits of the NEC's power over Labour MPs, even if it had wanted to play the role of 'custodian' of Conference decisions. In a steady stream of bulletins that were widely distributed throughout the party the CLPD would make this point:

> Under the present arrangements there is no way the Conference can effectively influence the parliamentary Labour Party. By its very nature Conference can, as a rule, do no more than lay down the broad outlines of policies. It has no machinery to ensure that its policy recommendations are acted on. However, the individual accountability of each MP to a regularly-held selection conference, backed up by the possibility of replacement, can bring this fundamental change which no Conference can accomplish.[15]

In the real world of parliamentary teams competing to put a government in office and keep it there, the real accountability of MPs was primarily – then as now – upwards to the Cabinet rather than downwards to those who nominated or elected them; and this was reinforced not only by the system of party whips but even more by the hope of prime ministerial patronage. The democratic party structure set out in the Labour Party constitution, according to which the Party Conference is sovereign, had no direct bearing on any of this. The only point at which the extra-parliamentary party directly impinged on the real world of parliamentary democracy was that CLPs decided (subject to endorsement by the NEC) who would stand as party candidates. The CLPD's goal was to use the requirement that sitting MPs should seek renomination to shift their accountability back towards the party rank and file. This would, they argued, overcome

> ... the central dilemma of the Labour Party. Namely, that many of its representatives in Parliament do not believe in the programme they are elected to implement. Others, while not actually opposed to the programme of their party, do not feel sufficiently strongly in favour of it seriously to resist attempts by Labour Cabinets to water down, neuter or reverse policies to which the Party is supposed to be committed. ... The purpose of mandatory reselection is to establish an open and honest relationship between the MP and his or her constituency party in the hope that, whatever the practicalities of office, our representatives in Parliament are never again allowed to lose sight of the ideals of the movement which sent them there. Such a relationship cannot develop overnight ... and it will depend as much on the enthusiasm of the party members as upon the MP.[16]

To make MPs 'truly accountable', said the CLPD, would require that the General Management Committees of CLPs should keep themselves well informed about what went on in the House of Commons, and in PLP and NEC meetings ('unless you know what your MP is doing and saying you cannot hold him or her accountable'), and also give MPs the opportunity to report back to them regularly both in person and through written reports which would be circulated at all branch meetings. A much more regularly active and informed local party was needed both to apply the sanction of deselection to an MP that ignored it, and to 'back the MP to the hilt' if following party policy meant challenging Government policy. 'It is no good taking important policy decisions by margins of one or two votes at ill-attended meetings where the results could easily be overturned a week or two later. ... Accountability is a two-way process which confers responsibility on the party as well as the MP.'[17]

An amendment proposing that CLPs should 'hold a selection conference at least once in the lifetime of every Parliament' had first been debated at the 1974 Conference, but was defeated by 3.5 to 2 million votes.[18] The NEC had recommended it be rejected, but Ian Mikardo was able to announce that he had already persuaded the NEC in 1973 to respond positively to the ferment in the constituency parties by adopting a 'self-denying ordinance' whereby it would only agree to hear an appeal by an MP against a CLP deselection decision if it could be shown there had been a breach of constitutional procedure. This was intended as a significant concession to the autonomy of the CLPs, and represented an

important break with the 'social democratic centralism' that had characterised the NEC under the right's control.[19] What the NEC still
opposed, however, was an automatic reselection procedure, on the
grounds that, as Mikardo put it, while the right to divorce should exist
when a marriage has broken down through incompatibility, 'divorce
should never be easy'.[20]

The feeling that emanated from the floor of the Conference reflected
the concern (later to be constantly expressed by the CLPD) that
precisely because the question of reselection was not a routine one, and
involved a special and cumbersome procedure, a CLP which tried to
exercise its right to deselect would risk an ugly public disputation which
would be played up by hostile media. This point was put sharply by
Peter Price, the delegate from Sheffield Brightside – the only constituency party in 1974 to have actually deselected its MP:

> It is not an experience I would like to recommend to any of you here. It is a
> very lengthy long drawn-out procedure, one which leaves the management
> committee to come under extreme fire and stress from the press and people.
> Dirt is thrown around, people are accused, you cannot walk down the streets
> without people accusing you of being Marxists, International Socialists;
> everything is thrown at you.... [Yet] I put it to you that it is the duty of
> your constituencies, the duty they have to the electorate, to put up a man in
> whom they have full confidence. There is nothing worse than a local party
> putting up a man who has lost their confidence. It breeds apathy not only
> among the workers but among the electorate.[21]

But the experience of Sheffield Brightside in deselecting Eddie Griffiths as its MP in 1974 would be as nothing compared to the uproar that
greeted the deselection of Reg Prentice in the London constituency of
Newham North East in 1975. Coming at the rate of only one a year
(Taverne in 1972, Eddie Milne in 1973,[22] Griffiths in 1974 and Prentice
in 1975), one might have thought that this kind of gradual reselection
process would not be seen as too troubling. But with the principle of
reselection having clearly now become a major intra-party issue, and
with the NEC apparently no longer willing to play its previous role as
the MPs' bodyguard, the parliamentary leadership virtually went to war
against the activists of the Labour new left in defence of Prentice (the
only Cabinet minister threatened with deselection). His deselection was
initiated just after the Referendum vote on the Common Market and
amidst the Cabinet's consideration of a statutory incomes policy as well
as public expenditure cuts in the summer of 1975, all of which made it
seem particularly necessary for the leadership to prove that senior pro-
European politicians on the right of the party like Prentice could be
protected. The day before his CLP's decision, 179 MPs (well over half
the PLP) were mobilised to sign a letter in his support. This included
twelve Cabinet ministers and thirty-five junior ministers, and it seems

to have been among the latter that the campaign was organised. One junior minister later told Hilary Wainwright that 'it was just assumed you would sign – especially if you were in the government – and that you accepted that the constituency party had been taken over or influenced by people without the party's best interests in mind'.[23] In a rare intervention, the Prime Minister made public a letter in which he charged that 'small and unrepresentative cliques' were at the heart of the problem – and this was only the most influential of many invitations to the media from within the parliamentary party to use red-scare tactics against the Labour new left. The press – not only the tabloids but even *The Guardian* – gladly picked up the charge and virtually 'overnight those who wanted Prentice to go were described as "extremists", "bed-sit revolutionaries", "members of the Trotskyist Militant", "unrepresentative of the Labour voter" and "enemies of democracy". These descriptions', Wainwright notes, 'with the term "hard left" added as a useful catch-all, have stuck for any group which challenges established political (especially parliamentary) power.'[24]

The Newham North East constituency party epitomised the type of moribund party that had been brought to life in the early 1970s by new activists with higher education who were part of the growing non-manual population in the area, and who differed in this respect from new manual working-class activists like those who had played the leading role in the Lincoln and Sheffield Brightside deselections. But as in these cases in the north, the new activists in London had also taken on leading positions 'not because of some organised infiltration and manipulation but because older party members welcomed this infusion of younger blood and encouraged them to become active as party officers and delegates'.[25] None of the twenty-nine delegates to the GMC that voted to deselect Prentice even belonged to CLPD at the time, and only four (none of them in a leading position) were Young Socialists who were supporters of Militant. Of the nineteen GMC delegates who supported Prentice, on the other hand, all but four were retired manual trade unionists, who were increasingly atypical within the community. Although the majority of the activists were no doubt well to the left of the average Labour voter, that did not prevent electoral success; indeed Labour did extremely well in local elections in Newham North East in the late 1970s when the party fared very poorly in most other places. After his deselection, Prentice crossed the floor and joined the Conservatives, became a voluble exponent of Mrs Thatcher's ideas, and later (having succeeded in finding a Tory nomination for a safe seat in 1979) became a loyal junior minister in her first administration. It was a passage that appeared to prove that parliamentary careerism trumped political principle, and it greatly aided those in the Labour Party who were advancing the case for mandatory reselection.

The 1975 Labour Party Conference met while the controversy over Prentice was still fresh. Despite twelve CLPs submitting resolutions on mandatory reselection, the issue was kept off the Conference agenda by the Conference Arrangements Committee (CAC) through the application of a 'three-year rule'. The CAC, which was still dominated – and would remain so – by 'moderate' second-rank trade union officials whose particular expertise was the 'management' of conferences, used this rule to exclude troublesome resolutions on the grounds that they had been debated at previous conferences. Although the rules allowed the NEC to override the CAC on any matter it considered of immediate importance, it refrained from doing so – a kind of passive protection for the parliamentary leadership that was maintained right through the Government's term of office. After the 1975 Conference, the NEC denied Prentice's appeal on the ground that no procedures had been breached.[26] But when Mikardo, having been convinced by the Prentice fiasco of the need to make mandatory reselection a routine procedure, moved that a constitutional amendment for this should be presented to the 1976 Conference, he was defeated by fourteen votes to eleven. This reflected, as Shaw has shown, not only the fact that a minority of left-wing MPs on the NEC were themselves 'either lukewarm or hostile to mandatory reselection', but also the multiple pressures to which the NEC was subject on this issue. The National Agent's Department had come out strongly against change, using 'the well-honed bureaucratic technique of questioning the feasibility of the reform rather than the principle ... [It] listed a battery of practical and administrative complications while refraining from suggesting how they could be overcome.'[27] The PLP also lobbied the NEC strongly in defence of their autonomy and job security. Press coverage of the NEC's decision against reselection, taken in the midst of the March 1976 leadership contest in the PLP, featured Callaghan's opposition as having determined the outcome, and Foot as having reluctantly voted in favour.[28] Probably most crucial was the fact that 'trade unions were mobilised to resist the measure' on the grounds, *horribile dictu*, that 'sponsored MPs might be unseated'.[29]

Thus even though forty-five CLP resolutions calling for mandatory reselection (the largest on any single subject) were presented to the 1976 Conference, the Conference Arrangements Committee still put the matter off by invoking the three-year rule. A challenge to this ruling from the floor of the Conference still only collected 2 million votes, which showed how little headway had been made on the issue among the unions. (By this point, the CLPD had affiliations from forty-five CLPs but only eight trade union branches.) Under the three-year rule, however, the matter had to come before the 1977 Conference (at which over ninety resolutions and constitutional amendments were submitted on this issue, with no fewer than sixty-seven CLPs submitting the

CLPD's 'model' resolution); but once again the campaign was frustrated by the CAC's application of another obscure rule that stated that constitutional amendments had to be referred to the NEC for a year before being debated. As for the remaining resolutions, the CAC, in a replay of the manoeuvring that had scuttled the twenty-five companies resolution at the 1973 Conference, formulated a composite motion based on a Militant Tendency resolution in such a way as to guarantee that the NEC would be bound to recommend its rejection. (Militant all along insisted on pushing for no limit on the number of reselection conferences that a CLP could hold in a single Parliament. As would repeatedly prove to be the case in the war against the Labour new left, if Militant had not existed, it would have had to have been invented.) Mikardo, however, offered the delegates a guarantee that in 1978 the NEC would present a constitutional amendment along the lines of the CLPD model.

But the battle was hardly over. All the same pressures were brought to bear once again on the NEC Working Party set up to resolve the issue. Indeed in some respects they were intensified. Although it was to cost Mikardo his seat on the NEC – as many CLP delegates at the 1978 Conference switched their votes in protest at his having reneged on his promise – he settled for a compromise according to which a competitive reselection procedure would be triggered only if an initial vote went against readopting the sitting MP. This would have still subjected GMCs to all the same pressures to avoid a selection competition – exactly what the CLPD wanted to avoid by making reselection conferences a routine procedure rather than an exceptional one. Mikardo had reluctantly accepted this compromise as the best he could get, given the support for it among union leaders; among them were the TGWU's Jack Jones (despite his strong stand in the late 1960s and early 1970s in favour of making MPs accountable) as well as his successor Moss Evans, who had a seat on the NEC Working Party. It also included the Engineers' Hugh Scanlon, who in any case considered the question of reselection to be 'chicken shit' in comparison with industrial and economic policy.[30]

But the CLPD had by now really begun to do its work in the unions, as was reflected in the fact that trade union branch affiliations to the CLPD, which had reached twenty-five in 1977, almost doubled again to forty-seven in 1978. The CLPD's allies in the unions played a key role in swinging the votes of the delegations to the 1978 Party Conference in favour of the CLPD proposal, including those of the TGWU and the Engineers. Victory was once again frustrated, however, when Scanlon 'miscast' the Engineers' block vote, sending the CLPD amendment down to defeat.[31] Given the uproar this caused at the Conference (not least among Scanlon's own delegation), and indeed throughout the labour movement, most observers at the time (and subsequently) treated this bizarre episode as an aberration from the trend, a last ditch, impossible to sustain, remnant of the old pattern of inter-elite intrigue between the parliamentary and union leaderships. In fact, it was a clumsily executed move in a growing counter-insurgency against the new left.

The Counter-insurgency Against the New Left

In this way the issue of mandatory reselection was put off until after the 1979 election. It is very important to note the success of the union and parliamentary leadership in securing this, and especially in ensuring that on the issues of intra-party democracy the NEC itself 'operated less as an initiator of reform than an arena of struggle'.[32] The forces identified with the status quo did not remain passive or merely defensive in face of the growing strength of the CLPD activists, and the NEC's adoption of the AES. This 'counter-insurgency' began not in 1981 (after the constitutional changes were effected, as most accounts have claimed) but five years earlier, in the fateful year of 1976; and it was conducted in terms of pure power politics. The Croslandite social democrats in the parliamentary party effectively withdrew from any serious debates on policy, and annual conferences were marked by 'the rows of empty chairs reserved for members of the parliamentary party'.[33] The abandonment of Keynesianism had left most Labour MPs in a state of political and ideological nakedness, and in this context 'the Government's parliamentary supporters were reluctant to come to the rostrum either to defend the Government's economic policies or to support the revisionist philosophy on public ownership which was so forcefully advocated in the late 1950s'.[34] The counter-insurgency, in other words, was a matter of organisational manoeuvring and media scare-mongering, not policy or principle.

Remarkably enough, the very same speech that pronounced the death of Keynesianism also launched the counter-insurgency against the new left. Callaghan concluded his address to the 1976 Conference by making it clear that he, unlike Wilson, would not be content with merely reasserting that the Government was only 'accountable in a parliamentary democracy to Parliament' and that MPs could not 'suspend their judgements in favour of extra-parliamentary bodies'. 'I do not want to retreat behind the stock defence that "the Government must govern", if that becomes a polite way of telling the party to go to hell.' Far from being embarrassed by having been dubbed a machine politician by the media,[35] Callaghan told the delegates that he accepted the designation of 'party man' as an 'accolade'. Contrasting the cooperative relationship that had 'grown up between the TUC and the Government in the past two and half years' with the critical stance of the party, he made it clear that his goal was to re-establish the dominance of the parliamentary leadership over the NEC and to restore the social democratic centralism of the party apparatus. To this end, he suggested that the NEC might need to be restructured, perhaps by including local government and regional council representatives. And he insisted that the NEC launch a formal investigation of 'those elements who misuse the word "socialism" and who seek to infiltrate our party and use it for their own ends ... not because I am on a witch hunt but because I want the Government and the party to work closely together'.[36]

This determination to use the issue of infiltration as a means of bringing the party into line with the Government meant that throughout the autumn of 1976, when amidst the trauma of the IMF crisis party members were going through the agony of watching their Government abandon the policy bedrock of social democracy, the public's attention was diverted to the issue of 'Marxist' infiltration of the Labour Party. What Stuart Hall called 'the conspiracy of the Red Scare' now became the prism through which Labour's parliamentary leadership and the mainstream media projected to the British public the meaning of the struggle taking place in the Labour Party. This was how

> the 'crisis' came finally to be appropriated – by governments in office, the repressive apparatus of the state, the media and some articulate sectors of public opinion – as an interlocking set of planned or organised *conspiracies*. British society became little short of fixated by the idea of a conspiracy against the British way of life. ... The tighter the rope along which the British economy is driven, the finer the balance between compliance with and overthrow of the 'social contract', the greater the power the conspiratorial metaphor has exerted over political discourse ...[37]

The 'conspiracy of the Red Scare' had, of course, been used throughout 1975 by those who fought against Reg Prentice's deselection, but by the autumn of 1976 both media and party attention had shifted to the selection as the party's National Youth Officer of Andy Bevan, a leading Militant figure in the Labour Party Young Socialists, and a capable and affable organiser who had won the support even of right-wing trade unionists.[38] Callaghan's insistent demand that the NEC override Bevan's selection, together with the leaking in November of a year-old internal report by the party's National Agent, Reg Underhill, on 'Entryist Activities', resulted in a flurry of sensationalist media stories. In the first week of December 1976 – the very week that the Cabinet went through its final agonising meetings on the IMF cuts – the Militant Tendency's activities within the Labour Party became 'officially' defined as a central strategic issue for the British state. A three-day series of lengthy articles and editorials devoted to this in *The Times* lent an aura of gravity to the issue that the hysteria of the tabloids could not match, and this was followed in the same week by two highly publicised speeches by Callaghan and Wilson, conveyed with the authority of Labour's only Prime Ministers since Attlee, castigating 'extremism' within the party and calling for urgent action to clear out 'left-wing infiltrations'.[39]

Of course, the issue had very little to do with Militant's real influence. While the question of what, if anything, to do about a small, classically entrist Trotskyist organisation has been a rather common minor problem for social democratic parties, its larger significance in the Labour Party and in the British state at this time was as a symbolic springboard for a counter-offensive against the Labour new left's far more serious challenge to traditional parliamentarism. As Roy Hattersley later honestly put it: 'The problem is not Militant, about whom we always talk, because Militant is so easily identifiable and so unpleasant that most people are prepared to squash it ... the problem is those organisations which talk in the language of democratic socialism.'[40]

Yet, while they were certainly successful in orchestrating the 'Red Scare' theme through their contacts with the media, the right-wing parliamentarians were incapable of mustering any effective counter-organisation to the new left within the party itself. Their Campaign for Labour Victory (CLV), launched in February 1977 as a counter to the CLPD, had no resonance whatever among the rank and file.[41] One supportive Labour front-bencher later admitted that the CLV was 'disastrous': it was 'an awfully elitist organisation ... [whose] failure was threefold ... it was London-based, a leadership organisation ... [and] had the Common Market obsession which ... is not the basis of [a] socialist programme'.[42]

But if the CLV was a dud, this was not true of the Trade Unionists for Labour Victory (TULV), whose origins go back to the same period.[43] In a calculated political initiative, originating at the 1977 conference of the General and Municipal Workers Union, the 'moderate' leadership of that union, with whom Callaghan had especially close ties, followed his lead at the 1976 Party Conference by issuing a call for an enquiry into the finances and structure of the Labour Party, including measures to 'reform' the NEC. Although this direct intervention by the union leadership in the NEC's sphere of authority was unprecedented, the ability of the GMWU's David Basnett to win the support of left-led unions (including the TGWU) provided the legitimation for it. The TULV, formally launched at the TUC's Congress House in August 1978, took upon itself the immediate task of coordinating union resources for the forthcoming electoral campaign and for purchasing a new party headquarters. But behind the TULV's concern with the party's financial problems was another: to try to contain the conflict between members and leaders that was now shaking the party.

It is crucially important to understand the role of the union leadership in this period. Whereas during the 1964–70 Labour Government's term of office a significant group among the union leadership had moved to the left, after 1974 these same leaders themselves moved back, as we have seen, to providing support as usual for the parliamentary leadership. Right through the 1970s, as Minkin has shown, it remained the case 'as it had been for much of the Labour Party's history, that a majority of union leaders were associated with the right and centre-right of the party'. And while the union leadership were now prepared to break with previous practice in terms of intervening in the NEC's internal party management, they still retained 'a sense of "rules" which inhibited intervention within the province of the PLP. . . . In any case, the Campaign for Labour Party Democracy was seen as a front for the left, and to be fought accordingly.'[44]

To be sure, even centrist and right-wing union leaders often found it prudent to satisfy the sentiments of their own activists by voting against government policies at party conferences, but then made it clear to the parliamentary leadership that these votes need not be taken too seriously.[45] As Callaghan put it, after meeting with the General Council before the 1976 Congress: 'I knew they would have difficulty in explaining the position to the delegates but I was very heartened by their private understanding.'[46] Even more left-inclined leaders were influenced by the precarious parliamentary position of the Government and their fear of an increasingly reactionary Tory leadership, as well as their ingrained reluctance to act as political not just industrial leaders. As a result, it was the Labour new left, not the Government, that was isolated from the union leadership.

Nor was it just a matter of the union leadership. At least until 1977–78 some of the same deep reserves of loyalty to a Labour Government, and many of the same fears and frustrations with the effects of high inflation on real wages and employment, were important in securing the acquiescence of many union activists to wage restraint. The vanguardist left recognised this at the time: Steve Jefferys, the industrial organiser of the Socialist Workers Party, admitted that even shop stewards shared 'the general conviction among workers that there was little you could do, you just had to put up with the Government's pay policy' and that 'in the face of the crisis there appeared to be no "practical" alternative'.[47] The role that the Communist Party had played in mobilising shop stewards in the late 1960s and early 1970s had been much undermined by its support for the Social Contract as well as by its declining membership; and the Institute of Workers' Control had little presence on the ground.

It was thus increasingly clear that not only the party but also the unions would need to be transformed if the new left's attempt to change the Labour Party was to succeed. Those who conceived the AES had understood from the very beginning that 'the old artificial division between "political" and "industrial" action has become a most harmful aberration' and that the AES required 'a determined effort ... to break it down from both sides'.[48] Benn himself had recognised all along that the source of 'the whole problem' for the new left, as he put it in 1975, was 'the relationship between the unions and the Government and the degree of political education within the trade union movement'.[49] Given Benn's immediate recognition of what a 'formidable leader' Mrs Thatcher was, he was extremely sensitive to the fact that, as he wrote in his diary on the last day of 1977, 'the country is moving sharply to the right'.[50] But even though there were enough union votes at Party Conference and on the NEC to endorse radical alternative policies, Benn knew that the trade union leaders were 'so enjoying their corporatist relationship with the Government that they don't want to hear anything about socialism'. The 'real battle', he concluded, lay not only within the party but within the broader labour movement; indeed it involved nothing less than 'a struggle for the soul of the movement'. Yet little progress could be made in this respect so long as the Government remained in office. The counter-insurgency that Callaghan had initiated had left the NEC in the last years of the Labour Government only barely 'hanging on to what remaining influence it has' (as Benn put it), let alone feeling strong and independent enough to lead a popular campaign for its alternative among the union rank and file.

Of course, the union leadership had begun to feel the effect of a membership revolt against its cooperation with the Government well before the 1978/79 'winter of discontent'. Jack Jones's defeat on the Social Contract at his union's 1977 conference was only the most dramatic of numerous union conference repudiations of cooperation with wage restraint that year; it was also the product of the more open and democratic regime that Jones himself had run inside the TGWU. The General and Municipal Workers' leadership's ability to stave off such a defeat was a direct reflection of that union's 'strong loyalist tradition and powerful mechanisms of internal control', but even in this case the pressures were such so as to bring about the defeat of the platform at that union's 1979 conference.[51] The implications of the CLPD's campaign for intra-party democracy for the union leaders' control over their own organisations could hardly be missed.

Yet the revolt against wage restraint did not mean that there was an automatic politicisation of a resurgence of rank and file militancy. As Gregor Murray concluded from his important study of the unions under the Social Contract, there was a significant layer of socialist activists in the unions who espoused the AES, but their impact was limited by their dependence on a

> complex organisational alliance with those [militants] whose opposition was fundamentally instrumental in character. They simply wanted more flexibility

to bargain and rectify anomalies that had created havoc in their pay structures. The mobilisation of opposition was rarely linked to any transformative project. What might be labelled 'social democratic economism' remained the predominant ethos in the bargaining strategies and political practice of British trade unionism. As Moss Evans, the TGWU General Secretary, phrased it in a report to the TGWU executive in the autumn of 1978: 'Our approach is carry on bargaining and backing Labour.'[52]

It was exactly what Jack Jones had said in 1969 – and a telling sign of how little progress had been made by the Labour new left in the unions. To be sure, a series of campaigns against cuts in public expenditure, led by NUPE, were impressive for the way they challenged traditional sectionalism and economism and reached out to community and women's groups.[53] But even this kind of action was politically contained. Key unions like the TGWU and GMWU kept their distance from the anti-cuts campaigns, partly out of a concern to protect the Government but also because the divisions between the interests of manufacturing and public service workers that the Government's policies promoted were reflected among their own membership. And although the unions made it clear to the Government that the Social Contract could no longer be sustained, they did not really embrace more radical policy alternatives. On the contrary, the TUC's Economic Reviews became more moderate in tone, and the TUC–NEC–PLP Liaison Committee's 1978 policy document, 'Into the Eighties', was far less radical than Labour's 1976 Programme. The TULV's emergence was not just about containing the campaign for intra-party democracy; it also partly reflected the union leaders' discomfort over the AES-style policies being developed by the party's research department, in contrast to the corporatist ones being advanced by the TUC.

Particularly important for the eventual success of the counter-insurgency against the left – and an important indicator that opposition to the Social Contract did not necessarily entail a shift to the left – was the election in 1978 of Terry Duffy and John Boyd, two classically anti-communist leaders, as President and General Secretary respectively of the Engineering Union. Although it was Terry Duffy who moved the resolution at the 1978 Party Conference rejecting wage guidelines 'until prices, profits and investment are planned within the framework of a socialist economy' (a resolution which was overwhelmingly passed), his endorsement of such phrases was purely cynical. On the very next day enough union votes were available, including those of the Engineers, soundly to defeat a resolution to amend the constitution so as to take the election of the leader out of the exclusive hands of the parliamentary party; and it was Duffy who leaned particularly heavily on Scanlon to ensure that the Engineers' vote was cast against reselection, in defiance of the wishes of the Engineers' conference delegation.

In light of Scanlon's behaviour at the 1978 Conference, Benn interpreted the 'abuse of the block vote by the trade union leaders [as] a very
important development because it will in the long run lead to a clean
up'.[54] But this assumed that the balance of forces would in the long run
swing back to the advantage of the left. At this Conference the left had
apparently been strengthened by the election of Dennis Skinner and
Neil Kinnock to the NEC's constituency section.[55] But little noted at
the time was the simultaneous election to the NEC's trade union section
of John Golding, a right-wing machine politician from the West
Midlands, a 'committee room Napoleon: a tough shrewd street-fighter'.[56]
At a PLP meeting to discuss the reselection issue in March 1978, Golding
had described how he had personally packed many GMC selection
conferences with union delegates and vowed that, if reselection went
ahead, 'it will be a traumatic experience because we shall start packing
GMCs to see that our people get in'. The Chief Whip, Michael Cocks,
endorsed Golding's cynicism by saying: 'He's right, you know, that's
what usually happens.'[57] Golding was a key player in the formation of a
hard-line right-wing group of union leaders, known as the St Ermin's
Group, determined not to compromise – as they feared the TULV's
more broad-based representation would require them to do – in the
counter-insurgency against the new left. He was to play the leading role
in challenging and eventually defeating Benn's and Heffer's leadership
of the NEC.

These developments within the unions enabled Shirley Williams to
assure the Foreign Press Association in a speech as late as February 1979
that as a social democrat within the Labour Party she was far from
politically 'dead', adding that '. . . many people have failed to notice the
extent to which there has been a considerable shift of power in respect
of our major unions. . . . They are clearly moving back to the centre. It
is only a small handful now which represent the far left.'[58] It was true
that, with the shift to the right in the Engineering Union, the leaders of
four of the six largest unions, accounting for two-thirds of the vote at
the Party Conference, were now unambiguously on the side of the leadership and against the new left. And the fact that the leaders of the
remaining two had joined the TULV was an important sign of their own
inclination to protect the parliamentary leadership. Even when the
1978–79 'Winter of Discontent' broke out, moreover, the union leadership made no common cause with the NEC on policy. They were as
embarrassed by their inability to control their membership and by the
damage the strikes were doing to the Government as they were angry
with Callaghan for having not listened to their warnings that their
members would not stand for another year of wage restraint. Indeed it
was the explicitly corporatist 'concordat' that the Government and TUC
reached in February 1979 that allowed Callaghan to reject with impunity

the election manifesto which the NEC had been so painstakingly preparing for three years.

Yet Shirley Williams spoke too soon. Or at least she relied too much on the power of union leaders to keep their activists in line on the issue of intra-party democracy in a conjuncture when they couldn't even keep them in line on wage restraint. The push for democracy in the party, together with alienation from the Government, had not left the unions entirely untouched; and it was further encouraged by the CLPD's campaign among union activists through its remarkable mobilisation of support in virtually every institution and in virtually every region of the Labour movement between the 1978 and 1979 Conferences (during which time CLPD union branch affiliations went up from forty-seven to eighty-five). This thwarted the full exercise of the repressive role of the 'union bosses' upon which the counter-insurgency against the new left so heavily depended. While the adhesion of the NUPE and TGWU's more left-wing leadership to the TULV no doubt looked (and was) very promising to the parliamentary leadership, their very sizeable block votes (NUPE's affiliation to the Labour Party grew sixfold to 600,000 members over the decade) were mandated to support reselection in 1979.[59] When the NEC resisted a behind-the-scenes attempt by the TULV leaders after the 1979 election once again to postpone consideration of the constitutional reforms, it did so knowing that the union leadership would not be able to hold back their delegations on the issue of reselection. At the 1979 Party Conference, mandatory reselection was finally passed by 4 million to 3 million votes.

The Limits of Constitutional Reform

It had taken five long and arduous years of dedicated organising to win just the first of the CLPD's constitutional reforms, entailing a change which, as one student of comparative parties would observe, was 'long-accepted as normal in most European social democratic parties . . . [and] extremely difficult to refute by any standards of democracy'.[60] In light of the determined opposition the CLPD faced in confronting deeply entrenched elitist aspects of the parliamentarist mode of representation in Britain, not to speak of the challenge it posed to the traditional arrangements between the industrial and political leaders in the Labour Party, it was certainly a remarkable victory for the Labour new left and the CLPD in particular. But if it took this long to secure this one modest intra-party reform, how long would it take to turn the Labour Party into an adequate vehicle for socialist advance – let alone to achieve socialism?

For this reform was won at a price. The CLPD had always been clear about the point of the internal struggle for accountability: 'Reselection was never conceived by us as anything other than a means whereby the party should be enabled to carry out its programme.'[61] But the CLPD's tactical brilliance, demonstrated by its resolutely sticking to the issues of democratic reform in order to maximise support, meant that it had to set aside the question of party members' understanding of and commitment to that programme, let alone the broader public's. Part of the reason for the CLPD's success in winning the reselection battle was its constant insistence on respecting party members' 'existing level of consciousness'. Yet the CLPD was well aware that party members' attitudes and understandings needed themselves to be developed and in some respects changed. For example, the case for affirmative action for women within the party was taken up by Vladimir and Vera Derer not only in terms of the importance of having more women candidates and MPs to attract more of the women's vote, but also in terms of the need to overcome the patriarchal values of party members, who were themselves not free from 'values whose general acceptance by the oppressed classes is the ultimate reason why we still live in a capitalist society. . . . If Labour Party members were free from the values and beliefs which dominate their capitalist social environment they would not have allowed Labour Governments to opt for the status quo.'[62]

The programme the CLPD activists were mainly concerned to secure was the one adopted during the 'turn to the left' of 1970–73; but we have already seen that Benn and his allies at the Department of Industry understood very well how little even shop stewards, let alone most union members, had been exposed to what the industrial strategy was all about. That was why they tried to initiate a campaign to popularise it from within the state, in face of Wilson's claim that it would be unpopular. Even among party members, the very fact that the CLPD thought they could win more support for democratising the party than for issues of policy proved that the programme they wanted the leadership to carry out rested on weak foundations. Nor could it be taken for granted, as that programme evolved into the Alternative Economic Strategy, that members would be able to defend it, let alone be motivated to try to popularise it. And if this was true of the party's direct membership, it was doubly true of the affiliated union membership.

After Benn had got the NEC to endorse Labour's 1976 Programme, the idea of an alternative strategy was kept alive through resolutions passed at the 1977 and 1978 Party Conferences, but although the unions voted for it, they did not popularise it among their members, and the NEC itself was constrained from sponsoring any sustained public articulation of that strategy. The problem was certainly not any shortage of attention to the detail of the policy. Under Benn's Chairmanship of the NEC's Home Policy Committee, a network of sub-committees and study groups laboured over hundreds of research papers prepared by the party's research department, headed by Geoff Bish, or by outside experts. But it was inconceivable that the NEC could in any major way really 'go public' with the AES so long as the Labour Government remained in office. All the work undertaken by the Home Policy Committee was confined to 'two main objectives: first, to influence and shape the work of our own Labour Government; second, to provide a detailed, well-researched basis for our Manifesto, so that the latter would reflect the views and priorities of the party'. In the event, as Bish later admitted, there was 'scant success' on either count: 'Despite all our efforts to prepare careful and detailed proposals, the status of the NEC *vis-à-vis* the Labour Government was, in practice, that of a mere pressure group, just one among many. . . . In many cases, indeed, the NEC was at a disadvantage compared to other major interest groups, including the CBI, the City, the TUC and others.'[63]

By 1978 there had begun to emerge a broad debate among socialists, economists and other intellectuals on the nature and viability of the AES – 'the first clear sign for a generation', according to Andrew Gamble, 'that serious strategic thinking about socialism had re-emerged on the British left'.[64] The fact that such thinking was generated by developments within the Labour Party, of all places, and while the 1974–79 Labour Government was still in office, showed the originality of the Labour new left. The formation of the Labour Coordinating Committee in 1978 by Meacher, Morell and others close to Benn was undertaken with the explicit purpose of popularising the AES. And through a number of working groups linking the Conference of Socialist Economists with the work being done in the party's research department, the contours of the AES were indeed considerably elaborated in 1978–79. What was crucially important about this elaboration was its explicit concern not only with economic policies but also with the development of strategies for engaging in struggles 'in and against the state' which would be directed at democratising state services and agencies.[65] The development of this strategic orientation formed part of a broader attempt on the part of a remarkably creative British Marxist left at the time to transcend the limits of both Labourist parliamentarism and Trotskyist and Leninist vanguardism.[66]

Nevertheless, the fact that virtually every contribution to the debate over the AES began by lamenting the absence of any single authoritative public statement of what was or was not included in the AES reflected the severe constraints under which the new left inside the Labour Party were permitted to operate. The founders of the LCC who worked as Benn's political advisers were carpeted by the Prime Minister himself. It almost seemed an achievement for them just to avoid being fired or expelled as they would have been in the 1950s. Even with a left NEC majority, the notion that they might have undertaken a campaign for the AES, under the auspices of the party and using its resources, was out of the question. Benn himself might try to get Hilary Wainwright or Peter Hain to join the Labour Party, but he was under no illusion that his power inside Transport House was such that he could even contemplate getting people of this calibre hired by the party to lead a political campaign to popularise the AES as a project for democratising the state as well as the economy. Even at Transport House, let alone in Whitehall and Westminster, Benn felt, and with good reason, that he was 'tiptoeing through the corridors of power'.[67]

The actual Manifesto on which Labour ran in the 1979 election was based on a hurried draft prepared by Callaghan's office at 10 Downing Street from which any trace of the AES was excised, as well as any reference to the commitment, approved by the Party Conference, to begin the democratisation of the British state by abolishing the House of Lords. This draft, first seen by the NEC on the day it was to be presented to the press, 'not only ignored many of the agreed decisions of the NEC–Cabinet Group, but also many basic planks of party policy'. In recounting these events, Bish admitted that while the refusal of the parliamentary leadership from the outset to concede any real measure of joint decision-making on policy or strategy to the extra-parliamentary party lay at the heart of the problem, it was also 'wishful thinking on our part' to imagine that the leadership would be prepared to run in an election on the radical policies it had consistently rejected: 'And the Government did have a point. For when a political party is in office, the Manifesto *has* to be seen as a development from the existing policies of the Government and not a sudden lurch towards a completely new strategy.'[68] But unless the NEC had been prepared directly to challenge the Government's credibility, the same logic also ruled out any serious programme of political education around the AES such as Bish recognised was necessary to 'build up ... the support [and] understanding we need, within the party, to help carry our policies through into the Manifesto and Government action'.

Perhaps the most telling indicator of where the balance of intra-party forces really lay on policy – and of the fact that the problem went beyond the parliamentary leadership's resistance to resolutions passed overwhelmingly by the Party Conference – was the way in which the NEC's statement on *Banking and Finance*, which as we saw earlier was overwhelmingly passed at the 1976 Conference in the thick of the IMF crisis, was so quickly driven off the party's agenda. The groundwork had been laid for it at the 1971 and 1975 Conferences, and there were grounds for thinking that the unions directly involved in the financial sector would be supportive. (For example, USDAW's annual conference

– which Minkin described as 'that weathercock of the British trade union movement' – passed resolutions in 1973 and 1974 specifically endorsing the takeover of the banks, the Stock Exchange, and the insurance companies.)[69] But Callaghan's immediate repudiation of the NEC statement, and his promise that he would veto its inclusion in the Manifesto, was bolstered by the reaction of the financial sector unions. When nine of them were consulted by an NEC working party, they were all found to be in varying degrees hostile to the proposal, including USDAW and such an ostensibly left-wing union as Clive Jenkins's ASTMS. This episode strongly suggested that it was highly unlikely that there would be a concerted push by even the left-wing unions in favour of the AES and against the party leadership.

All this showed how much policy campaigns, and campaigns to politicise the unions, not just campaigns for intra-party democracy, needed attention. No one in the CLPD would have denied this was eventually necessary. The real problem was how long even such a modest reform as reselection had taken, and how much energy it had consumed. Even in terms of intra-party democracy, the victory on reselection was only the first step in a much broader agenda for constitutional change that still had very far to go. The CLPD, as we have seen, had been quite pragmatic about choosing to concentrate on reselection first and foremost because it was likely to gain most support. The CLPD did take up the issue of the broader election of the party leader from 1976 on; and in the same year, the CLPD Women's Action Committee was formed through which much of the feminist impetus within the party was initially mobilised in the 1970s and early 1980s. There would be plenty of resentment, on the other hand, of the fact that the CLPD did not give as much priority or energy to winning democratic reforms for women as they did to reselection, or later to the electoral college for electing the party leader. The vesting of control of the party manifesto in the NEC and the issue of open and accountable decision-making in the PLP were also taken up immediately after the 1979 election. Other key issues of intra-party democracy – the way delegates to GMCs were themselves selected in the constituencies; the role of the general, non-active, party membership; the pattern of elections to the NEC; and the trade union block vote at Party Confer-ence – all these were at least implicitly, even if not explicitly, put into question by the CLPD's achievement in making the mode of represen-tation the immediate object of struggle. The CLPD was surely correct in thinking that mandatory reselection would never have been won, even after five years of campaigning, if all these issues had been allowed to come into play at once. Yet this made the CLPD vulnerable to the charge that it was prepared to tolerate and work within a broader constitutional framework which was hard to defend in democratic terms.

This criticism was thoroughly hypocritical when it came from people who had never exhibited any interest in intra-party democracy except that of putting a stop to it. It was hardly less frustrating to party activists when it came from left-wing critics outside the party who had previously shown little interest in (and still exhibited little understanding of) how power was actually exercised and manipulated inside the Labour Party – and who thus had little appreciation of the immensity of the task involved in winning even this one reform. Thus the issue of taking the final selection of candidates away from GMCs and turning it over to a general membership ballot (One Member One Vote) was only raised after it was clear that reselection was going to be passed, and it was advanced, especially within the PLP, primarily by those who had opposed reselection all along; their aim was further to delay the constitutional reform and to make accountability (which was the CLPD's main point) to actively engaged and well-informed local party members actually more difficult to achieve. As for the block vote, for the CLPD to have focused on a constitutional change to end it would not only have undermined the possibility of winning union support for reselection, but might not in itself have achieved much, given the way that union delegations in other social democratic parties tend to vote as a block in support of their leaders even when block voting is not constitutionally established. The CLPD's strategy was to try to demo-cratise the way the block vote was exercised in practice (by politicising issues at union conferences, mandating delegations to the Party Confer-ence, encouraging challenges by delegates to General Secretaries who tried to cast their union's block vote in line with behind-the-scenes deals with other leaders).

Yet it must be said that despite the fact that from year to year the CLPD did broaden the range of democratic reforms it put on the agenda, its determination to play by the existing rules, which was in fact the condition of its success on reselection, could easily be made to look like uncritical constitutionalism. There was some justice in Michael Rustin's criticism of the Labour new left in 1980 to the effect that 'constitutionalism within the party is the equivalent of parliamentarism within the state, in its inhibiting effects on political understanding and action'.[70] Developing an understanding among active party and union members about how the Conference really worked as a political institution, and about how the power of the 'platform' to control the agenda might be challenged effectively, marked an enormous advance over past practice. But there was an element within the CLPD whose world was contained by what transpired at annual party conferences, where constitutional rules and procedures could be as fascinating and imprisoning as parliaments can be for most MPs and political scientists.

There was also an element within the CLPD that was narrowly

parliamentarist in the sense that it thought that if a Labour Government would only implement the party programme, this would generate mass support just by virtue of the benefits it brought the majority of people; or, at least, that if and when undemocratic forces tried to stop the government from doing so, the people would rush to the defence of parliamentary sovereignty. To put the issue this way, as the CLPD only too often did, was seriously to underrate the necessity and difficulty of generating broad popular support for socialist policies, as opposed just to getting people to vote for a Labour government. But to dismiss the CLPD for its parliamentarism in this sense is to ignore the fact that it generated such 'hysterical overreaction' (as Derer not unreasonably called it)[71] precisely because it presented the most powerful practical challenge that had ever been mounted – certainly from within the Labour Party – to the most central characteristic of parliamentarism: 'the complete separation and non-participation of the masses in the work of parliament'.[72]

To organise even party activists to challenge this was no mean feat, especially in the British context; and it showed the seriousness of what was going on in the Labour Party that the emphasis fell on *organising*, which is a lot harder to do than to issue general populist calls for 'participation'. Most of the main issues had been rehearsed twenty years before in Ralph Miliband's debate with Robert McKenzie in 1958, but it had only been the CLPD's successful organisation of party activists that had finally made this one of the 'immediate issues' in British politics. Miliband had granted that intra-party democracy conflicted with the doctrine of parliamentary government as understood within the British constitutional order, as McKenzie had insisted. But, he had argued with his characteristic clarity, it was precisely this that had to be challenged in more fundamental democratic terms than that order allowed for: '... the electorate is a necessarily amorphous mass, which at least between elections, only acquires political meaning and *becomes capable of political initiative* through organisation, mainly political organisation'. The fact that only a minority of party members 'take an active part in the management of its affairs' was 'certainly deplorable' and needed to be overcome, but the situation was hardly likely to be improved by the application of the 'odd notion of democracy that the active minority should be penalised for the apathy of the majority'. The notion that intra-party democracy would mean that a minority of activists would force MPs to be their puppets was to ignore the MPs' advantages in terms of being able to maintain a high degree of independence from critical constituency activists, and the high degree of deference most GMCs accorded their judgements. 'But "intra-party democracy"', Miliband concluded, 'at least ensures that there *is* dialogue. The leaders of the Labour Party are at least required to argue the case with their followers and seek to persuade them, from reason and not authority, that the course of action they wish to see pursued is indeed opportune.'[73]

If there were grounds for doubting how far the CLPD's strategy and achievements by 1979 would succeed in turning the PLP more to the left, they were revealed in the way party activists actually approached the issue of the selection of candidates for the 1979 election. The interviews conducted by Bochel and Denver among almost 500 people who attended CLP selection conferences in eighteen constituencies in Scotland and the North of England between 1976 and 1979 were very revealing in this respect. In terms of the qualities selectors sought in a candidate, 'sincerity/integrity' (11 per cent), 'educated/intelligent' (9 per cent) and 'articulateness/good speaker' (9 per cent) came well ahead of any specifically mentioned political characteristics. Among the latter, being 'good on local problems' came first (6 per cent), ahead of 'left-wing/true socialist' (3 per cent); indeed even being a 'family man' (4 per cent) was more frequently mentioned. The selection conferences put 'a premium upon ability to communicate, "presence" and demeanour before an audience'; and the selectors, while regretting the fact that so many Labour MPs were middle class, went ahead and chose university-educated middle-class candidates because of 'the strong feeling among selectors that candidates should be well-educated. They do not wish to be embarrassed by an inarticulate, poorly educated candidate. There is a certain amount of deference in this . . .'[74]

In an effort to measure the degree of influence of the CLPD, selectors were asked whether their choice of candidate was designed to influence the balance between left and right in the PLP. Thirty-seven per cent said this had a bearing on their decision, and among those who placed themselves on the left of the party, 63 per cent said it did, a much higher proportion than among those who ranged themselves on the centre-left, centre-right and right of the party. This was taken by the authors of the study as a strong indication of 'the success of groups like the CLPD in alerting left-wingers in the constituencies to the importance of candidate selection as a weapon in the party power struggle'. But more significant, perhaps, in terms of who actually got selected as candidates in 1979, was the fact that only 51 of the 472 selectors interviewed on this indicated that they preferred a left-wing candidate as opposed to the 136 who preferred one on the centre-left, 224 who preferred one in the centre and 61 who preferred someone on the right. The reason for this was not that so few selectors defined themselves on the left (153 did), but that 'more left-wingers are electorally-oriented than are primarily ideological and 71 per cent of them at least partly take electoral considerations into account'. This figure was greater than the corresponding figure in any other group. Bochel and Denver appropriately drew the conclusion from this 'that left-wingers *are* decidedly more ideologically motivated than other selectors but that this does not exclude their taking into account electoral considerations as well'.[75] Overwhelmingly, the left-wingers preferred a candidate to the right of themselves because they recognised that voters were not as left-wing, and therefore believed 'that a candidate should be closer to the centre than their own position in order to have wider electoral appeal'. Even among those who favoured a left-wing candidate, 55 per cent did so because they believed that that candidate would be more attractive to the voters than any other before them. The analysis of the actual voting at selection conferences, moreover, did *not* indicate that left-wingers voted more cohesively as a group than did any other.

All this very strongly suggests that a far more serious question than whether MPs were about to be forced to become puppets of doctrinaire left-wing cliques in the constituencies would have been how many CLPs would continue to be deferential to their MPs, rather than keep themselves actively informed as to their MPs' voting behaviour and actively involved in making them account for that behaviour, as was necessary if reselection was to achieve its purpose. What can be said with certainty is that the claim conventionally made at the time by the social democrats within the party, and which has now become conventional wisdom, to the effect that the Labour new left in the 1970s were unconcerned with asking (as Tony Blair put it in 1995) how to make the party 'accountable and in touch with the people', is without any substance. Of course, it is true that many activists, and the CLPD itself, concentrated their very limited resources and enormous energy on the intra-party struggle, as they had to do in order to win mandatory reselection in the face of tenacious opposition and obstruction. But as Margaret McCarthy had told the 1970 Conference, the point of internal democratic reform was to establish the conditions whereby outward-looking campaigns for recruitment and support could be motivated and made credible. At the municipal level, where some of these preliminary struggles within the party would clear more space for a new politics than at the national level, this could be seen in the creative approach to local government initiated by many of the same people who were involved in the intra-party struggle at the national level.[76]

The most significant feature of this new local socialism was the stress it placed, not just on implementing radical policies, but on redefining (in the words of Maureen Mackintosh, commenting on the GLC experience) the 'way of working within the state [so] that [it] shifts the location of power, changes the access to information of different social groups, and develops the capacities of the previously less powerful. . . . This means actively encouraging new pressure groups among people who previously lacked the capacity to influence state structures.'[77] While the CLPD defined its political goals mainly in terms of ensuring the implementation of party policy by a radical government, this municipal socialist emphasis on the development of popular pressures and self-governing capacities, exemplified in many of the practices of the 'socialist republic of South Yorkshire' and the Greater London Council, came closer to the 'new politics' articulated by Benn in the early 1970s. But it would be wrong to draw too sharp a distinction between what they and the CLPD were about. The stress placed in Sheffield and London on accountability within local Labour parties, on the development of local election manifestos, on ensuring that the manifesto commitments defined the local governments' policy agenda, all showed that the kinds of intra-party reform the CLPD was advancing were a necessary condition for a municipal socialism that transcended 'parliamentary paternalism'. And it was (or should have been) obvious that this practice of municipal socialism could only be generalised and sustained with the active encouragement and support of the party at the national level. This is what David Blunkett had upbraided the Labour Government at the 1975 Party Conference for failing to do, and this point was made even more clearly by Ken Livingstone at the 1980 Conference when he insisted that only if the key constitutional issues of intra-party democracy were dealt with at the national level could local councillors achieve their goals at the local level.[78] As L.J. Sharpe suggested, in assessing how far the movement for a more decentralised socialism might go in the 1980s, the answer depended on whether the Labour Party would go on reinforcing 'unchanged cabinet hegemony', a practice which 'holds no terrors for the Conservative Party, indeed it is for it a logical relationship', but which for the Labour Party had meant cutting itself off from its original roots as 'part of a wider democratic awakening in the bowels of unrestricted capitalism, which its subsequent embrace of centralism has obscured'.

> The whole apparatus of British politics is tributary to the House of Commons, the majority within it, the Cabinet that heads the majority ... No other Western democratic system ... concentrates power so sharply and so decisively ... and the framework that supports it is the party. Thus the party is the beginning and end of the British system of government. Not only does any party which takes part in that system have to fashion its internal arrangements to suit the system, but the system's highly centralised character in turn fashions and shapes the way the party goes about its business and how it views the world: a centralised party for a centralised system.[79]

The CLPD's victory on reselection in 1979 was only the first, and in itself rather slight (albeit highly symbolic) instance of a much broader set of changes that would be required to begin an effective challenge to that system. Whether to try to take up that much broader an agenda for change was what the open confrontation within the Labour Party after 1979 between the supporters and opponents of that system was finally all about. It is quite incorrect to think that the further reforms, alternative policies and leadership challenges that followed were undertaken in blithe disregard of the need to popularise socialist and radical-democratic ideas, and to contrast them with the far-reaching changes articulated by Thatcherism, as conventional wisdom today constantly asserts. On the contrary, the confrontation that ensued over leadership and strategy at the national level within the Labour Party after the 1979 election was so highly charged precisely because of a widespread sense of the enormous implications which the failure of the old policies and politics was now having at every level of British society.

Superficially, the Labour Government's defeat in May 1979 could still have been seen (as it indeed was by those leaders whose ambition went no further than to cling to Labour's political role as a competing parliamentary team) as a mere 'continuation of the pattern established during the 1960s and 1970s of fairly rapid alterations of political power between the Conservative and Labour Parties'.[80] Even the unpopularity of the strikes in the 'Winter of Discontent' only accounted for about 1.5 to 2 per cent of the swing to the Tories in 1979, and while no doubt significant, this had but a small effect on the overall swing as compared, for instance, with the 7 per cent of the swing to the Tories that the Falklands war would account for in 1983.[81] Although Labour's percentage of the vote in 1979 fell to 37 per cent, its worst result since 1931, this was only a fraction less than what it had been elected on in February 1974. (It was the Liberals, rather than Labour, who seemed to suffer most from their association with the Callaghan Government.) And although the Conservative Party's share rose to just under 44 per cent (from its post-war low of just under 36 per cent in October 1974), this was still over 2 per cent *less* than the Tories had garnered in 1970 and some 5 per cent less than the 49 per cent polls they had secured in the 1955 and 1959 elections.

Lying beneath such gross figures, however, was substantial evidence that the rot that had so clearly undermined Labour's support during the 1966 Government had continued during the 1974–79 Government. At the core of this was Labour's declining support even among manual workers. Notably, the number of manual workers who spontaneously identified themselves as working class actually increased from 34 per cent in 1970 to 39 per cent in 1979 (having stood at 44 per cent in 1964), but this yielded no more of a stable base for the Labour leadership's electoralism than for its continuing commitment to corporatism. On the contrary, despite this increase in class identification, there was a further fraying of traditional party identification within Labour's main electoral constituency – precisely when it was most needed to sustain Labour through a period of crisis. The renewed fall in Labour's vote among manual workers in 1979, which had been temporarily arrested in 1974, left the party with only 50 per cent of the manual workers' vote.[82]

Shortly after the 1979 election, Patrick Seyd and Lewis Minkin (who then were devoted academic partisans of the CLPD) clearly expressed the perspective that guided much of the Labour new left's thinking at the time. They did not ignore the evidence of a decline in support for social expenditure and public ownership, even among traditional Labour supporters, but they rejected the conclusion reached by 'many in the parliamentary party, and many outside commentators ... that Labour would be better off accommodating' to this. They pointed to the evidence that showed that 'the drop in support for the party's values took place in two stages – 1964–70, and after February 1974. Between 1970 and 1974 there was a *recovery*, when Labour was in opposition and its policies moved to the left. The important point is that parties help to structure public opinion. The actions and speeches of Labour leaders prepare the ground for future appeals.' The leadership's 'obsession with the role of mass media', however, had devalued the party's own communication role and neglected the essential role of activists, who 'paid close attention to the political messages, and would, *if sufficiently stimulated*, spread them further among others', in the immediate environments of workplace, association and neighbourhood. Far from becoming obsolete, organisational capacities at this level were acquiring a new importance, they insisted, in a context where the relationships between class and party were becoming less habitual. It was precisely this that made the struggle for intra-party democracy so crucial:

> Democracy, accountability, and the health of Labour's grassroots are now inextricably linked. The membership is increasingly assertive and demanding a greater say in policy-making. This democracy encourages membership and raises morale. Conversely, making the party leadership accountable forces it to take an interest in the number, activity and elan of the activists. ... For the first time in fifteen years there is now an emerging consensus that the party activists are significant, and that it is in nobody's interest for the party's roots to shrivel.[83]

The expectation of an emerging consensus within the Labour Party on these terms was, however, a delusion – albeit one shared by a good many Labour intellectuals at the time. Stuart Hall's fear that the struggle to transform the institutions of the British left might prove 'too traumatic', and that the forces representing the status quo within the left would prove 'too rigid, deeply entrenched, and historically binding to be overcome', was to prove far more realistic.[84] It took almost a whole decade before the Labour new left finally won the constitutional reforms

163

on intra-party democracy. Yet these reforms could at best be only an organisational starting-point for a new mode of political representation whereby, to employ Seyd and Minkin's formulation, a socialist political leadership concerned to 'structure public opinion', would also seek to 'stimulate' party activists to spread the political message directly in their communities and workplaces. Yet far from generating such an intra-party strategic consensus, the modest constitutional changes that were achieved provoked such a violent reaction from those who were attached to the old mode of representation that the Labour Party was plunged into the sharpest internal polarisation in its history.

8

The Crisis of Representation: 'Between Agitation and Loyalty'

According to the prevailing myth, the new left in the Labour Party swept all before it following the 1979 election. An 'unstoppable' impetus for change is said to have built up inside the party, emanating from an 'elite' of far left local activists ('Stalinists, 57 varieties of Trotskyists, Tribunites, the emerging "soft left", the old utopian socialists and peaceniks'). Operating under the umbrella of the CLPD, and in alliance with an NEC dominated by Tony Benn, this elite is supposed to have 'wielded extraordinary power', culminating in the imposition on the party of 'that unbelievable document, Labour's 1983 Election Manifesto, which Gerald Kaufman memorably called the longest suicide note in history'.[1]

It is time this myth was dispelled. It is certainly true that after the 1979 election the new left engaged with the forces of the status quo in the party in a confrontation over party structure, strategy and leadership. The intensity of the confrontation, however, was not because the challenge came from the 'far left'. On the contrary, even by the turn of the decade most of the activists who were working to change the Labour Party from within were still regarded on the British left (and for the most part regarded themselves) as rather moderate and 'reformist'; left-wing intellectuals were quite clear about this. When Robin Blackburn interviewed Tony Benn in September 1979, he asked: 'Aren't your remedies very modest considering the magnitude of the crisis?'[2] Benn agreed – and so would have most of the activists who belonged to the CLPD or the Labour Coordinating Committee. And, as we saw in the last chapter, this was even truer of most constituency activists, including even the one-third who defined themselves as left-wing towards the end of the 1970s.

There was a surge of membership in the CLPD – from 443 in 1979 to 807 in 1980 and 1,016 in 1981 before peaking at just over 1,200 in 1982, while the number of CLPs affiliating doubled from 77 to 153 over the same period. The Labour Coordinating Committee (LCC) also continued to grow. Formed, as we saw, in 1978 by a group close to Benn, it had issued an alternative Manifesto in 1979 as part of its initial main goal of popularising the Alternative Economic Strategy. Under the influence of former Labour left student activists associated with the 'Clause IV' group, the LCC's active role in the intra-party struggles in the 1979–81 period was also directed at organising the new left as a counter to Militant and others in the party suspected of Trotskyist inclinations. By 1981, the LCC had 800 members and over fifty affiliated organisations.[3]

Of course, the activists in these groups remained a minority of all party activists. In this sense they could perhaps be called an 'elite', even if not a 'far left' elite; but then they were clearly an elite of a very different kind from the parliamentary elite who were resisting the intra-party campaign for democratic reform of the party. All political activity, including movements for the extension of democracy, involves leadership; the important distinction to be drawn is between those who mobilise support for it and those who oppose it. What is certain is that for a few years after the 1979 election it was the new left activists who had the ear of the party membership. But it was far less any commitment to doctrine, and far more the 'persistent and, sometimes, contemptuous disregard of the voice of the majority, as articulated by conference pronouncements . . . the rejection by the leadership of traditional majoritarian democracy', as Shaw puts it, that called into question the leadership's right to rule in the eyes of so many party members:

> After two instalments of Labour Government had failed to satisfy even their most moderate aspirations, a deep disenchantment with those who ran the party set in. After 1979, this became so ubiquitous, so palpable that it expanded from antagonism to particular leaders to an alienation from the very structure of authority within the party . . . Loyalism and the 'veneration of leadership' virtually vanished, to be replaced, amongst much of the rank and file, by a radically different collective syndrome: a psychology of mistrust, defiance, even of betrayal.[4]

It was in this context that the Labour Party finally had the great debate on democracy that Benn had called for almost a decade earlier, with the new left posing the question, more sharply than ever before, whether a social democratic party might yet be adapted into a political force for radical democratic change. Yet in the confrontation that followed neither the overall balance of power nor the greatest determination to win at all costs belonged to the new left. The deep aversion of the bulk of the parliamentary leadership even to having the debate, let alone seriously trying to refashion Labour's conventional interpretation of parliamentarism, was strongly supported by establishment opinion and virtually all of the British media.[5] Those who resisted change were also helped by the weakness of the old Labour left (epitomised in Michael Foot's brief tenure as leader) and of the union leadership, who still yearned for a better corporatist partnership. Moreover, the old characteristics of diffidence and deference on the part of most party members, while diminished, were by no means wholly eradicated. The result was that, although the new left won a few battles between 1979 and the beginning of 1981, it had lost the war before the latter year was over. Indeed, before the ink was dry on Labour's constitutional changes the counter-insurgency against the new left had become a counter-revolution. The balance of forces in the party had temporarily shifted enough to allow the new left finally to carry through two modest constitutional reforms – reforms that had first been proposed when Labour had gone into opposition a decade earlier. But it had not shifted anything like far enough to enable the new left to resist this counter-revolution when it came.

By 1981, the Foot–Healey axis that had been at the centre of the 1974–79 Labour Government still prevailed in the party's national leadership, despite the defection of the social democrats to the SDP. Indeed, it prevailed partly because of that defection, and because of the fear that more MPs would leave. Between 1981 and the 1983 election, party strategy was dominated by the concern to offer proof that the 'extremists' – a term that was now used indiscriminately to apply to anyone on the left from Tony Benn through the Greater London Council under Ken Livingstone to Militant – were being firmly relegated to their proper place at the margins of British politics. The primary tactic of the right throughout the confrontation with the new left was to use their close contacts with the media 'to discredit and isolate the [Bennite] left by tarring it with the brush of extremism, hence the imagery of "bully boys", the analogies with Eastern Europe and the accusations of intimidation and brutality'. While this tactic fostered 'a public revulsion from the left', as Shaw goes on to note, it earned the right in the Labour Party 'significant political dividends, although at the expense of gravely harming the party'.[6]

If the Labour new left was 'unrealistic', as has so often been alleged, it was especially so in underestimating how far the parliamentary leadership would be prepared to go in order to defeat them. The bitterness and intensity of the backlash against them led some of the Labour new left's original activists (and quite a few left intellectuals who had watched sympathetically from the sidelines) to become confused about what had been the point of struggle. Some of them eventually joined the 'dream team' of Kinnock and Hattersley, under whose leadership crude distinctions were drawn between a 'soft left', who adapted to the reimposition of parliamentary paternalism and social democratic centralism, and a 'hard left', who didn't. But this said more about the factors that rendered the Labour Party incapable of transformation than about what the Labour new left had actually wanted.

Defining the Project: 'Bennism' after 1979

We argued in Chapter 7 that the real significance of the CLPD's victory on reselection at the 1979 Party Conference was as a catalyst for realising broader objectives. In order not to lose overall perspective by getting bogged down in the details of conference votes on constitutional amendments, we need to ask at the outset how the new left in the party defined its aims at this time. There is no single authoritative source for this, of course, given that the Labour new left was a broad movement and lacked any single organisational core (i.e., it was *not* a party within a party).[7] But since the new left activists almost all enthusiastically embraced Benn as their tribune between 1979 and 1981, his speeches and writings probably convey a reasonably good impression of what the Labour new left in general were after. Eric Heffer played an important role on the NEC and at Party Conferences, but he did not share Benn's capacity to articulate the new left's vision and agenda. Ken Livingstone would later write about this period, when he himself had been putting together the radical coalition in the London Labour Party that went on to win control of the GLC in 1981:

> Most important of all was the agenda being set for the Labour movement by Tony Benn himself. . . . In those exhilarating years Tony seemed to be everywhere: on radio and television, writing books and in crowded meeting halls all over Britain. Audiences of hundreds and often thousands listened as he analysed, examined, predicted and gave confidence that we could achieve socialism and, yes, it did involve the very people in that particular audience . . . After the windy rhetoric of the Wilson/Callaghan years, Benn's speeches stood out like paintings by a great artist hung amidst a display of painting by numbers.[8]

What was Benn's agenda? It must first of all be noted that for all the sense of betrayal that fuelled rank and file hostility to the parliamentary elite, one of Benn's most insistent themes was that the problem could not be solved just by clearing out the old leadership. The problems, he insisted, were structural:

> In searching for the reasons why our society is now experiencing a crisis we should not . . . seek out a group of supposedly guilty men and women and demand their replacement by others who would not get to the root of the problem. The real answer requires the wide redistribution of political and economic power. The obstacles that now stand in the path of such a redistribution occur in the institutions of state power as well as in those which uphold private power. They exist inside the Labour and trade union movement as well as in the forces of capital.[9]

This was not, as so many of his detractors claimed, merely a posture, a cover for naked leadership ambitions. Benn was here saying what most of the new left actually felt. As in the early 1970s, it was Benn's capacity to listen to what these activists were saying and to articulate their ideas so effectively that made him their representative at a time when the whole concept of party leadership was being put into question.[10] Who would become party leader was important – no activist would have dreamt of denying it. But had that been the main thing the new left would not have pushed so tenaciously for the broad range of structural changes they did, only some of which would affect who became party leader – and all of which were designed to secure that leader's account-ability to both the parliamentary and extra-parliamentary party.

As for the crisis of economic policy, Benn told the 1979 Party Conference that this was 'the moment of truth, not only for the party, but for the nation', because the belief that the mixed economy could sustain full employment and rising public expenditure had turned out to be an illusion.[11] The ability of democratic governments to engage in national economic management on the basis of Keynesian and corpora-tist policy instruments had been undermined by what he consistently identified in his speeches as 'the international growth of industrial and financial power' as well as by 'the biggest acceleration of technical change the world has seen for many years, with the microchip cutting a swathe through administrative work and modernisation transforming the factories. Moreover, it is happening when we have an expanding labour force.'[12] Those who still concentrated on incomes policy as the means of securing non-inflationary Keynesian growth and full employ-ment (as the parliamentary leadership still did) were offering a prescrip-tion that ignored these fundamental changes.[13] As Benn put it in March 1980: 'The fact is that we have a capitalist system in this country which is no longer capable of sustaining the welfare upon which so much of our post-war politics rested. The real problem is not that the Tory government are pursuing their policy but that there is no alternative to their policy unless we are prepared to achieve a fundamental and irreversible shift in the balance of wealth and power in favour of working people and their families.'[14]

Benn recognised that it was harder to make the case for a radical alternative in these terms than it had been when he first coined this phrase in 1973. Immediately after the 1979 election he identified the primary task as that of restoring 'the legitimacy in the public mind of democratic socialism because the press were actually engaged in outlaw-ing any argument to the left of the centre of British politics'.[15] The new right had succeeded in popularising the claim 'that capitalism and democracy are inextricably bound up together and that both are now facing an attack by anti-democratic socialists. It is a measure of the power and influence of establishment propaganda, regularly put out by the media, that a good many people have been persuaded to accept that false analysis, which is the direct opposite of the truth.' The social democrats in the Labour Party fed this propaganda by designating every challenge to their narrow parliamentarism by the new left as anti-democratic. The central strategic task for the left, therefore, had to be to counter that image in the public mind by building a 'bridge which links democracy with socialism and merges the arguments for one with the arguments for the other'.[16]

How was this to be done? The answer at one level, of course, was by making the case for the Alternative Economic Strategy (AES). As one of its original architects, Francis Cripps, put it in 1981: 'The Alternative Strategy seeks to counterpose democratic national self-government against the anarchic pressures of a global market system,' since there was no possibility 'of democratic control at the international level [or] of effective resistance to market pressures at the local level'.[17] The Labour new left's most fundamental criticism of the social democrats who put the Common Market above everything else was their cavalier attitude towards the Treaty of Rome, which prevented such democratic controls. This is not to say that the Labour new left were oblivious to the importance of international cooperation in making national controls effective. Benn spoke of the need for 'close relations with countries which now make up the EEC ... but only on a completely different basis, through international institutions developed by international labour to meet its needs'.[18] Cripps put it this way: 'The mere fact that the Strategy is national in its scope is not sufficient to condemn it out of hand. Indeed, if successful, it would provide a progressive model for other countries with similar social and political institutions.'[19]

The common observation that the Labour new left's advocacy of import and capital controls proves that they ignored the forces leading to globalisation may be seen, in light of the above, to be superficial and misleading.[20] It was their sensitivity to the power of those forces, unless they were checked, to undermine national policy autonomy that led to the stress the new left put on controls over capital movements. Just as their emphasis on the growth of the multinational corporations was what made the Labour new left's analysis distinctive in the early 1970s, so did their emphasis on the growth of international finance at the end of the 1970s. At the centre of Benn's analysis was the growing scope of financial markets and their power, demonstrated during the IMF crisis in 1976, to force any progressively-inclined government 'to pretend that it wished to follow policies that have in fact been imposed by the pressure of world bankers'.[21] Of course, effective controls over capital movements require international cooperation. Yet the Labour new left's basic point remains valid: the first step towards any such cooperation must be to win support for such controls within each country and commit the state to working to that end. This is why Francis Cripps defined the battle over the AES as in the end really all about 'the nature of democracy itself', counterposing the new left's push for 'a participatory form of democracy' to the current 'passive model whereby professional leaders, proposing policies through the media, receive endorsements from a diffuse electorate'; the latter, he said, was a form of democracy which frustrates 'the left's aims because the media act as a deeply conservative filter of opinions'.[22]

Seen in this light, as they should be, the new left's proposals for reforms in the party form an integral part of their broader agenda for changing the structure of British politics. The reforms were designed to create the kind of party, with the kind of leadership, that would give priority to realising this broader agenda. There was considerable concern after the 1979 election to go beyond the intra-party debate, to reach outwards and try to get the new left's arguments aired among the broader public. It was no accident that, alongside reselection, the most important resolution passed at the 1979 Conference concerned 'the absence of genuine press freedom, access or diversity'; or that its mover, Bill Keys of the Graphical and Allied Trades union, explicitly made the connection between the debate on party democracy and the resolution's call for 'a national debate on alternative forms of democratic ownership and control of the press'.[23]

The principle of accountability, so central to the CLPD's campaign for intra-party reform, was a common thread that ran through the Labour new left's entire reform agenda. As we saw in Chapter 3, Benn had always defined the question of the democratisation of the media in terms of accountability, and this preoccupation also guided his wide-ranging proposals after 1979 for limiting prime ministerial power and patronage ('a constitutional premiership'), and ending bureaucratic control and secrecy ('a constitutional civil service'). This entailed a sharp challenge to Labour's traditional statism:

> ... democratic control must be established at every level in the public sector in order to create a wholly new vision of what society could be like if we lifted the stranglehold of market forces. It is not state socialism run from the top with a centralised bureaucracy as its instrument ... All societies, and all systems, require discipline if they are to work and the most effective of all disciplines is the self-discipline of real democracy. In this concept all power is held in trust and those who exercise it must be held to account for their stewardship by those over whom their authority is exercised. The basis of any new constitutional settlement must be the extension of democracy into the rest of society, in industry, the public authorities and the public services, organised wherever possible close to the people and away from the dictates of the centre.[24]

This vision matched closely the kind of 'in and against the state' ideas that inspired a good deal of the left in Britain in this period. They were famously taken up by the GLC under Livingstone, and at least until the defeat of the new left on the NEC in 1981–82 they also informed national party strategy, as the following quotation from an NEC Campaigns Committee document of June 1981 makes clear:

> On ... the management of public sector bodies, we believe this to be a crucial missing element of our past approach, very ably exploited by the Tories at the last election. There is, indeed, a clear sense of alienation felt by many Labour voters concerning the very institutions we will need to implement much of our programme – an alienation created by poor quality of service, buck-passing, allegedly wasteful expenditure, and off-hand, patronising treatment of clients and customers. Accordingly, in seeking to win support for public ownership and public services, it will not be enough to propagandise for more of the same. We will *also* need to demonstrate publicly that we do not regard the present operations of these institutions complacently but, on the contrary, that we are committed to finding more efficient, and more responsive, ways of running them.[25]

This, it should be noted, was in a document planning election strategy. The myth that (in Tony Blair's words) 'nobody asked how to make the party accountable and in touch with the people', is clearly belied by the explicit objective of this document, namely, 'to persuade Labour voters – and especially new, potential or wavering voters – that Labour is the party for them'.

All of the themes that had emerged out of the new left's turn to community and social movement politics in the early 1970s also strongly informed the Labour new left's agenda at the end of the decade. When Benn defined the key task after the 1979 election as that of restoring 'the legitimacy in the public mind of democratic socialism', he first of all thought in terms of making 'the Labour Party reintegrate with other activists with whom we sympathised, such as the women's movement and Friends of the Earth';[26] and he recognised, too, that this had to mean broadening out beyond traditional conceptions of the constituency for socialism. As he put it in the preface to a collection of speeches he published during the 1981 deputy leadership campaign: 'Inequality in Britain is not by any means confined to the class relations deriving from the ownership of capital.' Although this remained 'a central obstacle which must be overcome if any real progress is to be made', it was 'a pity that the nature of the argument for socialism should have been so narrowly conceived.... If democracy is based on a moral claim to equality, the issues opened up are as wide as life itself' – including women's inequality and discrimination against ethnic and racial minorities, and gays.[27] Benn expressed this in generous, not reproachful or recriminatory, tones; his aim was to allow people 'to draw new energy ... to take up the struggle with renewed faith and commitment'.[28]

Given the impact of feminist and black activists on community level politics throughout the 1970s it was hardly surprising that the struggles of women's and black sections within the party became the defining elements of the Labour new left's agenda.[29] Ken Livingstone actually went so far as to credit Benn with 'being the first to highlight the need for a wider Labour movement actively encouraging the involvement of women and black people alongside the traditional white male trade unionists'.[30] Be that as it may, the later charge that Benn was too narrowly tied to a defence of traditional trade unionism simply ignores what he was saying. It was actually large sections of the Tribunite left associated with Foot (and later Kinnock), not to mention Trotskyists and elements of the old CP broad left, who were more likely to be suspicious of the vision of the Labour Party as a federation of social movement groups that was being articulated by Benn. And while the others would sometimes actively play on working-class parochialism, Benn was often prepared to challenge it directly, particularly by strongly encouraging trade union involvement in 'the evolution of sensible strategies of development upon which communities depend for their lives and amenities', and arguing that this depended on forging strong links with activists engaged in anti-nuclear, ethnic, pensioners' and women's issues.[31]

In advancing this argument Benn was in fact making the most pointed criticism of the trade union leadership's embrace of corporatism to be offered by any leading European politician on the left. Not only rank and file workers, he argued, but even capitalists and bureaucrats had become disillusioned with the constraints of corporatism, leaving many trade union leaders defensively clinging to this 'sterile partnership'. He took up again the position he had articulated in the early 1970s, that unions should use their bargaining role to negotiate themselves into a position of power in the enterprise, with enabling legislation for the disclosure of company information and planning agreements backing up enterprise level bargaining over 'the whole range of company policy including decisions about research, development, marketing, investment, mergers, manpower planning and the distribution of profits with a requirement to agree on all these matters before company policy is decided'.[32] Today this could be called 'stakeholding with teeth', but Benn rejected the idea that this was all about 'co-partnership which seeks consensus in the interests of shareholders'. His model was rather workers' initiatives like the one at Lucas Aerospace; he hoped that decentralised planning of production at the company level would inhibit the re-emergence of corporatism. Such ideas informed the TUC–Labour Party Liaison Committee's *Industrial Democracy and Economic Planning* document of 1982, which also reflected the unions' concern, as Benn put it, that the Bullock Report of the last Labour Government had been 'too centralised in its conception and had failed to allow for the diversity of industrial circumstances and union attitudes which existed'.[33]

Benn warned, in this context, against union power structures that were 'top heavy, undemocratic and corporatist', and expected that the intra-party controversy ('Democracy always arouses controversy because it is about real power') would have positive effects inside the unions in terms of 'growing pressure ... to increasingly provide for regular elections, for reselection, for a full disclosure of information and for the strengthening of accountability and the democratic disciplines that that involves'. It was necessary to establish workplace branches of the Labour Party as quickly as possible to link these two internal processes of change.[34] There was a need for a massive expansion of trade union education ('conceived on the widest possible basis') and for programmes which would 'allow the trade unions to speak directly to the people about their problems, aspirations and work, free from the present distortion and imbalance'. He consistently urged that the unions had to pay careful strategic attention to the impact of strikes on popular attitudes ('The more picketing can be seen in its educational context, and the less it can be presented as a mere show of force, the better') and proposed imaginative new forms of industrial action which did not involve a blanket denial of public services, yet put effective pressure on management and capital.[35]

> If the trade union movement is seeking to offer an alternative industrial, social and political perspective for the future of Britain, it will be called upon to provide a far more positive and constructive leadership than its critics believe is possible ... If the sights of the trade unions are lifted above the defensive battles on the industrial front to a bolder perspective, the alliance with the Labour Party will need to be strengthened at every level. But if the lessons of the past are learned, democratic socialism will be seen to be quite different from the consensus corporatism that marked the evolution of labour power in the post-war years.[36]

But in rejecting corporatism Benn was in no way posing the old dichotomy between reform and revolution. At the 1979 Party Conference, recommending on behalf of the NEC that Conference reject a Militant-inspired resolution calling for the nationalisation of the 200 leading corporations, Benn described himself as 'a Clause IV socialist, becoming more so as the years go by'; but he insisted that if the Conference expected the PLP to take its resolutions seriously then the Conference had also to take the Labour Party seriously, as 'a party of democratic, socialist reform. I know that for some people "reform" is a term of abuse. That is not so. All our great successes have been the product of reform.' Taking reform seriously, however, meant coming to terms with

... the usual problem of the reformer; we have to run the economic system to protect our people who are now locked into it while we change the system. And if you run it without seeking to change it then you are locked in the decay of the system, but if you simply pass resolutions to change it without consulting those who are locked in the system that is decaying, then you become irrelevant to the people you seek to represent. ... We cannot content ourselves with speaking only to ourselves; we must raise these issues publicly and involve the community groups because we champion what they stand for. We must win the argument, broaden the base of membership, not only to win the election but to generate the public support to carry the policies through.[37]

This remarkably clear-sighted and thoughtful argument was ignored by the entire mainstream media, including *The Guardian*. Scarcely anyone who did not attend Labour Party Conferences, including most of the left, would have known he had made it. They would have heard it, however, if they were among the capacity crowd of 2,600 at Central Hall, Westminster who came to hear Benn and Stuart Holland debate with Paul Foot and Hilary Wainwright in March 1980 at the famous 'Debate of the Decade' between the left inside and outside the Labour Party. The revolutionary socialist groups, Benn insisted there, confused real reform with revolution. Their talk of revolution 'implies, and nobody believes it, that there is a short cut to the transfer of power in this country ... What the socialist groups really do is to analyse, to support struggle, to criticise the Labour Party, to expand consciousness, to preach a better morality. These are all very desirable things to do. But they have very little to do with revolution.'[38] The socialist groups had to come to see that they too were part of the problem, and that the limits of their own practices, just like those of the left in the Labour Party, could also be measured in the simple fact that 'we do not have a majority of support outside for any of our solutions'. It had to be recognised, moreover, that even those among 'the rank and file' who were acutely aware of the inadequacies of the Labour leadership's policies, and were sympathetic to socialist solutions, were not prepared to agitate for them at critical moments:

> The reality is that the rank and file of the labour movement do not want to put at risk the survival of a Labour government. We must be prepared to face the fact that *the problem of the balance between agitation and loyalty has got to be solved*. Unless we can deal with that problem we are going to continue to be radical in opposition and somewhat conservative in office.[39]

This was indeed the Labour new left's central dilemma. For the contradiction between agitation and loyalty existed not only when Labour was in office. An agenda for change as extensive as that which was being advanced after 1979 was obviously going to be fought tooth and nail, and the divisions this would engender would have to be covered over in good time before the next election if Labour was to have a chance of winning it. Benn recognised this, but hoped that after fifteen months of controversy, during which the new left would 'lay the foundations' of its agenda for change, the party would reunite to 'campaign together' for the 1983 election.[40] But this scenario assumed that the centre-right parliamentarians would be as loyal to the party as the long-suffering rank and file activists. This was very soon shown to be a huge miscalculation.

For those social democrats who stayed in the party, almost as much as those who left, evinced a very different mix of loyalty and agitation – and their agitation, unlike that of the rank and file activists, had the national media as its amplifier. Their claim that it was impossible to win elections with radical socialist policies was initially dented by the Mitterrand victory in France, and Labour actually ran well ahead in the opinion polls all through 1980 and most of 1981 despite the socialist policies it had adopted; but the social democrats' persistent denigration of the left through the media eventually took its toll on the party's popularity. The problem faced by the Labour new left in this context was captured by 'the usual problem of the reformer', just as Benn had identified it at the 1979 Conference. Those who set out to reform the party were concerned with keeping the party electorally viable in order to protect all those who looked to it for the protection of their immediate political interests; yet if they refrained from trying to change it, they would be locked into the decay of the system. It was the most intractable of dilemmas. That Benn was so acutely aware of it, and yet refused to give up, reflected not only the strength of his commitment but the depth of his understanding that accommodating oneself to this 'decaying system' (as he saw it, in moral as much as in material terms) was itself no long-term answer. This approach was made all the more poignant by his recognition – even on the optimistic scenario that the foundation for changing the Labour Party might be laid in as short a time as fifteen months – that the larger democratic socialist agenda could only be realised on the basis of a very protracted and long-term struggle. As he wrote in his diary on the eve of the 1979 Conference: 'I think we are going to be engaged in the most bitter struggle over the next ten years, and if this [new right] philosophy gains hold in the public mind then not only might we not win the next Election but socialism could be in retreat in Britain until absolutely vigorous campaigns for democracy are mounted again.'[41]

The battle for the Labour Party in the years after 1979 was really about the role it would play in relation to that long-term struggle. It was because it sensed this that the new left fought the battle with such determination.

Insurgency and Counter-insurgency: the NEC and the Union Leadership

As we have seen, all through the 1970s the National Executive of the Labour Party had itself been trapped in the contradiction between agitation and loyalty. It had often taken the lead in advancing radical policies, but it had tried to blunt the pressures for intra-party democracy. Immediately after the 1979 election, however, the NEC not only finally asserted its procedural right to facilitate the placing of constitutional amendments on reselection, and the election of the leader and deputy leader, on the agenda of the 1979 Conference; it also added an amendment asserting its own right to have the final say on what policy commitments were to be included in election manifestos.

The NEC's adoption of this position was unprecedented. As Minkin has put it: 'On all previous occasions in opposition, when the left had produced constitutional amendments to limit the power of the PLP, the NEC had successfully aided the fight to fend them off. On this occasion, for the first time in party history, the NEC put itself at the service of the insurrection . . .'[42] But in following Benn's and Heffer's lead in this respect, the majority on the NEC were only acknowledging the breadth and depth of sentiment among most party and union activists and were simply refusing to go on providing cover for the parliamentary leadership when this had become impossible.

What must also not be ignored is the way Callaghan himself threw down the gauntlet immediately after the election, playing his own part in inviting the headlines that were to define for the general public what was happening inside the party ('Jim opens war on Benn's NEC' was a mild one, in *The Guardian*).[43] Although he knew that an inquest on the death of the previous Government was inevitable, Callaghan immediately insisted that there would be no inquest within the Shadow Cabinet itself and that he expected collective Cabinet responsibility to be maintained.[44] Foot did not dissent from this (obviously, by virtue of the crucial part played by the 'Foot–Healey axis' in that government, he had even more incentive now than in 1970 to avoid 'a grand inquisition on all the delinquencies of the Government').[45] But for Benn, who had already decided not to stand for election to the Shadow Cabinet in order to be finally free of such restraints, this was 'the last straw'. The press sensationalised Benn's announcement of his decision as a naked bid for the leadership by the far left; and Callaghan used it as an occasion once again to challenge Benn with the information (which Benn presumed that MI5 were supplying through wire taps) that two members of the NEC were in touch with 'King Street' (the Communist Party office). It was clear that the counter-insurgency Callaghan had initiated in 1976 was to continue. Indeed, one reason he again gave for retaining PLP control over the state funds that were now being made available to support opposition party research was that if the funds were passed to the NEC, they would be sustaining a 'Marxist party'.[46]

This immediately gave rise to a highly contentious dispute with the NEC, but it had nothing whatever to do with Marxist infiltration. In 1970, when the party sponsored the research effort that had shifted policy leftwards, former Labour cabinet ministers had been placed on the defensive, and had sorely missed the research support they had got used to as ministers. The Labour Government of 1974 had introduced a programme of state aid for research by opposition parties (known as 'Short money' after Edward Short, who initiated the programme). Mrs Thatcher, when in opposition, had passed this money to the Conservative Central Office. Callaghan refused to follow this procedure lest it make the Shadow Cabinet dependent on the Labour Party's research department, rather than recruit their own researchers to help them pursue their own very different policy agenda. Perhaps the most telling signal of what the outcome of the post-1979 confrontation would be was that the union leadership took the parliamentary leadership's side in this crucial dispute.

Among the many misconceptions that persist concerning the strength of the challenge to the autonomy of the parliamentary leadership after the 1979 election, none is perhaps more ill-founded than the notion that the challenge came from the 'union bosses'.[47] We have already seen that the emergence of the Trade Unions for Labour Victory (TULV) in 1978 was central to the counter-insurgency, and that the union leaders had played a key role in repelling the CLPD's reforms and neutralising the NEC before the 1979 election. This did not change after the election, although even moderate union leaders now often took the lead in sponsoring socialist policy resolutions at Party Conferences which explicitly attacked the failed policies of the Labour Government. Indeed there was, if anything, at the same time an intensification of the pressure by the parliamentary leadership on the union leadership and by the union leadership on the NEC. The long-term goal of much of the centre-right of the PLP was, certainly, to establish a relationship between the party and the unions that entailed 'a much looser link, possibly along the lines between the Democrats and the unions in the US';[48] but in the short term, the strategy of Callaghan and Healey was, as John Cole put it in *The Observer*:

> to organise union votes to restore Labour stability to something nearer what existed in Attlee's day; recapture control of the NEC at first by fighting for union votes, later by restructuring. In other words ... to use Labour's creaking machinery, yet simultaneously appeal over it to arouse a new constituency in the country. It is a daunting task ...[49]

Just weeks before the 1979 Party Conference, some of Britain's most senior union leaders made an unprecedented personal visit to a meeting of the NEC's Organisation Committee. Benn's diary records the occasion as follows: 'At 11.30 in trooped this tremendous delegation – David Basnett, Moss Evans, Bill Keys, Alan Fisher, Clive Jenkins, Lawrence Daly, Joe Gormley – a huge and powerful group of people.' Basnett presented on behalf of the group the 'unanimous view of all the trade union leaders' associated with the TULV that all constitutional matters be once again put off until after a Commission of Inquiry into the organisation of the party had been established and reported. Benn commented:

> The enormity of that statement took my breath away. Not one of these individuals had consulted their trade union conferences or delegations. They were demanding that we neuter the Conference so that delegates would have no opportunity to vote on matters on which they had been mandated. That Jim Callaghan should wheel out the unions to crush the NEC was a grave warning of what could happen . . . [I]t was a démarche really. These men had come in to tell us what they expected the party to do.[50]

Remarkably enough, the NEC stood up to the pressure. While agreeing to the inquiry, the NEC refused to take constitutional issues off the agenda of the 1979 Conference (only Michael Foot joined Golding and four other trade union representatives in voting to do so). Given that 'from the right of the PLP there was an open invitation to union leaders to use the union money to bring the NEC . . . in line', as Minkin shows, and that some union leaders actually made financial threats of a 'naked character . . . unimpaired at this time by any remonstrance from the mass media for this behaviour', it took consider-able courage for the NEC, as Heffer privately put it, to refuse to be 'pushed around by union leaders'.[51] Given that the union intervention involved such prominent men of the left as Daly, Jenkins, Evans, Keys and Fisher, Minkin is right to insist that there was more to it than the kind of rooted political hostility towards the left that motivated the behaviour of the right of the PLP and their union allies. What motivated the left-wing union leadership was, rather, their managerial inclination to have as little mess and trouble as possible in the labour movement.[52] For this reason, they were especially responsive to Foot's entreaties from within the parliamentary team. They also were sensitive to the bad press the unions were receiving, and didn't want to be held responsible by the media for the constitutional reforms. Yet, those, like Minkin, who offer these considerations in defence of their action fail to appreciate how sad a commentary this is on these union leaders, given the severity of the crisis of social democracy and the appeal to many of their members of the new right's populist initiatives. What was needed in this context was political creativity and a commitment to intensive political education of their membership, not cautious and defensive managerialism hidden behind the insincere sponsorship of radical socialist resolutions at party conferences.

There was also more to it than just being honest brokers between left and right factions, as some of those involved in the intervention pretended. The corporatist aspirations that underwrote the TUC General Council's 'concordat' with the 1974–79 Labour Government had implicated them in the Government's 'delinquencies'; and the uprising against wage restraint at their own union conferences, as well as during the winter of discontent, was coalescing with the CLPD's mobilisation in the unions in support of the constitutional amendments on party democracy. Many union activists and officials, displaying little sympathy for the pressures their leaders had succumbed to, played an 'unusually influential role in this period' in securing union mandates for votes at Party Conferences on constitutional and policy issues that ran 'counter to the known wishes of the unions' most senior leaders'.[53] Benn was driven to the unpleasant conclusion that it was not only the traditional right-wing union leaders who were opposed to intra-party democracy, because 'it would take power out of the hands of the trade union bosses and give it to the rank and file', it also applied to left-wing union leaders, not least

> the ageing ex-communist left who are terrified of political initiatives. As a result of a lifetime of struggle, they have got themselves near the seats of power, but have lost their grassroots support now, and are afraid that if you stir it up they will be defeated either by an angry right-wing backlash or by a real new left. If you go along with that crowd, you are committing yourself to political decay of a very serious kind.[54]

The Labour new left did have some strong support within the unions, of course. On the General Council (and therefore also on the trade union side of the Liaison Committee) the leaders of a number of smaller unions combined with Walter Greendale, the Hull docker who was lay Chairman of the TGWU, to form a strong minority group supporting the positions of the NEC. The number of union branches which affiliated to the CLPD increased from forty-seven in 1978 to 112 in 1980; and financial support came from ten national union offices (including NUPE and ASTMS) and from regional or sectoral sections of numerous other unions. Motions to disaffiliate from the Labour Party put by several branches to NUPE's 1979 conference were countered by arguments not to opt out of the struggle but to 'campaign with increased militancy within the party for constructive democratisation'; while the TGWU's biennial conference in 1979 was 'marked not just by the very substantial number of resolutions on Labour democracy which were submitted from every quarter of the union's empire, but also by the unmistakable strength of grassroots feeling revealed in the course of the actual debate'.[55] In this context, the agreement of the union leaders to act as messengers to the NEC on behalf of the parliamentary leadership (or even, as they themselves no doubt saw it, as very influential mediators) led them into actions that were fundamentally undemocratic as well as contradictory. Moss Evans, who in 1978 had spoken from the platform of the newly formed Labour Coordinating Committee, and was apparently a 'believer in a participatory union membership and dispersal of power ... and, in general, sympathetic to the overall thrust of the left's constitutional case',[56] directly contradicted his union conference's decisions when he came to ask the NEC to take constitutional reform off the agenda of the 1979 Conference. Keys, Fisher and Jenkins were in much the same position.

The trade union leaders knew by the time they visited the NEC that they could not prevent reselection being passed if the NEC left it on the 1979 Conference agenda. What was really at issue when the union leaders visited the NEC was that they could not assure the parliamentary leadership that the other constitutional amendments would not pass as well – especially the one that proposed a broader franchise for the election of the leader – before the PLP had a chance to elect Callaghan's successor (who almost everyone assumed at the time would be Healey). Social democrats and media pundits who had always considered it a merit of the British political system that the opinions of 'swing voters' should determine Labour's electoral strategy now launched a tirade of abuse against swing voters in the Party Conference. The notion that a 'handful of delegates ... could decide the party's future shape' suddenly became abhorrently undemocratic.[57] Usually it was the Engineering union's delegates they had in mind – since a shift by just one or two of them would be enough for their delegation to defy their right-wing leadership's capacity to wield the union's block vote on behalf of the social democrats.

In the event, the union leaders' wishes most often prevailed with their delegations. This was partly due to their traditional power and prestige, but also because beyond the many union delegates who showed an inclination to vote for the CLPD's reforms, those who were prepared to provide more active support – offer information and advice, write letters, distribute CLPD material, lobby their union colleagues – were, as the CLPD admitted, 'still dreadfully scarce and desperately needed'.[58] Only three of the unions with over 100,000 votes consistently voted for all three constitutional reforms at both the 1979 and 1980 conferences (the TGWU, NUPE and ASTMS).[59] Yet, given the overwhelming support from the constituency delegates, this was sufficient in 1979 to win approval in principle for NEC control over the Manifesto, as well as finally to secure the passage of reselection. The proposal to expand the franchise for the election of the leader and deputy leader beyond the PLP was defeated, but the Conference's virtually unanimous decision to eliminate the three-year rule ensured that it would be back on the agenda in some form in 1980.

1980: The Year of Living Traumatically

The hopes entertained by the parliamentary leadership that between the 1979 and 1980 conferences the Commission of Enquiry which the TULV had forced upon the NEC would put an end to the constitutional revolt were also disappointed. They were dashed not only by the NEC choosing strong supporters of the reforms to sit as its representatives on the enquiry alongside Basnett, Duffy, Evans, Jenkins and Keys from the TULV; but also by the overwhelming support for all three constitutional reforms among the 2,460 submissions made to it.[60] In the end, the enquiry, unable to break the stalemate, had no recommendations to make to the 1980 Conference on any of the three constitutional reforms.

Much to the chagrin of the Shadow Cabinet and the centre-right of the PLP, however, there was no such stalemate on policy. While the enquiry was still meeting, an NEC policy statement, *Peace, Jobs, Freedom*, was overwhelmingly passed at a special policy conference in May 1980. Subtitled 'Labour's call to the people: how to stop the drift to catastrophe', *Peace, Jobs, Freedom* opened as follows:

> In the advanced, industrialised world, including Britain, mounting unemployment – now standing at more than 17 million – is the price of capitalist economic decline.
>
> In the poor, undeveloped countries the despair of poverty and hunger is deepening and threatens peace.
>
> The spread of weapons, spearheaded by the quickening race in nuclear weapons and their proliferation, makes the dangers of a Third World War very real.
>
> As peoples and countries become more dependent on each other ... international cooperation becomes more necessary but harder to secure and sustain.
>
> Britain should play a full part in making the world a fairer, safer, more co-operative international community. Under this Government it is not ...
>
> Instead of a Government dedicated to the fair treatment of people wherever they live or whatever their circumstances, we confront a Government determined to uphold the harsh attitudes of the market place ...[61]

The statement went on to set out ten central features of Labour's alternative: (i) 'the restoration and maintenance of full employment', brought about through (ii) economic expansion 'spearheaded by public expenditure'; (iii) a 'comprehensive and powerful system of price controls' supplemented by the 'closest cooperation' with the unions (thereby hinting at incomes policy); (iv) efforts to secure an international agreement for joint expansionary policies to stimulate world trade, supplemented by 'planning our trade in manufactures and our international payments to protect and promote industrial development in Britain' and assist Third World development; (v) 'strict controls over international capital movements' alongside working for 'international agreement to bring about greater currency stability'; (vi) statutory planning agreements to 'guide the activities of the huge companies which dominate the economy' towards a target of doubling manufacturing investment, while also extending public enterprise to secure 'a significant public stake – and a degree of control' in each important industrial sector; (vii) progress towards 'genuine industrial democracy in both the public and private sectors and commitment to repeal of the Tory Employment Bill'; (viii) 'work-sharing' through time off for study, longer holidays, early voluntary retirement and a progressive move to a thirty-five-hour working week; (ix) 'fundamental reform of the EEC', reconsidering continued membership only after using 'every means at our disposal . . . to convince our partners of the need for radical change'; and (x) since 'these policies cannot be implemented whilst the present unequal balance of wealth and power persists', commitment to a 'range of measures involving the strengthening of the House of Commons, the abolition of the House of Lords, and the introduction of a full Freedom of Information Act to strengthen democracy against privilege and patronage'.

To all this was added, in a statement issued at the height of the revived peace movement of the early 1980s, opposition to 'the manufacture of cruise missiles and the neutron bomb' and 'refusal to permit their deployment in Britain by the United States or any other country'; and a commitment to East–West negotiations for multilateral nuclear disarmament, including a pledge 'to ensure that cruise missiles and Soviet SS20s are both withdrawn'. This was the policy of the Labour Party as Thatcher's popularity plummeted ('The most unpopular Prime Minister since polls began', according to a headline in *The Times* on October 1980) amidst rapidly rising unemployment and rising charges for public utilities and local authority services.

This policy agenda was enthusiastically adopted and supported by the Tribune left in the PLP (including Foot and his allies on the NEC and the Shadow Cabinet), together with traditionally moderate as well as leftist union leaders. Indeed, especially as regards the Common Market and a non-nuclear defence strategy, it was they who took the lead in insisting it did not go far enough. In a speech to the May special conference on *Peace, Jobs, Freedom* Jack Straw argued that: 'as long as the Treaty of Rome remains unchanged and we are members, then it will be impossible for us to implement many of the ... excellent policies in the document. I believe we have to face up to the facts, that the prospects of radical change in the Common Market are very small indeed.'[62] Peter Shore echoed this at the October Party Conference: 'there is no longer any dispute about ... the incompatibility with socialist policies of what is enshrined in the Common Market'. Robin Cook demanded that the party adopt a clearer position on defence, deriding those who approached the nuclear issue in terms of mere electoral calculations ('I cannot think of a more frivolous position on which to make up our minds on the central issue facing mankind') while at the same time arguing that there was no hope of 'convincing the people in the streets, in the factories, in the pubs so long as they see us hedging and fudging our opposition to nuclear arms'. And Gerald Kaufman, whom history may well mainly remember for coining the derisive 'longest suicide note in history' phrase, insisted in 1980 (as the Shadow Cabinet spokesman responsible for countering the popularity among many workers of the Thatcherite policy of selling off council houses) that 'we must have a socialist housing policy – a policy based on need, not the market. Housing is not a commodity to be bought and sold.'

These MPs were following the pattern set in 1970–73, accommodating themselves to radical policies while at the same time also acceding to the parliamentary leadership's opposition to the demand for accountability and intra-party democracy. Yet the circumstances were now very different, thanks to the efforts of the new left activists over the course of the decade, as the formation of the Rank and File Mobilising Committee in May and June 1980 showed. The RFMC brought CLPD and LCC activists together with a broader range of left groups in the party to conduct a common campaign – including twenty rallies at different sites around the country in the run-up to the 1980 Conference – for five key constitutional demands: defence of reselection; control of the Manifesto by the NEC; election of the leader and deputy leader by the whole party; defence of the NEC's structure; and accountable and open decision-making within the PLP.

In this context, and as it became clear that the union leaders were not going to be able to frustrate all these demands, the social democrats were more and more inclined to vent publicly their long-standing misgivings about their relationship to Labourism. This was highlighted by the 'Gang of Three' – Shirley Williams, David Owen and Bill Rodgers – issuing an open letter in August 1980 which foreshadowed their later decision with Roy Jenkins to form a new party of the centre. Social democrats whose politics were above all defined in terms of their unqualified support for the EEC and NATO had put principle over party unity in supporting the EEC a decade before, and NATO two decades before. And if the General Secretaries could no longer protect their freedom to ignore the Conference on such matters, then in the early 1980s some of them were prepared to form a rival party.

This was not the position of the centre-right majority in the PLP and Shadow Cabinet, epitomised by Callaghan, Healey and Hattersley. They were still prepared not to take too seriously the kind of radical policy agenda that the NEC and the Tribune left were advancing. They knew how to 'speak socialist' on appropriate occasions, and were well aware that after a bout of dispiriting Labour government, Labour conferences traditionally were such occasions. But this is not to say they were anything but very seriously concerned about the impending departure of the social democrats and about the fact that the dynamic of both policy development and constitutional reform was moving leftwards. The Campaign for Labour Victory group of Labour MPs sent a message to the 1980 TUC Congress which accused the new left of having 'only one purpose – to seek to foist the views of an NEC clique on every other section of the party'.[63] And the more they expressed this concern, the more fearful the MPs in the Tribune Group grew about how large the split in the parliamentary party might eventually become. In this sense, the situation in the extra-parliamentary party was taken very seriously indeed by the whole of the parliamentary party.

In fact it drove some Labour MPs to distraction. What Dick Clements, the editor of *Tribune*, appropriately termed a 'collective hysteria' ran through the Labour Party from the summer of 1980 on – a condition which afflicted the PLP in particular.[64] As Jack Straw, looking back in 1995, put it: 'The Parliamentary Party was in a state of high neurosis ... a very important political institution [was] having a nervous break-down.'[65] Politicians who prided themselves on their realism made, with increasing frequency and passion over the course of the next twelve months, what Shaw appropriately terms the 'far-fetched and specious' claim (spread all over the media) that MPs were being turned into 'grovelling zombies' (Shore) who would do the bidding of a 'vanguard party' (Healey).[66] But it was not only cynical politicians who led the media in making such absurd charges, it was genuinely traumatised ones.

What traumatised them was that their very identity as professional representatives was being challenged. As *The Guardian*'s Peter Jenkins put it, what *had* seemed to have been settled in Britain almost a century before – that 'rule by the elite' would survive the extension of the franchise and the development of mass parties – was once again being challenged by an 'unrepresentative grassroots elite eager to seize power from the ruling parliamentary elite'.[67] What was being put in question by the confrontation in the Labour Party was nothing less than the political meaning of the word 'representative'. Raymond Williams analysed the situation brilliantly in a Socialist Society pamphlet at the time:

> In broad terms, a class of 'representatives' has been formed, initially in close relation to bodies of formed opinion, who at a certain point enter personal careers of being representatives, in what is really the old symbolic sense. They are persons of political experience and judgement. If they do not already (through some accident of career or election) have anyone or anywhere to 'represent', there is public discussion and private action about 'finding them a seat'. Thus it often happens that there are important political 'representatives' who do not yet represent anybody, in the carefully retained formal sense. Defined in this way, so that the representative amounts to a career, a position or a job, the actual process of representing formed opinions can be set aside or made subordinate, to the extent that the 'failure' to select or reselect such a person can be described as 'sacking' or 'firing' her or him, turning her or him out of her or his 'job'.[68]

In 1980, the backbench Labour MP was being forced to face the crisis of political representation that has appeared in every liberal democracy over the past two decades – and to face it more squarely than any others have had to do. At the 1980 Party Conference, Joe Ashton (who had been Benn's PPS in the 1970s) made a bid for the sympathy of the trade union delegates: 'If an MP gets the sack and he walks away into the sunset and says nothing – he does not get a penny redundancy pay or anything . . .'[69] David Owen saw the issue in less economistic terms: '. . . what really lay behind reselection . . . wasn't to have the reasonable accountability for a Member of Parliament who may be getting too old or out of touch and who ought to be called to account by his constituency, no no, they wanted [him] to be called to account by the thirty or forty hard-line lefties who dominated the Constituency Labour Party'.[70] The 'real' constituency that Owen had in mind was, of course, outside the party altogether – it was the amorphous and unorganised electorate. But even here the traumatised backbench MPs could not find much comfort, since if they had to bend to the wishes of the social democrats on the Common Market, the opinion polls on this issue gave them least claim to being 'representative' of public sentiment. The problem for the average MP, moreover, was not really that there were so many 'hard-line lefties' in his or her CLP; they were increasingly afraid that they might not be able to hold the support of the thirty or forty active party members who were mostly far from being hard-line lefties. A good part of the trauma that MPs were going through related to the fact that the centre-right parliamentary leadership no longer provided them with a set of arguments (as they had in Crosland's day) that gave them any confidence they could defend the votes that the Labour whips expected them to cast. The backbenchers' problem was the fear that they were likely to end up as the fall guys for a parliamentary leadership who had abandoned Keynesianism and had nothing else to offer, yet on whom they still depended for the advancement of their careers.

There was, on the other hand, plenty of grist for the media mill about 'hard-line lefties' in the postures which by no means very radical CLP delegates struck at the 1980 Party Conference. Patricia Hewitt, from the St Pancras North CLP, insisted that however angry people ought to be at what Thatcher was doing, 'many of us at this conference are also angry about much of what the last Labour Government did . . . And we have a right to be angry and to do something about our anger.' Pat Seyd from Sheffield Hallam opposed state funding for parties because it gave 'the parliamentarians the whip hand if they do not like what the mass party is saying'.[71] The prolonged standing ovation Benn received at the Conference – in sharp contrast to the hostility shown to most MPs – was expressive of a mood that Tom Sawyer, then a NUPE official, explained as follows: 'the only man who offered a big change was Tony Benn. . . . it was in our minds absolutely essential to take off in a new and different direction'.[72] The media represented such political emotion as endangering democracy and civil liberties, and portending the disintegration of the Labour Party. Experienced conference observers who knew the individuals involved were led, with Lewis Minkin at the time, to 'despair more about the condition of the mass media than the condition of the Labour Party'.[73]

The approval in principle of an electoral college for the election of the leader and deputy leader at the 1980 Conference, as well as the reconfirmation of reselection, appeared at the time to be a major victory for the Labour new left. But the victory was a highly qualified one. Even before the vote on the leadership election was taken, the decision of the 1979 Conference on control of the party Manifesto was reversed (albeit by a margin of only 100,000 out of over 7 million votes). The implications of this for the whole struggle over the democratic accountability of the Shadow Cabinet were enormous. But it also exposed the cynical practice of those 'moderate' union leaders who covered their flanks by supporting radical resolutions at Conference while leading the counter-insurgency against the new left. On the two issues to which both senior PLP figures like Foot and Shore, and up-and-coming ones like Cook and Straw, gave highest priority – EEC withdrawal and unilateral nuclear disarmament – the union block votes were there to pass overwhelmingly resolutions that went even further than the *Peace, Jobs, Freedom* statement in May. And in the name of the GMWU, David Basnett moved the main economic strategy resolution as the first item on the agenda at the 1980 Party Conference. It ostensibly committed the party to the position that 'Britain's economic and social problems can only be solved by socialist planning', including specifically restrictions on the export of capital, selected import controls, a wealth tax and the reflation of public sector spending.[74] Benn was not unjustified in pointing out to the delegates that every one of these economic policies had been advanced by the NEC before the 1979 election and yet had been ruled out of inclusion in the Manifesto by Callaghan. He publicly challenged Basnett to justify how he could put them forward as the centrepiece of economic strategy in 1980 while at the same time voting against the NEC's position on the issue of whether the Shadow Cabinet would be expected to include them in the next Manifesto.[75]

Perhaps even more ominous, at least in terms of prolonging and deepening the trauma, was that after endorsing in principle (again by a narrow margin of 100,000 votes) the broader franchise for the election of the leader, the Conference went on to defeat all three proposals on distributing the votes in an electoral college between the PLP, the unions and constituency delegates. Basnett moved an emergency resolution that a special rules revision conference be called in January 1981 to settle this. With the prospect on everyone's mind that Callaghan might resign before then to allow the PLP to choose his successor under the existing rules, Callaghan came to the rostrum and, after teasing the delegates about what he would do, offered this pledge:

> I think the proper course of action . . . is for the PLP to elect the leader in the traditional way in November, on the understanding and in the knowledge that, the Conference in light of whatever amendments are put forward at the Special Conference in January may want to reach different conclusions. I would hope that is clearly expressed, clearly understood without any bad faith at all, but with the intention of carrying on the business of the party in the best possible way.

Eric Heffer, speaking for the NEC to close the debate, immediately followed this by expressing his understanding that what Callaghan had said guaranteed that 'there would be no elections of new leaders in the sense of the term . . . Jim has made an important statement; let us take it on the basis of what he said, that the PLP must take into consideration the Conference decision on the question of the future leader.'[76]

The Election of Michael Foot

In the event, of course, these assurances were ignored. Callaghan did resign within weeks of the Conference, and despite a sixteen-to-seven vote by the NEC that the PLP suspend its standing orders to allow an electoral college vote after the January Conference, the PLP went ahead and in November narrowly elected Michael Foot as leader over Denis Healey. Foot immediately designated Healey as his deputy and this was followed in December by a secret agreement between Foot and the

TULV leaders that whatever the outcome of the Special Wembley Conference to be held in January on the method of electing the leader, the union leadership would support no challenge to Foot and Healey.[77] Thus, despite the disastrous effects of the 1974–79 Government, the Foot–Healey axis which had been its foundation was now invested with the leadership of the party; moreover this had been accomplished by the PLP and the TULV General Secretaries *alone*, and in defiance of the Party Conference's vote for a broader franchise.

Of course, the fact that Foot stood at all, let alone that he was elected by the PLP, was a reflection of the ferment at the base of the party and in the labour movement generally. It reflected a recognition on the part of enough MPs that only a leader traditionally associated with the parliamentary left could command sufficient support in the unions and the constituencies to contain and neutralise the Labour new left's momentum. If Healey had won, a challenge under the new rules might have been unstoppable, and once the choice lay with a broader-based electoral college Benn might have won.

For the first time since Bevan, Benn provided the left with the sense, as Michael Meacher has put it, that they 'had within their ranks someone clearly of leadership potential who was an inspiration, who had a grand vision, who had a sense of purpose and who was a brilliant communicator'. It was precisely this that made Benn so dangerous in the eyes of those who were determined to stop him at all costs. Peter Shore himself later admitted: 'He is Labour's lost leader. He is the man who was more superbly equipped than anyone else to fulfil the functions of a really dynamic and successful Labour leader.'[78] Foot had none of these qualities. But he had been the parliamentary leadership's 'link and buckle' with the General Secretaries for a decade.[79] Moreover, as Shore also admitted, Foot's 'long history of rebellion against previous party leaderships and his persistent advocacy of left-wing and radical causes had won for him an affection and regard in the constituencies that no other senior figure in the Labour Party – except possibly Benn himself – enjoyed'.[80] A campaign of letters, telegrams and phone calls initiated by Clive Jenkins and Ian Mikardo appears to have been decisive in persuading Foot to run, and to do so on the basis that – even at sixty-seven, only one year younger than the retiring Callaghan – he would not be just an interim leader. As Jenkins put it, speaking for Basnett and Evans as well as himself, 'none of us wanted [Healey] because we thought he was too aggressive and would split the party'.[81] But many of the MPs, still traumatised by the assault on their identity as professional representatives, turned to Foot for narrower reasons. According to Hattersley:

> The great thing you have to understand about the election of Michael Foot was that it was a conscious decision by the Parliamentary Party to abdicate.

Not to worry about the next election, not to worry about its popularity in the country, but to behave in a way which gave the beleaguered Members of Parliament the best chance of coming to an accommodation with their constituency parties.

In a sense, what he did with the party was for those people far less important [than] their ability to go back to the Little Thumpington Constituency Labour Party and ... say, I'm a left winger, reselect me because I'm the sort of man you want.[82]

In so far as this was true, and that it worked, it was of course further proof that the CLPs were *not* dominated by thirty or forty 'hard-line lefties'. On the contrary, what it demonstrated was how fragile was the Labour new left's whole project; how little most activists understood about the complex alliances at the top that had put the Foot–Healey axis at the very centre of the Labour Government they now felt so let down by; and how quickly they were prepared to bow to the demand for unity without careful consideration of the implications of this, either in short-run electoral terms, or, more importantly, in terms of longer-run socialist advance. This was equally true for Labour MPs. For it was not only MPs who would have normally voted with the centre-right of the PLP who 'abdicated', as Hattersley puts it; many of those who had supported the new left's project, and including Heffer as well as Mikardo, did so too.[83]

At a crucial meeting at Benn's house, on 12 October, the 'Sunday Group' that would constitute Benn's 'kitchen cabinet' for the next twelve months – Norman Atkinson, Ken Coates, Vladimir Derer, Stuart Holland, Frances Morell, Chris Mullin, Geoff Bish, Audrey Wise, Tony Banks, Reg Race and Jo Richardson – unanimously advised him against standing for the leadership if Foot stood.[84] Out of a tangled web of various tactical considerations – that Benn should not legitimate the PLP's defiance of the Conference decision, that Foot had the only chance of stopping Healey in a PLP vote, that anyone chosen by the PLP should be seen only as a caretaker until the electoral college came into being – a different strategic line was woven over the course of the subsequent weeks. It was that Foot ought to be politically embraced as leader by the Labour new left. Benn himself had wanted to stand in order to set the stage for a subsequent leadership battle the following year; his political judgement told him that if he did not do so he would not be able to win against the incumbent in the electoral college. Yet he reluctantly bowed to his advisers and voted for Foot as leader of the Labour Party. The night before the vote, he faced bitter hostility from both left- and right-wing MPs in the House of Commons Tea Room over what the impending departure of the social democratic MPs would signify in terms of a split in the party, and who would be responsible for it. It led Benn, as well, to the conclusion that the PLP were having 'a collective nervous breakdown'. But he also concluded something else: 'They are in a state of panic, and the hatred was so strong that I became absolutely persuaded that this was not a party I would ever be invited to lead, and nor could I lead it.'[85]

9

The Defeat of the Labour New Left

Virtually the whole British left were elated by Michael Foot's election as leader.[1] The Labour new left, for the most part, shared this feeling and enthusiastically celebrated his victory, even though Foot had opposed their project since the early 1970s. His main concern was not just unity among the parliamentary and union elite; he also genuinely opposed the new left's project, believing that its conception of democratic reform 'carried to its logical conclusion, would destroy Parliament'.[2] The Labour new left's confused attitudes towards Foot made it hard for activists and the general public to understand why they continued to pursue their project against his wishes.

A Foot–Healey leadership team certainly had greater capacity to stifle the Labour new left than a Healey–Foot team. But whether the gains in terms of 'party unity' justified putting the ineffectual Foot rather than the pugnacious Healey in the role of Thatcher's main opponent was doubtful. For either way, the real political position of their leadership, as Raymond Williams also wrote at the time, amounted to this: 'The current position of what is called the leadership – "don't rock the boat, let's unite to get Thatcher out" is not only an opportunist negativism; it is complacent in its assumption that it is bound to be the beneficiary, and that if it is it will know what to do (except go on being the leadership).'[3]

Yet Foot's election did entail some real costs in policy terms for the centre-right MPs, costs which those who left to form the SDP were not prepared to sustain – above all since having Foot as leader guaranteed that the Labour Party would finally adopt a non-nuclear defence policy. But the party's continuing commitment to NATO, together with the fact that the centre-right continued to dominate Shadow Cabinet elections, left considerable space for manoeuvre for the great majority of social democratic parliamentarians who opted to stay. Their staying was, however, conditional upon Foot and later Kinnock proving that the constitutional changes that had been adopted could be contained and rendered innocuous in terms of their implications for the autonomy of the parliamentary party; and on the Labour new left being defeated and marginalised.

Benn's Deputy Leadership Campaign

At the 1981 Special Conference at Wembley the CLPD's tactical brilliance and the RFMC's organisational efforts did prevent the adoption of an electoral college still dominated by the PLP. Another option, championed by David Owen, proposed that every individual party member should have the right to vote for leader (with the PLP alone determining who the candidates should be); but this received only 400,000 votes out of nearly 7 million. The insincerity of the social democrats was a factor here – just as with reselection, they advanced 'one member, one vote' (OMOV) only after their steadfast opposition to any broadening of the franchise had been defeated; but what really told against OMOV was that it meant entirely by-passing the unions. This was, at the time, a complete non-starter in every section of the party. Although there were elements within the RFMC coalition who supported OMOV (especially the ILP), most of the Labour new left preferred an 'electoral college' in which one-third of the votes would be cast by the unions, one-third by CLP delegates, and one-third by the PLP.

The CLPD's careful monitoring of what the various union delegations had been mandated to vote for led to a tactical decision to organise support for an option slightly weighted towards the unions (40–30–30) as the only way of defeating other options which were designed to leave the PLP with 50 per cent or more of the vote.[4] Although the Wembley conference decision to leave the unions controlling 40 per cent of the vote in the electoral college was a massive reduction from the 90 per cent of the vote they accounted for at the Party Conference, it was immediately presented by the social democrats and the media as a vote for the domination of the party by 'union bosses', and against the ostensibly most democratic method of 'one member one vote'. This completely drowned out the Labour new left's actual aim, which was not to adopt the ersatz plebiscitary democracy of an American-style primary system but to make MPs accountable to an informed and active local party membership, and to politicise and democratise the unions' role in the party, not jettison it.

The split in the parliamentary party occasioned by the Social Democrats' Limehouse Declaration at the end of January 1981 actually had the effect of tilting the balance in the Labour Party further against the new left. Those on the centre-right who stayed were determined to prove that the departing social democrats were wrong in believing that

193

under Foot's leadership the PLP would be too ready to compromise with the new left, and not be ruthless enough in undermining them. In a television interview shortly after the social democrats left, Healey 'talked about Dunkirk as if somehow *we* were Hitler', according to Stuart Holland.[5] And as Healey's demands for the expulsion of Militant were combined with those of Tribune MPs like Frank Field, Foot himself started to make intemperate attacks on Militant. This was in fact a complete red herring. Militant's influence in the party declined during 1980: as the Labour new left gained momentum after the 1979 election, activating members and bringing new ones in through its campaigns, Militant's sectarian appeal was drowned out.[6] The point of the attacks on Militant was, rather, to show that even under Foot it would be possible to re-establish the old regime of social democratic centralism.

The formation of the Solidarity Group of MPs at this time by Shore and Hattersley was explicitly designed to make 'the left-centre and the right assert itself' against the 'Bennite' left; it was soon demanding that the party should conduct a 'searching and independent inquiry'. The Solidarity Group's labelling as 'Stalinist' the CLPD's practice of urging local parties to ask their MPs to reveal their position on given policy and constitutional issues was typical of their strategy.[7] (That a practice such as this should have been construed as Stalinist, of all things, presumably implying some ultra-centralist organisational practice rather than the antithesis of it, was equivalent to Ronald Reagan's designation of the Contras in Nicaragua at this time as 'freedom fighters'.) The right-wing St Ermin's group of unions similarly began to take the initiative for the counter-insurgency from the TULV, flexing their muscles with well-publicised plans to reverse the Wembley decision and to secure right-wing control of the NEC at the 1981 Party Conference.[8] Benn, who sensed a 'new and very unpleasant' shift in the political atmosphere throughout the west since the beginning of 1981, increasingly felt that 'the struggle in the Labour Party was part of this'; and he thought it was necessary, in this context, to stop 'worrying so much about 40–30–30 . . . and see the movement broadly'.[9]

By 1981, in fact, the Labour new left was already much weaker than it had appeared to be in 1980. A sober assessment in February 1981 by a brilliant young CLPD activist, Jon Lansman, argued that while the RFMC's formation in 1980 had shown 'the potential strength of left unity in the face of concerted right opposition (as it appeared a year ago)', it had also demonstrated that there were actually very big differences between the CLPD and LCC activists and the members of organisations like Militant. What is more, however, the work of the Labour new left through 1980 had been done by 'too few people' and their concentration on the 1980 Conference and Wembley had demonstrated 'a lack of clear long-term aims'. The victory at Wembley was narrow and probably unrepeatable . . . In the CLPs we were weaker than for a long time, often through hostility to the level of trade union influence. In many unions our support was eroded through bureaucratic manoeuvres which we did not have time to counteract. . . . One of the major sources of our weakness at Wembley was dissatisfaction with and even hostility towards the trade unions' influence in the party which is rife even amongst the left in the CLPs. We need to defend trade union participation at all levels . . . whilst not condoning any undemocratic use of block votes (i.e. decision-making by too few). The most immediate application of this principle is the defence of the Wembley decision, but we also need to play a wider educative role to counteract the hypocritical attacks of the right.[10]

It is in this light that the purpose – and the eventual outcome – of Benn's fateful decision to stand against Healey for the deputy leadership needs to be understood. Lansman thought there would 'almost certainly' be such a contest and that the RFMC would have to involve itself in it, not by running 'a 'Tony Benn for No. 10' campaign', but supporting 'a candidate committed to conference policies'. This would entail defending the central role of the unions in setting policies and choosing leaders *'while not necessarily accepting existing levels of democracy within the trade unions'*.[11] The key point of Benn's campaign was, as Lansman put it, to 'actually save the [Wembley] decision' by testing the electoral college and by forcing Healey into a debate on policy: 'The right would be far more interested in stopping Benn than changing the proportions in a college. It is a big job to get people interested in constitutional changes; it is a much bigger job for the right than the left because the right don't have the activists on the ground, they don't have the active support.'[12]

Indeed, immediately after Wembley Foot had told the Shadow Cabinet that 'the Wembley decision will not be allowed to stand'.[13] Benn had by this point already privately decided that he would stand for the deputy leadership in a new electoral college, although he did not, then or at any time later, expect to succeed. To contest Healey was, of course, also to challenge Foot and the General Secretaries. They were not only fearful that Benn might win, and that this would force more of the social democrats out of the parliamentary party, but were also, as Bill Keys put it at the final meeting of the Commission of Enquiry in July 1980, 'sick to death of all this argument about party democracy'.[14] Foot pleaded with Benn to desist, but Benn did not find very convincing this 'typical Michael Foot state where everything you want to do will always lose us the next election. Well, as we followed his advice rigorously for the last five years of the last Labour Government and we did lose the election in May 1979, I can't say I found it very credible.' Benn's own rationale for standing for the deputy leadership was

> to force people to make choices. That's what's called polarisation, divisiveness, and all the rest, but ... you can't go on forever pretending you're a socialist party when you're not, pretending you'll do something when you won't, confining yourself to attacks on the Tories when that's not enough. People want to know what the Labour Party will do and I think this process is long overdue; the Labour Party are having a Turkish bath, and the sweat and the heat and the discomfort are very unpleasant.[15]

'You can't go on forever pretending you're a socialist party when you're not'; the words could be Tony Blair's or Peter Mandelson's: Thatcherism had exposed parliamentary socialism's evasions and obfuscations, as they also, in their way, understood.

Benn's campaign got off to a disastrous start. He had made the error of joining the Tribune Group at the beginning of February, not out of any new regard for it but for the purely tactical reason of mending his fences with at least part of the PLP. His 'Sunday Group' had advised him to join by a vote of ten to two – the dissenters being Ken Coates ('you shouldn't put new wine into old bottles with the Tribune Group') and Stuart Holland ('they may nominate someone else for the deputy leadership and then it would be difficult for Tony').[16] They were correct. The bulk of the Tribune Group was very hostile to Benn's running. Of course, the Tribune Group had greatly changed (as Mikardo put it: 'By that time ... it was no longer a left-wing group'); but even Heffer was distinctly unhappy with Benn's decision.[17] To avoid the Tribune Group nominating someone before he declared his candidature (they nominated John Silkin), Benn issued a press release at 3 a.m., and was ridiculed in the press as skulking around in the middle of the night to advance his personal ambition.

Benn knew he would not win. As he wrote in his diary the day after he declared: 'I am sure Denis will win – I will put that on record now – because the party never sacks anybody, and why should it sack its deputy leader, particularly when many people think he should have been the leader?' In the first days of the campaign he oscillated between thinking that he would carry 'a sizeable body of opinion which can't be ignored or neglected', and that his candidacy was going to amount to 'a great sacrifice and I will be humiliatingly defeated'.[18] In the event, despite being struck with Guillain-Barre Syndrome, which incapacitated him for over three months and kept him from public speaking until September, the campaign which the RFMC ran (under Lansman's leadership) was a remarkable success in terms of the politicisation and democratisation of the union activists' role within the party. What was involved here was the breaking down of the barriers between the industrial and political wings of the movement. However difficult, this was crucial to the Labour new left's project. It had always been difficult to realise, but during the deputy leadership campaign the Labour new left made more headway with it than ever before. This was seen in the debates and rallies held at all the main union conferences, in the very active support of a good many second-level union officials, in 1,200 trade unionists attending an LCC conference in July.

Healey ridiculed Benn for allegedly describing the campaign as a 'healing process'; yet in admitting that 'I learned more about the inner workings of the trade union movement in those six months than in my previous thirty-seven years of party work,' he inadvertently conceded much of the new left's case for extending the franchise for electing leaders beyond the PLP and for bringing the campaign into the unions.[19] Healey had disdained to put out a policy statement when he ran for the leadership in the PLP election the previous November, yet he was now forced to define his policies in response to Benn's – and this in turn exposed how far out of line they often were with party policy. The RFMC pointed this out at a rally it organised at the CND conference: 'If we lose, the applause . . . will extend as far as NATO and Washington. The fight for a democratic and accountable labour movement and the fight for it to take effective action, are not separate things.'[20] Labour's good showing in the local elections of May 1981, a month after Benn declared his candidacy, not only appeared to confound predictions that continuing the campaign for intra-party democracy was bound to bring electoral disaster, but gave a shot in the arm to constituency activists who mobilised large and enthusiastic rallies around the country.

Yet the very size and success of these rallies produced their own problems. Although the CLPD did not officially support Benn's candidacy because of its defining commitment to constitutional issues, Derer himself did so, but he was bothered by the personalised, even 'sycophantic' aspect of the rallies.[21] He thought they came across like American election primaries on television, giving the impression of 'a naked power struggle'. Seen as such, it certainly 'showed how bitterly the right will fight', as Michael Meacher said. 'There was never less than half a page of vitriol in the press per day and the source was the right wing of the Labour Party. They were feeding stuff into the press even though it did cataclysmic damage to the Labour Party. It was like a bombing raid flattening everything in sight. It was more a cause of the defeat in 1983 than the Falklands.'[22]

One particularly ugly tactic of the Healey campaign (which was run by the Solidarity Group of MPs) was to identify hecklers at his own rallies as agents of Benn's campaign. In fact, these most often were the same campaigners for the 'H Block' prisoners in Northern Ireland who had stridently heckled Benn at the Left's Debate of the Decade meeting a year before. Yet even Foot smeared Benn by asserting that he could have 'with a single sentence told them to leave Denis alone'. To which Benn responded: 'I think it's a ludicrous idea to expect somebody to denounce somebody over whom they have no control . . . But it was an attempt to make it look as though it was as if I was encouraging that which I was not.'[23] As Kogan and Kogan's account, highly sympathetic to the Labour right, acknowledged: 'The Healey campaign alleged that Benn supporters were undemocratic and thuggish . . . [They] misidentified their enemies and resorted to allegations that could not be justified.' This tactic blew up in Healey's face when he went so far as mistakenly to identify Lansman as one the hecklers. But this 'did not prevent the media . . . from assuming that all Benn's closest supporters came from the . . . Trotskyist groups'.[24]

This was the kind of thing that only increased the party rank and file's dislike of Healey. Amongst the party membership the Shadow Cabinet's open hostility, and Foot's angry demand that Benn should rather challenge him for the leadership, did them no good. Benn sensed immediately that they would be seen by the rank and file to be 'guilty of a serious overkill of vilification'.[25] But among the general public the damage done, not only to Benn, but to the Labour Party, was enormous. This included, of course, the impact on most union members. Benn's campaign in the unions was greatly resented by most of the General Secretaries; they regarded his going over their heads to their activists as an 'unfriendly act', in Clive Jenkins's words.[26] Some important second level leaders, most importantly the TGWU's representative on the NEC, Alec Kitson, also turned against Benn at this time. The Benn campaign's ability to win over so many union activists in the face of this was a remarkable feat, but they were under no illusion that they were also winning over the ordinary members.[27] On the contrary, what their campaign exposed was the structural flaw at the heart of Labourism, a flaw which trade union and party leaders had for so long avoided dealing with: their inability to engage politically with the large indirect membership that was attached to the Labour Party through the unions. The press happily conducted expensive polling among the membership of various unions to reveal an overwhelming degree of support for Healey over Benn, and had a field day searching out any discrepancies they could find between these polls and the preferences expressed by union conferences, executives and delegations. Although those unions which conducted ballots among their members found much more support for Benn than these polls suggested, the ballot results delivered a number of union votes (most crucially NUPE's) to Healey in the electoral college.

What this underlined – or should have – was how important it was that the campaign to politicise and democratise the institutions of the labour movement should continue, rather than be prematurely cut off. For the issue was not, in the end, about Benn versus Healey. It was about the unions, including especially the General Secretaries, themselves taking a host of political decisions and policy stances to which their members had not made any contribution whatever. The push for active and effective workplace branches of the Labour Party, endorsed by the Commission of Enquiry and passed by the Party Conference in 1980, came primarily from the Labour new left and their supporters in the unions. But there had hardly been time to get any started by the time of the deputy leadership campaign.[28] In any case, they could only have been significant if they had been part of a much more general process of democratisation of all the institutions of the Labour movement.

The Counter-revolution

The Labour new left's defeat at the 1981 Party Conference was not restricted to the deputy leadership contest. Indeed, the fact that Benn secured over 80 per cent of the constituency party votes on both ballots, and almost 40 per cent of the trade union votes (and even one-third of the PLP votes) on the second ballot (i.e. after Silkin was eliminated), could be seen as a remarkable victory, given the strength and determination of the forces marshalled against his candidacy. Much has been made of the fact that all Benn needed to win, in an outcome that gave Healey 50.426 per cent of the final vote to Benn's 49.574 per cent, was four MPs to vote the other way, whereas twenty Tribune MPs either abstained or voted for Healey on the last ballot. In reality, far more important for the defeat of the Labour new left was another set of votes for the National Executive, taken in the traditional manner.

The right-wing leadership of the Engineering Union finally fulfilled its promise (too late for Shirley Williams) to produce a right-wing delegation (although to do so it had to force a change in how its delegates were elected – from a more democratic basis in the branches to a less democratic one at the divisional level). That it went so far as to vote to remove Norman Atkinson, himself a member of the union, from the post of Party Treasurer, was an action, commented Minkin, 'wholly at odds with normal trade union representational behaviour'.[29] It was, however, only a small part of a much larger targeting and purge of those members of the NEC who supported the new left. After the TULV was unable to stifle the left in 1980, Basnett shifted the GMWU more closely towards the St Ermin's Group of right-wing unions, and broke a long-established pattern of voting with the TGWU whereby the big unions traded votes so that each secured places on the NEC and TUC General Council. Although no secret was made of what was going on since the spring of 1981 at least, the press made no demands for these votes to be referred to the union membership, as they had done in the deputy leadership election.

What Minkin calls the 'ruthless political character of the right wing's organisation' was especially in evidence as left-wing representatives were removed not only from the trade union section of the National Executive, but from the women's section as well. There was a particular irony in this. Women's representation in the Labour Party was always the most indefensibly undemocratic aspect of its structure (including the five women members of the NEC being elected largely on the basis of arrangements among the union leaders). The Women's Action Committee of the CLPD had been campaigning for reforms, but in a pattern reminiscent of the 1970s the Conference Arrangements Committee had kept their proposals off the conference agenda. The 1981 Conference opened, in the glare of massive international as well as national television and press coverage, not with the deputy leadership ballot but with a protest staged at the podium by women delegates. The horror on the faces of the union and parliamentary leaders at this feminist lack of deference showed very clearly that it was not the Labour new left who represented old-fashioned 'white male' traditional socialist politics.

Although it took until the 1982 Conference for all those targeted in the purge to be removed from the NEC, the success of the right-wing union machine at the 1981 Conference considerably enhanced the influence in the party of some of the least democratic and most ruthless elements in the labour movement. If the significance of their increased power was not immediately apparent, this was for two reasons. First because the successes of the new left in the party and the energising effect of the deputy leadership campaign attracted many activists from movements and pressure groups. For the first time in many years, the Labour Party was where the action was for young left-wing activists other than sectarian 'entrists'. This was especially reflected in the launch of *New Socialist*, a lively discussion journal, 'Bennite' in orientation, which gave the party a new intellectual presence among left activists.

Secondly, at the local level the rise and fall of the Labour new left followed a different tempo. As we saw earlier, Labour did well in the May 1981 local council elections in both the north and the south of the country, and this created new opportunities for Labour new left activists to try to put some of their ideas into practice. In particular, the Greater London Council under Ken Livingstone's leadership became the focus of national and international attention. The history of that remarkable experiment has been well documented.[30] Its most creative and innovative practices, including opening 'its buildings, its funds, its research and – very much more selectively – its decision-making process to some of the most radical and most needy sections of the public', were at this stage still embryonic and came to fruition only in the mid-1980s; and in the meantime, as Wainwright admits, 'There was much about the GLC's work for insiders and outsiders that was very messy and frustrating, as well as exciting and hopeful.'[31] As we argued at the end of the last chapter, the much-heralded municipal socialism in Britain of the early 1980s required a highly supportive national party, but by the time it really got going, the balance of power at the national level was such that any and all political 'messiness' was treated like the plague.

Indeed, the Labour new left's advances at the local level also provided a new front for the counter-insurgency – the main effects of which were felt initially at the national level of the party. Bitter right-wing Labour councillors, some of whom were about to defect to the SDP, fed the press minute details of every local political conflict (some of which involved cleaning up the rotten machine politics of the old Labour councils). And the press, centred in London, made a sensational national issue out of every unconventional statement or practice (personal or political) by young and often inexperienced new left activists in every London borough and constituency party as well as the GLC. At the Palace of Westminster, in-jokes with lobby journalists about the 'loony' local left became a handy means for Labour MPs to offer proof that they were 'sound'. Well before the 1981 Conference, headlines already began appearing like: 'Worried Labour men plot to oust "rent-a-quote" Livingstone.'[32] Livingstone later lamented: 'It would be nice to think that as the press attacks mounted we could have looked to the Parliamentary Labour Party for support. The more we were attacked the more the PLP dissociated itself . . .'[33]

Part of the reason for this was that the media's simultaneous gloss on the new sane, safe and determinedly centrist Social Democratic alternative also began to show its effect in the autumn of 1981. Although much of the SDP support involved picking up former Tory voters, their by-election successes and high opinion poll ratings, combined with the noisy defection of nine more MPs (all of whom had voted for Healey, of course), kept the PLP in its traumatic state. More had to be done to show that the new left was being vanquished. By the beginning of November the Manifesto Group of MPs sent a letter to the NEC demanding that it 'declare the activities and organisation of the Militant Tendency as incompatible with the constitution of the Labour Party', and that it refuse to endorse the selection of Patrick Wall as a candidate in Bradford North: '. . . if the Labour Party remains open to the bitter winds of extremism, it will perish as a force in British politics'.[34] And by the beginning of December, under pressure from former Chief Whip Bob Mellish – a trade union MP long allied with Callaghan, very much in the mould of Golding and the St Ermin's Group – Foot made his infamous peremptory repudiation of Peter Tatchell's selection as the Labour candidate for Bermondsey after Mellish retired. This was not a deselection. There was no breach of procedure. Tatchell was Secretary of the constituency party and not a member of Militant. In many ways he epitomised many of the finest characteristics of the typical young new left activist at the local level. There was an ugly homophobic side to the press's response to the charges brought against Tatchell by the old south London Labour machine, but Foot himself was caught instead on the bait of an article by Tatchell in *London Labour Briefing* which had been fed to the press and made the subject of a question to Thatcher in the House of Commons by a former Labour MP who had defected to the SDP. It is worth quoting Tatchell's article at some length, because it captures so well the spirit and style of what was being defeated:

> Labour has long lost the radical and defiant spirit of its early pioneers. We now seem stuck in the rut of an obsessive legalism and parliamentarism. This 'talking-shop' style of committee politics implies that the realisation of socialism can basically be left to a handful of wise and articulate MPs and councillors.... Work in committees often overshadows popular struggles. But these are vital, both inside and outside the forums of electoral democracy ...
>
> Though the party's marches against unemployment have been very worthwhile, surely the gravity of three million jobless justifies bolder protests? Perhaps we should be thinking more in terms of a 'Siege of Parliament' to demand jobs – a march on the House of Commons led by 250 Labour MPs and a thousand Labour mayors and councillors and involving an afternoon's sit-down occupation of the Westminster area. Or possibly the Labour-controlled GLC could sponsor a 'Tent City' of the unemployed and homeless in the grounds of County Hall and within the sight of the House of Commons.
>
> During the riots earlier this year, it seems remiss that neither the NEC nor regional EC held extraordinary meetings in response to the crisis. Shouldn't they have given a lead by calling an emergency mobilisation of the Labour Movement around appropriate demands such as 'Jobs and Better Housing for All, Democratic Control of the Police, and Freedom of Assembly and Demonstration'?[35]

It was an article, both in tone and substance, that Benn might have written, not only at the time, or even in 1971, but also at the time of the Notting Hill riots in 1958. Yet now he faced demands from both Foot and Healey that he repudiate the article. Of course, he refused, but reflecting its new composition, the NEC supported Foot's veto of Tatchell – even denying him the chance to attend and defend himself. And it immediately went on to instruct the new General Secretary (Jim Mortimer, who had himself once been expelled from the party in the old social democratic centralist days) to undertake a new enquiry on the activities of the Militant Tendency. The fact that the demand that Benn repudiate Tatchell's article was made in the context of justifying the need for an enquiry into Militant made it clear how much more was really at stake than Militant.[36] Indeed, all this went on amidst considerable hand-wringing and panic (quite comic if what it signified had not been so serious) over the application by the well-known Trotskyist activist and writer Tariq Ali for membership in the party (which was, of course, refused).

What was ultimately at stake was the very legitimacy within the party of the Labour new left's political discourse. The thread can be traced directly back to the counter-insurgency begun by Callaghan in 1976, and to the battle for control of the NEC and the restoration of social democratic centralism that began at that time. What was especially significant about what happened in the NEC in December 1981 is that it was at this point that Neil Kinnock made his really decisive move. Kinnock had already led the Tribune abstainers on the second round of the deputy leadership ballot – that is, to vote only for Silkin but for neither Benn nor Healey. In doing this, he was still signalling the distance he would keep from the right's counter-insurgency. But he now provided the one-vote margin that swung the balance in the NEC against Tatchell and in favour of the Militant enquiry. He did so on the grounds that the left, recognising that stringent measures were some-times necessary to defend democracy, also wanted a 'clean-up'. Of course it was not yet Kinnock, but rather John Golding, who set the agenda and the tone at these NEC meetings – although the connection between Kinnock's outlook and the ethos that Golding represented was tellingly revealed when the media quoted Kinnock as describing himself, in the context of the media focus on Tatchell's homosexuality, as being on the 'balls wing' of the party.[37]

The counter-revolution having thus succeeded, a joint TULV, NEC and PLP meeting at the beginning of 1982 yielded the 'Bishop's Stortford Accord', which announced the end of hostilities in these terms: 'There is a clear decision by all who participated ... to go forward with a new unity and sense of direction ... it is now anticipated that the Labour Party will put the period of division and self-examination behind us and that all sections of the party will recognise the need to avoid all statements or moves that might divide the party.' It was, significantly, David Basnett who told the press that 'peace had broken out' in the Labour Party. It was the usual peace between vanquished and victors. The two constitutional reforms were left in place, but through the course of 1982 the centre-right pressed its advantage. This was seen in the Register of Non-Affiliated Organisations set up in June 1982, which directly emerged out of the enquiry established by the NEC the previous December – the first concrete step to re-establish social democratic centralism in the Labour Party since the old Proscribed List was dropped a decade before.[38] This was overwhelmingly approved at the 1982 Conference as the new right-wing balance in the union block vote was also applied to clearing out the remaining supporters of the Labour new left from the trade union section of the NEC. Exactly one month later, at the NEC's first meeting after the conference, Benn, Heffer,

Richardson and Allaun were surgically removed from the key NEC committees in a long series of motions moved by John Golding and seconded by Healey.[39] The year that had opened with 'peace breaking out' in the truce of Bishop's Stortford ended with the Labour Party's own version of the 'night of the long knives'.

Of course, the strength of the new left was still such that it could not all be so easily dispensed with, although it now switched into a much more defensive posture – and as it did so, immediately seemed to lose a great deal of its confidence and creativity, at least at the national level. The fact that it was members of the Tribune left who now officially held the reins in the party also meant that there were limits to how quickly the counter-revolution could proceed and how thoroughly it could 'clean up' the mess created by the new left. Foot and Mortimer were strongly opposed to any expulsions under the register; they had even hoped to avoid having officially to proscribe Militant. The NEC did so in fact at the end of 1982 (after a very unseemly court battle over the principles of natural justice) and then proceeded to expel five party members on the editorial board of the Militant newspaper. Yet the concern that Foot and Mortimer displayed to avoid 'witch-hunts', that 'no one would be asked a question about ideology', was genuine. It not only reflected their own past sufferings at the hands of the right, but also the fact that they knew very well that the new left were much more genuinely committed to the core values of the party constitution than were the right. The fundamental reasons why ideological borders could not be established, as Shaw explains, was that 'the right's enthusiasm for Parliamentary institutions was not matched by any commensurate interest in socialist objectives, and, indeed, its enthusiasm for applying the Constitution did not extend to ... the commitment on social ownership'.[40] It would take another full decade before the political messiness that this entailed could finally be dealt with.

Perhaps the greatest cost of the defensive mode that the Labour new left was now forced into was that the search for a socialist strategy was abandoned when it urgently needed to be pursued. The Labour new left's concern for such a strategy was shown in two economic strategy documents produced in 1982. One of these was the TUC–Labour Party Liaison Committee's *Economic Planning and Industrial Policy*; the other was the Home Policy Committee's *Labour's Programme 1982*, both of which were published in the summer of 1982 as the culmination of two years of research work. The latter was a really detailed elaboration of the AES – as authoritative a statement of it as was ever produced. The former, as we indicated in Chapter 8, was directed at establishing an enabling framework for a radical extension of collective bargaining over the whole range of company decisions. There was a tension between the two documents – *Labour's Programme* being more oriented to working 'in and against' the central and local state, to advance democratic planning versus a 'public administration [that] is secretive and unresponsive'; while the *Industrial Policy* document reached for means of transforming collective bargaining into a vehicle for socialist advance. Benn's vision spanned both, and often the researchers more aligned to one conception rather than the other felt that his vision was, therefore, stretched too thin. There were plenty of generalities and evasions in both documents, in any case, a sign of how much work there was still to do and of what was tactically necessary if the NEC and TUC were to publish them at all in 1982. But nothing that has been produced by the British labour movement since this time comes anywhere near as close to making any significant progress towards the development of socialist strategy.

Both the Shadow Cabinet and the General Council, however, with their centre-right majorities throughout the 1970s and 1980s, had tolerated these studies only because of the strength of the new left. Now, even while they sponsored both documents at the 1982 TUC and Labour Party conferences, they were mainly concerned to get them out of the way and move on. At the same NEC meeting that removed Benn from the Home Policy and Liaison Committees, Healey sponsored a motion that 'in view of acceptance by Conference of Labour's Programme 1982, and in order to reduce costs and rationalise policy formulation, [the] committees of the NEC be instructed to review the number and composition of the sub-committees, study groups, etc., with the objective of achieving a substantial reduction in the number of such groups . . .'[41] This amounted, in practice, to the reassertion of the Shadow Cabinet's role as the fount of policy in the party, finally closing the chapter that had begun in 1970 when Holland, Hart and Benn first set out to find a way beyond the limits of Keynesianism and Croslandism.

This renewed Shadow Cabinet policy autonomy took shape in an attempt by Peter Shore, as Shadow Chancellor, to revive incomes policy as the centrepiece of Labour's alternative to Thatcherism. Moving on, it turned out, meant proudly and demonstratively going all the way back to the National Economic Assessment that had been conceived as part of the last corporatist 'concordat' agreed with the General Council of the TUC in the dying months of the previous Labour Government. It was all captured towards the end of the year in the title which the *New Statesman* gave to Foot's first major speech on economic policy, which it published in full: 'Come back Keynes, all is forgiven' (on the cover it featured a cartoon of Shore dressed as a magician pulling out of his top hat flags labelled 'national economic assessment', 'incomes policy', 'social contract', 'wage restraint' and – in the smallest print, barely visible – 'price controls').[42]

With an election looming in 1983, there was, of course, no time to get

Labour's other bothersome policy commitments on the Common Market and non-nuclear defence policy formally reversed – and in any case the centre-right could not be sure how far Foot would be prepared to go in dropping them. But all that really seemed necessary now was to let the Shadow Cabinet take as much or as little as they wanted from existing party policy in the run-up to the election – and if there was going to be a fight over this, it was better conducted in private. While the Bennite left in the PLP really shut up now – knowing that the right was just itching to blame them for an election defeat – and while at the CLP level a grand total of eight MPs were deselected before the 1983 election – the right was far less inclined towards calling off its counter-revolution. Golding and the Labour Chief Whip Michael Cocks were at the centre of a series of manoeuvres, in concert with regional officials from the GMWU, to ensure that in the redistribution of constituency boundaries in Bristol (which Cocks also represented) due to take place before the 1983 election, Benn would have to run for the most marginal seat – which indeed he lost in the 1983 election.[43]

Far more immediately harmful was the decision of Bob Mellish to resign early in order to force a by-election in Bermondsey before the 1983 election. This was done with the explicit intention of teaching the party a lesson after the CLP had renominated Tatchell and the NEC and Foot, faced otherwise with disbanding a CLP which had breached no procedure, finally allowed his selection to stand. The by-election was held at the end of February 1983, just four months before the general election, and the 'Real Bermondsey Labour' candidate put up by the old guard in the local party joined with the right-wing press to conduct a campaign which has become notorious as one of the dirtiest in British history. One poster, 'Which Queen would you support?', connecting the personal and political in one crude phrase, summed up the central themes in a relentless campaign of vilification. An army major from Belgravia who described himself as 'a Conservative of three generations' wrote to Tatchell expressing his hope he would win because the by-election 'was the most disgusting event I have ever known'. Another Tory who canvassed for their candidate wrote to Tatchell 'to deplore the sick and shameful campaign against you'. For none of this was anyone in the leadership of the Labour Party directly responsible (although those close to Mellish certainly were). But perhaps Tatchell was not mistaken in his belief that the 'actions of Michael Foot and the NEC, more than anything else, opened the door to the campaign of vilification and gave Fleet Street the signal that I was fair game'.[44]

The 1983 General Election

Thus was the scene set for the 1983 election. For over two years after the 1979 election, from August 1979 to the end of 1981, that is, right through the passage of the constitutional reforms and the adoption of radical policies and even the deputy leadership campaign, Labour had stood ahead of the Conservatives in the opinion polls. In October 1980, at the height of the PLP's trauma, the MORI poll found Labour support at 50 per cent, the Conservatives at 34 per cent and the Liberals 15 per cent. This, together with the elections in France and Greece of parties whose programmes were far more radical than Labour's, and the Labour new left's successes at the local level, emboldened the forces for change in the party. But a combination of factors rapidly transformed the electoral scene. The choice of Foot as leader – with opinion polls throughout 1981 consistently rating his performance below that of Mrs Thatcher, while her popular support was still lower than that of any post-war Prime Minister – proved a disastrous mistake in electoral terms. By the autumn of 1981 the new electoral option offered by the Alliance showed great initial potential to capture a sizeable portion of the vote: when Shirley Williams won a by-election in November its opinion poll ratings reached 44 per cent. Thus even though Healey had defeated Benn, the electoral reward for repelling Benn as the embodiment of the 'far left' went to the former Cabinet ministers who had abandoned the Labour Party, rather than to those who stayed.

Support for the Alliance began to decline immediately after November 1981 (indicating that media hype is not enough to sustain a party), although it still held a very slim lead over Labour, with the Tories a percentage point further behind, just before the Falklands war began in April 1982. The war, however, utterly transformed Mrs Thatcher's electoral prospects.[45] By June, Labour was 20 per cent behind the Tories, with the Alliance even further behind. A study by American psephologists at the end of the 1980s estimated that whereas the 'Winter of Discontent' had been worth about a 1.5 to 2 per cent swing to the Tories in the 1979 election, the Falklands war was worth over 7 per cent: it was 'the single most important event in staunching the decline of Conservative fortunes in the early 1980s, and paving the way for the party's landslide victory in 1983'.[46] Even after war fever died down, the mood of chauvinism did not – as the viciousness of the attack on Tatchell (a pacifist, an immigrant, and a homosexual) had shown. As W.L. Miller wrote, in much the most insightful analysis of the 1983 election campaign,

the Falklands crisis was no longer in the forefront of people's minds but it was evoked by all kinds of codes and symbols. Thatcher was photographed against the world's biggest Union Jack. She seized on the defence issue in order to portray Labour as divided and unpatriotic. . . . Winning the Falklands war could have been a disaster for a liberal pacifist like Foot, but it added a touch of verisimilitude to the tattered image of a nationalistic authoritarian like Thatcher. Image and event matched perfectly.[47]

The Labour new left had long understood that only a long-term campaign of mobilisation and education to refashion and reconstruct working-class and socialist identities could securely restore Labour's electoral base. But they had also imagined that this might still be accomplished through scraping back into office as Labour had done in 1974 – and was still doing at the local level in the 1980s, even after the 1983 election – and using the resources of the state to help empower popular forces. When it suddenly became clear that Thatcherism might not be a temporary interregnum, it also became all too clear that the Labour new left's attempted balancing act, between changing a party fundamentally while relying in the meantime on an anti-government vote to sustain the party's electoral viability, was no longer possible. The choice between a long-term campaign and immediate electoral viability became a stark one after 1981.

The dilemma became more acute as the effects of a new international economic crisis, and the commitment of western governments to give priority to defeating inflation through pushing up unemployment, began to make themselves felt. The attempt to change the Labour Party now ran up against the most intractable problem: that trying to change any party as fundamentally as the Labour new left proposed involves a long period of conflict within it; and even if it is the defenders of the status quo who do the worst damage, the fact remains that a visibly disunited party cannot win elections. And this was no small consideration when winning elections appeared ever more important in the face of Thatcherism and world-wide recession.

This logic was already dominant in the Labour Party well before the 1983 election campaign. Yet Labour's parliamentary team failed to restore Labour's electoral fortunes. They were unable to dispel the image of a party at war with itself. But the blame that was subsequently heaped on the Labour new left was not justified. The 1983 Manifesto was in some respects less radical than the 1974 Manifesto had been. The so-called 'longest suicide note in history' was not only considerably *shorter* than the Tory Manifesto, it contained little of the *elan* of Labour's Programme 1982, even though it often referred back to that document and retained much of the policy package. The terms in which the campaign itself was conducted were, of course, less radical still, as the Shadow Cabinet took centre stage. In fact, the internal strife that Labour actually exhibited during the 1983 election campaign itself was entirely within the Foot–Healey camp, as old conflicts resurfaced, now that the new left enemy had been neutralised. While the new left showed remarkable discipline in keeping a low profile, the tactics of the Labour old right wrought enormous damage.

Nothing could have defeated Mrs Thatcher by the time the campaign began. Tory support stayed between 45 and 47 per cent right through the campaign, before registering 43 per cent on the night of the election. But as Miller has shown, the drop in Labour support from 33 per cent at the beginning of the campaign to 28 per cent at the end, entirely to the benefit of the Alliance, which moved up from 18 per cent to 26 per cent, took place about halfway into the campaign.[48] The reason for this seems clear. Towards the end of May, the national press featured an alleged ultimatum by Healey to withdraw from the campaign if Foot interpreted the Manifesto as saying that Labour was in favour of unilateral nuclear disarmament. This was followed a day later by a calculated move by Callaghan, who, with all the authority of a former Labour Prime Minister who had 'been there', made a highly publicised attack on Labour's defence policy. And from the moment Healey and Callaghan took their stand election coverage was dominated by the obvious discomfort of Foot as he tried to bridge the gulf between himself and the right on defence policy – a gulf which had indeed been only thinly covered by a form of words in the Manifesto, designed to exploit popular support for getting rid of cruise and Polaris missiles, while at the same time minimising the impact of the unpopular expression, 'unilateral disarmament'.

It was thus ultimately an election campaign in which the radical democratic issues raised by the new left hardly surfaced, and in which voters did not even find Labour very much more credible than the Tories in terms of reducing unemployment (nor was this surprising with Peter Shore reminding everyone afresh of the futility of Labour's old rhetoric of 'national economic assessment'). Above all, however, as Miller concluded, it was

> ... dissension at the top rather than spontaneous desertion at the bottom [that] was the cause of Labour's very poor performance in 1983. That does not mean policies are irrelevant. If Labour leaders cannot agree policies amongst themselves on what they define as the central issues in politics then they will not succeed in convincing the electorate ... If they can agree on policies, however, they may well be able to turn public opinion in their favour or divert public attention to issues on which they do have public support. In particular the left must either convince the right or compromise with it, not because left-wing policies in themselves preclude electoral success, but because they need the support or acquiescence of all wings of the party before they can present a credible alternative.[49]

The Dissolution of the Labour New Left

The right wing of the party, however, would not accept left-wing policies. That was clear from the whole previous decade. As Wickham-Jones puts it in his comprehensive study of economic policy within the Labour Party during the period 1970–83, 'one central theme emerges ... It concerns the degree to which right-wingers within Labour remained opposed to what was official party policy.'[50] Given the collapse of Keynesianism, if left-wing policies were not pursued the party was bound to drift rightwards. When Neil Kinnock succeeded Foot as leader three months after the 1983 election this was not yet clear – even to Kinnock himself. He took the position that the problem was not policy, but disunity.

This was always the Tribune left's position, and it was what Kinnock now argued in every speech he made at the 1983 Party Conference. He stood for all the left's policies. His overwhelming defeat of Eric Heffer in the leadership election following Foot's resignation was related to this (Benn, having lost his seat, ruled himself out of the race). It was also related to the general sense, felt very strongly by Labour new left activists themselves, that the election campaign had shown that there was, as the newly elected Labour new left MP, Jeremy Corbyn, put it, 'great incompetence in the party machine'.[51] Heffer, who had chaired the NEC's Organisation Committee for so many years, astonishingly obtained only 7 per cent of the CLP vote – compared with Benn's 83 per cent in 1981. What was involved here was more than Kinnock's impassioned assertion that the task of winning the next election had to be a 'total precondition' of all strategic and policy decisions. He offered 'unity plus', the 'plus' being a youthful leader offering a modernised party apparatus better able to campaign for left policies. At fringe meetings, he even quoted Lenin and Gramsci on hegemony and passive revolution to underline his left credentials.

Yet the support for Kinnock also reflected a change of orientation among activists. Important signs of this began to appear even before the 1983 election. For instance, there were strong differences over whether to abide by the party's new Register of Unaffiliated Organisations; Derer, Lansman and the CLPD felt that Conference decisions had to be adhered to, while others, including Benn and those closest to him among the LCC leadership (but not the Clause IV group), thought the reimposition of social democratic centralism had to be opposed on civil libertarian as well as strategic grounds. Meanwhile, the leading Communist historian Eric Hobsbawm's interventions were influential in providing the intellectual underpinning for Foot and Kinnock's position.[52] On the basis of an acute analysis of declining proletarian culture, Hobsbawm called for the broadest political unity to oppose

Thatcherism while, like Foot and Kinnock, remaining silent about the issues raised in the debate on intra-party democracy and policy, as well as about the role played by the centre-right in the course of it.

Until the 1983 election the possibility of developing a new kind of socialist practice which would attract rather than lose votes had by no means yet been effaced in the party, or more broadly on the British left. In the immediate aftermath of Labour's crushing defeat in the June 1983 election, however, many of those who had supported the Labour new left became as fixated on the appeal to unity as they had been on the demand for change after the 1979 election. There was also a desire to look at the limits of the Labour new left itself, including the Alternative Economic Strategy, the contradictions of relying on the unions' votes while not being able to democratise them, and the need to give more weight to gender and racial issues. Especially among those who had been connected with the LCC – where the leading activists were more often intellectuals, some of whom were interested in a career in Parliament – there was a move towards the idea that some sort of 'Bennism without Benn' might be achieved under Kinnock's leadership.[53] In a March 1984 pamphlet the LCC criticised the left for having concentrated too much on democratic change in the party during the 1970s and early 1980s. What was needed now, they said, was to popularise socialist ideas *and* to accept Kinnock's leadership and avoid destructive conflict. In return, the LCC – revealing either astonishing naivety or pure wishful thinking – expected from Kinnock a 'committed attack on the nature of capitalist society itself'.[54]

Intellectual grounds for this were provided by a current within the widely read 'Euro-Communist' magazine *Marxism Today* which suggested that a Kinnock leadership would be open to GLC-style 'social movement' political activism and would distance itself from the old Labourist class politics. Ken Livingstone himself, as GLC leader, had no such illusions.[55] He knew very well how much the parliamentary leadership actively disliked (or at least feared being embarrassed in the eyes of the press by) black or feminist activists like those who took over the podium at the 1981 Conference. But the influence of *Marxism Today* helped to create a climate which undermined the kind of enthusiasm that supporters of the LCC had once had (and which *Marxism Today* had once encouraged) for intra-party democracy and for the Alternative Economic Strategy. The trouble was that the kind of thinking *Marxism Today* represented was incapable of producing (any more than Hobsbawm could with his more sober 'popular front' line) any *other* kind of socialist strategy. As Donald Sassoon, who still sees 'the iconoclasm' of *Marxism Today* as having been 'indispensable', admits: 'once the ground was cleared of old-fashioned leftism, the journal and its followers remained unable to go beyond it. ... In the manner of modern gurus they noted a trend (post-Fordism, flexible specialisation or charity events for Third World Countries), called it progress, and projected it into the future. By the time the journal folded in the 1990s, it had nothing left to say.'[56]

A core group of the Labour new left, including the newly formed Campaign Group of Labour MPs around Benn and Heffer, did not share the illusions of the LCC and *Marxism Today*. Their support of extra-parliamentary struggles and the links they formed with the independent socialist left – from the Socialist Society established in 1982 to the Socialist Conferences held in Chesterfield later in the decade – pointed towards a creative politics beyond Labourist parliamentarism. But having lost the initiative within the party, this residue of the Labour new left, continually fighting a series of losing battles against the party's drift to the right, lost such creativity as it had previously displayed. Benn himself, re-elected as MP for Chesterfield in March 1984, remained the left's 'prominent voice' and continued to focus on the need to democratise the state at every level. But this was not echoed by many members of the Campaign Group, and both it and the various socialist movements outside Parliament were politically marginal.

Most of the Labour new left's activists, especially those mobilised by the CLPD, were also more realistic about what Kinnock represented, much more than they had been about Foot. They were not impressed when Hobsbawm introduced Kinnock with fulsome praise at Fabian Society conference fringe meetings. Even when Kinnock promised them that unity would be based on retaining left policies, the party activists who voted for him did so with some sense of discomfort. At any meetings where Kinnock and Benn shared the platform, there could be no doubt about who was closer to the CLP activists politically – and this was revealed year after year in Benn's remarkably high vote in the constituency section balloting for the NEC. The CLP activists' support for Kinnock was quite pragmatic – he seemed to offer a chance to retain left policies and still win the next election. They could not know how far he would go in accommodating the counter-revolution, of course, and they could not know that unity meant what Healey had bluntly told the NEC immediately after the election in July 1983: 'The conference cannot tell MPs how to vote against their consciences . . . We want more tolerance of the Shadow Cabinet by the party and the NEC must accept the former's leadership role.'[57] They felt they had no option but to 'let Neil get on with it' in the name of unity – and to hope for the best in terms of left policies being retained.

Once the Labour new left's unity of purpose was removed its heterogenous make-up worked to fragment it into what became simplistically – and misleadingly – known as the 'soft' and 'hard' left. A number of its leading figures, including David Blunkett, Tom Sawyer,

Michael Meacher and Peter Hain, gradually parted from Benn and re-aligned themselves with Kinnock. In so far as they hoped, in doing so, to 'push him to the left', they seriously miscalculated. Eric Shaw, who witnessed the process from the inside, summed it up as follows:

> Members of the soft left joined the front bench in the hope of influencing party policy as well as to further their careers but, for some at least, it was *their* views that were more often altered ... Perhaps most important of all, many former Bennites changed their minds, because of the conclusions they had drawn after their experience of the strife of the early 1980s, in response to electoral defeats or because they no longer believed that the policies they had earlier espoused were workable, politically viable or electorally acceptable ... By damaging – probably beyond repair – the unity of the left, the effect of realignment was the isolation of the hard left who, by the end of the 1980s, were left as the only organised yet largely impotent focus of resistance to Kinnock's modernisation project.[58]

The massive vote for the Kinnock–Hattersley 'dream ticket' in the leadership election at the 1983 Conference (and for the expulsions of Miliant members); the marginalisation of Tony Benn and the absorption of a number of his erstwhile supporters into the Kinnock team; the election of a Shadow Cabinet with many new faces, but still dominated numerically by the centre-right of the parliamentary party – for those who had tried to change the Labour Party these were all severe defeats. By 1984 the number of individual members of the CLPD had already fallen to half its 1982 level, as had the number of CLP and trade union branch affiliations.[59] The initiative had passed to those elements, by no means any longer confined to the traditional centre-right, who attributed most of the blame for the election defeat to the process of change having gone 'too far', and who looked to policy 'moderation' as the basis for unity and electoral success.

The trouble with this strategy, however, at least initially, was that unity on these terms was unable to respond to the deep social polarisation that the Thatcher government was by then generating in Britain. Its 'counter-revolution' against the Keynesian/welfare state had produced such mass unemployment, destitution, alienation and conflict that the maintenance of public order came to depend on a stronger, more coercive state. Moreover, the fact that the Labour new left had been so clearly weakened lent support to the arguments of those who held that the battles had to be fought in the streets.

10

Disempowering Activism: The Process of Modernisation

Thanks to the division of the opposition vote caused by the SDP split, Mrs Thatcher easily won the general elections of 1983 and 1987, but her policies generated intense popular resistance in one area after another, from the miners' strike to the poll tax revolt that finally brought her down. This activism was a direct descendant of that of the late 1960s and early 1970s. The Labour new left had wanted to build a bridge between the party and that activism, to inflect it in a socialist political direction and to infuse the party with it. That project had now been defeated; the activism continued but could now only take the form of a series of defensive actions. This was a measure of the huge political cost of the Labour new left's defeat. Not only had it failed to democratise and transform the party, but this in turn meant that it had been unable to politicise the great industrial militancy of the time, or to 'nationalise' the myriad creative forms of community politics and local socialism.

This is not the place to retell the story of the great miners' strike of 1984–85, or the struggles over local democracy which continued through the abolition of the GLC and the other metropolitan counties in 1986, to the poll tax revolt of 1989–90 and beyond. But the scale and intensity of these struggles can hardly be overstated. The miners' strike, above all, focused the country's – indeed, the wider world's – attention on the nature of the Thatcherite project in a way that the Labour leadership singularly failed to do. As Raymond Williams observed at the time:

> In a period of very powerful multinational capital, moving its millions under various flags of convenience, and in a period also of rapid and often arbitrary takeover and merger by financial groups of all kinds, virtually everyone is exposed or will be exposed to what the miners have suffered.[1]

In a powerful review of the strike soon after it ended, Raphael Samuel noted that, in resisting the destruction of their jobs, the strikers found that they were involved not so much in 'an expression of community as a *discovery* of it...'. Most of the picketing, he pointed out, was the work of 'young single men, subsisting on a strike allowance of £1 a day,

[who] gave up serious drinking and abandoned the heavy metal clubs and the discos to take their place on the picket lines'.[2] The strike reactivated the retired, and famously mobilised the women of the mining villages, permanently changing many of them in the process.[3] It also galvanised activism – of a very different kind than electoral canvassing – among Labour Party members, on a scale not seen since 1945.

> From day one of the strike, support for the miners among grass roots party members, left, right and centre, was broad, determined and generous. Party branches, general committees, Labour groups on local authorities, women's sections and Young Socialists branches all threw themselves into fundraising and other support activities. Party members turned out again and again at local meetings and rallies, stood week in week out on high streets collecting money and food, sometimes facing police harassment and arrest for their pains.[4]

Similar things could be said about many of the struggles for local democracy. Only two out of five voters supported the Conservatives in the 1983 general election; in the same year a majority of Liverpool voters elected a far-left Labour council, and re-elected them again a year later. In an area of severe deprivation such as Merseyside, opposition to the whole thrust of the government's policy was widespread and deeply felt, and allowed the Militant Tendency to gain control of the council and propel it on a collision course with the government. Despite the Militant leadership's posturing and errors, even in 1985 more Liverpool voters blamed the government than blamed the council for the city's financial plight.[5] In London, where the local left leadership was more creative, three out of every four Londoners were opposed to the abolition of the Greater London Council, which the Government nevertheless pushed through two years later. The messy beginnings of the GLC's project, referred to in the previous chapter, generated not only innovative economic and social policies, but also the kind of democratic restructuring of the state's internal practices and its relations with the community that the Labour new left, at its best, had envisaged.[6] We saw in Chapter 2 that many activists had entered the Labour Party in the mid-1970s because they realised the need for political and material support for the grassroots labour and community organisations they belonged to. As Daniel Egan observes, in the best study of the GLC:

> The Labour left's critique of the failure of both the market and the state (i.e. Labourism) to meet social needs led to a conception of planning in which the state provides support and coordination for the development and implementation of strategy, but in which strategy is undertaken by trade unions and community organisations. During the Labour left GLC's tenure, the Industry and Employment Committee made over 700 grants totalling £19 million to about 300 labour movement and community organisations.[7]

Notwithstanding the concerted media denigration of all such local initiatives as the 'loony left', the Conservative attack on the autonomy of elected local government, most sharply expressed in 'rate-capping' legislation, produced resentment throughout the country. When the poll tax was introduced in 1988, this resentment came to a head with street demonstrations and mass refusals to pay.

In many of these struggles the tactics were almost inevitably modelled on the heady experiences of activism in the early 1970s, epitomised by the 1972 mineworkers' flying pickets at the Saltley coke depot in Birmingham, the Clay Cross councillors' refusal to raise rents as required by the Heath Government's Housing Finance Act, and the 'Pentonville Five' dockers whose threatened imprisonment nearly precipitated a general strike. But by now the context had changed radically. The Thatcher Government had a clear political project and was determined to carry it out. On top of a world-wide recession which brought the era of full employment to an end everywhere, the Government's monetarist policies, its assaults on trade union freedoms and its promotion of competitive individualism destroyed the conditions which had made the solidarity of the 1970s possible. During the protracted miners' strike, despite considerable financial and rhetorical support from most union officials, there was little practical cooperation in the way of sympathy action or even refusal to cross the miners' picket lines.[8]

Victory in such momentous contexts required the determination and planning that only a political party with an equivalently coherent project and organisational capacity could give. But the Labour leadership had nothing of this kind to offer: they were as paralysed in the face of popular activism as they had been a decade earlier, if not more so; the confrontations of the 1980s brought the Labour Party face to face with the question of whether to come out squarely against the Government's coercive tactics and against the bias of the police and the judiciary. This was always a wrenching question for a parliamentary party whose politics had been premised on the values of social harmony and moderation; it did not know what to do when faced by a reactionary and coercive state, on the one hand, and on the other by a stubborn refusal to back down on the part of a substantial section of the party's own constituency. Although its parliamentary leaders knew what they were supposed to say – that is, compromise, and look to the next election – the question was whether they could say it without creating a new scission within the party.

The NEC and the party General Secretary, Jim Mortimer, actively supported the miners; but Kinnock equivocated, condemning violence on all sides without taking sides. This meant that the Labour Party was not seen as fully behind the miners. Even less was it seen to be behind the local Labour left confrontations with the Government. It is true that there were elements of sectarianism and revolutionary posturing in the leadership of these industrial and municipal struggles, of the kind which always presents problems for a national party leader at moments of crisis.[9] But the task of democratic leadership must surely be to coordinate, subsume, balance, steer – in a word, to *lead* – popular struggles, not to shun them, let alone join in denigrating them. Kinnock saw himself as saving the party's electoral image from contamination by association with televised scenes of pit-head confrontations and press caricatures of 'loony left' councils. Yet the fact that one in five households in Conservative-voting suburbs were giving material support to the miners, and that Conservative county councils were among the leading opponents of the assault on local government autonomy, suggests that the electoral constraints were by no means necessarily so narrow.[10]

Kinnock's equivocations during the miners' strike contrasted painfully with his bravado at the 1985 Conference once Mrs Thatcher, the security apparatus, the police, the judicial system and the media had done their work.[11] His celebrated assaults on the NUM leadership and the Militant leaders of the Liverpool Council at this Conference represented, and were intended to represent, far more than a distancing of the party from what he derisorily called 'the generals of gesture' and 'the tendency tacticians' of the 'hard left'. His speech was, above all, a full redeclaration of independence by the party leader from the sovereignty that the Labour new left had claimed for the Conference, and for the extra-parliamentary party more generally. As Labour leaders had done so often in the past, but with even greater effect, given recent party history, Kinnock spoke as much over the heads of the delegates as he spoke to them. He was effectively saying, to the media, to the Tories and the Alliance, and not least to the right-wing social democrats who still dominated the PLP: You may say that the party is beholden to the unions, you may say the constituencies are dominated by extremists, but you can't pin that on me. And since within the British constitutional framework what matters once a party is elected is not so much what the party does or says as what the Prime Minister does and says, this was indeed the message these audiences wanted to hear, as the headlines made clear: 'NEIL SLAYS 'EM' (*The Mirror*); 'Kinnock speech a masterpiece, say moderates' (*The Times*); 'Kinnock beats left in show of strength' (*The Guardian*); and best of all, in the *Daily Mail*: 'THE COURAGE OF KINNOCK: Labour's most sensational speech in 25 years' – including a photograph of a happy and proud Glenys Kinnock saying, 'He's got guts and he showed it.'

The great majority of the delegates gave Kinnock a prolonged standing ovation, and this was more than a matter of playing their allotted role before the television cameras. Many of the same 1,800 people who attended a Labour Herald rally the night before to hear and cheer Benn and Scargill were the next morning on their feet applauding Kinnock. This political schizophrenia was due to the fact that Kinnock, like Foot before him, retained a substantial base among the rank-and-file of the party of a kind that right-wing parliamentarians never had, in good part because of his position on unilateralism and his defence of the welfare state. And however much the delegates might have preferred – indeed however much they continued to vote for – left-wing resolutions and NEC candidates, they also badly wanted to win the next election, to get Thatcher out at all costs.

The trouble with this, of course, was that it closed off the possibility of constructing out of the crisis anything resembling a socialist alternative to Thatcherism. Moreover, the media's adulation did not last. They sensed that the strength and depth of the previous socialist mobilisation in the party had been such that Kinnock's social democratic rhetoric would not be enough to enable the party to present a unified face to the electorate. The exorcism of the left could not be a one-off event. Despite Kinnock's attack on Militant and the mineworkers, *The Times* immediately turned its attention to women and black activists:

> ... the face of the Labour Party has not stabilised. What is offered to the voters in Brent, Haringey or Hackney is not Mr Kinnock's emollience but Miss Abbott's rhetoric of class struggle and skin-colour consciousness and the insurrectionary talk of Mr Bernie Grant. In a party with no boundaries, in a church with no catechism beyond the nullity of Clause IV, they have as good a claim to speak for 'socialism' as he does. Exit (perhaps) Mr Mulhearn, Mr Hatton and sundry other followers of the Fourth International; enter – with no one to bar their way – class and race warriors in thrall to the same Marxist doctrine.[12]

This was red-baiting of the crudest kind. It is very improbable that more than a handful of Labour new left activists, male or female, white or black, were ever 'Marxists' of any description. But *The Times*'s crudity stemmed from a passionate wish to write *finis* to the threat of 'socialism' in Britain. And this passion was shared by many on the right of the parliamentary party who also longed for an end to Thatcherism. There was work still to do in making the Labour Party a safe alternative government for the British establishment.

The Transition under Kinnock, 1983–92

This work Kinnock now began. He set in motion an organisational transformation that would culminate ten years later in the emergence of a new kind of party, more and more detached from what was left of the labour movement. The trade unions would lose much of their influence inside the party and would be told to expect no special favours from a future Labour government. Party membership would be expanded, and the influence of active members diluted and curbed. Control would be more and more frankly concentrated in the hands of a leadership elite of professional politicians, and above all, in the hands of the leader himself.

The central theme of all the changes was to allow the leader to determine party policy with only the formal approval of the party outside parliament – i.e. both its trade union wing, and its constituency activists – and to be seen by the media to be doing so. The Labour new left was to play very little part in this story. Some of its principal figures, as we have seen, aligned themselves with Kinnock. The 'soft' left supported him when he conspicuously dissociated himself from the mineworkers, closed the party's *New Socialist* magazine, and drastically reduced the influence of the NEC's policy committees – and the fact that they did so in the very midst of his distancing the party from the activist resistance to Thatcherism does put in question the strength of the commitment to extra-parliamentary politics of this particular stratum of the Labour new left. Others, including Benn, continued to articulate the new left's analysis and vision of the future, which still had some resonance in the labour movement and in a wide variety of social movements; but Benn and the remaining new left activists had now been effectively relegated to the party's margins, and no fresh generation succeeded them.

Kinnock later defended his establishment of an altogether novel degree of personal control over the party by saying, 'the condition of the party made management an obligation – so I got on with it'.[13] He was able to do this not only because he had been elected leader by overwhelming majorities in all three sections of the new leadership electoral college and so enjoyed a new kind of legitimacy, but also because the Office of the Leader of the Opposition now disposed of far more resources than ever before. Thanks to the unions' agreement to let the parliamentary leadership keep the new funding for opposition parties referred to in Chapter 8 (the so-called 'Short money'), by 1983 the Labour front bench had at its disposal £440,000 for research and assistance, and the trade unions added a further £100,000 per annum for the Office of the Leader. 'There were now, for the first time in party history, resources for a sizeable advisory staff available to the PLP leadership.'[14] By the end of Kinnock's term as leader, in 1992, the 'Short money' had risen to £1,455,000.[15]

Kinnock immediately set about removing control over policy-making from the NEC and the annual Conference. As seen by Patrick Seyd and Paul Whiteley, academic observers sympathetic to Kinnock, the party had become unpopular with the electorate because its policies reflected the views of its radical activists in the constituencies and the trade unions, who were unrepresentative of the electorate. Therefore

> The party leadership's first task ... was to reduce the activists' powers. It could not afford just to ignore them, because of their possession of significant constitutional powers. Yet it was electorally inexpedient for the leadership to rely on the block votes of certain trade union leaders to maintain its position at the party conference, because of the trade unions' general unpopularity, even among their own members.[16]

Kinnock's solution was to create a new system of Joint Policy Committees composed equally of NEC members and MPs. These effectively superseded the NEC's Home Policy and International Committees, with their myriad subcommittees; and although the Joint Policy Committees were chaired by NEC members, and assisted by secretaries drawn from both the party headquarters and PLP staff, effective control of their agendas and outcomes passed gradually into the hands of the leader and his professional advisers. As Lewis Minkin remarked,

> ... one must note the growing confidence, increasing resources and, at times, ruthless assertiveness of the PLP leaders, as they took full advantage of the mood change brought about by the defeat of 1983. From the first, the key Jobs and Industry Joint Committee was colonised by coopted supporters of the Shadow Chancellor and deputy leader. Key subcommittee chairs were taken by the Front Bench. An economic strategy emerged not only from the committee but in public speeches by Hattersley, in which the new direction was charted and new policy departures sometimes announced before they were taken into the party's procedures. Through his political and policy advisers, the new leader was able to exercise a selective but broad-ranging oversight ... the leader's assistants sat in on policy committees, formal and informal, taking initiatives, 'fighting fires', and letting others in the unions know 'what Neil wants'.[17]

The old tripartite NEC–PLP–TUC 'Liaison Committee', through which the NEC had formerly operated to secure pre-conference agreement with the unions and the PLP on policy issues, was gradually sidelined. What now became dominant was the Office of the Leader. And Kinnock deployed his new power directly against the party's so-called 'hard' left. After denouncing the Militant Tendency at the 1985 Party Conference he oversaw a series of measures to delegitimise and exclude it. The NEC expelled a small number of Militant leaders, after two years of exhausting internal conflict; then in 1987 a new National Constitutional Committee was set up, with exclusive and final powers to expel members, which worked its way without publicity through a further long list of Militant activists. The conflict over the expulsions was a significant factor further separating those who had aligned themselves with Kinnock from those, like Benn, who opposed the expulsions both on civil liberties grounds and out of a sense of solidarity with individuals who worked in a committed way on causes they held in common.

Perhaps the most important organisational change made by Kinnock, which would eventually drastically reduce the significance of not merely the NEC, but the whole extra-parliamentary party, was the creation in 1985 of a new 'Campaigns and Communications Directorate' (CCD) at the party headquarters. Directed by Peter Mandelson, the CCD had an annual budget of £300,000 at its peak in 1986–87 and operated in close collaboration with the leader's office, and with virtually total autonomy from the party's administrative hierarchy at the Walworth Road head-quarters. Mandelson also set up a 'Shadow Communications Agency' (SCA), coordinated by a professional market research and advertising specialist, Philip Gould, to provide information about the electorate and recommend ways of appealing to it. Mandelson devoted himself to getting the party to present itself in ways that the media would report positively. Gould provided 'interpretations' of the opinions and attitudes of voters.

The new strategists' growing influence – an influence which was far from politically innocent – reinforced two crucial shifts in the party's politics.[18] First, electors were now seen primarily as consumers of party programmes, with already-given attitudes and interests, rather than as people who could be persuaded to find their needs and aspirations met in the party's project for social change; and the electors who were seen to matter above all were 'swing' voters in marginal seats, who said things like 'it's nice to have a social conscience but it's your family that counts' and other Thatcherite-sounding statements.[19] Second, editors and jour-nalists were treated as the arbiters of what it was sensible for the party to advocate, in a way that even National Executive members were not.

The first tendency – treating voters so explicitly as consumers with pre-given wishes – followed logically enough from defining the party's overriding task as that of winning the next election: even if the leader and one or two senior colleagues had been thinkers of vision, with a body of new philosophy and practical thinking to draw on, winning electoral support for it would have required much more time than the interval between two elections. It represented, however, a decisive shift away from the concept of the party as a shaper and leader of opinion towards the idea of the party as marketing products – products which could themselves be more or less indefinitely modified in the light of 'market testing'. Similarly, accepting the power of editors to define what is sensible is also understandable, once their power to damage the party's short-term electoral prospects is taken for granted, and the power of senior party leaders to challenge and displace such definitions is dis-counted. But the significance of this conclusion can hardly be overestimated.

Then in 1987 came the further shock of the party's third successive election defeat. A slick media-oriented campaign, meticulously planned by Mandelson and Kinnock's press secretary, Patricia Hewitt, and widely judged to have been professionally superior to the Conservatives', failed to do more than beat back the challenge of the Liberal–SDP Alliance (which fell back slightly but still commanded almost a quarter of the vote). Labour's share of the vote rose from 27.6 per cent in 1983 to only 31.7 per cent; while the Conservatives slightly increased their share to 43.4 per cent and returned with another large parliamentary majority. Now, instead of merely trying to reduce the visibility and influence of the left wing of the party, Kinnock initiated a more radical change in party policy, and a more radical loosening of the links tying the leadership to the party outside Parliament.

On policy, Kinnock got the NEC – on which he had, by now, a reliable majority – to agree to submit the whole range of existing party policy to a new 'Policy Review'. This consisted of seven 'Policy Review Groups', each jointly chaired by a member of the NEC and a member of the Labour front bench. What was now at stake was how far the party should go in accepting the legacy of Thatcherism as a new 'settlement', as the Conservatives had once accepted that of 1945–51. The review, which was closely monitored and steered by Patricia Hewitt and Kinnock's personal staff, took two years, its final conclusions being adopted by Conference in 1989.

It removed three key planks from Labour's 1987 election platform: renationalisation of industries privatised by the Conservatives, the restoration of trade union rights abolished under successive Thatcherite laws during the 1980s, and unilateral nuclear disarmament, to which Kinnock himself (and notably his wife) had previously been strongly committed. Yet the results were still mixed. 'The market' was explicitly accepted, as a potentially neutral means of allocating resources; but emphasis continued to be laid on the need to redistribute wealth to give people more equal opportunities in the market. The state's role continued to be stressed in industrial policy, environmental regulation, regional policy, training, competition, and control of natural monopolies; and public ownership was not renounced, although employee share ownership schemes and cooperatives, and the public ownership of individual firms rather than whole industries, were endorsed. On industrial relations, a return to the pre-Thatcher system was ruled out, though trade unions were to get more rights under a new, specialised system of industrial relations courts.

Part of the reason why the results were mixed was that in the Policy Review process the dominance of the leader over policy-making was still incomplete.[20] But the review did create a precedent for explicitly reversing the flow of policy-making enshrined in the party constitution, according to which policy was the outcome of a process starting with resolutions submitted by local parties and affiliated organisations, as well as by the NEC, resolutions which were then 'composited', debated, and voted on at Conference with or without amendments. The seven Policy Review reports were presented to the 1989 Conference by the NEC to be adopted or rejected as a whole; no amendments were allowed. Later, Rentoul notes, the use of NEC 'Statements' to Conference, which under the party's rules could likewise not be amended, would become a common feature of party policy-making under Tony Blair.[21]

While the Policy Review was going on there was, admittedly, a curious exercise in seemingly 'bottom-up' policy-making called 'Labour Listens', mounted by the party's national headquarters in 1988–89. Meetings were organised throughout the country at which members of the public were invited to tell the party what they thought. The process was barely serious. There was no concern for the representativeness of the meetings, which were mostly poorly attended, nor were any mechanisms put in place to ensure that what people said was fed into the Policy Review.[22] The one thing that was clear was that the meetings were not for listening to Labour activists. It was an effort, however misconceived or even disingenuous, to link the party to the public over the heads of its active members, and to be seen to be doing so.

The grip of the leader's office on policy-making thus became more and more detailed and exclusive, and through Mandelson's management of press relations the media gradually came to treat the leader's views unquestioningly as party policy.

> Again and again the leader would let it be known through his private office what would and would not be Labour Party policy. The press grew accustomed to this and gave far more weight to these unattributable briefings than to the decisions of the annual Labour Party Conference. The Walworth Road policy directorate became an irrelevance.[23]

If anything, the media now looked only for discrepancies between the views of the leader and those of other front bench spokespeople, i.e. only for potential 'splits' *within* the PLP leadership, where power now clearly lay. As for the party's official policy-formulating machinery at the party headquarters, it was now thoroughly eclipsed by the 'teams' assembled by the Shadow Cabinet members. When Roland Wales, head of the party's Policy Directorate, finally resigned in October 1995, making little effort to conceal the fact that it was because the job had become pointless, his departure was treated by the media as barely newsworthy.

In addition to keeping tight control over policy formation in the short run, Kinnock also pursued two linked strategies designed to reduce the long-term influence of both the unions and active party members. First, under the slogan 'one member one vote' (or OMOV), he proposed that all individual party members should be able to vote in elections for the party leader, the selection of candidates for Parliament, and delegates to annual conferences; and the balloting would be done by post, not at meetings which only activists attended. Kinnock and his advisers assumed (rightly, as the 1995 Clause IV vote seemed to show) that less active members would be less left-wing. Kinnock also argued that OMOV would make more people want to be members; he envisaged a doubling of the membership from its then level of about 250,000 (at one time he rashly set a target of 1 million). Second, as individual membership rose, Kinnock proposed that the weight of the trade union block vote at annual conferences should be reduced.

These proposals addressed real problems. Party activists were indeed unrepresentative of the opinions of Labour voters, although Kinnock had been happy to rely on the activists' support while he still championed unilateral nuclear disarmament. On the other hand the trade union leaders' block votes were no less unrepresentative; they were casting millions of votes for members who were less and less politically involved – and moreover they often did so with little prior consultation with these members, and with no weight given to minority views among them.[24] Now that this means of curbing the power of activists had itself become unreliable it was declared to be indefensible. Kinnock's 'soft leftism' did not extend to wanting to democratise the trade unions and get their members more actively involved in politics, as the Labour new left had wished. He and his General Secretary, Larry Whitty, maintained that they not only wanted to increase the number of members but also to 'increase activism within the party'.[25] In fact, between 1984 and 1988, 60,000 members left the party and individual membership fell to its lowest level for forty years; and by 1991, when membership had very slightly recovered, a survey by Seyd and Whiteley revealed that 'four in every ten members felt themselves to be *less* active ... than they were five years [earlier]'.[26] What they actually wanted was a new source of *in*activist (and hence 'moderate') support for the leadership in the shape of a wider membership who could be directly consulted through postal votes. The changes really portended a North American-style party of professional politicians, supported by a membership who were essentially donors and election helpers, not participants in party policy formation, or leaders and mobilisers of local opinion.

Kinnock met too much resistance from both left and right, however, to be able to do more than initiate this transformation of the party. He was able to get the 1987 Conference to agree to a new system for selecting parliamentary candidates, which compromised between the principle of OMOV and the traditional weight accorded to the unions.

All individual members in the constituency would be balloted, but the final selection would be made, following the ballot, by a local 'electoral college' in which locally affiliated trade unions might have up to 40 per cent of the votes. Kinnock also got the unions to agree that in 1993 the weight of the trade union block vote at the annual conference would be reduced from 90 to 70 per cent, and that when individual party membership surpassed 300,000 consideration would be given to reducing this still further to 50 per cent. But this was as far as he could go. He was obliged to leave it to his successors to complete the party's transformation from one that still saw itself as the political wing of a social movement, to an elite-run electoral machine with a membership comprising a broad cross-section of the electorate.

The 1992 Election and John Smith's Interregnum

Labour's fourth consecutive general election defeat in April 1992, when its share of the vote still barely surpassed 35 per cent, not only forced Kinnock to resign but also reopened the issue of the power of the trade unions in the party, which the Conservative press continued to treat as its fundamental disqualification for office. Both the front-running candidates for the leadership, John Smith and Bryan Gould, called for the principle of OMOV to be extended, and Smith, having won the race, took up the question again. He established a Union Links Review Group which, urged on by Tony Blair in particular, eventually adopted OMOV for candidate selection, with only a slight concession to a continuing special role for the unions;[27] and a revised formula for leadership elections in which union members affiliated to the Labour Party, voting as individuals, would have a third of the electoral college votes (the other two-thirds being cast by MPs and Euro-MPs, and constituency party members, respectively). These changes were adopted by a narrow majority at the 1993 Party Conference (at which, in line with the previous agreement, the weight of the unions' block vote had already been reduced to 70 per cent).[28]

Apart from OMOV, however, John Smith's leadership called a halt to the centralising process and allowed a notable reopening of policy debate, at least within the PLP. Mandelson had already left the Campaigns and Communications Directorate in 1989 to become MP for Hartlepool; the directorate was now wound up, while Patricia Hewitt, Kinnock's former press secretary and a key architect of his centralisation measures, moved, after overseeing the Policy Review, to a new Labour-oriented think-tank, the Institute for Public Policy Research, and thence to a high-powered job in the private sector. A more traditional style of leadership was re-established.

... participants soon noticed a change in the way difficult issues were being handled. It was expressed in the look of confusion on the faces of some of the less bright committee members, the little-known functionaries sent along by their trade unions, who were not accustomed to having to make up their own minds on questions outside their immediate sphere of competence. For years, they had got by on telephone calls from Charles Clarke or Neil Stewart, in Neil Kinnock's office, which would tell them beforehand what the contentious questions were, and how they were expected to vote ... Having been bequeathed a huge majority on the NEC, with only Tony Benn as the last hangover of the former Bennite left, Smith had no need for such a tight operation.[29]

Nor did he appear to want it; on the contrary, he made it clear to the left wing of the party that in his view they had a legitimate voice in party affairs, and unlike Kinnock he maintained civil and even friendly personal relations with people like Livingstone and Benn whose politics he disagreed with.

The professionals who had come to play such a key role in the Kinnock years were deeply unhappy. All but one of Kinnock's office staff were replaced, but

there were numerous other advisers or researchers who regretted the change of face at the top. These were people who had entered politics to make a career of it ... fast risers who liked working to a clear chain of command, with a strong leader at the top as a source of quick decision-taking. Now they found themselves working to committees, in an atmosphere in which being bright, tough and disciplined did not necessarily count for so much as long, loyal service.[30]

Yet as McSmith, writing in 1993, presciently observed, the long-term outcome of the contest between the modernisers and the rest was not hard to foresee:

One side is well organised, with strong professional back-up. They have not one but two credible leaders in Gordon Brown and Tony Blair, and a clear idea of what they want ... On the other side there is not a disciplined army, but a jumble of right- and left-wing factions opposed to one part or another of the Kinnockite project.[31]

What McSmith could not foresee was how quickly the modernisers would return to power. On 12 May 1994 John Smith died. On 1 June Gordon Brown decided not to run for the leadership and on 21 July Tony Blair was elected leader with 57 per cent of the total votes cast.[32]

'New Labour': The Modernisation Project of Tony Blair

When Tony Blair succeeded to the leadership the power to set policy was placed in the hands of a leader who, for the first time in the party's history, was almost completely free from the influence of the party's traditional 'labourist' ethos – the mix of values and practices, evolved over some 150 years of collective political effort, which had hitherto shaped party policy. Not everything in this ethos was admirable – as Henry Drucker pointed out in 1979, it contained a great deal that was archaic, formalistic and anti-intellectual;[33] but it also comprised some of the most egalitarian, humanistic, internationalist and brave elements of progressive British culture. Previous party leaders had been influenced by this ethos to different degrees: none was as untouched by it as Tony Blair, either before he became leader in July 1994 or afterwards.[34] In the Leader's Office, and in his most intimate political circle, he operated in a milieu with a different ethos, that of professional politics based on higher education, management skills, and the culture of the communications industry. Some of the chief exponents of this ethos more or less openly despised that of the old labour movement. In particular, they rejected the idea that capitalism might one day be replaced by a superior social and economic system. For them, the task was only to manage it; socialism – a word most of them avoided – meant at most a set of values that should govern this task. Blair agreed. This meant, first and foremost, completing the process of taking power away from the party's activists, nearly all of whom thought capitalism should either be replaced, or at least – through a return to a more 'mixed economy' and far greater state intervention – radically modified.[35]

Blair restored the Kinnock regime. Young staffers from the Leader's Office were once more omnipresent, policy documents handed to members of the NEC at the door had to be signed for and returned at the end of the meeting, and Shadow Cabinet members were required to clear all their speeches with the Leader's Office in advance. Key players in Kinnock's team also reappeared. Mandelson returned to centre stage as one of the new leader's closest advisers, after a celebrated role (officially kept 'secret' because of his unpopularity with many senior party figures) as Blair's campaign manager in the leadership contest. He was appointed a junior whip, and in July 1995 was given charge of running a by-election campaign in Littleborough and Saddleworth which gained instant notoriety for appealing to right-wing authoritarianism and anti-tax attitudes, and for its use of negative personal attacks on the ultimately successful Liberal Democrat candidate. In October 1995 he was appointed to the front bench in the deputy leader's office and also given overall charge of running the forthcoming general election campaign – a move which led shortly to the departure from the party headquarters of both the Policy Director and the Director of Campaigns and Media inherited from the Smith era.[36] Patricia Hewitt remained in the private sector but returned to the inner circle as a member of an unofficial group of policy-makers run by Mandelson for Blair, and was soon adopted as parliamentary candidate for the safe Labour seat of Leicester West.[37]

Meantime the 'OMOV' strategy began to show results. Tom Sawyer, who replaced Larry Whitty as General Secretary of the party when Blair assumed the leadership in 1994, launched a sustained membership drive inspired by the 'Sedgefield model' developed by Blair in his own constituency, and by American-style management thinking. Blair had got the NEC's permission for the Sedgefield constituency party to recruit members by accepting whatever they were willing to pay by way of subscriptions, and making up the difference between this and the national membership subscriptions by local fundraising. The effect was to increase Sedgefield's membership to 2,000 by 1995, compared with an average of 470 members per constituency for the country as a whole. If, as critics complained, the price was that time had to be spent 'organising barbecues instead of meetings', the benefit was a broadly-based membership, attached to the party as much by social as by political ties – as members of the Conservative Party traditionally were – and run by Blair and his core of loyal supporters, not by activists with political ideas and agendas of their own.

As for the management approach to membership, it was reflected in constant advertising for members in the national press, and in a revealing interview given by Tom Sawyer in which he said 'he favoured management consultants [he mentioned the Cranfield Institute of Management] to help inject new thinking into the party's targeting of new members, including judgements on whether members are best recruited in marginals or heartlands, to raise funds or to be active. Different marketing techniques will be used for different goals . . .'.[38]

By the middle of 1995 Sawyer reported that 113,000 new members had joined since Blair became leader; total membership had reached 350,000. On the other hand, in the same period 38,000 members had left. This was a serious exodus, but a price the leadership was not unwilling to pay; an interesting example, perhaps, of a government dismissing an unpopular electorate and choosing one it likes better. The new members do not seem to have been very different in their attitudes from members of longer standing. A survey in May 1995 found that 57 per cent were in favour of Labour setting a rate for a minimum wage before the next election (an indicator of sympathy for trade union demands, since Blair was resisting making such a commitment), while only 40 per cent said they 'agreed with the direction the party was going under Blair' (23 per cent disagreed, and – perhaps most significantly – 37 per cent didn't know).[39] But their role in supporting Blair's successful campaign to rewrite Clause IV of the party constitution was to prove crucially important.

Clause IV famously stated that the party's central object was 'to secure for the workers by hand or brain the full fruits of their industry and the most equitable distribution thereof that may be possible upon the basis of the common ownership of the means of production, distribution and exchange...' Gaitskell had tried unsuccessfully to change it in 1960; ever since it had continued to be treated, as Harold Wilson had cynically remarked, like Genesis, as part of the Bible (and 'you can't take Genesis out of the Bible'). Soon after Blair's election as leader in July 1994, he resolved to return to this battle and indicated as much, in slightly veiled language, at the Party Conference in October. The NEC somewhat reluctantly agreed and called a special Conference for April 1995. A campaign of opposition to any change was begun by twenty Labour Members of the European Parliament in an advertisement in *The Guardian* in January 1995, and taken up by the Socialist Campaign Group of Labour MPs and others outside Parliament. Blair responded by undertaking a unique series of thirty-five highly publicised meetings throughout the country, attended by a total of some 30,000 party members, at which he urged that Clause IV no longer represented the range of values that the party stood for in the 1990s, while on the other hand it committed it to something – public ownership – that people no longer believed in: 'I don't think anyone now believes that vast chunks of industry should be taken over by a Labour government'.[40]

The latter argument was distinctly tendentious. The polls showed that a majority of the electorate still favoured public ownership of energy, water and railways, and the fact that the modernisers used the same implausible rhetoric as the Conservative press suggested that they were unwilling to discuss the issue on its merits; Peter Mandelson, for example, in a debate with Arthur Scargill on the new Clause IV in May 1995, after its adoption, said: 'The old Clause IV threatened the end of private corner shops, newsagents, markets. That would mean buying our chips at the Common Ownership Fryers.'[41] But it worked; at the special Conference on 29 April 1995, 90 per cent of the constituency delegates' votes were cast for the change, offsetting the much narrower majority (54.6 per cent) cast in favour of it in the unions – a striking inversion of the old pattern, in which right-wing union leaders could be relied on to back the leadership against the left-wing activists in the constituency parties.[42] The old Clause IV was replaced by a portmanteau commitment to a range of other values (a dynamic economy, a just society, an open democracy and a healthy environment); including, crucially for the media, an endorsement of 'the enterprise of the market and the rigour of competition', and 'a thriving private sector' – even if, as Hugo Young noted, no one at the special Conference which finally endorsed the new wording displayed any notable enthusiasm for any of these.[43]

Blair's decisive victory enhanced his authority and enabled him to contemplate further changes. One was to pursue the further reduction in the weight of the unions' block vote at party conferences to 50 per cent, already agreed in principle once the total individual membership of the party exceeded 300,000, which it now had;[44] this change came into operation in 1996. Another was to put pressure on the unions to ballot their members on issues to be decided at party conferences: 'There will have to be discussions to ensure that from now there is a much greater consistency of view between what ordinary members think and the votes cast by their leaders.'[45]

Blair also moved to end trade union sponsorship of MPs, the system whereby in over 150 constituencies unions undertook to pay some of the expenses of the local party organisation – sums generally around £600 a year, and £2–3,000 at a general election. Although sponsored MPs received no financial benefits for themselves they were expected to represent the interests of the union concerned in Parliament, even though most sponsored MPs claimed that they were never asked to do so in any specific context. Blair, himself sponsored by the TGWU, saw sponsorship as an unnecessary hostage to the Conservative press, which always treated it as evidence that Labour was in thrall to the unions; by February 1996 he had secured the unions' agreement to switch from sponsoring individual candidates and MPs to giving financial support to local party organisations in marginal seats.

Further changes included getting the PLP's agreement to let him choose the party's Chief Whip and Deputy Whip, hitherto elected by the MPs. A further tightening of Blair's control over the party resulted from controversies over candidate selection. As a means of increasing the number of Labour women MPs the 1993 Conference had voted to have 'women-only' shortlists for prospective candidates in 50 per cent of marginal seats and in 50 per cent of all seats held by Labour MPs who were standing down before the next election. This met resistance, partly from male candidates with strong local support (including some anti-feminist 'backlash'), and partly from left-wing activists, both male and female, who saw it as a way of 'parachuting' middle-class women modernisers into their constituencies.[46] Eventually, after Blair let it be known that he would abolish women-only shortlists after the next election, they were declared illegal by an industrial tribunal in January 1996.[47] In one case, however, Liz Davies, a London-based lawyer who had been selected from a women-only shortlist by the party in Leeds North-East, was vetoed by the NEC explicitly on account of her left-wing politics.[48]

The Reaction to Modernisation Under Blair

The left in the party had long since become inured to prolonged periods of self-denial, 'in which those who differed from the party line kept their mouths buttoned up to avoid giving comfort to the enemy';[49] but signs accumulated after the special Conference on Clause IV in April 1995 that their toleration was being stretched to its limits and beyond, however much they wanted to give the new leader the benefit of every doubt. Blair had even risked a joke at their expense, after the vote at the special Conference, when he said that contrary to rumour, 'the [party's] name was not going to change' – i.e. from Labour to 'New Labour', as the party was now called on the covers of all its publications – thus implying clearly enough that it lay within his power to change it if he chose to. A demand from leading trade unionists, that there should be a pause in the 'modernisation' process after the special Conference, was snubbed; on the contrary, Tony Blair told the members of the General and Municipal Union in June, 'he was elected on a platform of change and modernisation. When people asked if he would ever stop, "I say the answer is never".'[50] But the relentless centralisation of power had costs in terms of participation. Party agents and workers reported that in many areas constituency party General Council meetings, once the focus of rank and file participation, were increasingly inquorate – as, interestingly enough, were meetings of NEC committees too.[51]

Finally, three events in 1995 broke the issue open: Blair's indication in June that he would seek an end to trade union sponsorship of MPs, Peter Mandelson's conduct of the Littleborough and Saddleworth by-election in July, and Blair's acceptance in the same month of an invitation to address a conference in Australia of Rupert Murdoch's News International group.

Murdoch's newspapers had vilified Labour throughout the Thatcher years with unremitting lack of scruple (it was of Murdoch that Dennis Potter said, in his blistering final television interview with Melvyn Bragg, 'There is no one person more responsible for the pollution of what was already a fairly polluted press');[52] and Blair's willingness to fly to Australia as his guest was of a piece with Mandelson's ruthless pursuit of votes at the Littleborough and Saddleworth by-election in July. Both exercises had the mark of Mandelson's famous 'unsentimentality', and both stuck in the gullets of many party activists. The issue of trade union sponsorship of MPs had a slower-burning fuse, but in the context of the impending reduction of union voting strength at party conferences, and hints that Blair would call for further reductions in future, the fact that he had chosen also to call for the end of union sponsorship was seen as further evidence of a party take-over by a London-based, middle-class coterie around the leader.

Open resentment was eventually triggered by an article in the *New Statesman* in July 1995 by a mildly left-wing backbench MP, Richard Burden, in which he criticised the 'amorality' of the Littleborough and Saddleworth by-election campaign as a manifestation of New Labour's top-down, centralised power structure, and of a party 'desperate to be elected as representative of mainstream opinion, and yet with its own inner sanctum holding a virtual monopoly on defining what such mainstream opinion consists of'.[53] This was followed by a short outburst of articles and statements also voicing what had previously been said publicly only by the party's left wing; and thereafter by periodic episodes which momentarily brought into the open the resentment felt by many MPs of the rightward drift in party policy and the centralisation of power in the hands of the leadership.[54]

What was striking was the way some of the old Labour right, personified by Roy Hattersley, the former deputy leader under Kinnock, shared in the discontent. Hattersley was careful to remind Blair that he was no advocate of inner-party democracy. 'As always', he said, 'the complaints have been directed at a series of surrogate targets – the arrogance of the young men and women in the leader's office, the increasing detachment from the trade unions, and the most wizened of old chestnuts, "the lack of democracy in policy-making".'

The real problem, he asserted, was a concern about policy; the present leadership had abandoned ideology so completely, and was so preoccupied with winning middle-class support, that its commitment to the fundamental needs of the 'disadvantaged' was no longer clear. 'Ideology', he declared:

> is what keeps parties consistent and credible as well as honest. In the long term, the party's public esteem would be protected by a robust statement of fundamental intention. Socialism – which is proclaimed in the New Clause IV – requires the bedrock of principle to be the redistribution of power and wealth ... When the going gets rough, it is not the new recruits from the SDP who will stay at his [Tony Blair's] side. They will jump ship as soon as they realise that he is not the reincarnation of David Owen [the former SDP leader, now Lord Owen]. The necessary support will come from members of the real Labour Party who, rightly, think he shares their basic beliefs.[55]

Hattersley's intervention was a good indication of how far the leadership had moved away not just from the party's left (old and new), but also from its 'labourist' and 'revisionist' right. Blair's response was predictable. He 'pledged to continue with his wide-ranging "modernisation" of the Labour Party in order to ensure victory in the general election, making it clear that he was undeterred by criticism of his leadership style ... election victory could only be gained by shaking off old-fashioned links and building up voters' trust in the new-style party ...'[56]

Retreat was excluded by the logic of his sustained effort to woo 'middle England', and by his judgement that ridding the Labour Party of its last vestiges of anti-capitalism was the acid test of his merits as a leader. Hattersley's 'real Labour' members might be alienated, but catering at all significantly to them would be pilloried by the media and could jeopardise the party's electoral prospects, which were strong – so the modernisers argued – precisely because 'old Labour' had been so clearly dethroned.[57] The new recruits (wherever they came from) might indeed prove fickle, but the party's capacity to attract them was probably also an index of its ability to win new voters. Thereafter party members might become as relatively unimportant as they are in the Conservative Party or any other bourgeois political party endowed with sufficient funds to fight election campaigns, which are in any case increasingly decided in the media.

Modernisation: The Penultimate Phase

Blair secured three more major changes before the 1997 election. One was to build on his success in going directly to the membership over Clause IV by getting the NEC to agree that the entire party membership should be asked to endorse a 'pre-manifesto programme'. The document was finalised by a joint meeting of the Shadow Cabinet and the NEC and submitted to the annual 1996 Conference, which not surprisingly – since the document had to be accepted or rejected as a whole – endorsed it unanimously. It was then sent out to the whole membership in a 'yes-or-no' postal ballot. Although presented as a way of consulting the membership more widely, the primary aim, commentators agreed, was 'to bind the rank and file into [Blair's] vision of New Labour';[58] or in the words of the document itself, *The Road to the Manifesto* (described by Blair as 'his contract with Britain'): 'There must be no doubt whatever at the end of this process that the party and its constituent parts accept and agree this programme.' In the ballot in October 1996 61 per cent of party members responded, 95 per cent of them voting in favour.[59] Although this process was ostensibly grafted on to the existing policy-making authority of the Party Conference, its thrust was clearly to institutionalise a new, plebiscitary relationship between the leader and party members in relation to which the Party Conference would eventually become less important.

A second change was directed at Blair's critics in the parliamentary party. New rules of conduct were drawn up for MPs, which created the open-ended new offence of 'bringing the party into disrepute'; strong hints were also given that in future local constituency Labour parties might be expected to select parliamentary candidates only from a central list compiled by the National Executive.[60]

The third change, launched publicly on the eve of the 1997 election, concerned the composition and policy-making role of the National Executive and the role of the annual conference. This was the denouement of a review begun almost two years earlier on the initiative of the General Secretary, Tom Sawyer. The essence of the changes proposed in his document, *Labour into Power: A Framework for Partnership*, and endorsed by the NEC in January 1997, was to make the extra-parliamentary party an auxiliary to the parliamentary party, rather than the other way round. Instead of being a potential alternative source of authority to a Labour government, the NEC should be its 'partner', committed to making the party support it. To this end, the NEC should no longer consist of members elected by the annual conference but of representatives directly elected by a range of party 'constituencies', including the unions, the Cabinet, the PLP, the European PLP, local government, socialist societies, the Youth Section and black and Asian members. In particular, constituency labour parties should be represented by ordinary members chosen at the local level; in other words not by people with high enough national profiles to win broad-based support at annual conferences. The 'Old Left' Derbyshire MP Dennis Skinner – the only dissenting voice on the NEC when the report was adopted – noted that after surviving 'off and on' as an NEC member 'for about twenty years by a democratic process', under the new proposals he would not 'even be allowed to stand' (because as an MP he would not be eligible to be a constituency party representative).[61] The activists' last bridgehead in the party's centre was thus marked down for elimination.

Labour into Power also proposed that the party's policy-making process should be permanently changed to something like the Policy Review of 1987–89. A Joint Policy Committee of the Cabinet and the NEC – like the one established by Kinnock, but in future to be chaired by the leader or his deputy – would originate policy documents in a two-year 'rolling' review cycle, steering them through a consultative process in which the chief role would be played by the National Policy Forum, a hitherto informal body of a hundred members who were, *Labour into Power* noted, 'drawn' – i.e. not elected – 'from all parts of the party and country', and who met in private.[62] The revised documents would finally be submitted to the annual conference; but the document clearly did not envisage that they would be hotly debated there. Though the conference was the 'sovereign policy-making and decision-making body of the party', it must become better adapted to the fact that it was also a 'hugely symbolic event' and a 'showpiece'; it must avoid 'gladiatorial conflicts and deeply divisive conflicts' which gave the press opportunities to emphasise 'the alleged power and influence of key individuals, unions or groups'. It should be more of an occasion to listen to the leaders, get educated on policy issues, and show support.

Without detracting from the democratic decision-making powers of the Conference, we need to beware of providing opportunities for external opponents and critics of the party to pinpoint Conference as an example of difficulties for the party in power. We believe there is room for the Party Conference to become a more valuable and rewarding experience for all who take part. It could provide a serious opportunity to set out and publicise Labour's achievements and plans, be the occasion of in-depth consideration of policy, contribute to mutual political understanding, offer opportunities to hear the views of experts or key figures from inside and outside of the party and be a clear exemplification of partnership in practice.[63]

The bland 'corporate' style of *Labour into Power* was evidently meant to soften the impact of what it proposed.[64] But rather than conceal its real intentions, the document's laboured and often disingenuous language tended if anything to draw attention to them.[65] Formally, Conference would remain 'sovereign'; in practice policy would be set by the leadership, discussed (privately) in the Policy Forum, and presented to Conference in such a way that open disagreement would be minimised; and NEC members would cease to be primarily high-profile figures representing important segments of party opinion.[66] This was very much what James Callaghan had proposed in his famous conference speech at the time of the IMF crisis amidst the last Labour Government's conflict with the Labour new left majority on the NEC.[67]

The Union Link in Question

When Callaghan launched his counter-insurgency against the Labour new left in 1976, he depended on the help of the union leadership. But as we saw in Chapter 8, this really implied a broader counter-revolution which would entail the ultimate disengagement of the party from the labour movement itself.[68] *Labour into Power* had now finally put this clearly on the agenda. Already at the TUC Annual Conference in October 1996 the party's industrial relations spokesman, Stephen Byers, had speculated to journalists that the party might ballot its members on severing the link.[69] While this was immediately denied, most commentators thought it was a serious possibility, particularly if the union leadership failed to agree on a 'code of conduct' that would avoid strikes, including binding arbitration and second ballots, that the Labour leadership was said to be urging on them in private discussions; meanwhile 46 per cent of Labour supporters said they favoured ending the trade unions' voting rights at Labour conferences.[70] Publicly, Blair said 'New Labour will, in government, as now in opposition, be respectful of the unions' part in our past, but will have relations with them relevant for today'.[71]

Underlying this Delphic pronouncement was an important shift that had meanwhile been occurring in the party's finances. While the trade unions were still crucial, their contribution to total party income had fallen from 77 per cent of a total of £5.8 million in 1986, to 54 per cent of a total of £12.5 million in 1995, the difference being made up by fundraising activities and donations from individuals and businesses.[72] By 1997 money from people wealthy enough to pay £1,000 or more a year to join the party's 'Thousand Club' (whose members enjoyed periodic meetings with the leadership), or up to £1,000 a head for a dinner with Blair and Brown, had become a significant element in party fundraising, and individual donations to Blair's private 'Leader's Office Fund' had also become substantial.[73] Thus quite apart from the policy shifts that had distanced the party from the unions, its dependence on donations from wealthy businessmen was already large enough to raise questions about the degree to which the unions could expect any major returns from their heavy financial commitment to the party; it seemed only a matter of time before the increasingly anomalous nature of the relationship was called in question. While a formal break with the trade unions would mean a major drop in union funding, their contribution might be replaced by state funding (as practised elsewhere, and advocated by Denis Healey, the former deputy leader, among others) – something that the escalating costs of media-dependent electioneering might well necessitate in any case.

In any event, Labour's days as the political wing of a broad-based social movement, seeking to educate public opinion and to lead a popular drive for social transformation, were clearly over.

11

Tony Blair: The Transition from Socialism to Capitalism

The organisational changes pushed through by Kinnock, Smith and Blair to disempower the activists paved the way for a policy accommodation with neo-liberalism. The modernisers confirmed in this way how correct the Labour new left, for their part, had been in seeing intra-party organisational change as a precondition for effective policy change – in their case, with the goal of making the party into a vehicle for socialism. By the 1997 General Election the shift of party policy away from socialism and towards capitalism had reached the point where the differences between Labour and Conservatives on social and economic issues had become extremely narrow.

The Policy Review of 1987–89 had already abandoned three of the party's long-standing commitments: unilateral nuclear disarmament, the restoration of trade union immunities, and renationalisation of most privatised industries. Immediately afterwards, Labour also completed the reversal of its original hostility to the European Community when in 1989 Kinnock and John Smith (then Shadow Chancellor) both announced their support for British membership of the Exchange Rate Mechanism. This, in turn, meant ceasing to treat full employment as an overriding aim, and so full employment disappeared, even as a long-term goal, from the NEC's 1990 policy statement *Looking to the Future*. Labour's socialism, if it still existed, was now confined to a different way of managing an economy that was no longer a 'mixed' one and that it no longer even proposed to modify significantly, let alone replace.

Thus by the beginning of the 1990s attention was already focused on the question of what exactly the difference between the two major party policies would amount to. In the run-up to the 1992 election, the Conservative Party and press successfully translated this into an issue of taxation policy; and their election victory was widely seen as due to their success in convincing voters that the detailed 'Shadow Budget' released by John Smith three weeks before polling day meant an increase of £1,000 a year in the average family's tax bill. This made a deep impression on the modernisers and would have fateful consequences in the run-up to the next election.

Smith succeeded Kinnock as leader in July 1992, with the strong support of most sections of the party, including most of the modernisers, but especially the trade unions. He took a relatively sanguine view of what the election result implied. As we have seen, he decided to commit himself to complete Kinnock's unfinished project for 'OMOV', but it stretched his credit with the unions to the limit, and after this his priority became party unity. He appointed an independent Commission on Social Justice, under the chairmanship of Sir Gordon Borrie QC, to report on how the Welfare State should be adapted to the changed economic circumstances of the 1990s; and various internal working parties, including one on electoral reform and one on Europe. But his inclination was to 'play the long game', waiting for the Conservatives to outstay their electoral welcome while Labour gradually re-coalesced on the more limited social-democratic terrain that remained available after the abnegations of the Policy Review. A Commission on Electoral Reform, set up by Kinnock, reported in 1993, recommending the Supplementary Vote (similar to the Alternative Vote used in Australia); the Party Conference voted in favour of holding a referendum on the issue.[1] The Borrie Commission on Social Justice was still meeting when in May 1994 Smith died.[2] The modernisers who took charge of policy-making under Tony Blair in July had a very different view of the 1992 election result. They thought the election had been lost because neither the party nor its policies had yet changed enough to match the needs and the spirit of the times. 'For Blair, [the election result] confirmed his view that Labour still had a lot to do, and no time to lose.'[3]

The significance of the changes that had been made in Labour's internal power structure was vividly illustrated at Blair's accession to the leadership. In the past, when a new leader assumed office, attention was focused on how far his known views coincided with the positions recently adopted by annual conferences. In Blair's case, all that journalists wanted to know was what he thought. They took it for granted that if he disagreed with previous conference decisions, these could no longer be seriously considered to be party policy. When Blair expressed the view that Regional Assemblies should be established in England only if they were supported by a majority of the voters in each region, this effectively superseded Labour's former commitment to introduce them by a simple Act of Parliament. Similarly, the party's commitment to restore elected local government control over schools which had 'opted out' under the Conservatives' legislation was abandoned after internal discussions between the leader and the party's 'shadow' education minister; the schools would keep their opted-out status, but with a change of name ('foundation schools'). Many other policy commitments

– such as the introduction of a minimum wage, the abolition of general practitioner 'fundholding' within the National Health Service, the creation of a Scottish Parliament with power to raise and spend taxes and the restoration of a 'publicly owned' railway system – were significantly diluted in statements by Blair and his front bench colleagues. Lists of policy commitments abandoned or significantly modified under Blair's leadership featured regularly in the press, and hardly any of the changes resulted from debates at party conferences. They were often announced first in the media, which could then be relied upon to treat any critical reactions within the party as evidence of a 'split', making opposition difficult.

As a result, policy change was driven forward by Blair and his closest colleagues with – as we have seen – only 'regular and ineffectual spasms of Old Labour discontent'.[4] The unions complained strongly about Blair's refusal to set a specific figure for the minimum wage which the party was committed to introduce (as well they might, given that the party's commitment to a minimum wage had been a quid pro quo for their accepting the leadership's earlier decision not to restore their former legal immunities). Roy Hattersley, the former deputy leader under Kinnock, complained bitterly about David Blunkett's decision, as shadow education secretary, to leave the grant-maintained schools outside Local Education Authority control, and his failure to give unambiguous assurances that they would not be allowed to pick and choose pupils for admission. Alan Simpson, the secretary of the Campaign Group of MPs, protested against the leadership's apparent willingness to entertain the possibility of Britain joining the planned European Monetary Union without a prior democratisation of the EU's political structures. But all these remained, or became, 'New Labour' policies.

The Neo-Liberal Context

What was the world to which 'New Labour' was determined to accommodate? Underlying everything was the abandonment of Keynesianism by Callaghan and Healey which had paved the way for Thatcher's decision in October 1979 to abolish government control over capital movements, leading the rest of the world towards economic globalisation. Huge capital outflows followed; by the end of the eighties Britain had become once again a major rentier nation, with far the largest stock of overseas direct investment relative to GDP of any OECD country, and had decisively opened its economic policies to the arbitration of the capital markets. In conformity with market sentiment, the government made low inflation its chief aim, and control of the money supply (as opposed to fiscal policy or demand management) its only means of achieving it. Industrial output fell and did not recover to the previous peak level of 1973 till 1988, and thereafter fell again, only overtaking the 1973 peak in 1993. Unemployment rose from about 1.3 million in 1979 to 3.4 million in 1986; after dipping to 1.8 million in 1990 it rose again to over 3 million in 1993, and seemed destined to return to roughly this level in every recession.[5]

As the demand for unskilled workers fell, moreover, the proportion of households with no one in work rose to 20 per cent: a major new form of marginalisation was created, with 30 per cent of all children living in poverty, most of them in these workless households. What is more, as unemployment fell, the number of people claiming sick pay rose, until in 1997 their numbers equalled those out of work; a significant proportion of these were clearly older people who had become ill under the stress of anxiety about redundancy, increased work intensity, or deteriorating conditions.[6] The job mix also deteriorated for those in employment, with only 38 per cent of new jobs being full time and permanent.[7]

One effect of these changes was the 'ghettoisation' of the unemployed, separating workers from those out of work; another was a steep decline in trade union membership, from over 12 million in 1979 to under 7 million by 1996, accelerated by a series of Conservative measures that stripped the unions of the legal immunities on which their strength had rested. After the defeat of the miners in 1985 and the printers in 1986, strike action dropped to insignificant levels. Simultaneously, the Conservatives stripped local government of most of its powers. Not only were secondary schools encouraged to 'opt out', but all schools were transferred from local authority management to management by boards of governors. Local authority housing was compulsorily sold to tenants or could be transferred, if tenants agreed, to Housing Associations or Trusts. Local services were privatised, local spending tightly controlled and cut. Although the Conservatives were defeated in most local council elections through the 1980s and 1990s, in the long run all these changes probably cost Labour – at least, considered as a potential instrument of progressive social change – more dearly. By the late 1980s the party's two traditional bastions of support, local government and the trade unions, had been savagely reduced.

Thatcherism also 'colonised the life-world' during these years through a radical shift from non-market to market principles in every sphere. The privatisation of the big utilities, starting with British Telecom, was crucial in changing public perceptions. The publicly-owned utilities had become inefficient and unpopular, largely because they had been systematically starved of funds, which fed through into low morale, poor management, overmanning and bureaucratism. As private companies they quickly became profitable (thanks to being sold cheap, cutting jobs, and being put under 'light touch' – i.e., generous – regulation), and this enabled them to invest. Service improved and although the selling price had been kept low the proceeds were used to cut income tax, and millions of voters took advantage of the cheap offer to make a profit by buying the shares and quickly disposing of them again. And gradually more people did come to own shares, which also made these voters less likely to share the general outrage at the huge salaries and share options of the utility company directors, or the grotesque bonus payments given to the famously 'yobbish' share and exchange dealers in the City following its 'Big Bang' deregulation in 1986.

Radical changes in the state were also important. 'Operational responsibility' was increasingly devolved from ministries to 'executive agencies', nominally independent of ministerial control and subject to quasi-market incentives, charging each other for their work, paying their managers by 'performance' and intensifying the 'throughput' of their junior staff. In the National Health Service, higher education and personal social services, 'quasi-markets' were instituted, based on designating some public servants as 'purchasers' and separating them from service 'providers'. Instead of the distribution and performance of services as a whole being politically accountable to elected representatives in local authorities or Parliament, the providers – hospital staff, school teachers, social workers – now became routine targets of scapegoating, as they tried to meet the tasks assigned by the 'purchasers' with the ever-diminishing resources resulting from central government cuts. A huge new industry of 'auditing' grew up, as the Audit Commission stretched the concept to cover the pseudo-technical monitoring of every sort of performance.[8] The public were encouraged to think of themselves not as users of collectively-provided services such as patients, school parents, or people with disabilities, but as 'customers'.

These radical changes created a relationship between the state and the citizen diametrically opposite to that which the Labour new left had envisaged. It was a relationship which fitted the privatised, individualised culture of Thatcherism. This was the world to which 'New Labour' now aimed to adapt the party's policies.

The Intellectual Context

Four strategic ideas governed this adaptation. First, the next election *must* be won at all costs. This meant catering to the voters' existing ideas, rather than seeking to build support for new ones; moreover the electorally crucial ideas were those of voters who must be won back to Labour, not those of voters who had suffered most under Conservative rule, most of whom would vote Labour in any case. Second, it must be accepted that voters' preferences had been shaped not just by twenty years of new right propaganda, but also by profound changes in the real world. On this view, people no longer identify themselves primarily in terms of social classes or as producers, the workforce is no longer predominantly male, jobs are no longer permanent or secure at any level, the state is no longer regarded as a benign or reliable ally through life's vicissitudes. 'New Labour' policies must reflect these realities. Third, the aim must be to win at least two successive elections, not just the next one, so that long-term policies, such as education and training policies, would have time to bear fruit. This meant that Labour must win acceptance by 'business' as a suitable, and if possible a preferred, governing party, so that investment would be forthcoming to support the growth on which everything else depends. This in turn meant being 'realistic' about the constraints imposed by globalisation – the impossibility of 'Keynesianism in one country', the need to keep corporate taxation and regulatory burdens no higher than elsewhere, and the need to keep British wage levels down to compensate for lower productivity.

Finally, they accepted that today's media – even radio and television, which are supposed to be politically neutral – make it hard for new policies to be appropriately propounded and rationally debated. As Labour's leading media expert, Peter Mandelson, put it, 'politicians' ability to make a persuasive case ... is much diminished because of the limitations of the thirty-second soundbite, repeated by a dozen or more different channels and news bulletins in a single day', while the overwhelmingly right-wing tabloid press systematically misrepresented everything Labour said.[9] Giving all issues the best media 'spin' was seen as an electoral necessity, and this meant keeping tight control over all policy pronouncements.

This strategic perspective gave a new colouring to the evolution of Labour ideology and policy that had begun under Kinnock. There was a different rhetoric, symbolised by the 'New Labour' label itself (adopted by Blair in imitation of Bill Clinton's self-description as a 'New Democrat'), and it had different intellectual roots. There were probably fewer intellectuals in the Blair leadership team than at any previous time in the party's history; people of the independent intellectual authority of Richard Crossman, Tony Crosland or Tony Benn were notable by their absence. Nor was New Labour obviously indebted to any conspicuously original or creative thinkers outside the ranks of the leadership. Instead, and symptomatically, there was a proliferation of new 'think tanks', pools of what might be called 'average' intellectual labour power, which aimed at bringing useful ideas from a wide variety of sources to the attention of the Labour leadership, and doing 'policy relevant' research and reflection for them. By the end of the 1990s at least four such groups were in business: the Institute of Public Policy

Research (IPPR) and Charter 88 (both founded in 1988), Demos (established in 1993), and Nexus (formed in 1996).

Although it was formally a non-party institution, the IPPR's first director (Tessa Blackstone) and deputy director (Patricia Hewitt, fresh from supervising Labour's Policy Review) were both prominent Labour figures; its task was to provide Labour, following its purge of old policies, with a body of solidly researched policy documents. Its publications have a characteristic blend of 'realistic' (in the 'modernisers'' sense) assumptions about the permanence of global capitalism, and well-documented analyses of economic and social problems, and suggestions for their amelioration within the limits of the possible. David Miliband, the secretary to the Borrie Commission on Social Justice which was funded through the IPPR, became head of research in the Leader's Office under Tony Blair, and was said to be an important link between the IPPR and New Labour; but if the fate of the Borrie Report was any guide (in the words of an ironic song sung at Labour social gatherings, it was 'never seen again'), the IPPR should probably be understood more as a useful source of data and analysis than of important new ideas or principles.[10]

Even less central to New Labour's thinking, perhaps, was Charter 88, which focused on issues of democratic rights and liberties and open government.[11] These themes had been put on the agenda by the Labour new left: Charter 88's concentration on proportional representation and a written constitution (advanced by Benn, but pretty much alone), to the exclusion of the Labour new left's wider agenda, took it in a different, more purely liberal, direction. Its work on issues like devolution and quangos undoubtedly contributed both to New Labour thinking and to building public support for constitutional reform. But New Labour – in this respect like the Labour new left itself – disliked PR, as it threatened Labour's electoral monopoly on the left. This made Charter 88 unpopular with Blair and his team.

The case was different with Demos, launched in early 1993. Geoff Mulgan, its founder-director, was formerly adviser to Gordon Brown, Blair's Shadow Chancellor of the Exchequer, and formed part of a small group of intellectuals with good access to Blair. Mulgan founded Demos because he felt that 'public policy and political thinking' had 'become too short-term, partisan and out of touch'. 'In the past,' he wrote, 'creative thinking often came from within the traditional institutions of parliament and parties, and from within the main political ideologies. But these are no longer able to keep up with the pace of change in society, the economy, technology and culture. Society has become more porous and complex, as old traditions and hierarchies have broken down. Demos is a response to this new situation. It draws on ideas from outside the political mainstream.'[12]

Mulgan's work, reflected in the general output of Demos, had certain distinctive features. One was a general lack of attention to political economy, which he regarded as a 'weak' field.[13] The result was utopianism, though this was presented, paradoxically, as 'realism'. The question posed was predominantly one of what to do about various trends that are inexorably working themselves out through the dynamics of modern capitalism and the technological changes it brings – this was the 'realism' part. What was utopian was that few of the practical constraints that affect the options considered were analysed, and no agents of change were specified. Second, there was a constant stress on complexity, differentiation, pluralism and choice. Partly this was code for abandoning analysis in terms of classes; partly it seemed to be a postmodern embrace of difference and particularity (which goes with a rejection of 'grand narratives', of which critical political economy is one). But whatever its sources, the result was a dramatic eclecticism. The topics, concepts, analyses and perceptions that Mulgan drew from so many diverse fields were not brought into any kind of unity, but recurred in kaleidoscopically changing rearrangements. A third characteristic of Mulgan's work was a fascination with the new. For him, what was wrong with past socialist thought was above all that it was 'out of touch' with the 'pace of change'; being 'in touch' is the supreme virtue, and it is mainly found in the younger generation – another recurring theme in 'New Labour' rhetoric.

It seems more likely that there was an affinity between the thinking of Blair and Mulgan than that Mulgan was a significant influence. Nevertheless these same characteristics – utopianism, eclecticism and a constant stress on the 'new' – were very marked features of his speeches too.[14]

Nexus, a fourth potential source of New Labour thinking, was in some ways the most characteristic. Founded early in 1996 following a meeting between Blair and some eighty intellectual sympathisers organised by the formerly LCC journal, *Renewal*, by early 1997 it consisted essentially of a 'database' containing details on some 1,000 individuals who had responded to a call for a pooling of expertise.[15] The idea was for them to work in groups, meeting from time to time in seminars or conferences, but especially exchanging ideas and working papers on the Internet. One could only wonder how far such 'networking' would yield useful answers to some of the questions that Nexus 'theme groups' were posing, such as 'What version of equality does the left now espouse, if any?'; or 'The centre-left stands urgently in need of a new organising ideal – a working model of the kind of society it aspires to create. Can the notion of a "stakeholder society" fill the gap?'[16] What was interesting was that such incontrovertibly crucial questions were seen as quite open – and as capable of being answered by such means. Nexus was perhaps most significant as an index of the extent to which 'New Labour', having distanced itself from most of Labour's 'traditional intellectuals' (now largely dismissed as 'old Labour'), had few deep intellectual foundations of any kind.

New Labour's intellectual limitations were, however, treated with remarkable indulgence by most political commentators – whether because they were impressed by Blair's rhetoric, or tacitly yearned for a change of government, or even (in some cases) hoped to influence it, is impossible to say. They were perhaps also affected by New Labour's heavy investment in media management. Peter Mandelson, in his role as director of the party's Campaigns and Communications Directorate in the late 1980s, had been Labour's answer to Mrs Thatcher's Press Secretary Bernard Ingham, tirelessly 'managing' news and tempting, cajoling or bullying journalists and editors to give favourable treatment to the Labour leadership (a role enthusiastically resumed by Blair's new Press Secretary, Alastair Campbell, from 1994 onwards). Because Mandelson had a very close personal relationship with Blair he came to play an exceptionally powerful role in policy-making. The most distinctive aspect of his thinking was that he accepted the electoral logic of social democracy in the age of global capitalism with a consistency and wholeheartedness of which most Labour MPs, let alone rank and file activists, were incapable. He took it as given that globalisation imposes very severe limits on all social and economic policies, so that the only ones worth promoting are those that capital – 'the market' – will accept. He included in this the power of the increasingly globally-owned media, and was determined that Labour should do whatever it took – including Blair's highly symbolic visit to the annual meeting in Australia of Rupert Murdoch's News Corporation International – to win a less venomously hostile treatment than Kinnock received from the one-third of British national newspaper circulation controlled by Murdoch. In his view, to oppose this was sentimental self-indulgence which the party cannot afford; his notorious alleged remarks about the Party Conference or the unions being dispensable were deliberate provocations to those who resist this logic.[17] It was a logic that Blair accepted (and it paid off, inasmuch as Murdoch instructed the *Sun*, whose attacks on Kinnock were widely believed to have tipped the balance in the 1992 general election, to declare for Blair in the 1997 election).

Mandelson's 1996 book, *The Blair Revolution: Can New Labour Deliver?*, co-written with the former Social Democrat Roger Liddle, was the most ambitious attempt so far to give New Labour a coherent philosophy.[18] Its central thesis was that a new kind of social solidarity was needed for success in global markets:

What are we doing to prepare for inevitable change? Are we going to gain from it and create a sense of social order alongside it, as New Labour wants, or are we going to let change wash over us, with the result that we slip further backwards economically and disintegrate further socially? The Conservatives ... argue that their stress on deregulation and low labour costs is the only way to prepare Britain for a competitive future. Their instinct is to accept the situation of increasing insecurity – even welcome it and further promote it – as the price of remaining competitive in the modern world. New Labour utterly rejects this counsel of despair. The more secure, more cohesive and, as a result, more equal our society, the better our chances of economic success. This is not to delude ourselves that wealth is somehow created by governments or society. Wealth comes from personal effort and entrepreneurial flair, exercised through companies that have found the right formula (which differs from business to business) ... But just as good companies can pull countries up, bad government policies can drag companies down ...[19]

– that is, by not educating and training the workforce adequately, maintaining employment levels and hence consumer demand, removing the causes of social alienation and crime, and so on. The relative coherence of the argument is evident in this passage; at the same time, so is its relative superficiality – for instance the assertion that wealth 'comes' only from 'personal effort and entrepreneurial flair', a formulation clearly aimed at signalling an unconditional renunciation of Labour's 'interventionist' past. Both features could also be seen in the ideology of 'New Labour' propounded by Blair and his front bench team.

New Labour's Ideology

Although Blair claimed in March 1995 that 'a clear reconstruction of a modern ideology' was 'near to completion', this was not evident from his speeches down to that time;[20] they showed the signs of having been 'developed' by speech-writers and 'souped up' by spin-doctors for presentation. His speech to the 1995 Party Conference seemed, admittedly, an extreme example – at least until his speech to the 1996 Conference. Its peroration went like this:

I want us to be a young country again.
Young.
With a common purpose.
With ideals we cherish and live up to. Not resting on past glories.
Not fighting old battles.
Not sitting back, hand in mouth, concealing a yawn of cynicism, but ready for the day's challenge.
Ambitious.
Idealistic.
United.[21]

One of the key words in Blair's emergent ideology would – for a time – be 'stakeholder'.[22] Already in the March 1995 speech cited above he had said: 'I believe that you cannot create a responsible society unless everyone has a stake in it'; and had gone on to list some of the kinds of 'stake' people needed to have, such as secure housing, education, and a welfare system that encouraged independence. Here, having a stake seemed to be just a prerequisite of people feeling responsible for their role in society; in other words, it was an ethical concept, though Blair did add that there were costs involved in not giving people these stakes. In January 1996, however, in a speech to the business community in Singapore, he linked the idea of having a 'stake in society' to the idea of economic efficiency, arguing that the one is necessary for the other:

> We need to build a relationship of trust not just within the firm but within a society. By trust, I mean the recognition of a mutual purpose for which we work together and in which we all benefit. It is a Stakeholder Economy in which opportunity is available to all, advancement is through merit and from which no group or class is set apart or excluded. This is the economic justification for social cohesion, for a fair and strong society, a traditional commitment of left of centre politics but one with relevance today, if is applied anew to the modern world.[23]

'One nation politics', he said, was 'not some expression of sentiment, or even a justifiable concern for the less well off'. In 'a global economy' it was necessary to make everyone cooperatively productive:

> Working as a team is an effective way of working; or playing a sport; or running an organisation. My point is that a successful country must be run the same way. That cannot work unless everyone feels part of the team, trusts it, and has a stake in its success and future.[24]

Even in his Singapore speech, however, Blair's main emphasis was still on the immorality of social exclusion; 'an underclass of people, cut off from society's mainstream, living often in poverty, the black economy, crime and family instability, is a moral and economic evil ... wrong, and unnecessary, and incidentally, very costly'. But this speech marked the potential emergence of a distinctive New Labour argument. Instead of being concerned for the underclass simply as a matter of class interest (old Labourism), or of moral obligation (Blair's 'socialist ethics'), concern for the poor (now renamed 'the excluded') was now presented as necessary for national competitiveness.

This formulation also fitted quite well, on the other hand, with Blair's recurring stress on the *duties* owed by the individual to the community – a theme he plainly found more congenial. In return for having a 'stake' in the community, he argued, individuals have obligations towards it – to take the jobs it offers (which, Blair maintained, also made 'workfare' justifiable); to ensure that one's children attend school (Blair supported penalties for the parents of truant pupils); to be polite to one's neighbours (Blair strongly backed a Labour Party proposal to give local authorities powers to evict repeatedly abusive tenants); to be law-abiding (his most famous slogan was 'tough on crime, and tough on the causes of crime'). He rejected what he called 'early left thinking' which, he claimed, had focused on rights guaranteed to individuals by the state to the exclusion of the responsibilities owed by individuals to the community. He also rejected the 'social individualism' of the 'libertarian left', 'where you "did your own thing"'.[25] Whether there is any sense in which Blair's ethical stance can be considered 'left' is questionable; but it undoubtedly corresponded quite well with the sentiments of many of the voters of 'middle England'.[26] The new right's opposition between collectivism and individual freedom was displaced by a new articulation between the two, but with the collectivity defined as a community of individuals whose economic life remains individualised. For example:

> Let us talk of rising living standards. And let's make that mean cash in the pocket. But let's make it mean more than cash too. Let's make it mean rising standards of behaviour, rising standards in schools and hospitals, rising standards of mutual respect. Those are the living standards that make us one nation – a nation bound together by what unites us, not pulled apart by what divides.[27]

As critics of all stripes pointed out, the most characteristic trope of New Labour rhetoric was the rejection of what it held to be false or irrelevant oppositions – between left and right, capitalism and socialism, capitalists and workers, state and market, good and bad structures – with, as a rule, little supporting argument.[28] The result is a distinctive kind of idealism, co-existing with the insistence on 'realism' about the new globalised economy. The 'realism' consists essentially of the assertion that global capitalism is a permanent and irremovable fact of life, not an inhuman and ultimately self-destructive system: correspondingly, politics is the art of living with it, not a vocation to overcome it. The idealism consists in the assertion that socialist ethics offer an economically superior basis – one more conducive to national competitiveness – for living with global capitalism.

The flavour was well summarised by Henry Porter in a very favourable survey of Blair's first year as leader: 'Nothing seems the same as it was; even the old distinctions between left and right no longer matter as much as generational differences appear to.' And what was distinctive about the new generation? Porter quoted 'a close political ally' of Blair:

> ... Tony had been thinking along these lines long before he was made leader. In fact he was impatient under John Smith to reform the Labour Party. He understood that a whole new generation of people in their thirties and forties had arrived and that they had attitudes and a whole culture which are light years away from the old Labour Party. Intellectually *they accept the restrictions in responsible policy-making that now exist.*[29]

Blair, said Porter, had 'realised that things are not as clear as they appeared to be in the eighties and that many of the new home-owners and new parents – in his words, "the moderate middle-income majority" – are also consumers of Murdoch's various media products. They are . . . concerned with social and economic issues . . . but perhaps the emphasis is more on the good management of a society than on fairness or compassion. And this is exactly the direction Tony Blair has taken Labour, arguing that a compassionate society is firstly a competently run and prosperous society . . .' – and so on. Or as Blair put it, in the soundbite language of 'modernisation':

> What we are about is a partnership between the public and the private sectors, rather than a battle between the two. We are about reforming the welfare state, making it a platform of opportunity. Tough on crime and tough on the causes of crime. Rolling back the quango state. It is extremely important to make sure before you start getting lost in the thicket of policy that the public has really got the big picture.[30]

The word 'socialism' now figured rarely in party literature or the leader's speeches, and always in carefully circumscribed language, usually emphasising the degree to which it was *not* socialism as it used to be understood. For Blair, in particular, socialism (or 'social-ism' as he sometimes liked to write it), referred not to a social system (that was 'old Labour' dogma) but to an ethical ideal; and 'modernising' Labour policy meant dropping all previous ideas about the *application* of that ideal, i.e., not just 'old Labour' ideas about public ownership or the welfare state, but also, indeed even more categorically, all the ideas of the 'new left' in the 1970s about participative democracy. Andy McSmith, in a sympathetic essay, nevertheless drily summed up Blair's Christian socialism as follows: 'Although he is a radical Christian, he does not promise a future in which the first shall be last and the last shall be first. In Blair's Britain, the first shall face fair, non-punitive rates of taxation and the last shall have enhanced opportunities for re-skilling and self-improvement.'[31]

Lest this leave too stark an impression of moral conservatism combined with electoral opportunism, let us conclude this section with a quotation from one of Blair's speeches which paints the kind of broader picture that he favoured (what Porter, perhaps unkindly, calls 'political cinemascope'). Celebrating the fiftieth anniversary of the 1945 Labour Government, which he identified as having drawn its strength from a broad national consensus, Blair declared: 'I passionately want to lead a party which once again embodies and leads the national mood for change and renewal.' He concluded:

> Socialists have to be both moralists and empiricists. Values are fundamental. But socialism has to be made real in the world as it is and not as we would

like it to be. Our commitment to a different vision of society stands intact. But the ways of achieving it must change. Those should and will cross the old boundaries between left and right, progressive and conservative. They did in 1945. What marks us out are the objectives and the sense of unity and purpose by which we are driven. Our task now is nothing less than national renewal. Rebuilding our country as a strong and active civil society. We should gain confidence from the government of 1945; confidence in our values, in our insights and in our ability to deliver change. The generation of 1945 has set us an example which it is an honour to follow.[32]

What Blair did not acknowledge, but what his rhetoric could not conceal, was that 'New Labour' lacked at least two crucial assets which the Government of 1945 possessed: a coherent project for social reform, distilled by several generations of socialist thinkers, advocated by tireless propaganda and endorsed by a large majority of the public as a result of bitter experience; and a world trade and investment regime of the kind laid down at Bretton Woods which gave national governments some freedom to pursue such projects without necessarily having the total approval of the financial markets.

New Labour's Policies

What all this implied was a dramatic convergence towards the policy positions of the Conservatives in every economic and social arena.

i) Economic policy

Gordon Brown, as Labour's shadow Chancellor of the Exchequer, explicitly accepted that the globalisation of financial markets means that if inflation rises, or the ratio of public debt to GDP rises, the cost of borrowing will rise still further; therefore he would 'take no risks with inflation': 'the war on inflation is a Labour war ... Brown's law is that the government will only borrow to invest, public debt will remain stable and the cost effectiveness of public spending must be proved ... nobody should doubt my iron resolve for stability and fiscal prudence'.[33] On the other hand, he pointed out that the risk of inflation was higher in Britain than elsewhere because chronic under-investment restricted productive capacity. Therefore a medium-term growth strategy must accompany anti-inflationary monetary and fiscal policies. This should consist of a range of measures to raise investment levels, such as a national investment bank, tax incentives for savers to save and for companies to invest, making pension fund managers more responsible for the long-term investment strategies of the companies in which their funds are invested, and putting the onus on take-over bidders to prove that the effect will be to increase efficiency and serve the public interest.

But almost all these measures were suggested, not promised; they were 'possible options', there was 'a strong case' for them, the party would 'consider' them. This caution was due to fear of adverse market reactions to almost any measure that might be represented as limiting market freedoms; and there was the further constraint of the Maastricht convergence criteria (which Labour significantly did not, unlike the Swedish social democrats, propose modifying).[34] And during the year prior to the 1997 election New Labour in effect stopped even 'considering' all the various options that it had previously outlined for state-led measures to increase investment and achieve 'supply-side' reforms; what had been a distinctive industrial policy previously worked out by the party's 'Industry Forum' almost completely disappeared. As Colin Hay put it in 1996, 'Where in 1992 Labour's principal economic goals were to raise investment in the domestic economy, to boost productivity, and to reduce long-term unemployment, its primary aims now are to control inflation and promote macroeconomic stability.'[35] Brown eventually adopted an inflation target of 2.5 per cent, below the level actually achieved by the Conservatives.

New Labour was also obsessed by the electoral need to shed the 'high tax' image which was thought to have lost it the 1992 election. Both Brown and Blair repeatedly declared that the aim must be 'fair taxes, not high taxes'; 'the days of reflex tax and spend politics are over'.[36] People 'do not want nor will they get a Labour Government that will add to the burden of taxes on ordinary tax payers';[37] on the contrary, New Labour proposed to cut the lowest rate of income tax to 15 or even 10 per cent.[38] There would also be 'no return to ... penal rates of high personal taxation' for the rich – indeed, Blair and Brown eventually decreed that there would be no increases at all in personal taxation; while corporate tax rates must also remain internationally competitive.[39]

But if taxes cannot rise, and borrowing is limited to investment spending, current public spending cannot expand except through growth leading to more buoyant revenues, which may well take a long time to appear – and which New Labour no longer had any distinctive policies to bring about; and so, consistently enough, Blair indicated that virtually no new spending commitments would be made by the next Labour government unless they were matched by corresponding savings or cuts. He told the Scottish Labour Party Conference in March 1996 that he had

asked the Shadow Cabinet to submit to me written bids spelling out their priorities and their legislative demands. And I tell them ... some of them will be disappointed. We will not be able to do everything overnight but we will make a start and make a difference ... I have asked colleagues to submit proposals that will make such a difference at little or no cost. And I have asked them to look for savings in their own departmental areas. Government is about hard choices.[40]

As the election drew nearer, Brown took the still more self-denying step of making an unqualified commitment to stay within the Conservative Government's spending plans for the next two years. Given the generally recognised unrealism of the forecasts on which these spending plans had been based, most economists thought this implied drastic spending cuts. The forecasts had also assumed that there would be further privatisations; nothing loath, Brown announced that Labour would 'conduct an urgent review' of state assets with a view to further sales.[41] And a natural further casualty of this policy stance was New Labour's only remaining commitment to public ownership. At the party's 1995 Conference, Blair promised that 'there will be a publicly owned and publicly accountable railway system under a Labour government'.[42] Six weeks later the party's shadow transport spokesman rephrased this as 'a 'publicly controlled and publicly accountable' system, 'and in due course publicly owned also';[43] six months later renationalisation even of part of the system was made conditional 'on the availability of resources, and as priorities allow'.[44]

In seeking policies that would 'make a difference at little or no cost' New Labour assigned special priority to measures to reduce unemployment, which would not only reduce suffering and wasted lives but also cut social assistance spending and raise tax revenues. Included among such measures were shifts in the welfare budget aimed at ending the 'poverty trap'. The principle of universal payments was abandoned; the aim was now to 'target' public spending on the long-term unemployed, offering subsidies to employers who take them on, and changing the incentive structure of benefits and taxes to make it worthwhile for unemployed people to take jobs.

What New Labour's economic policies – or lack of them – revealed most strikingly was how severe were the limitations which New Labour's strategists were convinced they must accept. Mandelson and Liddle acknowledged, in *The Blair Revolution*, that New Labour policy contained 'no single big idea, no clever policy wheeze, which [was] going to transform Britain's prospects overnight'; but they asserted, with an optimism it was not easy to share, that 'small step-by-step changes in a consistent direction will produce gradually more impressive long-term results'.[45] No wonder that Blair was concerned to emulate Mrs Thatcher's success in winning a long spell in office: 'My ambition is not to win an election but to transform a country. To win one term and then be rejected would be the biggest failure and betrayal of all.'[46] Yet it was difficult to imagine that such a pinched and tentative series of marginal adjustments to the Thatcherite economic legacy could make a significant impact, let alone transform a country, even over two parliaments.

In a systematic review of New Labour's 'supply-side socialism' the economic historian Noel Thompson identified four defining elements: first, abundance and choice become the ends, and equality, community and other socialist values means; second, these ends and these means are held never to be in conflict (what we have called New Labour's characteristic *trope*); third, because of this, the power of private capital is not seen as a problem, against which the state must be able to deploy countervailing power (hence New Labour's assertion that *regulation* of markets can achieve all that public ownership – now 'discredited' and in any case no longer affordable – could do); and fourth, that wherever New Labour economic thinking does, even if inadvertently, assign priorities, it is the 'traditional City–Treasury goal of stability' that comes first.

> Fair is efficient, cooperative is competitive, deflation means growth ... Of course ... low inflation, currency stability and the expectations they will engender may lay the basis for a sustained rise in (mainly) private investment and that, in turn, will engender a supply-side miracle and a strong economic performance. But what if, in the short run, deflation means a rise in unemployment? What if objectives conflict? ... in the real world, when the crunch comes, as it so often does soon after a Labour government takes office, it will, like its forbears, have to confront the problem of how best to deploy scarce resources among competing ends ... In such circumstances and with no clearly articulated priorities and with the crucial levers of power in the hands of others, the danger is that ... it will move along the line of least resistance ... the deflationary line which provokes least resistance from the City, the IMF, the US Federal Reserve and the US Treasury.[47]

Or in the less restrained language of the journalist Iain Macwhirter:

> A decade and a half of free-market Thatcherism has reproduced levels of social inequality unseen since Victorian times, and the social fabric is being destroyed by mass unemployment. New Labour has no particular remedy other than to ask businesspeople to be more responsible. Yet the reality of the market is that it lacks a social conscience. The interests of the wider society always have to be imposed from without by democratic control ... Two Conservative parties is one too many.[48]

ii) Industrial relations

The convergence of Labour and Conservative policy with regard to the trade unions was particularly striking under Blair's leadership. Not only did he reaffirm the party's undertaking not to reverse the anti-union legislation of the 1980s, but under pressure from the Conservatives during the 1997 general election campaign, he declared: 'The changes that we do propose would leave British law the most restrictive on trade unions in the Western world.'[49]

As the unions' weight in party decision-making was progressively reduced the party's remaining policy commitments to them were also watered down. A commitment to legislate in the first year of a Labour government to give workers the right to be represented by a union was withdrawn, as were commitments to give part-time workers the same legal rights as full-time workers and to allow workers to claim unfair dismissal after six months' employment, rather than two years. Support for the right of workers dismissed during a strike to be reinstated afterwards was reduced to the right to take their case to an industrial tribunal, and support for the right of public sector workers to strike was abandoned, while the party contemplated introducing compulsory and binding arbitration for public sector disputes.

The commitment to a minimum wage was progressively diluted, first by refusing to adopt a specific figure in advance of the next election, as the trade unions wanted, and then by announcing that the figure would eventually be set only after a referral to a commission which would include business interests. Even the party's promise to sign up to the Social Chapter of the Maastricht Treaty, which dealt with working conditions, and from which John Major had negotiated a special right for Britain to 'opt out', was increasingly qualified: in November 1996 Gordon Brown told the CBI that Labour had 'no intention of importing any European-style legislation that would threaten jobs' and that 'we must never return to a situation here in Britain where ... one party is seen as pro-business and the other as anti-business'.[50] In March 1997 Blair produced a separate election manifesto specially directed at businesspeople.

iii) Education

Blair stated repeatedly that education would be his 'passion' in government; straining for maximum soundbite effect, he told the 1996 Party Conference that his priorities were 'education, education and education'.[51] Education certainly is, together with technical training, a key 'supply-side' policy area, as well as an issue of social justice. It was also one that, in New Labour thinking, offered scope for improvement at modest expense (it was symptomatic that Blair repeatedly cited a speech by the former Permanent Secretary at the Department of Education, who had 'argued that there was room for a 30 per cent improvement in the education system within existing budgets').[52] Thus one idea was to switch educational spending to improve the employability of the least-favoured category of unemployed young people by abolishing the 'assisted places scheme', under which £120 million per annum would be switched from enabling a small number of children from lower-income families to attend private schools to helping reduce class sizes for five- and six-year-olds in state schools. Another idea was to abolish the 'child benefit' paid to the families of all children aged seventeen and eighteen continuing in full-time education – a predominantly middle-class group – and use the savings to finance new schemes aimed at encouraging many more young people to continue in education after age sixteen. And the one new tax that Gordon Brown was willing to countenance, a one-time 'windfall' tax on the profits of the privatised utilities, was to be spent on a new set of options for long-term unemployed young people, in which vocational training would be a major element.[53]

The fact remained that although the education system had been seriously underfunded under the Thatcher and Major governments, no significant expansion of spending on education was envisaged (unless we count Gordon Brown's suggestion that the country's estimated £3.2 billion backlog of school building and equipment repairs should be tackled by a government partnership with merchant banks – whose possible motive for putting their money to this use was not explained).[54] Improvements were to be achieved, therefore, primarily by better efforts from parents (who, for example, would become formally responsible for ensuring that their children did specified amounts of homework and would be fined if their children played truant); by more inspections and 'league tables'; and by the removal of 'failing' teachers and head teachers, and the closing of 'failing' schools.[55] And as already mentioned, New Labour also abandoned the party's earlier pledge to restore the comprehensive principle in secondary schooling by restoring local authority control over schools that had 'opted out' of it with Conservative encouragement; and to end the de facto two-tier system of educational provision caused by their ability to select pupils for admission. The absence of 'clear water' between Labour and Conservative thinking on education – and the increasing tendency to seek improvements through stronger central control, and a 'tougher' regime for teachers – was particularly striking, not least for a party whose base in the state education system and the teaching profession had once been so strong.

iv) Health

A similar logic underlay New Labour's approach to the National Health Service. It was an area where Labour enjoyed an electoral advantage (people overwhelmingly supported the NHS and wanted it 'rescued' from financial strangulation and market-oriented restructuring). But partly on the grounds that the NHS staff should not to have to undergo any more reorganisation, and partly because they seemed to believe it was more 'efficient', Labour policy-makers proposed to retain the 'purchaser–provider split' introduced by Mrs Thatcher in 1990, but to abolish its financial aspect. In place of actual purchasing, there would be bulk 'commissioning', in which GPs and local health authorities would order services from hospitals but no money would actually change hands; and the resulting savings in accounting bureaucracy would be used to reverse the run-down of resources for 'front-line' health care provision.[56] The ownership of the hospitals would revert from the independent hospital trusts to the National Health Service, but hospital management would remain in the hands of the trusts' managers.

Whether these distinctly marginal modifications to the marketised NHS would have significant effects seemed questionable; but it was also possible to doubt whether New Labour would stick even to them. Faced with vociferous opposition from the spokesmen for 'fundholding' GPs the party's health spokesman backed away from the previous firm commitment to replace it with GP 'commissioning', agreeing to leave fundholding alone unless fundholders volunteered to give it up.[57] One could also doubt whether a Labour government would in practice be prepared to face down the equally vociferous hospital managers' lobby, at whose expense the administrative savings that were expected from ending the internal market would have to come.[58]

Yet apart from such savings any other improvements in health care would, as in education, have to come from the more efficient use of existing funds; higher spending was ruled out. Both health authority and hospital trust boards would be made more representative of the communities they served (i.e. they would no longer be composed predominantly of Conservative businessmen, as hitherto); Labour's proposals also asserted that these boards would, as a result, be 'genuinely accountable', though since they would still be appointed, not elected, this claim also seemed questionable.[59] Thus even in health policy the 'creeping privatisation' initiated by Mrs Thatcher and continued under Mr Major was not to be significantly challenged.

v) Social security

The overall commitment of New Labour was to reduce the share of GDP spent on the Welfare State; to the extent that unemployment could not be drastically cut this meant that any improvement in welfare provision would have to come from improved 'targeting' (i.e. shifting away from universal provision). In general, New Labour accepted the view that welfare expenditure was a drain on the competitive economy that could no longer be afforded at its former levels.[60]

The chief focus of debate here was state-provided old age pensions, which successive Conservative cuts had, by de-linking them from the growth of GDP, made so inadequate that several million retired people had been reduced to living on means-tested public assistance. New Labour policy-makers resisted all proposals for re-establishing state pensions at a more realistic level, and re-indexing them to the growth of average earnings, on the grounds – hotly contested by 'old Labour' critics – that this would mean intolerable new spending commitments; instead they proposed to improve the lot of the poorest 700,000 old people through targeted special assistance, and to look to occupational and private sector pension schemes to make up the growing shortfall in state pension levels.[61] A determined effort to get the 1996 Conference to support a major improvement in the state pension, spearheaded by the former Labour minister for social services, Barbara (Baroness) Castle, was repulsed with the aid of the trade union vote, and with the promise of a further 'review'.

With respect to the unemployed, the leadership declined to commit themselves to reverse the Job Seekers Allowance, introduced by the Conservatives in November 1996, which made state support for the long-term unemployed conditional on undergoing training and accepting whatever work (including state-subsidised voluntary work) might be available afterwards, on pain of losing state support entirely. The Conservative view was that it was up to individuals to improve their employability, with state help if necessary, or price themselves into work by accepting less and less. Except for the one-off scheme, mentioned earlier, to create jobs for 250,000 young people financed by a windfall tax, it was hard to see that in practice New Labour disagreed.

New Labour and the State

Rather than pursue New Labour thinking in other policy fields, from the environment to crime – in virtually all of which minor, low- (or zero-) cost modifications to the Thatcherite legacy were similarly proposed – it seems more useful to focus attention on the one area where there were significant differences between New Labour and the Conservatives: the constitution. Even here, however, the limitations of the 'project' and its tendency to constant dilution were no less clear.

A speech by Tony Blair in February 1996 pulled together what seemed at first sight to be an ambitious programme of state reform: local government 'renewal', including a qualified end to central government-imposed ceilings on local taxation, elections of a third of council members every year, and encouragement for referenda, citizens' juries and other innovations; re-establishing a strategic authority for London; elected mayors for London and other major cities; elected regional authorities in England, subject to approval in regional referenda, for strategic planning and to oversee regional quangos; a Parliament for Scotland elected by proportional representation, and an Assembly for Wales (without tax powers, but also to be elected by proportional representation), to take over the functions currently performed by the Scottish and Welsh Offices and their related quangos; a Freedom of Information Act; the incorporation of the European Convention of Human Rights into British law, permitting British courts to adjudicate cases under it; abolition of the voting powers of hereditary members of the House of Lords, with a view to the subsequent creation of an at least partly elected upper house; and a referendum on the electoral system.[62]

Most commentators saw this as a radical and far-reaching programme. Yet its limitations were significant. For example, there was no proposal to restore significant *powers* to local government, even for London.[63] The party's former commitment to reform the judiciary, beginning with the creation of a new Ministry of Justice, separate from the anachronistic office of the Lord Chancellor, had been abandoned (as had an earlier commitment to establish a Ministry for Women). There was also an ambiguity in Blair's commitment to a Freedom of Information Act; would it give citizens a general right to all state-held information, or only to information held by the state about themselves – and what priority would it have once it was a Labour government that possessed the information in question?[64] The original commitment to an elected upper house was very soon abandoned. Instead, the leadership pledged simply to abolish the voting rights of hereditary peers (which had been memorably mobilised to pass Mrs Thatcher's notorious poll tax against general opposition from the life peers of all parties) and deal later – at some evidently distant time – with the wider issue of reform of the House of Lords which, it was next hinted, need not be purely elected.[65]

Yet as a Labour victory in the 1997 election grew more and more likely, the party's parliamentary managers began to fear the potential of the party's constitutional proposals to consume inordinate amounts of parliamentary time, and to offer too much leverage to a Conservative opposition for thwarting other measures; on the other hand, the long-run credibility of a Labour administration required some substantive accomplishments, which these relatively cost-free and eminently 'moderate' measures offered a chance to get. So a front-bench heavyweight, Donald Dewar, was made Chief Whip, with a mandate to minimise the difficulties, and another, shadow Foreign Secretary Robin Cook, was mandated to negotiate for Liberal Democrat support on a package of constitutional measures. The negotiations were successfully concluded in March 1997. The Liberal Democrats undertook to support Labour's main constitutional proposals – devolution for Scotland, Wales and the regions, a Freedom of Information Act, early incorporation of the

European Convention, and the abolition of hereditary peers' voting rights;[66] while Labour agreed to hold its promised referendum on the electoral system reasonably early in the next parliament – but did not promise to support a change to proportional representation. The risk for the Liberals was that without Labour support for PR, it might not secure a majority of votes – or at least not a clear enough majority to oblige the government to act.[67] But it was as much as they could hope to get, and it would put the issue on the agenda; and other elements in the agreed constitutional package (including the prospect of proportional representation in the Scottish Parliament and the Welsh Assembly) might well increase public support for it.

There were also some significant silences. For instance, no undertaking was given to reconstruct the state to make it capable of mastering the market, rather than serving it; there was no promise to reverse the Thatcherite transfer of authority from the central civil service to commercially-oriented and substantially unaccountable 'executive agencies'. And although in Scotland and Wales unelected quangos would be largely replaced by a parliament and an assembly, in England there were no plans to abolish them, or to substitute election for appointment of their members; in the end it was not clear that Blair's call for 'rolling back the quango state' meant more than making quangos less purely Conservative in composition, and – perhaps – somewhat less secret. In general, the proposed reforms would at most make modest adjustments to Britain's centralised, elite-managed and undemocratic state.

Conclusions

In the run-up to the 1997 election most commentators were, of course, no longer very interested in Labour's transition from socialism – or, more accurately, from 'parliamentarist' social democracy – to capitalism; most of them welcomed it and thought it overdue. What interested them was the possibility that a New Labour government might at least bring a significant change of tone – even honesty – to politics at Westminster after seventeen years of prejudice-driven and increasingly venal Conservative rule. And there was still some inclination to believe that behind the Blairite talk of a 'radical politics of the centre' there might indeed lie a prospect of 'national renewal'.

Yet there was a pervasive uneasiness. New Labour's policy package could not help giving an impression of insubstantiality. It is difficult to appear weighty and forceful if what you propose is essentially to do better with less. The magnitude of the goal envisaged in Blair's rhetoric of 'national renewal' – and the scale of the means proposed – from a more representative group of advisers for the Bank of England, to compulsory school homework – were just too disproportionate. Staying within the constraints that Labour's modernisers accepted ruled out radical proposals; but without radical measures, there could hardly be a radical improvement in the performance of Britain's economy. The results of a hundred and one minor modifications to existing supply-side policies would be neither massive nor swift. It was a telling symptom of Labour's failure to offer a convincing alternative to the Conservatives' overall legacy that in the autumn of 1996 the leadership allowed itself to be drawn into a 'Dutch auction' with their opponents on the issue of who were the strongest champions of 'moral values', with Tony Blair and the shadow Home Secretary, Jack Straw, going out of their way to sound distinctly tougher on crime than on its causes.[68]

New Labour's relentless pursuit of electoral advantage through constantly trimming its policies to what opinion research showed that voters – above all, 'swing' voters – wanted, carried other risks as well. It had not worked in 1987 or 1992; and had the Conservative Party not been so irreparably split in 1997 it was not a foregone conclusion that it would work then either. 'Positioning' Labour so that it could present itself as a cleaner, less ideologically-driven alternative to the Conservatives, another 'party of business' (as Blair said it must be), left the initiative in setting the political agenda in the hands of the Conservative right.[69] Labour, with no distinctive solutions of its own to the continuing weaknesses of British capitalism, might well gradually succumb to the stresses of office and open the way for a further instalment of neo-liberalism and social authoritarianism.

The Blair leadership team placed great confidence in their ability to avoid this outcome, taking their new-found electoral strength as evidence that Labour was poised to displace the Conservatives as the 'natural' party of government. But the weight of historical experience was against this. The hope of achieving even modest successes in office presupposed that all the relevant players would be interested in collaborating with a Labour government. In reality, innumerable vested interests would vigorously resist any significant changes, and 'business opinion' remained on balance distrustful of Labour and supportive of the Conservatives in spite of all Labour's blandishments. It was hard to share the faith exhibited by both Brown and Blair in the rewards they could expect for economic 'honesty', reflected in their pledge not to 'play politics' with public finances. The Conservatives clearly felt no such need, having played politics with the public finances, when in office, at every election since the 1950s, without ever losing the support of either the City or the CBI. Brown's promise to follow the 'golden rule' of borrowing only for investment was an obvious bid for business approval, but it seemed doubtful that actually following the rule would induce most British businesses to support Labour. Meanwhile, the frustration that would arise when the pent-up hopes of Labour's core supporters were denied, and the internal conflicts to which the continuing plans to centralise party decision-making could still give rise, would also take their toll.

Moreover Conservative efforts to undermine Labour's position would not be confined to rational debate on the merits of its policies. An intemperate far-right election campaign in the shape of a national-populist attack on Labour as being willing to 'surrender' British interests to 'Europe' had begun as early as the beginning of 1996, laying the ground for continuing attacks on this issue, with strong support from the Conservative press, on the new Labour Government after May 1997.[70]

A radical way forward, which would be logically consistent with New Labour's assessment of the constraints imposed by globalisation, would have been for the new Labour Government to seek alliances with other progressive parties, especially in the EU, to try to ease those constraints by working towards a new, more progressive international trade and investment regime. This would include a new set of conditions governing capital flows that would allow governments rather than multinationals to have the decisive say in their countries' economic and social development.

But in real life this option would require the party to have campaigned for it – to have already generated a powerful groundswell of popular support for it, instead of focusing entirely on assuring 'business' of Labour's enthusiasm for the market.[71] And here New Labour's lack of a strong emotional and ideological bond with their newly-enlarged membership would also be a problem. Blair's rhetoric had hegemonic aspirations but it was far from having a strong hold on the feelings and dreams of Labour members, let alone a mass public. This was due in part to the inherently elitist character of the modernisers' project. Drawing all power to set policy into the hands of an increasingly tightly-coordinated circle of senior politicians had been accomplished at the expense of no longer having a potent force of engaged and committed opinion-leaders in the party rank and file. Yet given Labour's weak presence in the institutions of the state and in 'business', the only effective weapon a Labour government can deploy against entrenched opposition to its policies is the strength of mobilised public opinion. This, however, New Labour had given up trying to generate. Its endorsement of the market had reinforced the ideology of the market – including its hegemony over the minds of the party's leaders and their professional staffs.

12

Beyond Parliamentary Socialism

What succumbed in these defeats was not the revolution. It was ... persons, illusions, conceptions, projects from which the revolutionary party ... was not free ...[1]

Only a great optimist, it may be thought, could see the events reviewed in this book as a step towards socialism, rather than as a definitive defeat. To most people, socialism looks finished; many if not most of its intended standard-bearers, the western working class, no longer think of themselves primarily as workers, while the parties that once mobilised them have either collapsed (in the case of the Communist parties), or have abandoned the socialist dream. From this perspective, the Labour new left's attempt to change the party, its defeat, and the triumph of the 'modernisers', might well seem no more than a minor spasm in the final death-throes of the socialist project.

Yet it takes no less optimism to suppose that global capitalism is creating a rosy future. Do people really suppose that its contradictions have disappeared? Is its indispensable need for growth ecologically sustainable? Do people really expect full employment to return; or – alternatively – can we foresee a new consensus on transferring a steadily growing share of the surplus to support the poor and the unemployed, so that the increasingly alienated and dangerous 'relative surplus population' is reintegrated into 'the community'? Has the secret been discovered, which will prevent the steadily worsening inequalities from leading to more and more crime, violence and wars, as they always have in the past? As the liberal Italian theorist Norberto Bobbio put it, 'Democracy ... has overcome the challenge of historical communism. But what means and what ideals does it have to confront those very problems out of which the challenge was born?'[2]

From this perspective the essence of the socialist project – the idea of a social order capable of transcending the alienation and escalating risks of capitalist accumulation – is anything but finished; it seems more likely that it is just beginning to come into view again as a necessity – but freed, precisely, from conceptions and illusions still clinging to it from the late nineteenth century.

What has come to an end in Britain, we might say, is not socialism, but a particular kind of 'parliamentary socialism' – *and* the idea that a party dedicated to it can be changed into a party of a different kind. Labour's conception of parliamentary socialism had three essential elements: acceptance of the 'Schumpeterian' conception of democracy, as a contest between competing teams of elites; treating the extra-parliamentary party as, in the final analysis, a servant of the parliamentary team; and conceiving of citizens primarily as mere voters, not as active participants in self-government, whom the party must develop as such. What the events of the 1970s and 1980s made clear beyond all doubt is that socialism cannot be achieved by parliamentarism understood in this way.

This conclusion is reinforced by New Labour's broad acceptance of the Thatcherite reconstruction of the state, with the civil service now 'hollowed out' into a congeries of 'executive agencies' attuned to serving not citizens but 'the private sector'; the neutering of elected local government by the removal of its most important functions in housing and education, and the virtual elimination of its remaining financial autonomy; and the vast new tier of appointed 'quangos', with little or no effective accountability even to the government, let alone the voters. Any socialist advance will now require a radical reconstruction of the state, which only a party with a radically changed conception of democracy, such as the Labour new left envisaged, could hope to mobilise enough popular support to achieve.

The reasons for the defeat of the Labour new left's project need to be confronted. In one respect it was undertaken in favourable circumstances – in the context of a profound crisis of the ruling ideas of the previous twenty-five years, in which a significant mass of the population was exceptionally open to new thinking and aspirations. Yet it was doomed to fail.

This was not because of any fundamental inappropriateness of the new left's analysis. In particular, new left thinkers in the Labour Party like Tony Benn and Stuart Holland understood well before their opponents how the globalisation of the economy from the late 1960s onwards was destroying the 'Keynesian capacity' of all nation-states, on which the social democratic management of capitalism depended;[3] it was this that clinched their determination to try to change the party into one with a different conception of its task. Moreover in the context of the 1970s – well before capital controls had been abolished anywhere – their proposals for import quotas and tighter controls on transnational company activities, etc., were far from unreasonable. It is historically false to assert – as even a historian of left-wing sympathies such as Donald Sassoon does – that the Labour left were defeated because they were unaware of globalisation, and 'profoundly conservative' about national sovereignty.[4] Labour's new left had quite clear ideas about both globalisation and Europe; it was perfectly possible – indeed it still is – to be against the European Community or Union (the 'Europe of the bankers'), while being *for* a closer European union designed to defend society against being undermined by global market forces. To deride the Labour new left as proposing a 'siege economy' incapable of winning electoral support, as Sassoon does, wrongly implies that they were unaware of the need for international support.[5] And how was such support to be won without first securing it at home? This kind of criticism avoids all the difficult questions which have to be confronted by those who actually do put the problem of countering the power of international capital at the top of their agenda – and inside the Labour Party, only the Labour new left did so.[6]

It was not enough, however, for the Labour new left to have rational ideas. The party leadership, besides being much slower to grasp the implications of globalisation, were more committed to the centralised and elitist state than to socialism, while most of the union leadership still believed in the possibility of corporatism. And in their struggle against the new left they had several decisive advantages.

In beating back the left's challenge the Labour leadership had the wholehearted support of the state (the civil service and the Bank of England, the judiciary, the police and the military); of all sections of capital, from the CBI to the City; and, crucially, of the media. Not just the partisan tabloid press but all 'mainstream' media, including the supposedly 'neutral' radio and television channels, were ranged unanimously against Labour's new left, pillorying it as communist, fascist, self-interested, naive and mad, all at once.

And as the struggle dragged on the Labour new left lost the advantage that international conditions had initially given it. Throughout the industrial west the crisis was being resolved in favour of capital, and the British left could not be immune from the consequences. The international conjuncture was no longer encouraging, and the inspiration that had once also been offered by the examples of left-wing movements elsewhere gradually gave way to the depressing influence of their failures.[7]

For its part, the Labour new left contributed to its own defeat through some major weaknesses. The most important of all was, evidently, that in concentrating on trying to change the Labour Party it became trapped in that struggle. It never solved the problem of having to fight for its goals through unending party committees and conferences without becoming absorbed by them. For many it was a point of principle to try to win the party over to a new democratic socialist project by persuasion and the fullest use of the party's existing democratic processes. But the bitterness of the right's resistance prolonged the struggle over so many years that almost a whole political generation consumed their energies in this way.

Another problem was that the Labour left was far from homogeneous or united in its thinking. We have stressed Benn's speeches, because they did inspire and give coherence to the whole project; and the role of the CLPD, because it was the decisive element in achieving the gains – especially reselection of MPs – that were made. Yet there was no broad unanimity. Some elements were sectarian – and by no means only the Militant Tendency. These currents brought some strengths – activists who were class-struggle oriented, capable and tough. Too many of these, however, had undemocratic political habits; and they also tended to speak in a 'bolshevik' language (of 'demands', 'lines' and so on) that was not only incapable of reaching out beyond the ranks of organised labour, as Benn could, but also repelled many people who needed to be persuaded. Other elements also adopted a style that made others feel excluded; this was true of some of those who bought the new 'identity politics' into the attempt to change the Labour Party, and of the 'aggressive proletarianism' that Dennis Skinner famously adopted on the NEC, which antagonised the middle-class right of the PLP and many union leaders too.[8] The negative light which the defeat of the left casts retrospectively on all these practices is certainly a gain. On the other hand any major progressive project will always attract some problematic elements, and working out how to minimise these difficulties without limiting participation is a task that still needs to be undertaken.

A related but somewhat different problem was the role of the unions. The Labour new left wanted to see the unions democratised and made into agencies of political education and popular mobilisation; but although they worked to encourage this in various ways – through their links with the Institute for Workers' Control, the work of the CLPD in the unions, campaigns at union conferences, the push for party branches at workplaces, and so on – they did not get very far. Yet it is hard to envisage that any socialist project can make headway unless organised labour plays a major role in it. The problem was posed in a very poignant way by the intense industrial militancy of the 1970s – direct action, flying pickets, work-ins and the like. How could these various actions have been made less defensive and more transformative?[9] Why was it left so much to Benn to point up the links between the issues being pursued by industrial and non-industrial movements? In general, if the future of socialism depends on social movements taking on each other's agendas, what does this mean in practice? Is there any alternative to a political party of some sort taking on the task of fusing diverse issues and struggles into some sort of unity? If so, what kind of party might be capable of doing this, and be accepted in that role? The Labour left did not solve any of these problems; its achievement was only to put them on the agenda for the future more concretely than before.[10]

On the positive side, it was no small thing that the Labour new left did confront the problem of globalisation, not only before most of the Labour leadership but even before most politicians of the far right who would later become enthusiasts of globalisation. They were not always clear whether they wanted a democratic socialist reform or a 'radical bourgeois' one; indeed, we can quite easily see 'stakeholder capitalism' prefigured in some of the Labour left's statements of the period, especially in relation to the need to subordinate the City to democratic policy-making – which is ironic in view of the way they were routinely called 'socialist fundamentalists'. This was true also for the GLC under 'Red' Ken Livingstone's leadership, and the 'socialist republic of South Yorkshire' under David Blunkett's; they were never entirely clear whether they were for municipal socialism or municipal capitalism.[11] But it was a creative ambiguity; they worked on it, without limiting themselves to easy slogans about 'transforming' the state (let alone 'overthrowing' it). The point is that the Labour left's project was not a utopian or idealist affair; it sought to respond – but to respond radically – to the world as it actually existed.

The project's greatest achievement, however, was its vision of a radical broadening of the public arena, tapping the talent and energy of ordinary people and bringing them into new positions of power and responsibility in the state. No doubt this vision was imperfectly shared, but there is also no doubt that when Benn articulated it he struck a powerful chord. If there was one thing more than any other that unified the drive to change the Labour Party – and, no doubt, also united the centre and right against the Labour new left – it was this intimation that people wanted, needed and deserved a more active role in the government of their lives, that it was no longer safe or acceptable to leave it to a small elite of professional 'representatives'.

Did this conception of democratic socialism expect too much of ordinary people? Did it imply 'too many committees', as Oscar Wilde complained it must? It is very possible that most people in the Labour new left saw democratisation largely in terms of just having elected delegates take over functions from bureaucrats.[12] But this was really secondary; what was crucial was to see that the key to any alternative to capitalism lay in rejecting the dominant ideology according to which 'activism' is considered something to be discouraged and, if necessary, suppressed. What democratic alternatives there may be to periodic elections of representatives – what other forms of participation, openness and accountability, what alternative expectations and habits socialism may require – are questions that the Labour left could not resolve.[13] They were very far from having discovered 'the political form . . . under which to work out the emancipation of labour' – or of women, or anyone else – in the twenty-first century.[14] But they did show that finding new forms of democracy is an indispensable requirement for the renewal of the socialist project.

What they did not do was consolidate their ideas and achievements in any enduring institutional forms. This was partly because they were too focused on the Labour Party, which they failed to change; and partly because whatever they did achieve inside the state – such as Benn's regime in the Department of Industry in 1974–75, and Livingstone's at the Greater London Council – was ruthlessly extirpated. The consolidation of Thatcherism through the 1980s also radically altered people's perceptions of what could be achieved in the short run and made it seem urgent to try to salvage as much as possible of what was left of the postwar settlement. This led some Labour new left figures, especially those who had always aimed at political careers, to align themselves with the 'modernisers', a move sanctified by the cultural 'retreat from class' promoted by *Marxism Today* and its offspring such as Demos – the so-called new 'radicalism of the centre' as a 'counter-hegemonic' project. It led others, such as most of the Campaign Group of MPs, who maintained a genuinely radical stance, to fall back more on those elements within the labour movement whose class politics made them reliable in the hard 'new times' – but often at the expense of setting aside their broader vision.

As for the sequel, New Labour, the reader who has got this far will not want much further summary. In so far as the 'modernisers' could assure it, the extra-parliamentary party had been de-fused and made safe, for the purposes of party management, by far-reaching changes in the party's constitution, as well as through regular assertions of the leader's will. Policy could now be set, in effect, by a handful of people close to the leader – and set not merely to the right of the policies of the Liberal Democrats but even, if it seemed expedient, to the right of the Conservatives as well, with little fear of serious repercussions from the remaining party activists in the constituencies, or the unions, or the Parliamentary Labour Party. It remains to be seen how far all the diverse elements that were comprised in Labour's broad alliance will remain not merely acquiescent but supportive of the new government led by the modernisers.[15] Donald Sassoon, who tends to join the modernisers in disparaging the Labour new left, sees things more clearly when they occur on the other side of the channel. With regard to the French socialists under Mitterrand, he says:

> To give up the ambition of abolishing capitalism . . . is not much of a strategy. Modernisation as a slogan sounds appealing, but it has done so for over a hundred years. No party of the Left in post-war Europe (and hardly any

party of the Right) has ever been against modernisation. One suspects the watchword, devoid as it is of any practical content, is used purely symbolically: to be for modernisation means to be for progress without abolishing capitalism.[16]

The story recounted in this book suggests that the route to socialism does not lie through transforming the Labour Party. This does not mean that progressive elements in it should not be supported, but supporting them should not be confused with the main task. New organisational forms must be developed, and a new conception of parliamentarism and its relation to extra-parliamentary politics needs to be worked out. It is not a question of parliamentarism versus extra-parliamentary struggle, but of what kind of parliamentary practice, complemented by what kind of non-parliamentary practices, is capable of moving us forward.

Some people will see it as a counsel of desperation, if not a betrayal, to argue against concentrating one's main efforts in the Labour Party. But the fact that the social democratic parties exist, with their accumulated resources of traditions and loyalties as well as funds and premises, is not necessarily an asset; not only because these resources are regularly deployed *against* the left, but also because their sheer weight and presence tends to conceal the fact that these parties are no longer, if they ever were, vehicles of socialism. Even when this is recognised, the very fact that they exist is sometimes in itself almost enough to block other initiatives.

It is not entirely far-fetched to see important parallels between our situation today and that of Europe in 1850. Then, national economic conditions did not yet make it possible for the workers to take power, as the socialist revolutionaries of 1848 had imagined. Today, the conditions do not yet exist for socialism to be achieved in face of the power of global capitalism. Now, as then, there is an urgent need to study the current phase of capitalism and understand the new forms taken by its contradictions.

This in no way implies a project of intellectual work cut off from immediate practical struggles; on the contrary, one of the lessons of the Labour new left's defeat is the need to give attention to new ways of uniting theory and practice. Nor does it mean trying to work out some comprehensive schematic 'model' of the contradictions of global capitalism, from which the conditions of success for socialist struggle can be 'read off', as in the evolutionist and 'catastrophist' Marxisms of the Second International. Nevertheless, part of the current sense of disorientation on the left is due to the lack of any kind of general model of the main contours and dynamics of global capitalism. There is a rather hysterical literature on global change – technological, social and cultural ('postmodern', 'post-industrial' etc.) – but not a very coherent literature on global political economy, let alone a persuasive reading of its resulting political dynamics. There is a huge intellectual task to be undertaken here – synthetic and analytic, empirical and theoretical, individual and collective.

In general it is obvious that deregulation has released the logic of capitalist accumulation from the constraints of the Keynesian welfare state within the Bretton Woods system of capital controls and national economies; it now operates once more on a global plane, with national-level effects previously felt only by colonies and underdeveloped countries. But there is a great deal of controversy, even among mainstream economists, about these effects;[17] and the political implications have barely begun to be systematically explored.

For instance, the victims of the chronic unemployment that has now been re-established in the OECD countries – the 'losers', in neo-liberal parlance – will not be left to starve. Many of them will be segregated in crime- and drug-ridden inner-city districts (and 'ghost' company towns and mining villages), in humiliating state-supported poverty. Yet even they will still be interpellated by the ideology of consumer society, through its television, music, tabloid press, professional sport and so on. They will not spontaneously turn against 'the market', so much as against other people, including each other. This, however, is ground to work on: a deep sense of injustice, a memory that it was not like this only a few decades ago, and a suspicion that the 'new reality' of 'global competition' is actually a deliberately constructed reality, to which there *must* be – contrary to what politicians reiterate with revealing over-insistence – an alternative. This may be thought an extreme example, although with a third of all children in Britain living in officially-defined poverty, it can hardly be considered insignificant. But we do need to map and analyse the various different forms of exclusion, exploitation, oppression and alienation that globalised capitalism is creating (or restoring), as arenas of political struggle through which a new alternative conception of society, a new socialist project, will be gradually built up.

Analysing the contradictions of globalised capitalism and their political effects is not the same as constructing a renewed socialist project, even though the two tasks are intimately interconnected. At least two additional elements are involved. One is the need to think through some fundamental issues that must be resolved in any conception of an alternative future to the one the neo-liberals are creating for us. For instance, socialists need to have a view about how far they accept the ideas of continued growth and consumerism; of income being derived from work; of inequality or equality; of markets or bureaucracies as instruments of the distribution of resources; and so on. The other requirement is to start imagining, in realistic and concrete terms, feasible socialist utopias capable of touching a nerve in people's actually existing consciousness.

A socialism that offers no credible vision of an alternative future is meaningless; constant reductions in social services, chronic unemployment, increased stress, longer hours and increased insecurity at work will eventually rob 'market society' of its appeal, but in the absence of a credible alternative it will still seem inevitable. And any alternative must be credible not only to ascetics, saints, anti-car crusaders and tree-lovers, but to people with ordinary desires and dreams. In particular, it will be important to work out what people really want and are willing to sustain in the way of democratic participation – in what arenas, taking what forms, shared with whom, occupying how much of their time. On the other hand, ordinary people have deeper feelings, more regard for the whole society they live in, longer historical memories and higher aspirations than professional politicians often give them credit for; and it is on these things that the renewed socialist project must ultimately be founded.

The extraordinary growth of the post-war years created the illusion that full employment and permanently increasing incomes were now assured; an illusion that was partly sustained by the very thing the new right were determined to abolish – the regulated regime of trade and investment of which the Keynesian welfare state was a key element. It has taken almost two decades of deregulated global capitalism to begin to put a question-mark against the consumerist dreams of the 1950s and 1960s; the first reaction to disillusionment, however, is not political action but fatalism, in face of what are presented as global forces beyond anyone's control. But this mood, which New Labour has played on almost as much as the new right, will sooner or later change to resentment and anger, and a rediscovered will to act, to which a new socialist project must respond. How far can the building of this project be the collective work of ordinary citizens? It is true that in every past social advance, the ideas of one or two exceptional individual thinkers have played a vital role. But these theorists have always incorporated the thinking of hundreds of lesser thinkers, and the practice of thousands of activists who were also, in a less abstract way, intellectuals (i.e. people who think seriously about their society); they have summed it up and made it coherent, vivid and, finally, 'natural'. Such major thinkers add something indispensable, and their emergence cannot be planned or arranged. But they always work on 'thought material' already developed by others; and this, in the meantime, we have to try to produce.

It is not clear how this ultimately collective task can be institutionalised. Unless the principles which are to govern it are first worked out very clearly any organisation which is formed for this purpose seems liable to bog down in the usual mutual complaints between self-styled intellectuals and self-styled activists, and become an arena for the re-running of outworn sectarian disputes which bore everyone to death and achieve nothing. The nature of the organisation (or organisations) that might avoid this is not self-evident, but there is no reason to suppose that progress in this direction is impossible. There are plenty of historical models to reflect upon while experimenting with new ones.

Vital to this will be democratic debate and collective thinking of precisely the kind that has been virtually extinguished in the Labour Party since the defeat of the new left project. But what that defeat also shows is that the debate that is needed must go beyond the issue of intra-party democracy and touch all the institutions of society. Crucially, this means addressing the pressing need to decommodify the media of political communication. To the extent that the left has no access to the mainstream media, and no popular press that articulates its understanding of reality or its visions of the future, it is not being heard – and in politics, what is not heard may as well not have been said.[18] Decommodifying the broadcasting of news and public policy debate, ending the abuse of 'freedom of expression' represented by the tabloid press, is essential for restoring the possibility of effective communication between the left and the rest of the community.[19]

Such changes will depend on renewed socialist organisation and mobilisation on a scale which cannot be expected to emerge quickly. Major defeats take time to recover from. Yet it would be surprising if the organisational forms worked out for working-class mobilisation in the late nineteenth century and early twentieth century were still just what was needed to carry the struggle for socialism forward more than a hundred years later. We need to be ready to think long-term again, not just about the periods between elections. This can, of course, be criticised as sacrificing the interests of today's generation to the imagined interests of future generations – the objection always made by 'practical' men and women against 'utopians'.[20] But to put it like this is to pose a false dilemma. The need to support what exists, to value small gains (or even the limitation of losses) in the present, is not inconsistent with seeing the main task as lying elsewhere. It is not a matter of choosing one or the other, but of learning how to act in the present in such a way as not to undermine our capacity to build a different future.

Epilogue: The Dénouement

The 1997 election seemed to confirm that the era of 'TINA' was really over – that there was, after all, an alternative. New Labour came to power amidst considerable popular support, and enjoyed a remarkably long honeymoon. Its huge majority of 179 seats transformed the social character of the parliamentary party, and altered popular expectations about its performance in power. The new PLP was both younger and more female than any before it. Of its 419 MPs, 173 were between forty-one and fifty, 54 were still in their thirties and 10 were under thirty; 101 were women. Their social background, on the other hand, was more overwhelmingly middle-class than ever, with 239 university graduates, 104 former academics/teachers and 32 former barristers or solicitors; only seven were former miners, and two former dockers. Labour's percentage of the popular vote (44.4 per cent) was lower than the party had achieved in its previous big victories (48.3 per cent in 1945 and 47.9 per cent in 1966); the main cause of the landslide in seats was the collapse of the Conservative vote. Nonetheless, the scale of the victory – and the rhetoric of modernisation and national renewal which accompanied it – led to a heightened expectation of change. The euphoric comments of some centre-left journalists in the immediate wake of the election tapped a widespread sense of new beginnings. Andrew Rawnsley, for example, wrote: 'on Friday morning Britain woke up a different country. It may be a trick of the light but it feels like a younger country.'[1]

New Labour in Government

The early euphoria was generated by the promise of change in New Labour's election manifesto, which contained what Tony Blair had earlier called the 'four building blocks of a more secure and successful Britain'.[2] These four cornerstones were presented as a coherent 'New Labour' policy package, a new 'third way' in British politics that was neither Thatcherite nor 'old' Labour:

- On *economic policy*: to 'provide stable economic growth with low inflation, and promote dynamic and competitive business and industry at home and abroad' by sticking for two years to the tight spending limits previously set by the Tories, avoiding income tax increases for five years, helping small businesses, and introducing both regional development agencies and a national minimum wage.
- On *foreign policy*: to give it an open and ethical dimension to 'help in tackling global poverty', and to 'give Britain the leadership in Europe which Britain and Europe need' by pushing for EU reform, offering a referendum on a single currency, strengthening NATO and reforming the UN. [3]
- On the *constitutional* front: to 'clean up politics, decentralise political power throughout the United Kingdom and put the funding of political parties on a proper and accountable footing' by introducing devolved government in Scotland and Wales, elected mayors in English cities, and a Freedom of Information Act; and by removing hereditary peers from the House of Lords.
- On *social policy*: to make 'education our number one priority ... rebuild the NHS ... be tough on crime and on the causes of crime ... build strong families and strong communities, and lay the foundations of a modern welfare state' by raising spending on education and health in real terms each year, moving people from welfare to work (250,000 young unemployed off benefit and into work), aiding single parents and introducing fast-track punishment for persistent young offenders.

The break with 'old' Labour was heavily emphasised in the run-up to the election. There was to be no return either to the governmental habits of previous Labour administrations or to the policy agenda of the Labour Party during its brief turn to the left after the 1979 election. There would be no reversal of privatisation, no planning agreements, price commissions or tripartite pay bodies. Nor was there to be any return to the 'beer and sandwiches' corporatism characteristic of 'old' Labour in power. The Conservatives' labour law would be largely left in place: there would be 'no return to flying pickets, secondary action, strikes with no ballots, or the trade union laws of the 1970s'[4] – no return, that is, to any 'winters of discontent' of the kind that had undermined the electoral credibility of earlier Wilson- and Callaghan-led governments.

New Labour thus entered office having reset the emphasis of its economic policy away even from that of the Kinnock and Smith years: away from the 'old' Labour trinity of growth, employment and welfare towards a distinctly Blairite concern with international competitiveness in the new global order; and away from tripartism towards a new set of arrangements in which 'one looks in vain for labour's stake⁵. Indeed, New Labour was enthusiastically pro-business and pro-market, and distinctly cool towards the party's traditional union supporters, to whom it promised only 'fairness, not favours'.

But New Labour also entered office adamant that its policy realignment did not mean that it was simply offering Thatcherism Mark II, as even sympathetic commentators quickly began to argue (before long even Will Hutton – who, as editor of the *Observer*, had greeted the election result as a new dawn – was saying that 'the Tories are kind of governing through their surrogates, New Labour').⁶ The New Labour Government presented itself as radically different from the Conservatives on all three key domestic fronts. Constitutionally it was to be more democratic and innovative. Socially it was to be more pluralist and inclusive. Economically it was to be more interventionist, albeit in a market-enhancing way. Against Thatcherite neo-liberalism it presented itself as a strong advocate of the 'new growth theory' – combining a neo-liberal enthusiasm for flexible labour markets with a belief that investment in human capital held the key to competitiveness and growth. New Labour presented itself as the vanguard of a new political 'third way' that was neither Keynesian corporatist nor purely neo-liberal in inspiration. This 'third way', as Blair told a Dutch audience in 1998, offered Europe the capacity to combine

> economic dynamism with social justice in the modern world. This Third Way is more than a free market plus decent public services – laissez faire economics with a warm heart. It is about active government working with the grain of the market to ensure a highly adaptable workforce, good education, high levels of technology, decent infrastructure, and right conditions for high investment and non-inflationary growth. It is about securing the flexibility that the market offers with the 'pluses' that only an active government can add.⁷

So the claims that New Labour leaders made for themselves and their project were great; and initially, at least, many people were prepared to give them the benefit of the doubt. Perhaps New Labour stood for a new kind of politics: one that could transform the UK's political class and lift the economy on to a high-wage, high-investment, high-productivity growth path. The length of New Labour's honeymoon in the opinion polls was an indication of how general was the desire to see such a project succeed. But slowly this latest exercise in the politics of hope over experience began to unravel; and as that unravelling quickened in the second half of New Labour's first term in office, the honeymoon came to an end.

Indeed, there were early signs that the euphoria was unwarranted. The New Labour Government lost the moral high ground quite quickly by the way it handled the Bernie Ecclestone affair on tobacco advertising and party finance (the Formula One racing tycoon Bernie Ecclestone had donated £1 million to the party, then benefited from a policy 'U-turn' exempting Formula One racing from an impending ban on tobacco advertising in sport – Blair was obliged to order the return of Ecclestone's money).[8] Its image was also damaged by its decision to introduce student fees for higher education, its release of fighter aircraft to the Indonesian military, and its cutting of welfare funds to single parents (its first domestic internal dispute, late in 1997). New Labour's capacity to postpone contentious and potentially unpopular issues by the setting up of 'working parties' to study them kept the jury out for most of that first year, however: it was only those who were closely watching the detail of New Labour policy who could already see the signs of further disillusionment to come. For although it went generally unnoticed, Tony Blair very quickly positioned the New Labour Government well to the right of European Social Democracy as a whole – travelling to Malmo as early as June 1997 to call for labour market de-regulation in Europe, and persisting in an enthusiastic endorsement of globalisation as a process, and labour market de-regulation as a goal, after the European summit.

This sponsoring of American-style capitalism within Europe was tempered by New Labour's failure to deliver on its initial intention to put Britain 'at the heart of Europe', but it was more generally indicative of the fact that British foreign policy would continue to be very closely aligned with that of the USA. On every significant international issue – and most dramatically on Iraq and Kosovo – New Labour took the lead in endorsing American imperial policy, and participated enthusiastically in its military interventions.[9] Amidst such strategic choices, Robin Cook's initial commitment to an 'ethical' foreign policy could not last long, and was eventually abandoned.[10]

Elements of the initial radical promise of New Labour's social programme remained on the policy agenda – we will come to that – but, as with foreign policy, its core economic and industrial policies showed a basic consistency with those of the Major Government that preceded it. New Labour quickly confirmed its acceptance of the previous Government's levels of direct taxation and its planned spending limits for the first two years, and issued a competitiveness white paper[11] that was remarkably similar in both tone and detail to those issued by the Heseltine-led Department of Trade and Industry after 1992. The parallels between the white papers of the two governments are striking – both in the substance of the policies proposed, and in the modesty/timidity of those policies when set against the scale of the problem identified. For just as Thatcherite monetarism was foreshadowed after 1976 by the Callaghan Labour Government, so New Labour's 'third way' in industrial and economic policy was foreshadowed by the Major Government's rediscovery after 1992 of the need to strengthen the UK's industrial base. There was a change in presentational style between the Major and Blair Governments, and a larger role for the Department for Education and Employment (DfEE) in the delivery of industrial policy. But significant elements of New Labour's 'third way' industrial policies looked distinctly Heseltinian.

The New Labour Government also quickly surrendered its freedom of manoeuvre on monetary policy by handing control over the setting of interest rates to the Monetary Policy Committee of the Bank of England. Declining to strengthen in any way its capacity directly to control or restructure private capital, New Labour left itself only the space to intervene in and restructure labour markets – and here its initiatives (even set against those of previous Labour governments) were both modest and conservative. New Labour introduced only one tranche of industrial relations reform: establishing a parsimonious national minimum wage, giving back to the trade unions some of the recognition rights removed under Thatcher, and marginally extending worker rights in relation to paternity leave and redundancy. But as it did so, leading New Labour ministers also made it clear that this was as far as they were prepared to go in departing from the Thatcherite labour codes; and that in consequence – as Tony Blair proudly asserted when introducing the white paper *Fairness at Work* – the UK would continue to possess the most lightly regulated labour market in Western Europe. In opposition, Blair had been adamant that New Labour would break decisively with a Thatcherite growth strategy based on low wages and European opt-outs;[12] but in power, New Labour was just as reluctant as its Tory predecessors to embrace European directives on labour rights, and just as keen to exempt the UK labour force from EU-based regulation.

Where New Labour was more active than the Major Government was in the field of (particularly youth) unemployment. Gordon Brown, at the Treasury, made 'welfare to work' the cornerstone of his first budget: offering young unemployed workers a 'new deal' of four different education or training options, plus job counselling, and providing a six-month job subsidy to employers taking on the long-term unemployed. Other government initiatives followed, including job support to single parents, money for individual training accounts, and proposals for a University for Industry; and the DfEE accompanied these with a series of initiatives aimed at improving the educational standards of students prior to their entry into the labour force. Significantly, however, whereas there was heavy pressure on the young unemployed (and slightly less heavy pressure on single parents) to take paid work (via the threat of loss of benefit), there was no compulsion at all on firms to pay for training.

The resource flows associated with these initiatives were equally indicative of New Labour's priorities and thinking, containing as they did a well-resourced government commitment to get young people into work (financed by a special tax on privatised utilities), but a less well-resourced commitment to equipping them with the skills which ministers regularly claimed workers needed for economic survival and prosperity in the DTI's new 'knowledge based economy'. That is to say, New Labour, as in other parts of its industrial and employment policy portfolio, restricted itself to the 'exhortation and encouragement' of employers in the pursuit of competitiveness, while signalling a greater propensity actively to 'manage' employees to the same end. This proclivity for managerialism was fully in line with the practice of past Labour governments, which were equally liable to end up courting the business sector and subordinating trade union demands to the requirements of capital accumulation. In terms of these basic policy *continuities* – stretching back through Thatcherism to the 'old' Labour governments – it is unmistakable how conventional New Labour had really become.[13]

This might have mattered little had New Labour's economic and industrial policies finally triggered a qualititative transformation in economic performance, but they did not. It is true, as the Government claimed, that the creation of a million new jobs in the UK economy in the three years after May 1997 brought unemployment down to a pre-Thatcher level. It is also true that living standards over these years went up (10 per cent on average, according to the Government). But much of the reduction in unemployment was the product of movement into low-paid, low-skill service jobs. Job insecurity and work pressure remained high, and manufacturing employment continued to decline, particularly in the Labour heartlands of Scotland and the English north. Living standards, though rising, remained low in comparison with countries like France, Germany and the Netherlands, and income inequality remained acute – and actually grew in Labour's first two years in office.[14] The UK's capacity to attract foreign investment is still guaranteed only by a mixture of comparatively high interest rates and long working hours. Until the Tory spending limits were removed after 1999, the social fabric and economic infrastructure (housing stock, public transport networks, hospitals and schools) were left under-resourced, while the prices of manufactured goods were well above the western European average.

Yet on social policy, the promise of change seemed more secure. The New Labour Government instituted the practice of issuing annual reports, recording the fidelity of its actions in office to its promises in opposition. The July 2000 report recorded 177 election promises, and reported '104 of them met or done, 71 on course and 2 not time-tabled'[15]. In education: rising spending per child, falling class sizes, and tough new performance thresholds for reading and maths. In the health sector: rising real spending, reduced waiting lists, more doctors and nurses, and curbs on tobacco advertising. In welfare provision: reductions in long-term unemployment, and in the scale of benefit fraud, and so on. On top of all this, by the spring of 2000 the government was in a position to undertake a dramatic expansion of public spending, and had brought in a budget in which the health sector received an extra £13 billion and education an extra £12 billion.

Yet somehow, none of this was enough to maintain the enthusiasm of the original support for the Government. Part of the reason was the incipient authoritarianism which accompanied so much of New Labour's social agenda. The language of 'responsibilities' slipped easily, in the New Labour lexicon, into the politics of compulsion. The 2000 Annual Report made much of falling crime figures, and the more rapid processing of offenders from arrest to jail, and even presented its new highly coercive refugees policy as an improvement in the way in which the UK handled asylum seekers. As Anna Coote wrote about New Labour's social initiatives: 'nearly into its third year ... it is still not clear whether it is predominantly a liberally-minded democratizing government or an authoritarian, centralizing, government'. Would more time in office 'make New Labour more at ease with the idea of openness and power sharing', or could it make it 'more arrogant about its capacity to push through its policies, and to prod all of us dumb beasts into action'?[16] In the arena of social policy, it was compulsion rather than power sharing that stood out in such things as the detail of the 'New Deal' for youth employment and school reform, and the outright coercion in New Labour's policies on immigration, and on law and order. There was a hard edge to New Labour's project, which left the Government looking less the radicalising moderniser, and more the martinet.

New Labour's claim to being a radical democratising government was, of course, stronger on its constitutional than on its social and economic agendas; though here, too, the slippage between promise and performance eroded much of the initial enthusiasm. New Labour did introduce devolved government for Scotland and Wales. It introduced an element of proportional representation into the electoral systems for those devolved assemblies and the European Parliament. It held elections for a London mayor. It abolished the rights of all but 92 hereditary peers to vote in the House of Lords. It incorporated the European Convention on Human Rights into UK law; and it produced (after much procrastination and backsliding) a Freedom of Information Act. But even here, much of what the New Labour Government did was parsimonious, reluctant and inadequate: as Anthony Barnett put it, the constitutional 'revolution is not full-blooded because New Labour does not want it to be'.[17] The issue of proportional representation for the House of Commons was deflected into the Jenkins Commission, and then postponed. The full reform of the House of Lords went to the Wakeham Commission, with the same effect. The Freedom of Information Act eventually introduced by Jack Straw left vast swathes of government business immune from public scrutiny. The crucial opportunity comprehensively to democratise the British state with a written constitution was deliberately missed. New Labour came into office in 1997 promising a young country. At the millennium, it still felt like an old one.

New Labour and the Party

As the shine faded from New Labour's project, so did the enthusiasm of the party's leadership for further experimentation with constitutional change – and this was compounded by the willingness of regional and local electorates, and local Labour Party activists, to use the Scottish and Welsh elections and the London mayoral election to punish the Government. In any case, New Labour's commitment to democratising the state has always been in contradiction with its own antipathy to popular mobilisation, and to democratic participation inside the Labour Party itself.

In office, the New Labour leadership was determined to enhance still further its power over the party inside and outside Parliament. Building on Kinnock's dramatic expansion of the power of the leader, the Prime Minister's Office took over where the Leader's office had left off. Ministers were expected to clear all their speeches with the PMO, and all MPs were equipped with pagers and expected to respond to frequent summons from Millbank Tower – home of the party's Media Unit – to ensure that they were 'on message' at all times. The selection of candidates for the Scottish and Welsh elections, and for all parliamentary elections and by-elections, was closely controlled from the centre to ensure that as far as possible only loyal 'modernisers' were nominated. A list system of proportional representation for elections to the European Parliament – which, in effect, allowed the party leadership to exclude all but impeccably 'New' Labour MEPs – was adopted without consultation with the existing Labour MEPs, some of whom were expelled from the party for publicly opposing the change. The leadership also tried to impose candidates of its choice for leader of the Welsh Assembly and the new Mayor of London.[18]

The fact that in both these cases its efforts backfired showed that there were some limits to the power of the leadership, but they were not extensive. MPs became subject to new disciplinary rules, and – apart from Blair's close ally Peter Mandelson, and Gordon Brown (who, despite rumours to the contrary, was politically close to Blair) – no senior minister now enjoyed much independent authority. Powerful intellects and forceful characters were unlikely to find the new dispensation congenial and, more importantly, there was no longer a labour 'movement' in the old sense to afford such people a significant independent power base. 'Millbank' controlled which leaders had access to the main television and radio programmes, and what they said on them. The Cabinet was also now less than ever an arena for serious debate; Cabinet meetings typically lasted no more than an hour, and endorsed decisions already arrived at in bilateral meetings between the Prime Minister and the individual ministers who chaired the various specialist Cabinet committees.

It is easy to see that decision-making power had become highly centralised. It is less obvious who was really generating the policies decided on. Part of the answer lies in the murky area of ministers' 'special advisers' (whose numbers increased under New Labour from 38 to 74, at a total annual cost of £3.9 million by mid-2000) and the opinion pollsters, focus group interpreters and 'spin doctors' employed by the party. Patrick Wintour noted that while the new National Policy Forum was producing for the party's 2000 annual Conference a set of documents full of beatitudes about the Government's achievements in office with virtually no concrete proposals for the future, a young 'special adviser' called Ed Richards had been appointed by Blair to draw up 'a second term programme' – in collaboration, to be sure, with the fourteen highly secret 'spending reviews' then being undertaken by the Treasury.[19] Not a few such 'special advisers' were drawn from moderniser-friendly 'think tanks' – especially the Institute of Public Policy Research, the Fabian Society and Demos. Colin Hay observes that these think-tanks limited themselves to thinking about what can be done within 'the parameters of a free-market liberalism whose ascendancy they refuse to challenge. The result has been a welter of detailed policy prescription and very little else.'[20] But what else could they do, if their chief aim was to assist the 'modernisers'? The modernisers' 'radicalism of the centre' did not call for major departures from the status quo, despite their incessant celebration of the 'new'. What it required was a range of modest inflections of policy that would find favour with voters in key seats, and do some good without offending business. The think-tanks and the special advisers presumably met some of this need.

How useful the opinion researchers were seems more debatable. For one thing, the Government had to balance following public opinion against the risk of upsetting significant political or economic forces. For example, opinion polls revealed strong support for the abolition of fox-hunting, but the fox-hunting lobby showed itself a formidable opponent through its ability to mobilise the so-called 'Countryside Alliance', so the pledge to ban hunting was left to a free vote, and then deferred. In another example, the Government's own polling showed that university tuition fee increases would deter a significant minority from going to university, but – presumably for reasons of 'credibility' with the financial markets – it chose to conceal this evidence and impose the increases.[21] On the other hand, there were reasonable grounds for distrusting a good deal of the apparently 'hard' evidence produced by opinion surveys, not to mention the interpretations of it offered by 'focus group' leaders convinced that they were plumbing the innermost feelings of 'middle England'. When the cloudy and subjective nature of the advice tendered to Blair on this basis by Philip Gould, the party's chief opinion researcher, was momentarily exposed to public scrutiny in July 2000, it did not encourage confidence in his reports, or in the Prime Minister's judgement in relying on them.[22]

New Labour's obsession with 'presentation' – which lay behind the enormous power enjoyed by the Prime Minister's belligerent chief press officer, Alastair Campbell, and was transmitted to all ministers and back-benchers by the Prime Minister's Office and the party's Media Unit – had its origins in the media's feeding frenzy over Labour's internal conflicts in the 1970s and 1980s. As this book shows, the right wing of the Labour leadership had often invited this by encouraging media attacks on the left. The 'modernisers' grouped around Kinnock were equally hostile to the left, but realised that it was essential for the party to regain a measure of control over the way it was represented to the public in the media. The Media Unit was one result. Blair's accommodation with Murdoch before the election was another. A third was an almost neurotic preoccupation with avoiding the least sign of discord that could be represented by the media as a newsworthy 'split' – hence the insistence that all public statements must be vetted by the centre to ensure that they were 'on message'. A more general consequence was a pathological intolerance of criticism from any quarter seen as 'progressive'. Labour-inclined journalists were particularly singled out for intimidation on this score, but so too were progressive experts in various policy fields.[23]

It is hardly surprising that the 'Millbank tendency' – as New Labour's chief 'modernisers' and their assorted advisers and spinners were ironically called, in honour of the old 'Militant tendency' – was unpopular. A 'senior Labour veteran' was quoted by Michael White in November 1997 as saying: 'They're self-righteous pragmatists with no base. There's a lack of wisdom there. It will get us into trouble.'[24] The speaker was referring to the 'Ecclestone affair', but he or she might equally have been thinking about the decision to go ahead and build the Millennium Dome, a project which was opposed by a majority of Labour supporters but backed by the undoubted founder of the 'Millbank tendency', Peter

Mandelson, and which would fail so ignominiously and expensively when the millennium arrived. Hugo Young passed a similarly jaundiced judgement on New Labour's 'special advisers':

> Thirty years ago, when the species emerged ... the typical adviser was a professor who knew more about pensions or housing or education than the Civil Service ... Today's political advisers are different. With some exceptions they have little interest, and often no expertise, in policy. They're the minister's personal familiars, whose prime talent, if any, lies in explaining what the minister wants to get across; the guardians of access and the messengers of perception.[25]

The leadership's errors of judgement in imposing Alun Michael as leader of the Welsh Labour Party and Frank Dobson on the London Labour Party as candidate for Mayor similarly testified to the dangers of listening to the new kind of 'advisers', rather than to experts – or to people with an elective base in the party's rank and file.

The view of the 'modernisers' was that a 'tight ship' steered by a band of dedicated professionals was the price a reforming party had to pay if it wanted to win and keep power in the face of a hostile press and the 'new reality' of globalised financial markets. The implications for the rank and file were clear: members were less and less significant, except as subscribers and donors; and in spite of great efforts to prevent a decline, their numbers fell from 405,000 in December 1997 to 361,000 in December 1999. Some who left were recent recruits; others were veterans who felt disappointed by the Government's record – for instance, by the cuts in lone parents' benefits and disabled people's allowances in early 1998. The downward trend in membership was not peculiar to Labour, of course; party membership continued to fall in all 'post-industrial' countries, and activists were drawn increasingly into 'single-issue' social movements instead. Perhaps it is inevitable that for political parties of the kind New Labour is building, 'an American prospect beckons where most "activists" are paid and democratic participation by members in deciding party policy is strictly limited'.[26]

The US Democratic Party under Clinton was always an important point of reference for Labour under Blair. The American party model depends, however, on massive donations from business. In office, New Labour continued to move in that direction: the trade unions' contribution to party funds continued to fall as a proportion of the total – from 54 per cent in 1995 to 30 per cent in 1999 – while 'major donations' grew to account for 20 per cent (about £4.5 million), and members' subscriptions and 'small donations' for 40 per cent.[27] But dependence on rich donors and corporate funding comes at a price, as the Ecclestone affair had shown all too clearly. Moreover, although New Labour's 'credibility' with the City and the CBI had greatly improved, making it more like the 'party of business' that Blair had declared it wished to be, it was not (at least, not yet) *the* party of business, and could not count on corporate funding on the same scale as the Conservatives, however weak the latter currently were.[28] New Labour still needed members and their subscriptions, and the trade unions and their subscriptions.

The question was how far it could offer enough to either in return. The long-term solution initially favoured by Blair was state funding, and a legal ceiling on spending on general elections by party head-quarters. In the meantime, New Labour had to juggle the conflicting interests of capital and labour as best it could, relying, as always, on the awareness of both union leaders and activists that they would be worse off under a Conservative government.

Indeed, in the euphoria following the 1997 election victory, the changes to the party's constitution prepared by the 'modernisers' before the election, to restrict the power of the unions and party activists (see Chapter 10), were accepted by the annual Conference. From then on, the trade unions would control the election of only 12 National Executive Committee (NEC) members out of 33 – that is to say, they would no longer control a majority on it. Moreover, MPs were no longer eligible to stand for the six NEC places reserved for Constituency Labour Party (CLP) representatives, which eliminated this traditional power base of nationally popular left-wingers critical of the party leadership. Only three back-bench MPs were now included in the NEC, elected by all the Labour MPs and MEPs, which effectively ensured that they would be New Labour supporters.[29] A few left-wingers who were not MPs but had some national prominence, such as Mark Seddon, the editor of *Tribune*, won election to the NEC as CLP representatives; but the overall effect of all these changes was to end the era of serious policy contestation in the NEC. They also ensured that the NEC served as an effective agent of the leadership in disciplining members – through suspensions or expulsions for activities seen as disloyal – and in vetting all would-be Labour candidates.

The weight of the trade union 'block' vote at annual conferences was also reduced to 50 per cent of the total votes cast; but this was less significant than a new rule which largely confined Conference to debating only resolutions submitted through a new structure of 'policy forums', overseen by a Joint Policy Committee (JPC) of the NEC and the Government. The procedural details need not detain us. They included, for example, what might at first sight seem a curious 'guideline' which stated that members of the 175-strong National Policy Forum (NPF) were expected to 'respect the privacy of other members of the forum by protecting anonymity of views';[30] in effect, this rule extended to the members of the NPF – which met for three weekends a year – the principle of 'Cabinet responsibility' which Wilson had used to try to curb Benn's and Foot's independent authority within the party immediately after the 1974 election (see Chapter 5). Another rule said that unless at least 35 NPF members supported it, no resolution other than one endorsed by a majority in the NPF (described as 'the consensus') could normally be proposed at Conference.[31] What matters is the overall effect, which was to associate a number of rank-and-file members with what appeared to be a policy-forming process – one firmly managed by the JPC, under the leadership's close control, and one whose content was kept secret, not only from the press but also from other party members – in such a way that when Conference found itself debating only resolutions that the leadership already approved, it could be claimed that this was the result of an extensive democratic discussion within the party. (Anyone who doubts that this is a reasonable interpretation should study the NPF's *Reports* to the 2000 Conference, which contained only resolutions which 'glowingly render[ed] the Blair government's achievements to date' – often repeating verbatim the contents of government publications – and had virtually nothing to say about future policy choices.)[32]

By the time the 2000 Party Conference was being prepared, these developments had gone so far that a 'Labour insider' was quoted as saying: 'The conference has become a US-style convention instead of making policy. Millbank wants an audience, not activists.'[33] He or she was responding to the fact that by April 2000, in what was seen as 'an unprecedented protest by Labour's rank and file', over 200 Constituency Labour Parties – a third of the total – had still failed to nominate any delegates to the forthcoming Conference. 'At least now they will have more seats to sell to corporate sponsors,' the Labour insider quipped. But the problem was a serious one. Some trade unions also declined to increase their affiliation fees in protest at the Government's policies on issues like pensions and university tuition fees,[34] and in June 2000, trade unions unhappy with New Labour's neglect of their members' interests had found enough support from other elements in the NPF to secure the necessary 35 votes for 'hundreds' of 'alternative' resolutions, proposing different positions on a wide range of government-favoured policies, from proportional representation (to oppose the promised referendum on it) to pensions (to restore the link to earnings, rather than prices) and many other sensitive issues. Government supporters were quoted as saying: 'It looks horrific'; unions and CLPs had 'worked out how to use the system and they [were] exploiting it'.[35]

So an 'old' Labour solution was needed. In return for various concessions, arrived at in private meetings (with the Prime Minister himself, in at least one case), the trade union leaders backing the troublesome alternative resolutions agreed to drop their support for them, so that they did not go forward to the Party Conference. On proportional representation, the Government agreed to postpone any referendum until the systems already in operation for Scotland and Wales, the European Parliament and the London Assembly had 'become familiar', and 'all their consequences' had been felt. This was hardly a big 'concession', since Blair himself did not favour PR. On other issues – such as pensions, employees' rights in company mergers, and the minimum wage payable to young workers – the leadership promised 'reviews'.

The unions' allies in the threatened 'insurrection' inside the NPF – a surviving handful of CLP 'activists' – were predictably upset, and Patrick Wintour commented that there was 'a danger that the drive for consensus turns the forum into a means of filtering out disagreement from conference debate'.[36] But preventing the Conference from being an arena of disagreement had been the openly stated aim of the party's then General Secretary, Tom Sawyer, and the other 'modernisers'. So, given that consensus on important issues is unattainable, the effect of the new system was that the private deals between the union leaders and the party leadership, which used to underlie the block-vote-based settlements at annual Conferences, were now done in the final phase of the NPF – with much less media coverage, and with both activists and unions drastically weakened.

The impotence of the unions was underlined when conflict did reach the conference floor. On the issue of the state pension, for instance, it turned out that by backing down at the NPF, the union leaders had left themselves free, under the new rules, to reintroduce the issue at the 2000 Conference in the form of a 'contemporary issues' resolution (what used to be called an 'emergency' resolution). In spite of much behind-the-scenes arm-twisting, Unison, supported by the GMB and the TGWU, insisted on a debate, and won a 60–40 vote in favour of relinking the pension to average earnings, rather than just inflation. Gordon Brown, however – arguing that it was cheaper and fairer to let the basic pension, paid to rich and poor alike, decline relative to earnings, and use tax revenues to boost the incomes of the poorest pensioners by other means – immediately declared that he would not be bound by the Conference decision. His comment on the vote – 'It is for the country to judge, it is not for a few composite motions to decide the policy of this government and this country' – made it clear why, for him, focus groups could be more important than Party Conference decisions.[37]

Perhaps reflecting what their focus groups were telling them, the leadership's rhetoric did, however, undergo some change at this conference. Echoing Al Gore at the American Democratic Party convention a month earlier (attended by some key Labour Party policy advisers), there was some return to the language of redistribution and fairness. As Roy Hattersley noted of Blair's conference speech:

Government expenditure has been elevated from vice to virtue. Taxation, which was once a detriment to progress, has become the engine of the social justice that is essential to economic success ... Tony Blair is not going to glide back into office on windy talk about young country and fresh start ... the whole bogus concept [of New Labour] was dramatically played down last week – by everybody except Peter Mandelson ... who stood heroically on the burning deck of 'the project' ... He clearly sees himself (as Benn once saw himself) as the advocate of a philosophy that although right and true is gradually being abandoned by the government.[38]

This shift in rhetoric could hardly amount to much in a party whose leaders had so radically detached themselves from rank-and-file activists, and seemed closer in government, both politically and socially, to the CBI than to the labour movement. The 'new social movements' also found New Labour not much more sympathetic to them than the Conservatives had been.[39] New Labour's ideology of 'youth', 'the people', 'community', 'pluralism' and 'choice' was a very long way indeed from entailing alliances with the women's, ecology or peace movements, let alone the sort of active 'community politics' pioneered by the Liberals in the 1970s. On the contrary, in the name of giving power to ordinary people as individuals, real power was more than ever concentrated in the hands of a professional party elite. By the year 2000, precisely one hundred years after the formation of the Labour Representation Committee, the Labour Party leadership stood before the electorate as a largely self-appointed 'management team', to be judged on the basis of the current share price of Britain plc.[40] When that price dipped (metaphorically speaking, of course) – as it did in September 2000, for example, in the unhappiness over the cost of petrol – the managers lost support. The voters' famous new 'volatility', demonstrated in their sudden swing to the Conservatives in the opinion polls in that month, was a not inappropriate response to New Labour's chosen relationship with them.

Yet the causes of the voters' capriciousness were not immediately obvious. The seemingly unshakeable popularity produced by three years of rising disposable incomes and significant measures to alleviate acute poverty appeared to have been shattered by nothing more earth-shaking than a cold reception to a speech by Blair to the Women's Institute, a Conservative campaign against asylum seekers, and a new 'oil shock'. Part of the problem was 'spin': every policy initiative was bathed in hype, to the point where the media and the public had grown cynical. But there was something else besides: the leadership could not expect the kind of deep loyalty from Labour supporters that would have been extended to tried and trusted spokesmen for working people, the bearers of long-nurtured collective hopes, such as the Labour Party had produced when it was still grounded in a mass movement.

New Labour and the 'Third Way'

After all the hype, some popular disenchantment with New Labour was sooner or later inevitable. What was perhaps more significant was a deeper sense of disappointment that gradually came to the fore among so many of those who had been most enthusiastic about the 1997 election result. The fact that this was not a socialist government could hardly account for it. For most of this century, social democratic parties in general – as Donald Sassoon rightly insists – needed to be primarily 'conceived as an attempt to regulate capitalism' rather than replace it, and this was true long before they 'discarded radical anticapitalist rhetoric'.[41] No doubt the facile way in which New Labour insisted, with its invocation of the 'Third Way', that there was no necessary contradiction between the commitment to market efficiency and the goal of social justice – and that any suggestions to the contrary were evidence of antiquated thinking – was particularly irksome. But such squaring the circle was also nothing new: from the party's very beginning, most Labour politicians, echoing Ramsay MacDonald's insistence on the principle of class harmony rather than class conflict, engaged in similar rhetorical evasions. Nor could it be fairly said, despite the continuities in policy discussed above, that New Labour's political practice was simply neo-liberal. Its commitment was to an effective state within the framework of capitalism, not to a minimal one; nor could its concern to enhance the incomes of the poorest families, or the eventual increases in health and education spending, be ignored.

The deeper disappointment with New Labour reflected, rather, an emerging awareness that in so far as this version of social democracy did reflect a definitive break with the past, it did so in terms of repudiating crucial concerns which social democracy had contributed to the struggle for democracy and social justice in the twentieth century. Even if social democracy has always been mainly about regulating capitalism, the point of the earlier regulation was normally to oppose or limit the power of capitalists, the writ of the market and the commodification of social life. The type of regulation New Labour engaged in, however, based its validity on capitalist criteria – or, as Blair put it, 'working with the grain of the market'. Whereas mainstream social democrats traditionally saw competition as a constraint on their goals, giving rise to social costs and posing problems that needed to be managed or coped with, New Labour actively embraced competition as its own main objective.

One of the things that was abandoned in the process was the ethical socialism which, Labour Party politicians were always proud to insist, had motivated them so much more than Marxism. For all the language of 'values' and 'morals' that tripped off the tongues of New Labour leaders when it came to how families were supposed to behave, what went missing was any sense of what was unethical about an economic strategy which fostered the export competitiveness of one's own national economy with little thought to what this might mean for less successful competing economies. The embrace of competitiveness was presented in the context of coming to terms with globalisation, but for all the rhetoric of internationalism, the project of pitting the workers of Britain plc in a competition against all comers in the 'new economy' was, if anything, more narrowly nationalist than traditional social democracy. In adopting this new kind of mercantilism, New Labour was again content to follow the lead of the American state, the main promoter of this competitive version of globalisation.

It used to be the case that a social democrat, seeing someone hungry and homeless on the street, would think not in terms of that person being untrained, uncompetitive and un-entrepreneurial but, rather, in terms of there being something wrong with the system. The immoralities of a social order which is founded on economic competition, and defines 'success' accordingly, were now obscured by an ideology which designated whole economic regions as not entrepreneurial enough, not well-trained enough, not competitive enough. The very tension – so long present in social democratic labour movements – between pride in the dignity of work and concern with the alienation of work disappeared in the embrace of an ideology of competitiveness which alone defined the necessity of work, the purpose of work, the nature of work. To be sure, at the margin of New Labour's strategic orientation, such as giving tax credits to the poorest families, an ethical concern to help those most in need was still visible. New Labour policymakers sometimes spoke in terms of 'leaning against the natural inequality that today's market economy brings about', but they did this more in private than in public, and in any case never went so far as to use the old language of 'redistribution'. But what really characterised New Labour was its complete acceptance that this systemic inequality was indeed 'natural'.

Moreover, however much New Labour insisted that 'the Government has a key role to play as a catalyst, investor and regulator to strengthen the supply side of the economy', what it above all came to accept, as part and parcel of its embrace of competition and the market, was the notion that 'business must lead'.[42] This was even reflected in New Labour's definition of the substance as well as the limits of the public sector itself (for instance, by ceding to business the leading role in defining how to 'continuously upgrade skills' in schools and training schemes, or by adopting programmes to 'vigorously promote the commercialization of university research').[43] But, more fundamentally, what accepting the leading role of business really involved was the abandonment of any notion of *shifting the balance of class forces*. Mainstream social democracy in the post-war era, however moderate, retained some commitment to this; indeed, Crosland's *The Future of Socialism* was entirely premised on the achievement of a relative balance between labour and capital, and the displacement of business from its predominant position *vis-à-vis* government. Such a strategic conception had now utterly gone – and at a time when the balance was continually shifting the other way.

This was closely related to New Labour's posture towards the party and the labour movement – and had extremely troubling implications not only for social justice but also for democracy. The history of modern democracy in Britain cannot be told without the Labour Party. The party could not have come into existence if the vote had not been extended to working men, and once it was formed, the party played a major part in the struggle to extend the vote to the great majority of the population who were still denied it. Inextricably bound up with the realisation of democracy was enhancing the power of the working class by building institutions through which it could express itself. However parliamentarist the Labour Party's strategic conception was, the institutions of the extra-parliamentary party, with their organic linkages to the trade unions' own representative institutions, constituted the central arenas where working-class people and their representatives met to debate and define the various and common interests of the class. And while it was through these institutions that a senior Labour minister, such as Stafford Cripps in 1949, could direct an appeal to workers for wage restraint in the name of 'Christian values' as well as the 'national interest', the same institutions provided the space where a woman cleaner in Whitehall, a delegate of the Transport and General Workers Union, could take the floor to proclaim that while the vegetarian Cripps might 'live on orange juice and radish tops ... the workers of Great Britain cannot be expected to follow his example to that extent'.[44]

Under New Labour, the old idea and practice of the party as something separate from government has been reduced almost to vanishing point. This is a major blow to the substance and process of democracy in Britain. The extra-parliamentary party has not disappeared; nor has it been merely bypassed or marginalised.[45] It has, rather, become more and more an agent of government; its role as an arena for substantive debate, discussion and decision – let alone for class formation and shifting the balance of class forces – has been drastically curtailed.

In fact, what is happening is the Americanisation of British politics. In the American model, of course, the party system does not reflect class identities and divisions; but, more than this, the broader currents of dissent and protest find neither clear electoral expression nor expression within the institutions of a mass party. The cry 'TINA' was launched two decades ago as a campaigning slogan by the British political right; today, it is a lament on the political left, and the lack of party alternatives is now felt as strongly by the British left as it has always been by the American left.

The mass socialist and labour parties formed in Europe a century ago created institutional means through which working people could develop the capacity to govern their lives collectively, to learn to be active participants in democracy. Because other institutions did not grapple with the stunting of that capacity in a class society, this was the most impressive – and the most daunting – of all the goals mass socialist parties set themselves.[46] Little trace of it can any longer be found in social democratic parties in general, or New Labour in particular. New Labour still speaks in terms of developing capacities. But the capacities it explicitly seeks to develop are those of 'entrepreneurship' and 'competitiveness'.[47]

Although most of New Labour's characteristics were in evidence throughout the whole history of the Labour Party, in the past they were always disputed. However much the party as an arena of class formation and as a developer of popular democratic capacities may have atrophied over the decades, it remained the main forum of debate and contestation in Britain about what kind of regulation of capitalism there ought to be, and about the continuing relevance of a conception of socialism as another kind of society. The fact that the protagonists in these debates, on all sides, came to be dismissed as 'old Labour' makes it very clear that what is above all regarded as antiquated and no longer acceptable is the party as a contested terrain, as an arena of democracy and as an incubator of popular democratic capacities.

Given this dénouement, it is now clearer than ever just how high were the stakes in the conflict within the Labour Party in the course of the transition from 'new left' to New Labour. The outcome was perhaps inevitable, given the weaknesses of the 'new left' and the scale of the obstacles confronting it in its attempt to change a party whose policies and practices had, in any case, always been limited and had become increasingly unviable. By the year 2000, the old parliamentary socialist project which the 'new left' had wanted to supersede was well and truly dead – at first weakened by its internal contradictions, and finally killed off by the 'modernisers'. The project for a much fuller democratisation of British state and society through the much fuller democratisation of the Labour Party had also been decisively defeated. Every previous phase of the party's history was characterised by prolonged struggles between the leadership and recognisably distinct, organised and pro-grammatically informed left oppositions. New Labour has restructured the party so that virtually no room is any longer allowed for this.

But New Labour's project is itself unstable in a world where market efficiency cannot be easily squared with social justice, and the absence of any real 'third way' means that the contradictions of capitalism continually and painfully reassert themselves in so many parts of the globe – and, indeed, in Britain too. It is increasingly evident that the New Labour project is not only vulnerable to economic recession but, given its nature as an elite management exercise, also vulnerable to loss of direction and fatigue under the constant pressure of market forces, including those of the media.

By 2000 there were growing signs of renewed vitality on the left. When young people engaged in mass protests around the world, including Britain, increasingly called themselves 'anticapitalist', it was a Labour Party which had closed itself to the idea that there is any future but a better capitalism that began to look antiquated and incapable of engaging creatively with these new political forces. This opened space for renewed socialist politics outside the Labour Party, as seen in Ken Livingstone's victory over New Labour as an independent candidate in London's mayoral election, and also in the growth of the Scottish Labour Party. New socialist projects are on the agenda at the beginning of the twenty-first century. Lessons will have to be learned, both from the limits of parliamentary socialism (as well as authoritarian communism) and from the defeat of the new left inside the Labour Party. In the wake of that defeat, as happened many times before, many people lost the capacity to think ambitiously about social change. Once this capacity is recovered, and as new institutions are being constructed, the purpose and vision of those who had wanted the Labour Party to become a genuinely democratic socialist agent of transformation will be better understood and appreciated.

Notes

1. From New Left to New Labour

1. Stuart Hall, 'The Great Moving Right Show', *Marxism Today*, January 1979. See also 'Thatcherism – a new stage', *Marxism Today*, February 1980.
2. 'In 1977 the income of the richest 20 per cent of Britons was four times as big as the income of the poorest 20 per cent; by 1991 that multiple had increased to seven' (and it has increased further since); '. . . the gap between the highest- and lowest-paid male workers in Britain is at its widest since the 1880s when such figures were first compiled' (*The Economist*, 5 November 1994).
3. See e.g. Alec Nove, *The Economics of Feasible Socialism Revisited*, London 1991; Michael Albert and Robin Hahnel, *Looking Forward: Participatory Economics for the Twenty-First Century*, Boston 1991; Pranab K. Bardhan and John Roemer, eds, *Market Socialism: The Current Debate*, New York 1993; Paul Hirst, *Associative Democracy: New Forms of Economic and Social Governance*, Cambridge 1994.
4. But see e.g. Hilary Wainwright's concluding chapter in Sheila Rowbotham, Lynn Segal and Hilary Wainwright, *Beyond the Fragments*, London 1981; and 'The London Edinburgh Weekend Return Group', *In and Against the State*, London 1980.
5. See Lin Chun, *The British New Left*, Edinburgh 1993.
6. Ralph Miliband, 'Moving On', *The Socialist Register 1976*, p. 128. There were very few links between the Labour new left and most of the original new left's leading figures, including E.P. Thompson, John Saville, Raymond Williams, Miliband himself, Stuart Hall and later editors of *New Left Review*, until the early 1980s – after the Labour new left had already been defeated at the national level of the party.
7. Raymond Williams, Edward Thompson, Stuart Hall and Ralph Miliband had noted as early as 1968 that past efforts by the Labour left had always bogged down in the same way; the left 'becomes of necessity involved in the same kind of machine politics, the same manipulation of committees in the name of thousands . . . It is also . . . directing energy into the very machines and methods which socialists should fight . . . And this has prevented the outward-looking and independent long-term campaign'

(Raymond Williams et al., eds, *The May Day Manifesto*, Harmondsworth 1968, pp. 173–4).

8. The first expression is from Tony Blair's commentary on the BBC's series, 'The Wilderness Years', in the *Observer*, 17 December 1995; the second is from Peter Mandelson's and Roger Liddle's *The Blair Revolution*, London 1996, p. 214.

9. *The Blair Revolution*, p. 2.

10. 'They have not won their political battles; they have not carried their main points, they have not stopped their adversaries' advance; but they have told silently upon the mind of the country, they have prepared currents of feeling which sap their adversaries' position when it seems gained, they have kept up their communication with the future' (Matthew Arnold, cited in Fred Inglis, 'The Figures of Dissent', *New Left Review*, no. 215, January–February 1996, p. 82).

11. Tony Blair, 'True Story of the Wilderness Years', *Observer*, 17 December 1995.

12. Tony Benn, Fabian Autumn Lecture, 3 November 1971, in *Speeches* by Tony Benn, 1974, p. 275.

13. Tony Crosland, *Socialism Now and Other Essays*, London 1974, pp. 27 and 72–3.

14. Tony Benn, *The New Politics: A Socialist Reconnaissance*, Fabian Tract 402, September 1970, pp. 8–9; for the paragraph from which this phrase is drawn, see Chapter 3, page 50. It is also worth noting that Benn's pamphlet of 1970 anticipates in all essentials the argument of Stuart Hall's famous essay of November 1978, 'The Great Moving Right Show', first published in *Marxism Today*, in which, however, Hall also wrote as if the Labour new left had nothing relevant to contribute to the task of combating the new right.

15. Michael Crozier, Samuel P. Huntington and Joji Watanuki, *The Crisis of Democracy: Report on the Governability of Democracies to the Trilateral Commission*, New York 1975.

16. David Hine, 'Leaders and Followers: Democracy and Manageability in the Social Democratic Parties of Western Europe', in William E. Patterson and Alastair H. Thomas, eds, *The Future of Social Democracy*, Oxford 1986, pp. 278–89.

17. Quoted in R.W. Johnson, *The Long March of the French Left*, New York 1981, p. 159.

18. See Stefano Bartolini, 'The Membership of Mass Parties: The Social Democratic Experience, 1889–1978', in H. Daalder and P. Mair, eds, *Western European Party Systems: Continuity and Change*, London 1983, esp. pp. 185–91.

19. Ralph Miliband, 'A State of De-Subordination', *The British Journal of Sociology*, vol. xxix, no. 4, December 1978, pp. 399–409.

20. Trevor Blackwell and Jeremy Seabrook, *A World Still to Win*, London 1985, pp. 113–14.

21. See R. Cayrol, 'The Crisis of the French Socialist Party', *New Political Science*, vol. 12, Summer 1983, pp. 11–16.

22. See M. Spourdalakis, *The Rise of the Greek Socialist Party*, London 1988, especially chapter 6.
23. Jonas Pontusson, *The Limits of Social Democracy: Investment Politics in Sweden*, Ithaca and London 1992, especially chapter 7.
24. Robert Michels, *Political Parties: A Sociological Study of the Oligarchical Tendencies of Modern Democracy* (1915), New York 1962.
25. Max Weber, *Gesammalte Aufsatze zur Soziologie und Sozialpolitik*, quoted in G. Carchedi, *Class Analysis and Social Research*, Oxford 1987, p. 12.
26. Lewis Minkin, *The Labour Party Conference: A Study in the Politics of Intra-Party Democracy*, London 1978, p. 14.
27. R.T. McKenzie, *British Political Parties: The Distribution of Power within the Conservative and Labour Parties*, London 1955.
28. Robert McKenzie, 'Power in the Labour Party: The Issue of Intra-Party Democracy', in D. Kavanagh, ed., *The Politics of the Labour Party*, London 1982, pp. 196–7.
29. Ibid.
30. J.A. Schumpeter, *Capitalism, Socialism and Democracy*, 5th edn, London 1975, pp. 269 and 285.
31. Perry Anderson, 'The Antinomies of Antonio Gramsci', *New Left Review*, no. 100, November 1976–January 1977, pp. 28–9.

2. Origins of the Party Crisis

1. *The Forward March of Labour Halted?*, London 1981, p. 18. But Hobs-bawm's concentration on a fatalistic discussion of long-term sociological trends undermining the 'forward march of Labour', led him to neglect to offer any explanation of the Wilson years. This was not surprising perhaps, since the 'popular front' strategy he was in fact putting forward in the late 1970s and early 1980s was not terribly dissimilar to that which the Labour Party had fashioned for itself in the early 1960s.
2. 'Election Agenda', *Socialist Commentary*, May 1962, p. 5, emphasis in text.
3. 1961 *Labour Party Conference Report* (hereafter *LPCR*), p. 155.
4. 1964 *TUC Report*, p. 383.
5. Swansea, 25 January 1964, reprinted in Harold Wilson, *The New Britain: Labour's Plan, Selected Speeches*, London 1964, p. 19; on Benn's contribution to this speech, see Robert Jenkins, *Tony Benn, A Political Biography*, London 1980, p. 99.
6. 1963 *LPCR*, p. 198.
7. See esp. *Tribune*, 8 January, 5 and 19 February, 23 April, 28 May 1965.
8. Perry Anderson, 'Problems of Socialist Strategy', in P. Anderson and R. Blackburn, eds, *Towards Socialism* (1965), Ithaca, N.Y. 1966, pp. 222, 261, 284.
9. After the first breakthrough in Labour's vote to over 30 per cent in the 1920s, and the second breakthrough to over 40 per cent in the 1940s, Labour's support showed no tendency to a steady rise or fall until the experience of the 1966 Wilson Government. Labour's percentage of the vote

fell from an historic high in 1951 of 48.8 per cent (when they lost the election) to 46.4 per cent in 1955 and 43.9 per cent in 1959, but in its standing in the opinion polls between elections it pretty consistently ran ahead of the Tories through the 1950s, hovering around the percentage of the vote it had obtained in 1951. The first Wilson Government in 1964 was elected on 44.1 per cent of the vote, and the second in 1966 on 48.1 per cent of the vote, barely less than 1951 and distributed in such a way this time to yield an overwhelming majority in the House of Commons. (The longitudinal data employed in this discussion are mainly drawn from A. Heath, R. Jowell and J. Curtice, *How Britain Votes*, Oxford 1985, Tables 1.2 and 3.1 and Diagram 1.3, pp. 3–5, 30.) The class voting patterns in the mid-1960s remained strong enough to seem to justify leading psephologists, with their typical tendency to extrapolate the present into the future, in the view that Labour was being invested by demographic changes with a permanent majority. (See, for example, David Butler and Donald Stokes, *Political Change in Britain*, London 1969.)

10. Their first findings were published as 'Affluence and the British Class Structure', *Sociological Review*, July 1963.

11. Mark N. Franklin, *The Decline of Class Voting in Britain: Changes in the Basis of Electoral Choice*, Oxford 1985, p. 174. David Weakliem's more recent study confirms that the critical moment in determining the decline in working-class voting for the Labour Party took place between 1964 and 1970, when the Labour Party lost a similar degree of support among what he identifies as 'class-conscious' working-class voters as among those whom he defines as 'class-aware'. (The views that were expressed by 'class-aware' voters are similar to the new working-class consciousness Goldthorpe and Lockwood identified as 'instrumental collectivism'.) See David Weakliem, 'Class Consciousness and Political Change: Voting and Political Attitudes in the British Working Class, 1964 to 1970', *American Sociological Review*, vol. 58, no. 3, 1993, esp. pp. 391–5.

12. Robert Jenkins, *Tony Benn, A Political Biography*, London 1980, p. 109.

13. *A World Still to Win*, London 1985, p. 133.

14. Cynthia Cockburn, *The Local State*, London 1977, p. 5. See also John Gyford, *The Politics of Local Socialism*, London 1985, p. 25.

15. Interview with Ken Livingstone, in Kogan and Kogan, *The Battle for the Labour Party*, London 1982, p. 122.

16. In his autobiography, Healey attributes the phrase (with which he believed everyone was familiar) to the comedienne Hermione Gingold. He admits that his 'careless tongue' in this respect caused him considerable public embarrassment – especially with the People's Republic of China – and haunted him throughout his political career. See *The Time of My Life*, London 1989, p. 444. Healey first used the phrase in February 1976 to deride those who said the real divisions in British politics cut through the Labour Party: see Tony Benn, *Against the Tide: Diaries 1973–76*, pp. 521–2.

17. Ian Mikardo, 'Watch the Unions: That's My Tip', *Tribune*, 8 October 1965.

18. Lewis Minkin, *The Labour Party Conference*, London 1978, p. 294.

19. See Lewis Minkin's definitive account, *The Contentious Alliance: Trade Unions and the Labour Party*, Edinburgh 1991, esp. chs 5 and 6.

20. Eric Shaw, *Discipline and Discord in the Labour Party*, Manchester 1988, p. 296.
21. See Minkin, *The Labour Party Conference*, esp. pp. 125–6.
22. She concentrated instead on asking (to howls of laughter): 'Are we to get no thanks for the fact that the price of beer has been stabilised in the past two and a half years?' The price of the beer they were imbibing had not been the main topic of conversation among the union delegates during their 'extra-curricular' conference activities. 1968 *LPCR*, pp. 127, 149, 153.
23. Jenkins, *Tony Benn*, p. 214.
24. The most significant instances of disaffiliation took place among the railway, miners, textile and sheet metal workers' unions. Moreover, although the unions maintained the level of block affiliations to the party, the actual number of individuals who contracted out of the political levy portion of their dues also increased (most markedly from 240,616 in 1966 to 320,983 in 1970 in the engineers' union).
25. Jack Jones, 'Keeping Trade Union Links with Labour', *Tribune*, 9 February 1968.
26. In 1969 both the Transport and Engineering unions announced that they were reviewing their panels of MPs in response to rank-and-file dissatisfaction. As the TGWU carried through its review, this produced an unholy row with George Brown as he and three other MPs lost their sponsorship before the 1970 election. It marked the beginning of complaints about union 'abuse of parliamentary privilege': *The Times* news accounts of these events began quoting Erskine May; and editorials began appearing arguing that the notion that 'active trade union membership is a better basis for judging public affairs than membership in the House of Commons ... smacks of contempt' (Editorial, 'Sponsored MPs', *The Times*, 6 December 1969). The trade unions' concern with the behaviour of their MPs was, of course, not unprecedented. Within two months of the fall of the Labour Government in 1931, the London Trades Council had issued a political manifesto suggesting that trade unionists and local parties 'should carefully consider how strenuously did their former member of Parliament fight the battle of the wage earners ... Those who desire an exclusively political career had better look elsewhere for their nomination and support.' (Quoted in John Scanlon, *Decline and Fall of the Labour Party*, London n.d., p. 18.)
27. Quoted in Geoffrey Goodman, *The Awkward Warrior, Frank Cousins: His Life and Times*, London 1979, p. 515.
28. Interviews with Michael Foot, 5 August and 11 November 1971, conducted by Leo Panitch for *Social Democracy and Industrial Militancy: The Labour Party, the Trade Unions and Incomes Policy, 1945–74*, Cambridge 1976.
29. Tony Benn, *A New Course for Labour*, Institute for Workers' Control pamphlet, Nottingham 1976, p. 10.
30. Official figures on individual party membership were notoriously inflated, not least because they reflected from 1963 to 1979 the introduction of a new party rule which required constituencies to affiliate on the basis of a minimum figure of 1,000 although most CLPs had memberships far less than that. The 680,000 figure around which the party's individual membership hovered by the end of the 1960s probably needed to be discounted by

at least one-half, perhaps by as much as two-thirds. (See *Report of the Committee on Financial Aid to Political Parties*, Cmd. 6601, London 1976; and Paul Whitely, *The Labour Party in Crisis*, London 1983, ch. 3.)

31. See Stefano Bartolini, 'The Membership of Mass Parties: The Social Democratic Experience, 1889–1978' in H. Daalder and P. Mair, eds, *Western European Party Systems: Continuity and Change*, London 1983, figure 7.3, p. 188.

32. Quoted in Patrick Seyd and Lewis Minkin, 'The Labour Party and Its Members', *New Society*, 20 September 1979, p. 614.

33. There was a loss of 150,000 members from 1964 to 1969. Once the inflated official 680,000 membership figure of 1969 is appropriately discounted (i.e. at least by half), we can see that Ken Livingstone's estimate that the party lost half its members in these years may not have been too much of an exaggeration.

34. Seyd and Minkin, 'The Labour Party and Its Members', p. 613.

35. David Widgery's *The Left in Britain 1956–68*, Harmondsworth 1976, provides a useful glossary of left-wing groups and publications up to the early 1970s, pp. 477–505.

36. Marjorie Mayo, 'Radical Politics and Community Action', in M. Loney and M. Allen, eds, *The Crisis of the Inner City*, London 1979, pp. 132–5.

37. Barry Hindess, *The Decline of Working Class Politics*, London 1971, pp. 98, 108.

38. Quoted in ibid., p. 116.

39. Shaw, *Discipline and Discord in the Labour Party*, pp. 294–5.

40. Ibid., p. 296. The Russell case was initiated by the NEC's Organisation Committee itself in reaction to his sponsorship of a World Disarmament Conference in Moscow in 1962. Often other expulsions were initiated by right-wing local party leaders and then endorsed by farcical NEC 'Enquiries', as was Ken Coates's expulsion in 1965. Yet by 1969, when Coates's long struggle to re-enter the Labour Party was won, this was the very time that most other independent socialists saw the Labour Party as the last place to be active. As for the organised 'entrists', by the late 1960s the only Trotskyist group of any size involved in 'entrism' was Militant (which had only some 100–200 members).

41. Palmer, the *Guardian*'s long-standing European correspondent on Brussels, was to become in the 1980s a key figure in Ken Livingstone's administration of the GLC. On Coates's expulsion, see his *The Crisis of British Socialism*, Nottingham 1971, pp. 80–98. On the IS and Militant at the time see Widgery, *The Left in Britain*, pp. 210–11, and Michael Crick, *Militant*, London 1984, pp. 55ff., 131.

42. Howard Elcock, 'Tradition and Change in Labour Party Politics: The Decline and Fall of the City Boss', *Political Studies*, vol. xxix, no. 3, 1981, p. 440.

43. David G. Green, *Power and Party in an English City*, London 1981, p. 36.

44. Quoted in A. D. Glassberg, *Representation and Urban Community*, London 1981, p. 50.

45. Green, *Power and Party in an English City*, p. 70.

46. Cockburn, *The Local State*, p. 90.

47. 'The enormity of their defeat effectively knocked the bottom out of their world; some of them drifted out of politics altogether in despair whilst those who remained were now vulnerable for perhaps the first time in their political lives.' John Gyford, *The Politics of Local Socialism*, London 1985, p. 26.

48. Tony Benn, *Out of the Wilderness: Diaries 1963–67*, London 1988, pp. 491–2.

49. David Blunkett, 'Why I am a Socialist: Sheffield Steel', *New Socialist*, November/December 1982, p. 56.

50. Illtyd Harrington, 'Young Turks of Town Hall', *New Statesman*, 16 July 1971, p. 77.

51. See P. Abramson, 'Intergenerational Mobility and Partisan Preferences in Britain and Italy', *Comparative Political Studies*, vol. 6, 1973, pp. 221–34.

52. David Lockwood, *The Black Coated Worker*, London 1958.

53. Hindess's portrayal of Labour's new middle-class activists as displaying a technocratic mentality was not only appallingly reductionist, it was far too monolithic. The 'new middle-class' Labour activists in fact reflected various ideological orientations, as did Labour's working-class members, and Hindess's study thus proved remarkably unprescient with regard to the radicalisation of the constituency parties that took place in the 1970s. For useful studies of party membership trends in this period which also present insightful critiques of Hindess's view of Labour's new middle-class activists, see Geoff Hodgson, *Labour at the Crossroads*, Oxford 1981, pp. 55–9, and T. Forester, *The Labour Party and the Working Class*, London 1976.

54. Quoted in Cockburn, *The Local State*, p. 126.

55. Ibid., pp. 118, 159–61.

56. Quoted in Gyford, *The Politics of Local Socialism*, pp. 34–5.

57. Mayo, 'Radical Politics and Community Action', pp. 141–2.

58. Quoted in Gyford, *The Politics of Local Socialism*, p. 35.

59. See esp. Green, *Power and Party in an English City*, pp. 36, 40, 85–6, 108, 118, 126; and Gyford, *The Politics of Local Socialism*, pp. 35, 43–4.

60. Interview with David Blunkett in M. Boddy and C. Fudge, *Local Socialism*, London 1984, pp. 244–5.

61. Cockburn, *The Local State*, p. 90.

62. See Radhika Desai, *Intellectuals and Socialism: 'Social Democrats' and the British Labour Party*, London 1994, pp. 190–92.

63. Quoted in John Carvel, *Citizen Ken*, London 1984, p. 46.

64. Ibid., p. 40.

65. David Skinner and Julia Langdon, *The Story of Clay Cross*, Nottingham 1974, pp. 17–18.

66. They ran a tight ship in the Labour Group where council policy was decided, but at the same time they made themselves all answerable to monthly meetings of the local party: 'it had all to do with not losing touch with the people, with practical politics in action' (ibid., p. 20). Local party membership grew tenfold. The average age of councillors was under forty. They dispensed with the formalities of officialdom and dropped all perquisites for councillors. According to local mythology, the chain of office that

Dennis Skinner refused to wear as chairman of the council had been melted down and the money obtained put into the housing account.

67. Ian Gordon and Paul Whitely, 'Social Class and Political Attitudes: The Case of Labour Councillors', *Political Studies*, vol. xxvii, no. 1, 1979, pp. 99–113. On other issues there was rather less common agreement amongst them: 49 per cent thought that 'Labour should adjust policies to capture the middle ground of politics'; 50 per cent thought 'Labour should establish a legally backed incomes policy'; 58 per cent thought 'Labour should condemn political activities which break the law'; 49 per cent thought that 'Britain should withdraw from the Common Market' and 33 per cent from NATO; 36 per cent thought that 'Britain should retain nuclear weapons'; and 47 per cent thought 'the P.L.P. should accept conference decisions as binding'.

68. 'Weighing 'em up', *Labour Organiser*, vol. 50, no. 578, January 1971, pp. 3–4.

69. 'The implications of this committee's activities, even the fact that it existed at all, are far reaching. Ignoring for a moment the imperfections of the Party's candidate selection procedures, the truth is that in most cases local activists try their best to make a fair and democratic choice, within the confines of the system. Yet, for a considerable period at a vital point in the history of the Party, a group of distinguished and prominent people at the very heart of its affairs were able to exert a dominating influence over the selection of particular candidates, marshalling their local forces, instructing delegates, calling for and receiving aid from the Party's full-time officials, sifting and sorting the individuals available for selection on the basis of their character, associates and political views and generally centralizing a system specifically designed for a considerable measure of local control.' Peter Paterson, *The Selectorate, the Case for Primary Elections in Britain*, London 1967, pp. 65–6. The committee included the party Chief Whip as well as other senior parliamentary colleagues of Gaitskell's, senior officials from the General and Municipal and the Mineworkers' unions, the chairman of the Co-operative Party and the ever-present Gaitskellite fixer, Bill Rodgers, later a founder member of the breakaway Social Democratic Party in 1981.

70. Dick Taverne, *The Future of the Left*, London 1974, as quoted in Alison Young, *The Reselection of MPs*, London 1983, pp. 69–70, 75.

71. Bryan Gould, *Goodbye to All That*, London 1995, p. 215.

72. Shaw, *Discipline and Discord in the Labour Party*, p. 295.

73. The initiative came from Sheffield where activists in the Trades and Labour Council had also tried and failed a year earlier to launch a Campaign for a Democratic Labour Party at the national level. The Labour MP most closely associated with Socialist Charter was Frank Allaun who had been elected to the NEC in 1967 and consistently made the Government's disdain for Conference resolutions an issue on the Executive. Among the union leadership, Daly, Jones, Seabrook and Scanlon all lent their names to Socialist Charter when it was founded in 1968. But most constituency activists were far more inclined at the time to leave the party rather than try to change it. In 1972, at a 'convention' attended by twenty-three people, Socialist Charter was taken over by the Revolutionary Communist League.

(See Widgery, p. 498; Minkin, *The Labour Party Conference*, pp. 35, 406 n.16, and *The Contentious Alliance*, pp. 161, 181, 206 n.13; D. Kogan and M. Kogan, *The Battle for the Labour Party*, London 1982, pp. 20–21.) Some of the founders of Socialist Charter moved on, however, to organise, with far more success, the Campaign for Labour Party Democracy in 1973 – which we shall examine in detail in chapter 7. A group of 'Young Chartists' who had briefly headed Socialist Charter in 1971 also went on, via *London Labour Briefing*, to play an important part in swinging the London Labour Party to the left in the late 1970s and early 1980s.

74. E.P. Thompson, 'Yesterday's Manikin', *New Society*, 29 July 1971, pp. 200–202.

3. Tony Benn: Articulating a New Socialist Politics

1. See Trevor Blackwell and Jeremy Seabrook, *A World Still to Win*, London 1985, p. 53. The same might be said of Stuart Hall's writings on the rise of Thatcherism.
2. At least not until the Campaign Group of MPs in the mid-1980s, by which point the Labour new left's project had already been defeated.
3. The term is Minkin's, *The Labour Party Conference*, p. 329.
4. 'Secrecy and the National Executive', *Tribune*, 15 June 1973, reprinted in *Speeches by Tony Benn*, Nottingham 1974, p. 302. Benn concluded this book with these words.
5. Tony Benn, *Years of Hope: Diaries 1940–62*, London 1994, pp. 182, 315.
6. Ibid., pp. 321, 372.
7. Interview, 10 October 1985. In any case he did not share many of the Bevanites' defining political positions. In his first speech at a PLP meeting in 1951, Benn pronounced Bevan's and Wilson's resignation from the Cabinet on the '"principle" of a free health service' as 'nonsense'. Nor did he initially oppose Britain's nuclear weapons testing, only gradually moving throughout the 1950s, in an opposite trajectory from Bevan himself, 'in an anti-bomb direction'. See *Years of Hope*, pp. 147, 232–3.
8. See *Years of Hope*, pp. 175, 179, 209, 245. When, in 1960, a ban-the-bomb demonstration outside an NEC meeting 'almost drowned out the proceedings', Benn resented this for having 'introduced an element of mob violence into our affairs' (p. 347).
9. This was Benn's harsh judgement in contemplating Bevan's 'defection' from his own group by joining with the party leadership and coming out against unilateral nuclear disarmament at the 1957 Party Conference: 'Certainly you could form no effective left-wing simply on the basis of unilateral renunciation of the H bomb. The total failure of Nye Bevan to offer constructive thought or generous political leadership has destroyed the group and relegated him to the position of captivity in which he now finds himself' (*Years of Hope*, p. 251).
10. *Years of Hope*, p. 244.
11. Ibid., p. 320. When Benn spoke in the debate after Gaitskell's speech, he put

the issue in terms of 'peace, colonial freedom and modernising Britain ...
[without] mentioning nationalisation one way or the other', thereby placing
himself outside the mainstream of debate between left and right at the time.

12. Ibid., p. 323.

13. Ibid., p. 287.

14. Ibid., p. 286. Benn's orientation also had led to a remarkable confrontation
with Crosland in the same year. In response to a proposal at a Fabian
Society meeting to emulate the successful practices of Universities and Left
Review (ULR) in attracting hundreds of young people to meetings in 1958,
Crosland took the position that 'he could see nothing of interest in the
ULR except that "there's a man who seems to be able to run a coffee
house". He thought that political activity under the age of thirty-five was
not of great interest to the Fabians. ... All this was said in the most bored
and offensive way and was greeted with a titter of laughter. ... I admit I
was by now in a high temper and began by saying that if Tony's view was
the Fabian view – then I certainly wasn't a Fabian in any sense. But for the
life of me I couldn't see how you could run any political organisation on
the assumption that the political views of people under thirty-five didn't
matter. "Boredom [Benn is here quoting himself speaking at the meeting]
seems to me unforgivable. But an affectation of boredom is quite incompre-
hensible and lunatic in a political organisation." ' *Years of Hope*, pp. 294–5.

15. Quoted in Robert Jenkins, *Tony Benn*, pp. 40–41.

16. Quoted in ibid., p. 77.

17. Ibid., p. 89. Benn's own account is offered at the end of *Years of Hope*,
pp. 356–419 in the form of interviews conducted with him at the time by
David Butler.

18. Quoted in Jenkins, *Tony Benn*, p. 193.

19. *Speeches by Tony Benn* (Joan Bodington, ed.), Nottingham 1974, p. 99.

20. Quoted in Jenkins, *Tony Benn*, p. 45.

21. *Speeches by Tony Benn*, p. 267. But for a senior Labour minister to try to
carry a substantive debate on Marxism into the NEC as Benn did by writing
a paper for the Executive on 'Marxism and the Labour Party' in 1976 during
the dispute over Andy Bevan's appointment as the party's first national
youth officer, was a dramatic break with party tradition. He sought to
legitimise Marxism as 'one of the main sources of inspiration' of the Labour
movement and cited Attlee, Bevan, Morrison, Laski, Crosland, Brandt and
Palme to make the case that being influenced by Marxism did not preclude
a commitment to democracy, but he made it clear that there was more to it
than that weak reed allowed. When the NEC refused to circulate the paper,
he published it in the national press and this enraged the custodians of party
discipline.

22. See Ben Pimlot, *Harold Wilson*, London 1992, p. 150, and Tony Benn,
Against the Tide: Diaries 1973–76, London 1989, pp. 12, 692.

23. Tony Benn, *Talking About Socialism*, based on a interview with John Foster,
Glasgow 1996.

24. Tony Benn, *Out of the Wilderness: Diaries 1963–67*, p. 422.

25. Ibid., p. 437.

26. Ibid., p. 461. Benn considered this luncheon address a 'pre-introduction

model' of a major speech he later gave 'on every possible occasion', for which see ibid., Appendix IV, pp. 552–3.

27. *Out of the Wilderness*, p. 463.
28. Ibid., p. 459.
29. 731 *HC Debates*, 14 July 1966, col. 1789.
30. See *Out of the Wilderness*, p. 464.
31. Quoted in Jenkins, *Tony Benn*, p. 153.
32. Interview, 10 October, 1985. For Benn's rather different account in his diary on the day, see *Office without Power: Diaries 1968–72*, London 1988, pp. 154–5.
33. *Office without Power*, p. 153.
34. Speech to the Annual Conference of the Welsh Council of Labour, Llandudno, 25 May 1968, in *Speeches by Tony Benn*, pp. 201–7.
35. Interview, 10 October 1985. This was, of course, not a new theme for as iconoclastic an MP as Benn had always been. When chastised for moving a motion of censure on the Speaker for having refused to allow a debate on the Government's military intervention in Muscat and Oman in 1957, Benn had delivered a disquisition on the party system in parliamentary government: 'the modern party system, even at its most oppressive, does not in any way limit our right to speak. It may limit how we vote at the end of the day [but] the right of free thought and free speech ... is left unfettered by the party system. ... I am not forming an anti-party faction at all ... I am one of a thousand flowers asking permission to bloom.' (Quoted in Jenkins, *Tony Benn*, p. 53.) But how far Benn could take this now as a minister was immediately questioned by Wilson, who at the first Cabinet after Benn's Llandudno speech, upbraided Benn for having 'caused a lot of trouble because the Cabinet was responsible for the system of government and if the latter was attacked, it was an attack on Cabinet'. Michael Stewart, the Foreign Secretary, raised the question of 'whether the role of political science lecturer was compatible with Cabinet Office'. *Office without Power*, p. 73.
36. Jenkins, *Tony Benn*, p. 57.
37. *Office without Power*, p. 74.
38. Ibid., p. 249. Benn later in the year used this quotation on the cover of his Fabian pamphlet, *The New Politics*.
39. *The New Politics: A Socialist Reconnaissance*, Fabian Tract 402, September 1970, p. 9.
40. Ibid., p. 12.
41. 'Democratic Politics', Fabian Autumn Lecture, 3 November 1971, in *Speeches by Tony Benn*, pp. 277–9, emphasis added.
42. *Speeches by Tony Benn*, pp. 223–4.
43. Ibid., p. 278.
44. Quoted in Jenkins, *Tony Benn*, pp. 186–7.
45. Interview with Tony Benn in Allan Freeman, *The Benn Heresy*, London 1982, pp. 174–5.
46. Quoted in Hatfield, *The House the Left Built*, p. 70.
47. See Leo Panitch, *Social Democracy and Industrial Militancy*, Cambridge 1976.

48. *Tribune*, 17 May 1968, quoted in David Coates, *The Labour Party and the Struggle for Socialism*, Cambridge 1975, p. 210.
49. See Shaw, *Discipline and Discord in the Labour Party*, esp. pp. 156–67.
50. Quoted in Hatfield, *The House the Left Built*, pp. 36, 41.
51. *Labour – Party or Puppet?*, July 1972.
52. Simon Hoggart and David Leigh, *Michael Foot: A Portrait*, London 1981, p. 163.
53. Quoted in Hatfield, *The House the Left Built*, p. 114.
54. 'Democratic Politics', *Speeches by Tony Benn*, pp. 281–4.
55. Ibid., pp. 275, 281, 285, 287–8; *The New Politics*, p. 28.
56. He added for good measure: 'The generalised discontent among women has now assumed the proportions of a real national – indeed international – movement. Whether we support it or not – and I am arguing strongly that we should do – it is a political force to be reckoned with . . . This is the stuff of which revolutions are made, because it involves a change of values which threatens the existing patterns of male domination . . . We ought to make this year "Women's Year" in the Labour and Trade Union Movement, allying deliberately and specifically with women in this country in their struggle for equality. And it would be a good start to give women their proper role in the Labour and Trade Union Movement where they still do not enjoy full equality.' *Speeches by Tony Benn*, pp. 188–95.
57. *Against the Tide*, p. 44.
58. TUC *Report*, Brighton 1972, pp. 401–2.
59. *Speeches by Tony Benn*, pp. 16–25.
60. Ibid., p. 285.
61. *Office without Power*, p. 454. For Jones's view in this respect, see Minkin, *The Contentious Alliance*, esp. pp. 180–81; and Jones's autobiography, *Union Man*, London 1986, esp. pp. 220–27. This is not to say Jones was closely allied with Benn. Benn found Jones 'very remote and hard to get through' and Jones soon took the view that some of Benn's ideas were 'airy fairy'. Benn was closer to other key TGWU figures with whom he shared platforms at the time at IWC and other conferences. He formed an especially close and long-lasting tie with Walter Greendale, a remarkably creative socialist docker from Hull who was very influential as a secondary leader in the TGWU. Ken Coates of the IWC was a critical figure in linking Benn to such trade union leaders, having contacted Benn after he spoke out so clearly in favour of industrial democracy as well as publicly supporting the many workers' sit-ins at the time.
62. Interview, 10 October, 1985.
63. *Speeches by Tony Benn*, pp. 165.
64. Ibid., pp. 255–6.
65. 867 *HC Deb.*, 10 January 1974, cols 305–9.
66. This letter is reprinted in full in *Office without Power*, p. 302, and it is worth noting, in light of later developments, that in it Kinnock also suggests that he is less optimistic than Benn, and adds: 'I don't think my failure to reach assertive answers manifests any lack of courage – it is more probable that, after that first month in parliament, my worst fears were over-realised

and I fell victim to the "It's all bloody hopeless and we might as well be in Disneyland" syndrome. I think I'll get over that. I'd better get over it.'

67. *Office without Power*, pp. 384, 386.

68. Ibid., pp. 447–8.

69. Ken Coates was at the time most prominent for his leadership of the Institute for Workers' Control. He had contacted Benn in the context of his support for industrial democracy at the time of the UCS occupation, and brought Michael Barratt Brown and John Hughes to his home to discuss the situation. That Benn was just now coming into contact for the first time with such leading socialist economists in the party itself says a great deal about the lonely path he had travelled in his transition from radical liberalism to radical socialism. As for Coates, he had been expelled from the party (and three other left-wingers suspended) in the mid-1960s at the initiative of a right-wing Labour-controlled council in Nottingham. Coates had been long well-known nationally (including for his close ties to Bertrand Russell), and had extensive ties among trade unionists. He was one of the few prominent new left intellectuals who became active in the Labour Party after leaving the Communist Party. Although Trotskyist entrism was the charge against him (Coates was a founder of the International Group in Nottingham, the forerunner of the IMG, and editor of *The Week* with Robin Blackburn), Eric Shaw's definitive *Discipline and Discord in the Labour Party* (pp. 83–8) has shown that 'the International Group was less a disciplined faction than a small ideologically heterogeneous group, [which] in turn, was part of a broader left caucus, a loose knit association of people with disparate views held together by opposition to the ruling local establishment'. As for Coates's 'revisionist Trotskyist' ideology in the 1960s, Shaw is certainly correct that it 'vaguely connoted an attachment to Marxism with repudiation of Soviet-style "socialism"' rather than the hard dogma it was intended to connote as the term was deployed indiscriminately by the right wing. Coates's long struggle for readmission to the Labour Party came to fruition by 1969, and he became the leading advocate among new left intellectuals in the 1970s calling for socialists to join the Labour Party. Benn thought Coates 'a naive person in many ways, too ready to see good in me', and he at first wondered, when contacted by Coates, whether this would convince MI5 (whom he thought must have been tapping Coates's telephone regularly for a long time) that 'I have suddenly gone sharply to the Left. It may well be that some of the hostile press is coming from that source. I say that without any real evidence and that indicates what a state of paranoia one can get into.' *Office without Power*, pp. 382, 447. The evidence, and plenty of it, was not long in coming. See esp. Stephen Dorrill and Robin Ramsay, *Smear! Wilson and the Secret State*, London 1991. Cf., Benn, *Against the Tide*, pp. 547 and 623–4 for how intelligence reports on Coates and other Trotskyist influence were used against Benn by Wilson and Callaghan.

70. See Benn, *Against the Tide*, p. 486.

71. Hatfield, *The House the Left Built*, p. 68.

72. See Hollingsworth, *The Press and Political Dissent*, pp. 37–76, esp. 71–3. Benn himself recognised that his speech to the 1972 Party Conference

strongly criticising the media 'did me a great deal of damage'. Benn's diaries at the time show he was genuinely hurt by what he saw as the 'really perpetual, obsessional hatred', such as that launched by Bernard Levin at *The Times*, who appears to have been the first to apply the term 'loon'. *Against the Tide*, pp. 19, 25–6.

73. Hollingsworth, pp. 45, 54, 56–7. For Peter Shore's criticism of his colleagues for their 'outrageous' and 'intolerable' behaviour in explicitly setting out to get Benn in trouble through statements to the press, see Benn, *Against the Tide*, p. 29. Shore later became a bitter opponent of Benn, but at the time they were, as Shore puts it, 'allies on many, if not all, issues'. Peter Shore, *Leading the Left*, London 1993, p. 106.

4. The Search for an Alternative Strategy

1. Michael Hatfield's valuable book on *The House the Left Built* was not so much on the structure of the 'house' as the process of painting it red. He correctly discerned that the 1970 defeat 'signalled the erosion of the reformist social democrats' hegemony over the formulation of party policy'. But his study did not concentrate on the crucial issue which was raised at this time – and would continue to be insistently raised for the next decade – of whether the Labour Party, its parliamentary leadership, and indeed parliamentary democracy itself in its heretofore hegemonic form could be reconstructed to make a more appropriate 'home' for radical policy. In a similar vein, David Coates's *Labour in Power? A Study of the Labour Government 1974–79*, London 1980, saw the attempt to change the party almost entirely in terms of economic policy victories of the new left alliance in the party ('a series of clear policy commitments more radical in tone and in aspiration than any the party had endorsed since 1945') which he judged as inadequate in terms of the crisis of international capitalism. Cf. Mark Wickham-Jones, *Economic Strategy and the Labour Party: Politics and Policy-making, 1970–83*, London and New York 1996.

2. Quoted by John Campbell, *Roy Jenkins: A Biography*, London 1983, p. 141.

3. 1971 *LPCR*, p. 236.

4. *Agenda for the 69th Annual Conference of the Labour Party*, Blackpool 1970, Resolutions 18–23, 29, pp. 13–15. The solutions proffered ranged from overhauling the agency service to concentration on political education at all levels; from better forms of publicity to the need for a national daily Labour newspaper. A particularly notable resolution was one from Nottingham which called for an enquiry into Labour's List of Proscribed Organisations in light of Labour's tendency 'to become more and more divorced from socialist thinking' and the need for open discussion among socialists in order to 'establish clearly the relevance of socialism in modern conditions'. No fewer than six of the resolutions asserted the primacy in the party of conference decisions. These went to the core of the matter in respect of the shift to the left at the base of the party in relation to a parliamentary party dominated by social democrats who, in so far as they

thought about socialist analysis and prescription at all, only wanted surgically to excise it.

5. 1970 *LPCR*, p. 176.
6. 1970 *LPCR*, pp. 182, 184.
7. Lewis Minkin, *The Labour Party Conference: A Study in the Politics of Intra-Party Democracy*, London 1978, p. 343.
8. 1972 *LPCR*, p. 103.
9. 1972 *LPCR*, p. 112. On the whole of this paragraph, see also pp. 136–8, 158–64, 178–81, 190–93.
10. The decline in the number of ministers on the NEC, from fifteen to ten, by 1968, together with the election of left-wing MPs and trade unionists in 1967 and 1968 (Frank Allaun, Joan Lestor, Lena Jeger, Alex Kitson) began the shift. In 1972, Joan Maynard – who came to be called 'Stalin's sister' by the right – replaced Eirene White on the women's section; Tom Forrester of DATA (later AUEW–TASS) was elected at the same conference to fill a vacancy on the trade union section; and Sam McCluskie of the Seamen's Union came on to the executive in the same way in 1974.
11. Minkin, *The Labour Party Conference*, pp. 343–4.
12. See *Resolutions for the 72nd Annual Conference of the Labour Party*, Blackpool 1973, pp. 3–4.
13. One resolution on the sovereignty of Conference decisions was allowed on to the final agenda and briefly debated at the 1973 Conference, but as we shall see it was subject to quite cynical manipulation by the platform. On the enquiry, see 1974 *LPCR*, pp. 38–41 and Appendix 1.
14. Minkin, *The Labour Party Conference*, p. 406 n.16. Few groups attempted to stimulate resolutions from the constituencies in this period. The most successful campaign of this sort came from the Child Poverty Action Group which in 1973 'produced 24 resolutions and 5 amendments which could be traced to its circulation. This was an unusually high figure'.
15. Benn, *Against the Tide*, p. 40.
16. See Peter Taaffe, *The Rise of Militant: Militant's Thirty Years*, London 1995, pp. 53–5. This recent 'official' history by one of the organisation's main leaders is a useful addition to the considerable literature on Militant, as is Andy McSmith's 'The Long Trudge of Ted Grant' in his *Faces of Labour*, London 1996. But see also the indispensable earlier studies by Michael Crick (*The March of Militant*, London 1986) and by John Callaghan (*British Trotskyism: Theory and Practice*, London 1984; and *The Far Left in British Politics*, London 1987). An outstanding journalist's account, published at a key moment in the history of the Labour new left, was Patrick Wintour, 'Militant's Resolutionary Socialism', *New Statesman*, 18 January 1980.
17. Hilary Wainwright, *Labour: A Tale of Two Parties*, London, 1987, p. 153.
18. Benn, *Against the Tide*, pp. 20–21.
19. 1971 *LPCR*, p. 236. His resolution passed on a show of hands without a card vote. So was a resolution moved by Sid Weighell of the Railwaymen which involved a complete U-turn on traditional party policy by calling for the renationalisation *without compensation* of those parts of the public sector sold to private industry by the Heath Government. This moment, with Weighell moving and Benn accepting for the NEC, is in retrospect

replete with historical irony. For it was Weighell who was one of the leaders of the brutal campaign against the left majority on the NEC and Benn in particular in 1981; and it was Benn who was to be dismissed from the Shadow Cabinet in 1981 for enunciating in the House of Commons the party's policy on renationalisation without compensation.

20. Anthony Crosland, *Socialism Now and Other Essays*, London 1974, pp. 27, 72–3.
21. Quoted in Susan Crosland, *Tony Crosland*, London 1982, pp. 225, 227.
22. See Roy Jenkins, *A Life at the Centre*, pp. 298–9, 335, and John Campbell, *Roy Jenkins*, pp. 148–50.
23. Quoted in Crosland, *Tony Crosland*, p. 227.
24. Benn diaries, *Office without Power*, pp. 325–6.
25. See James Callaghan, *Time and Change*, London 1987, pp. 309–10, and Benn, *Office without Power*, p. 316.
26. Benn, *Office without Power*, p. 414.
27. Ibid., p. 345. Cf. pp. 360–61, 380–81, 425–6.
28. Ibid., p. 436.
29. *Labour and the Common Market*, report of a special conference of the Labour Party, Central Hall, Westminster, 17 July 1971, p. 38; and Robert Harris, *The Making of Neil Kinnock*, London 1984, p. 73.
30. Benn diaries, *Against the Tide*, 1973–76, p. 94.
31. Interview, 10 October 1985.
32. 1980 *LPCR*, p. 148.
33. Mikardo and Pitt went so far in trying to shift the locus of policy-making in the direction of the NEC's committees and the research department that they lost Benn as an ally in respect to a joint staff–NEC working party report (chaired by Mikardo) in 1971 which sought to set up three administrative 'overlords' at Transport House. Benn was suspicious of 'empire building' (interview, 10 October 1985). The report was scuttled by Hayward after he was appointed General Secretary. See 1972 *LPCR*, pp. 8–9.
34. Quoted in Hatfield, *The House the Left Built*, p. 55; on Crosland's position, see pp. 57–8.
35. Ibid., p. 118.
36. The working group's initial composition, apart from Mikardo and John Hughes, included: Harold Lever and another moderate MP, John Roper, and ex-MP and bank clerk Alistair MacDonald; Muriel Turner from ASTMS; and the established Keynesian luminaries among the economics profession, Professors Balogh, Kaldor, Artis, Opie, Nield and Robinson. Later, Michael Barratt Brown was added to bolster the left, but so were Peter Jay, Professor Robert Field, Ian Wrigglesworth MP and Frank Welsh, a merchant banker – all bolstering the right. David Lea was also added from the TUC's research department, but in fact neither he nor Barratt Brown, nor Jay nor Muriel Turner, ever actually attended a committee meeting. See 1972 *LPCR*, p. 42 and 1973 *LPCR*, p. 47. See also Hatfield, *The House the Left Built*, esp. pp. 168–9, and Wickham-Jones, *Economic Strategy and the Labour Party*, pp. 120–29.
37. Also on the Public Sector Working Group from the beginning were Mikardo, Lord Delacourt-Smith of the Post Office Engineering Union, and

Margaret Jackson as secretary (she became MP for Lincoln in 1974). Later Balogh and Robinson were also to be added for 'balance', but so were Tony Banks, then a researcher with the AUEW, and Albert Booth, a Tribunite MP. Both Pryke and Holland had worked in Wilson's Cabinet Office, but Pryke had cut his ties with the social democrats (and especially Balogh) when he resigned and publicly attacked the July 1966 deflation and wage freeze and the abandonment of the National Plan. See Richard Pryke, *Though Cowards Flinch: An Alternative Economic Policy*, London 1967. Holland still worked with people like Rodgers and Jenkins after the 1970 election and in fact wrote a speech for Jenkins promoting the idea of a state holding company. But it soon became clear, especially after a two-day meeting of the Industrial Committee at the Bonnington Hotel in London in February 1972, that what Holland and Pryke were advancing was beyond the social democratic pale. Holland's ideas were elaborated in *The Socialist Challenge*, London 1975.

38. Both quotations are from Hatfield, *The House the Left Built*, pp. 111, 130.
39. TUC–Labour Party, *Economic Policy and the Cost of Living*, February 1973.
40. The TGWU's Walter Greendale proposed to Benn in June 1973 that a national shop stewards conference might be called to discuss how to implement the 'twenty-five companies' proposal, but Benn preferred to try 'to stimulate debates actually in the factories or workshops, or among shop stewards of one particular company at a time, so one could begin to test the extent to which support would build up within a company for public ownership of that company. If such debates could really be started, it would be tremendously effective in strengthening our hand politically ...' Benn, *Against the Tide*, p. 47.
41. Quoted in Hatfield, *The House the Left Built*, p. 216.
42. Benn, *Against the Tide*, p. 46. Jones makes no mention of the twenty-five companies episode in his autobiography, *Union Man*, but to confirm Benn's impression, see Minkin, *The Contentious Alliance*, pp. 172–3.
43. Hatfield, *The House the Left Built*, p. 49. Cf. Benn, *Against the Tide*, pp. 4, 47; and Simon Hoggart and David Leigh, *Michael Foot: A Portrait*, London 1981, p. 164.
44. *Speeches*, pp. 82–3. By pointing to the very great discretionary powers the Heath Government had assumed *vis-à-vis* industry, which he saw as the essence of the 'corporate state'; by putting forward new mechanisms of parliamentary control over the Cabinet; and by explicitly raising the question of 'in whose interests is the economy managed?', Benn's speeches tried to point the way to overcoming the popular fears aroused by a press and business campaign against 'bureaucratic socialism'. See Tony Benn, 'Heath's Spadework for Socialism', *Sunday Times*, 27 March 1973.
45. Hatfield, *The House the Left Built*, p. 211.
46. Ibid., pp. 183–6. It was notable that not one trade union representative on the Executive, despite the unions' support for, and even their sponsorship of, very radical resolutions on public ownership at the party conferences, joined with Benn, Joan Lestor and Frank Allaun from the constituency section, Hart and Maynard from the Women's Section, and Peter Doyle

from the Young Socialists in voting against Healey's amendment. This was an important signal of the union leadership's real priorities, now that they had secured from Wilson a rejection of a statutory incomes policy.

47. See Healey, *The Time of My Life*, p. 370.

48. Militant walked right into the trap. They were not alone. One of the other two more vague composites incorporated part of Sheffield Hallam CLP's resolution: 'This Conference rejects the whole concept of shopping lists of industries or companies for social ownership however long or short' and left out the rest of it: 'except as illustrations of the minimum encroachment to be made on private privilege, property and power'. David Blunkett, speaking for the first time at a party conference, did so from the position of seconder of a composite resolution, therefore, which was taken as endorsement of Wilson's position when it was passed: 'It is up to me to say that my constituency included the words "shopping list". They did so not because they wished to restrict or to criticise the twenty-five companies but, in fact, because they wished to say that this should be a minimum demand, and not our full complement in this State.' Blunkett was the Conference Arrangements Committee's unwitting and unhappy tool. See *LPCR*, p. 177.

49. Benn's diaries show clearly the private despondency he felt at his almost complete isolation among the leadership. See *Against the Tide*, pp. 45–82.

50. 1973 *LPCR*, p. 301. The resolution was carried, against the NEC's objection, by 3,166,000 to 2,462,000 votes. A similar motion had been passed on a show of hands the previous year with the NEC's support.

51. 1973 *LPCR*, pp. 310–11, 160, 122, 129–30.

52. Harris, *The Making of Neil Kinnock*, pp. 71–2.

53. Coates, *Labour in Power?*, p. 3.

5. The Labour New Left in Government

1. Benn, *Against the Tide: Diaries 1973–76*, pp. 115, 118. It should be noted that Wilson split the Department of Trade from the Department of Industry, which meant that Benn's appointment signified that he was being accorded less status and power than Peter Walker had held in heading the DTI 'superministry' in the Heath Government. Moreover, since the Department of Trade had responsibility for the newspaper industry, keeping Benn away from it meant that there need be no fear that the media might be subjected to the kinds of democratic reforms he had proposed at the 1972 Party Conference.

2. Benn, *Against the Tide*, pp. 75–6.

3. 'The doctrine of the mandate and the manifesto always has to be applied cautiously and it is now being actively perverted to divide the nation. In these circumstances, when the national economic crisis comes, what chance is there that this Labour Government, with so many on the left for the first time in the places of power, will be in a position to put the interests of the nation first?' Ronald Butt, 'Why the Tory Choice Matters', *The Sunday Times*, 10 November 1974.

4. Paul Whiteley, 'The Decline of Labour's Local Party Membership and Electoral Base, 1945–74', in D. Kavanagh, ed., *The Politics of the Labour Party*, London 1982, p. 132.

5. 'Every day they were in', James Maxton is reported to have said of the 1924 Labour Government, 'led us further from Socialism.' John Scanlon, *Decline and Fall of the Labour Party*, London 1932, p. 76.

6. *The Times*, 5 March 1974.

7. *The Times*, 17 June 1974.

8. This was in marked contrast to the later practice of some left-controlled Labour Groups at the local level: after winning an election they would have their manifesto carried by the first council meeting, so that it instantly became the orienting policy guide not only for the Labour majority on the council but for the whole local government. This was a factor of considerable value in terms of the message thus sent to permanent officials.

9. W. Keegan and R. Pennant-Rea, *Who Runs the Economy? Control and Influence in British Economic Policy*, London 1979, p. 205.

10. Quoted in Barbara Castle, *The Castle Diaries*, London 1980, p. 181.

11. Keegan and Pennant-Rea, *Who Runs the Economy?*, p. 123; see also Marcia Falkender, *Downing Street in Perspective*, London 1983, p. 227, who describes Healey as a 'political bully'. Also see Denis Healey, *The Time of My Life*, London 1989, esp. p. 397 for his account of his own role as well as Michael Foot's in negotiating wage restraint with the TUC in 1976.

12. *The Castle Diaries*, pp. 694, 712.

13. The Secretary of the Treasury in the Labour Government, Joel Barnett, later avowed: 'Michael's position was unique. He was tremendously loyal to both Harold Wilson and later Jim Callaghan and the Government could never have survived so long without him. At the same time, if Michael felt very strongly on a subject, both Prime Ministers would be ready to make concessions to him. That would not include concessions on the central economic strategy ... It was precisely because Michael was on the losing side on the big issues that the Prime Minister must have felt it reasonable to give way to him on lesser issues.' Joel Barnett, *Inside the Treasury*, London 1982, p. 15. Cf. James Callaghan, *Time and Change*, London 1987, p. 438; and Simon Hoggart and David Leigh, *Michael Foot: A Portrait*, London 1981, pp. 166–7, 187–9, 199, 201.

14. See quotation from Cousins in Chapter 2 above, p. 25.

15. Jack Jones, *Union Man*, p. 295. Cf. pp. 282–7.

16. 1975 *LPCR*, p. 164. On Foot's peacemaking role and the importance he accorded to party unity, see Hoggart and Leigh, *Michael Foot*, pp. 150–51, 154–6, 168–70, 188, 202.

17. *The Castle Diaries*, p. 378.

18. *Against the Tide*, p. 115.

19. Michael Foot, *Loyalists and Loners*, London 1986, p. 118.

20. This is confirmed not only by Tom Forrester's excellent study (*The Labour Party and the Working Class*, London 1976) of this campaign from the perspective of the Labour new left itself but by the memoirs of participants in the Government as ideologically distant from the Labour new left as Joe Haines (who as Wilson's press secretary saw it from the perspective of the

Prime Minister's Office), Edmund Dell and Joel Barnett (who saw it from the perspective of the Treasury). See also Mark Hollingsworth, *The Press and Political Dissent: A Question of Censorship*, London 1986, p. 43; and on Sir Anthony Part's role, Stephen Dorril and Robin Ramsay, *Smear! Wilson and the Secret State*, London 1991, pp. 278–9.

21. Quoted in Forrester, *The Labour Party*, pp. 90–91; see also Joe Haines, *The Politics of Power*, London 1977, pp. 31 ff. The term 'Bennery' actually may have been coined by Michael Ivens, Director of Aims of Industry, who passed it on to a Fleet Street journalist during a telephone conversation; see Dorril and Ramsay, *Smear!*, p. 43.

22. Barnett, *Inside the Treasury*, pp. 18–19. For Benn's sober account of his officials operating in this way against him, see *Against the Tide*, esp. pp. 333–4.

23. Ibid., pp. 79, 146.

24. Foot, *Loyalists and Loners*, p. 116, emphasis added.

25. See Mark Hollingsworth's excellent discussion of the media treatment of Benn, in *The Press and Political Dissent*, ch. 2.

26. Greg Philo et al., *Really Bad News*, London 1982, p. 105. The assertion that the Civil Service controlled the Government was, as we have seen, hardly uncommon even among centre-right Labour ministers.

27. Dorril and Ramsay, *Smear!*, p. 273. Cf., esp. pp. 232, 246, 278–81, 292–3, 299. See also David Leigh, *The Wilson Plot*, London 1988; P. Knightley, *The Second Oldest Profession: The Spy as Bureaucrat, Patriot, Fantasist and Whore*, London 1986, pp. 350–53; and Ben Pimlott, *Harold Wilson*, London 1992, pp. 693–723.

28. Quoted in Knightley, *The Second Oldest Profession*, p. 351. Nor was it just a matter of the 'Secret State', but of the growing presence of 'the coercive apparatus of the state' in general, in British society. At about the time the exchange between Foot and Benn took place, Edward Thompson was writing: 'As a historian I can say that I know of no period in which the police have had such a loud and didactic public presence, and when they have offered themselves as a distinct interest, as one of the great "institutions" and perhaps the first in the realm. And I know of no period in which politicians and editors have submitted themselves so abjectly or ardently to their persuasions.' Thompson laid a large part of the blame for this development, and the 'dulling of the nerve of outrage' in respect to it, on the 'bureaucratic statism towards which Labour politicians increasingly drifted ... The dividing line between the Welfare State and the Police State became obscure ...' Thompson did not forbear from implicating Michael Foot in this. In making the case that Parliament could and should have intervened against the Labour Attorney General's guidelines on jury-vetting, whereby the practice of checking jury lists against the records of police was legitimated, Thompson insisted that the managers of parliamentary time had not allowed this to come before the House. He added, pointedly, that the man mainly responsible for this, as Leader of the House, was 'that noted libertarian, Michael Foot'. See E.P. Thompson, 'The Secret State' (1978) and 'The State of the Nation' (1979), in *Writing by Candlelight*, London 1980, pp. 164–5, 201, 215–16.

29. 1973 *LPCR*, pp. 298–301.
30. *The Castle Diaries*, pp. 57–8.
31. Ibid.; and Benn, *Against the Tide*, p. 135.
32. On the basis of Wilson's own account (*The Governance of Britain*, London 1976, pp. 74–5 and Appendix I) it appears he relied for precedent on a memorandum issued by Lord Simon to a War Cabinet Committee. Simon's logic was quaint, but it reflected that particular combination of class and patriarchy that socialist feminist theorists have correctly insisted is such a crucial ingredient in composing state authority: 'A husband is responsible for his wife's debts even though he does not know where she goes shopping or how big a bill she is running up ... The same thing applies in a Cabinet. Ministers who are not in the inner circle trust those who are ...' Wilson also reveals here how he sought to assure financial markets about his own total lack of accountability to the extra-parliamentary party: 'Under the constitution of the Labour Party the Executive has a duty to work out policy for submission to the Annual Conference. Inevitably, an Executive elected by Conference includes a substantial number – frequently amounting to a majority on particular issues in 1974–76 – who were concerned to prepare policy statements on almost every subject under the sun, home and abroad, inconsistent with, sometimes sharply critical of, Government policies. This was liable to cause confusion from certain quarters, including national and international financial markets, where there are many who are singularly uninformed, not to say naive, about our political institutions, and on where power really lies. Quite often, therefore, I had to make this point clear, by answers to questions in Parliament or published replies to anxious letters from City-based financial institutions such as the British Insurance Association or the merchant banking community, on more than one occasion drafting the letter, to which I was at pains to reply myself.'
33. In March 1976, as part of his campaign for the leadership after Wilson resigned (which occurred in the context of Jack Jones's, Hugh Scanlon's and David Basnett's much publicised joint appeal for support of the Government after thirty-five Tribune MPs abstained on a vote on a White Paper announcing massive public expenditure cuts), Benn made this memorandum public 'so that members of the party can be informed about the position'. See Tony Benn, *A New Course for Labour*, Nottingham 1976, pp. 7–9.
34. Harold Wilson, *Final Term: The Labour Government 1974–6*, London 1979, p. 144.
35. Cited in Hatfield, *The House the Left Built: Inside Labour Policy-Making 1970–75*, London 1980, pp. 228–9.
36. Benn's paper was published in its entirety in *The Times*, 23 May 1974.
37. *The Castle Diaries*, p. 103.
38. Quoted in *Against the Tide*, p. 194. Cf. Edmund Dell, *A Hard Pounding: Politics and Economic Crisis, 1974–1976*, London 1991, p. 97.
39. Michael Hatfield, 'Minute by Treasury Started Benn Campaign', *The Times*, 17 June 1974. For the origins of this, see Dell, *A Hard Pounding*, pp. 90–91.
40. See Hollingsworth, *The Press and Political Dissent*, pp. 39–45.
41. Even as late as the autumn of 1975 Judith Hart would still insist to the Labour Party Conference that not only British management but even 'the

world financial institutions' could be convinced that the Labour new left's economic strategy was feasible by stressing its Swedish and French 'accent' and by pointing to the alternative of a bankrupt Britain unless the investment this strategy promised to generate was secured. 1975 *LPCR*, p. 212.

42. *State Intervention in Industry: A Workers' Inquiry*, 2nd edn, Nottingham 1982, p. 160. This valuable study of the Labour Government's industrial policies (sponsored by the Trades Councils of Coventry, Liverpool, Newcastle, and North Tyneside) was written by Hilary Wainwright, Paul Field, Slim Hallett and Eddie Loyden.

43. Ibid., p. 40.

44. *The Times*, 15 May 1974.

45. *The Times*, 23 May 1974.

46. *The Times*, 1 July 1974.

47. Harold Wilson, *Final Term*, pp. 141–2.

48. Interview, 10 October 1985. See also *State Intervention in Industry*, esp. pp. 70–74, on how convenors from an engineering factory at Kirkby and the Triumph Meridan plant at Coventry, both subject to closure, almost immediately showed up at the Department. The Meridan workers had already been engaged in a five-month occupation of the factory and had hatched the idea of a cooperative as a bargaining lever and a means of gaining time for government support, but as one of the leaders put it: '. . . as the weeks of picketing and working-in stretched into months, workers saw real possibilities and advantages of setting up a cooperative. The idea began to catch hold of people.' Within a fortnight of the February 1974 election, Benn had met with the leaders and not only assured them of his Department's support, but sent a government accountant to work with them on an application for financial assistance. Similarly, as an AUEW convenor at Kirkby explained: 'I really believed the slogan "back to work with Labour". I thought there would be more consideration for industry and the regions . . . With the ideas of workers' control and industrial democracy around at that time, especially through people like Tony Benn and Eric Heffer, we gained enough confidence to put forward the idea of a cooperative. With all the chopping and changing of management, and of products, all the waste and lack of commitment involved with this, we'd become convinced for some time we could run it better ourselves.' For his civil servants' attempts to obstruct his support for these co-ops, see Benn's *Against the Tide*, esp. p. 297.

49. See Dell, *A Hard Pounding*, pp. 139–41, and Benn, *Against the Tide*, pp. 333–4. On the billions advanced in the rescue scheme during the secondary bank crisis in 1974–75, see Jerry Coakley and Laurence Harris, *The City of Capital*, London 1983, pp. 70–73.

50. Hilary Wainwright and Dave Elliot, *The Lucas Plan: A New Trade Unionism in the Making?*, London 1982. For the information and quotations in this and the next paragraph, see esp. pp. 82–4.

51. In January 1975, the Tyne Stewards' Conference was formed, involving between sixty and ninety stewards from thirty-five major companies based on Tyneside, to discuss, distribute information on, and meet monthly to

develop campaigns for the radical version of planning agreements, the NEB, industrial democracy and nationalisation. The feeling that they had 'allies in government, a source of political power over their managements', led these stewards to the belief 'that here was a new opportunity to win control over the companies' decisions, as a means of guaranteeing job security for the future. The assumption was that workers could prepare their own proposals and then win the backing of the Department of Industry.' But the Tyne Conference was a unique initiative; indeed one of the problems it repeatedly pointed to was lack of education and information on the industrial strategy coming from the union offices. See *State Intervention in Industry*, pp. 47–9.

52. A typical example of the defence of exclusive official trade union links to the state occurred in the summer of 1974 when Benn proposed to make use of £25,000 made available by the Common Market for academic studies on regional labour market mobility by offering instead a six-week sabbatical to shop stewards in Wales to undertake such a study. Not only did this upset the Department of Industry's Permanent Secretary, who threatened to report Benn to the Public Accounts Committee if he used the money this way; it also provoked the wrath of Len Murray, who told Benn he had no right to give money to trade unionists without the TUC's permission. Interview with Tony Benn, 10 October 1985.

53. Lewis Minkin, *The Contentious Alliance: Trade Unions and the Labour Party*, Edinburgh 1991, pp. 124, 170.

54. Quoted in *Against the Tide*, p. 166.

55. Quoted in *State Intervention in Industry*, p. 121. See also Jones's speech to the TUC's special Conference on Industrial Policy in October 1977, in TUC, *The Trade Union Role in Industrial Policy*, p. 33.

56. The White Paper was published as Cmnd. 5710, 15 August 1974.

57. Wilson, *Final Term*, p. 34. Cf. Hoggart and Leigh, *Michael Foot*, p. 173; Eric Heffer, *Labour's Future: Socialism or SDP Mark 2?*, London 1986, p. 12; and Benn, *Against the Tide*, pp. 212–14.

58. The first resolution passed at the Tyne Shop Stewards Conference in January 1975 included an appeal for the original industrial strategy proposals as opposed to 'the watered down version before Parliament at present'. And the TUC General Council supported Benn's more radical hopes for the NEB at a meeting with Wilson in March 1975. Wilson reassured them by offering them 'absolutely contradictory pledges' to those he had given the CBI a week before. See Benn, *Against the Tide*, pp. 336–7; and Dell, *A Hard Pounding*, p. 143.

59. Partly because of the names attached to the new institutions and procedures established in the legislation, although they now amounted to new labels for old corporatist forms of intervention, the City of London still vociferously opposed the watered-down version of the bill while the press denounced it as 'Benn's Great Grab Plan'; see Hollingsworth, *The Press and Political Dissent*, p. 43. Cf. Dell, *A Hard Pounding*, pp. 139–41.

60. See Wilson, *Final Term*, p. 98 and *The Governance of Britain*, Appendix III; and Callaghan, *Time and Change*, pp. 303–7, 316–18.

61. See *The Common Market ... Loss of Self Government, the Full Text of Mr.*

Benn's New Year Message to His Constituents, 29 December 1974, London 1975, pp. 3–4.

62. Lord Kaldor, *The Economic Consequences of Mrs. Thatcher*, London 1983, p. 3.

63. The Foreign Office had tried to get Benn to agree that the Common Market Commission ought to look at and approve the Industry Bill before it was published. *Against the Tide*, pp. 177–8.

64. This quotation is from *The Castle Diaries*, pp. 346–50, but see also John Campbell, *Roy Jenkins: A Biography*, London 1983, pp. 38–9, 172–3; Roy Jenkins, *A Life at the Centre: Memoirs of a Radical Reformer*, New York 1991, pp. 323–4, 386–8; and Wilson, *Final Term*, pp. 104–8.

65. Wilson threatened in this context to resign as leader of the Party (but not as Prime Minister, thus raising, as Wilson later put it, 'a most interesting constitutional situation'). See Wilson, *Final Term*, pp. 104–8; *The Castle Diaries*, pp. 346–50; and Hoggart and Leigh, *Michael Foot*, pp. 178–9.

66. Nor was it surprising given the press's unequal treatment of the two sides throughout the campaign. As David Butler and Owe Kitzinger's study of the press coverage (*The 1975 Referendum*, London 1976) revealed, '. . . as far as sympathetic column inches were concerned . . . the mean balance turned out to be 54 percent for the EEC and 21 percent against which didn't even reflect public opinion or the final result'. Midway into the Referendum campaign, the pertinent issues of the debate and the debate itself almost seemed to be reduced to the simple question of whether you were 'for' or 'against' Tony Benn. Benn was portrayed by the press as personifying the entire anti-EEC movement and, in the final days before the vote, the press's reports consisted almost entirely of quotes by pro-marketeers who accused Benn of lying about the effect of EEC membership on employment. The *Daily Mirror* labelled Benn the 'Minister of Fear'. See Hollingsworth, *The Press and Political Dissent*, pp. 47–50.

67. In May 1975, Wilson had already tipped off the *Daily Telegraph*'s political correspondent Harry Boyne of his plans to sack Benn from Industry; see Hollingsworth, *The Press and Political Dissent*, pp. 45–6.

68. On Foot's opposition to Wilson's Cabinet reshuffle, see Hoggart and Leigh, *Michael Foot*, pp. 180, 182–3. On Jones's opposition to the 'victimisation' of Benn – and his failure to do anything about it when it nevertheless happened – see Hatfield, *The House the Left Built*, pp. 148–9.

69. *The Politics of Power*, p. 31. Eric Varley, who was very close to Wilson at the time, told Benn: 'I think Harold entered into some commitments with the City or somebody, and he has to get rid of you.' Wilson's former PPS, Joe Slater, told Benn that Wilson had said that he had to move Benn from Industry 'because of all his Trotskyite connections'. This was a charge that Benn had never heard before, but which he presumed related to Ken Coates and this confirmed his suspicions that his phone was bugged and reports fed through to Wilson. See Benn, *Against the Tide, Diaries 1973–76*, pp. 390, 547. Not a minor factor seems to have been Wilson's personal 'hatred' and 'loathing' of Benn by this time, which had apparently reached almost hysterical proportions. See Healey, *The Time of My Life*, p. 446; and Benn, *Against the Tide*, p. 525. For somewhat different accounts, see Susan

Crosland, *Tony Crosland*, London 1982, p. 293 and Falkender, *Downing Street in Perspective*, pp. 169–70, 209–10.

70. Quoted in Mikardo, *Backbencher*, pp. 195–6.
71. Kathleen Burk and Alec Cairncross, *'Goodbye, Great Britain': The 1976 IMF Crisis*, New Haven and London 1992, p. 19.

6. The Abandonment of Keynesianism

1. The actual Bretton Woods framework fell fall short of the early proposals put forward by Keynes and his counterpart as chief American negotiator, Harry Dexter White, for an effective system of cooperative capital controls, whereby member states would be obliged not to accept capital fleeing from the controls imposed by another member country. The American Government, and Wall Street in particular, were not prepared to go further than a certain permissiveness for individual countries to retain capital controls as part of their reconstruction strategies, with the presumption that these would be limited and temporary. The Bretton Woods arrangements had left enough space, in other words, for the re-emergence of extensive international financial markets by the 1960s. See Eric Helleiner, *States and the Reemergence of Global Finance*, Ithaca 1994, esp. pp. 33–8. Cf. James Crotty and Gerald Epstein, 'In Defense of Capital Controls', *The Socialist Register 1996*.
2. Helleiner, *States and the Reemergence of Global Finance*, p. 111.
3. Ibid., pp. 115–20.
4. Healey, *The Time of My Life*, pp. 419–20.
5. See Burk and Cairncross, *'Goodbye, Great Britain'*, pp. 145–6; and Keegan and Pennant-Rea, *Who Runs the Economy?*, pp. 133–4.
6. See esp. Simon Clarke, 'Capitalist Crises and the Rise of Monetarism', *The Socialist Register 1987*, pp. 393–427.
7. Clarke, 'Capitalist Crises', pp. 395–6.
8. Burk and Cairncross, *'Goodbye, Great Britain'*, p. 5. The data in this paragraph are drawn from this authoritative account.
9. Clarke, 'Capitalist Crises', p. 410.
10. See Dell, *A Hard Pounding*, pp. 55ff.; Burk and Cairncross, *'Goodbye, Great Britain'*, pp. 13, 219; Keegan and Pennant-Rea, *Who Runs the Economy?*, pp. 157–8.
11. Quoted in David Coates, *Labour in Power? A Study of the Labour Government 1974–1979*, London 1980, p. 27.
12. Dell, *A Hard Pounding*, p. 120.
13. Healey, *The Time of My Life*, pp. 378–9.
14. This, according to Edmund Dell, Healey's deputy at the Treasury, who went so far at the time to deride 'the dope of expansionist demand management' at a Conference on Business Strategies sponsored by *The Times* and the CBI in April 1975. Dell, *A Hard Pounding*, pp. 138, 237.
15. Keegan and Pennant-Rea, *Who Runs the Economy?*, p. 159.
16. Benn, *Against the Tide*, p. 404.

17. See Ralph Tarling and Frank Wilkinson, 'The Social Contract: Postwar Incomes Policies and Their Inflationary Impact', *Cambridge Journal of Economics*, vol. 1, no. 4, December 1977.

18. Benn, *Against the Tide*, p. 415.

19. Dell, *A Hard Pounding*, p. 171.

20. Jones, *Union Man*, p. 298.

21. Burk and Cairncross, *'Goodbye, Great Britain'*, p. 15.

22. Keegan and Pennant-Rea, *Who Runs the Economy?*, p. 159.

23. Dell, *A Hard Pounding*, p. 193.

24. Ibid., p. 185.

25. Burk and Cairncross, *'Goodbye, Great Britain'*, p. 223.

26. Healey, *The Time of My Life*, pp. 401–2.

27. See Dell, *A Hard Pounding*, pp. 188–9; Benn, *Against the Tide*, pp. 356, 461; Crosland, *Tony Crosland*, pp. 299, 307.

28. Burk and Cairncross, *'Goodbye, Great Britain'*, pp. 30–31.

29. Fay and Young, *The Day the Pound Nearly Died*, p. 34.

30. Burk and Cairncross, *'Goodbye, Great Britain'*, p. 10. Cf. pp. 37–8 where Arthur Burns, the Governor of the Federal Reserve, is quoted describing himself as 'a neanderthal conservative and naturally suspicious of a Labour Government. I thought it was a profligate government . . .'.

31. Dell, *A Hard Pounding*, pp. 220, 250; Burk and Cairncross, *'Goodbye, Great Britain'*, pp. 39, 172–3. Callaghan later claimed that he received at the time 'well authenticated reports that a prominent front-bench Conservative spokesman, who has since served in Mrs Thatcher's Cabinet, was in Washington trying to influence the administration very strongly against the Labour Government'. See *Time and Change*, p. 431.

32. Burk and Cairncross, *'Goodbye, Great Britain'*, pp. 8, 42.

33. Fay and Young, *The Day the Pound Nearly Died*, p. 35.

34. Dell, *A Hard Pounding*, p. 231. Cf. Leo Pliatzky, *Getting and Spending*, Oxford 1982, p. 150.

35. Burk and Cairncross, *'Goodbye, Great Britain'*, p. 54.

36. 1976 *LPCR*, pp. 188–9; see also Callaghan, *Time and Change*, pp. 425–7.

37. Peter Jay, 'In Search of the Thatcher Factor', *Times Literary Supplement*, 30 May 1986, p. 580.

38. 1976 *LPCR*, p. 189.

39. Quoted in Crosland, *Tony Crosland*, pp. 355–6.

40. Benn, *Against the Tide*, p. 633.

41. See Benn, *Against the Tide*, pp. 303, 324–5.

42. The others included the maintenance of price controls, selective assistance to industry on a larger scale, work sharing and temporary employment subsidies, progressive tax increases, cuts in overseas defence spending and a further downward float of sterling.

43. Benn, *Against the Tide*, pp. 325–6. Cf. pp. 302–3.

44. John Eaton, Michael Barratt Brown and Ken Coates, *An Alternative Economic Strategy for the Labour Movement*, *Spokesman* pamphlet no. 47, February 1975, p. 12. Francis Cripps also saw the alternative economic strategy primarily in terms of its contribution to building a participatory form of democracy. See his 'The British Crisis – Can the Left Win?', *New*

Left Review 128, July/August 1981. And for the most remarkably detailed and inspiring version of the strategy presented in these terms, see Raymond Williams, 'An Alternative Politics', *The Socialist Register 1981*.

45. See *The Castle Diaries*, pp. 420–28, and Benn, *Against the Tide*, pp. 403–4.

46. See Benn, *Against the Tide*, pp. 165–6.

47. Ibid., p. 380. Cf. Eaton, Barratt Brown and Coates, *An Alternative*, p. 3.

48. The charges from the pro-Common Market forces that this was a narrowly conceived protectionist project which was bound to provoke retaliation and a trade war misrepresented the New Cambridge argument (as Crosland understood in crossing the lines on this issue). The case for import controls rested on the understanding that when a country tried to maintain its domestic employment and income in the face of contraction in other countries, it would draw in more imports while experiencing a decline in demand for its exports. Where this would result in a very large and destabilising drop in the exchange rate (which would certainly drive the country back to deflation) import restrictions were justified. Even in this regard, the Cambridge Economic Policy Group drew 'an important distinction between import restrictions preventing an *expansion* of imports beyond a level that cannot be financed by exports, and restrictions which reduce imports below the level of exports which is a policy of exporting unemployment. The former policy is designed to allow expansion towards full employment, implying a fall in the import ratio but not necessarily a fall in the absolute level of imports. It is not therefore a beggar-thy-neighbour policy ... [and] need not then provoke retaliation.' Anthony P. Thirlwall, *Nicholas Kaldor*, Brighton 1987, p. 281.

49. See Benn, *Against the Tide*, p. 657; Burk and Cairncross, '*Goodbye, Great Britain*', p. 89; Thirlwall, *Nicholas Kaldor*, pp. 250–54; and Dell, *A Hard Pounding*, pp. 126–9, 259.

50. Cambridge Political Economy Group, *Britain's Economic Crisis*, Spokesman pamphlet no. 44, September 1974.

51. Benn, *Against the Tide*, p. 518. Cf. p. 498.

52. When Michael Meacher, Benn's parliamentary under-secretary at the Department of Industry, wrote an article on saving jobs at the beginning of 1975 that included reference to the 'anarchy of capitalist markets that had developed after 1970' Sir Anthony Part objected to Benn on the grounds that this was a political phrase and inappropriate for use by a Government minister. Benn, *Against the Tide*, pp. 294, 329.

53. Minkin, *The Contentious Alliance*, p. 171.

54. Ibid., pp. 169–70.

55. Crosland ended his reflections on the politics of the situation in the summer of 1976 (see n.39 above) with the following words: 'Don't see much role for myself on the home front – concentrate on being competent Foreign Secretary.' Crosland, *Tony Crosland*, p. 356.

56. Benn, *Against the Tide*, pp. 415–16. Cf. p. 518 for the quotation immediately below.

57. Mikardo, *Backbencher*, pp. 198–9.

58. Minkin, *The Contentious Alliance*, pp. 183–5. Cf. Jones, *Union Man*, p. 300.

59. Thereby showing a degree of independence from the party leadership in office which seems breathtaking from the perspective of the 1990s.

60. By a vote of seventeen to three, even though Benn avoided attending in order not explicitly to defy the Government with his vote.

61. 'For 25 years the Doctrine of the Unripe Time has been used as an excuse for refusing to grasp the nettle. The lack of any outright commitment in Labour's October 1974 Manifesto other than "to ensure that banking and insurance makes a better contribution to the national economy" need not prevent the Annual Conference from adding to the party's official programme. In doing so Conference should be aware of the extensive influence of bankers and financiers anxious to preserve the "status quo", and their own privileged place within it . . .' *Banking and Finance*, a statement by the NEC presented to the Labour Party Annual Conference, Blackpool 1976, pp. 1, 24.

62. Fay and Young, *The Day the Pound Nearly Died*, pp. 33–4. On the other hand, Benn found on a trip to the US in February 1976 that the 'general view in Washington is that Wilson has swung to the right and all is well in the world. I tried to explain that there was a real debate going on.' In New York he attended a dinner at the Salomon Brothers offices which he described as 'a fantastic gathering of all the great money houses in America, the banks, the oil companies, the merchant bankers, the brokers, and so on. . . . They were hard, tough men . . .' One wonders if Benn told them there was a debate going on? In any case, he took full measure of the challenge: 'The market economy is now so complex and interconnected that everybody is reacting within a fraction of a second to what everybody else does. If one is serious as a socialist and one wants to get control of this system, one has to see it against a background of a whole investment industry with its own interests.' *Against the Tide*, pp. 519–20.

63. *The Social Contract 1976–77*, Report of the Special Trades Union Congress, 16 June 1976, pp. 12, 23, 40.

64. Benn, *Against the Tide*, p. 599.

65. 1976 *LPCR*, p. 157.

66. 1976 *LPCR*, p. 313.

67. Dell, *A Hard Pounding*, p. 238.

68. In his memoirs, Callaghan reveals that in a telephone conversation the day after his speech to the Party Conference, President Ford complimented him on his 'helluva speech yesterday' and offered to help with the IMF, but wanted to raise 'one more serious point'. Callaghan then presents the following verbatim quotation of their dialogue:

> 'President: 'Are you contemplating import restrictions?'
> Prime Minister: 'Not for the moment, but this is the alternative strategy that is being dangled in front of people.'
> President: 'We would have reservations, and hopefully, Jim, you could avoid the trade limitation.'
> Prime Minister: 'If the alternative strategy were adopted it would call into question Britain's role as an Alliance partner which I am anxious to preserve.'
> President: 'We certainly need you standing tall and strong, and I assure you, Jim, I will work with that.'
> Callaghan, *Time and Change*, pp. 429–30.

69. Quoted in Fay and Young, *The Day the Pound Nearly Died*, p. 30.
70. See Burk and Cairncross, 'Goodbye, Great Britain', pp. 90ff.
71. Crosland, *Tony Crosland*, pp. 379–80.
72. Dell, *A Hard Pounding*, p. 261.
73. Burk and Cairncross, 'Goodbye, Great Britain', p. 103; Benn, *Against the Tide*, p. 685. In a personal communication, Benn wrote that it accorded 'very strongly with my recollection' that Crosland's actual words were: 'It is mad but we have no alternative.' Benn also recalls that, at the decisive Cabinet meetings of December 1 and 2, Callaghan 'was very clever in putting me on first and I had the whole Cabinet to myself when my colleagues tore the alternative policy to shreds and, thereafter, Callaghan was able to say, "We agreed there was no alternative but to accept the IMF terms." This meant that the wobblies in the middle who did not like the IMF terms were already bound by their decision earlier in disposing of my paper.' Tony Benn letter to Leo Panitch, 20 October 1986.
74. Dell, *A Hard Pounding*, pp. 226, 273.
75. Burk and Cairncross, 'Goodbye, Great Britain', pp. 192, 213. The Letter of Intent is reprinted in full as an appendix at pp. 229–35.
76. Helleiner, *States and the Reemergence of Global Finance*, p. 144.
77. Keegan and Pennant-Rea, *Who Runs the Economy?*, p. 169.
78. Barnett, *Inside the Treasury*, p. 73.
79. See Colin Leys, 'Thatcherism and British Manufacturing: A Question of Hegemony', *New Left Review*, no. 151, May/June 1985, esp. pp. 16–17.
80. 'Great pressure was put on us to restructure, and we believed that the NEB, holding 20% of a new merged company, would at least operate more in the workers' interests. But I wouldn't touch them with a barge pole now ... Eventually the credibility of the NEB as it was constituted was practically nil with us.' Harry Blair, Secretary of the Parsons Corporate Committee, quoted in *State Intervention in Industry*, p. 93.
81. The kinds of penalties that were originally conceived as being applied to firms which failed to provide information and to invest in conformance with the planning agreements were only applied to firms which failed to observe the wage norms.
82. Jones, *Union Man*, pp. 325–6.
83. See A. Heath, R. Jowell and J. Curtice, *How Britain Votes*, Oxford 1985, pp. 132–3; and Ivor Crewe, 'The Labour Party and the Electorate' in D. Kavanagh, ed., *The Politics of the Labour Party*, London 1982, p. 39, Table 1.1.
84. Quoted in Hollingsworth, *The Press and Political Dissent*, p. 50. Cf. pp. 54–6 on how journalists used the defence that Labour leaders agreed with them to justify their characterisations of the left.
85. For this shift in attitudes among Labour identifiers along each of these dimensions see Crewe, 'The Labour Party and the Electorate', p. 39, Table 1.1.
86. Benn attributes this expression to Healey at a Liaison Committee Meeting in March 1976. *Against the Tide*, pp. 521–2. Cf. Healey, *The Time of My Life*, pp. 444, 502ff.
87. See Burk and Cairncross, 'Goodbye, Great Britain', p. 228; and Healey, *The*

Time of My Life, pp. 378–81, 434. Callaghan maintained that the Labour Party approached the doctrine of monetarism 'with caution' and merely 'tiptoed around the edges'. He had difficulty recalling 'anyone [in Labour] who fiercely embraced the faith'. *Time and Change*, p. 477.

88. Benn, *Against the Tide*, p. 313.

89. Benn's main contribution as Energy Minister to the broader struggle was that of leading by example: demonstrating that a radical minister could run a department efficiently with much less secrecy and much more participation than was the norm in Whitehall; encouraging the National Union of Mineworkers to produce their own plans for 'democratic self-management' and actively involving them in the development of the Tripartite Plan for Coal; challenging the nuclear power lobby by insisting that ecologists could not be dismissed as cranks and subversives and clarifying that the 'development of nuclear power ... is neither self-evidently inevitable nor self-evidently wrong (but) the decision must be a political one, otherwise we are abnegating our responsibilities to the experts'. Above all, despite his inability to persuade the Cabinet to nationalise British Petroleum, there is no doubt that Benn's greatest success as Energy Minister, working closely with the industrialist Lord Kearton as head of the British National Oil Corporation, was in securing remarkably favourable terms from the multinational oil corporations and considerable public control over the exploitation of the North Sea oil fields. See Robert Jenkins, *Tony Benn: A Political Biography*, Ch. IX, 'Dissenting Minister', pp. 232–7, 242–54.

7. The Conflict over Party Democracy

1. Stuart Hall, 'The Great Moving Right Show' in Stuart Hall and Martin Jacques, eds, *The Politics of Thatcherism*, London 1979, pp. 26–7. The essay was first published in *Marxism Today*, January 1979, pp. 14–20.

2. Stuart Hall, 'Thatcherism – A New Stage?' *Marxism Today*, February 1980, p. 27.

3. 'The Decline of Labour's Local Party Membership and Electoral Base, 1945–79' in D. Kavanagh, ed., *The Politics of the Labour Party*, London 1982, p. 122.

4. Thus while there was certainly no significant increase in individual party membership through the decade, Seyd was correct in emphasising the importance of new activists joining the party who either were 'relatively young, higher-educated, public sector employees, often with a working-class parental background ... [who had] first been made aware of Marxism in their intellectual studies but then adopted the ideas as part of their political perspective'; or represented 'a new generation of manual-worker trade unionists, often living in council housing, [who] had joined the party to defend their standards of living and were less deferential than previous generations to their party and trade union leaders'. Patrick Seyd, *The Rise and Fall of the Labour Left*, London 1987, pp. 46, 74.

5. 'CLPD Priorities for 1979', discussion paper prepared by the Secretary,

17 December 1978, p. 1. The following account is based on original CLPD documents and interviews with CLPD activists, including Vladimir and Vera Derer. Cf. Seyd, *The Rise and Fall of the Labour Left*, esp. pp. 83–9, 103–21; David Kogan and Maurice Kogan, *The Battle for the Labour Party*, London 1982, esp. chs 5 and 6; and A. Young, *The Reselection of MPs*, London 1983, esp. chs 7 and 8.

6. 'CLPD Priorities for 1979', p. 1.
7. 'The Case for Public Ownership', a Campaign for Labour Party Democracy pamphlet (written by Nicholas Costello, Tony Cutler, Vera Derer, Irene Hong and Seumas Milne), September 1986.
8. 'Secretary's Statement', *CLPD Bulletin*, 11 January 1986, pp. i–x.
9. Vladimir Derer, 'Paper No. 2', prepared for Labour Left Liaison, Summer 1988.
10. Frank Allaun was the CLPD's first 'President'. He was replaced in 1975 by Joan Maynard. Jo Richardson, Audrey Wise and Ernie Roberts (who became a victim of reselection in the 1980s) were 'Vice-Presidents'. As a Cabinet minister, Benn had to keep his distance, of course. But he had in any case, as we saw in Chapter 3, been wary of concentrating on precise constitutional formulae in advancing the case for intra-party democracy. Within the NEC, especially after 1976, he became one of the strongest supporters of the CLPD's campaign. But very few MPs were CLPD enthusiasts. Even some of those close to the founders via their association with Socialist Charter, like Stan Newens and Arthur Latham, initially didn't like the idea of reselection and in any case wanted to see if the CLPD really was a serious project. For his part, Derer respected their concerns about being 'used' to front for projects that had no real support.
11. Robert Michels, *Political Parties* (1915), New York 1962.
12. Seyd and Minkin, 'The Labour Party and Its Members', p. 614.
13. Campaign for Labour Party Democracy, Statement of Aims, June 1973.
14. 'CLPD Priorities for 1979', pp. 1–2.
15. CLPD, *Campaign Newsletter*, 2 May–June 1975, p. 2. Or as another bulletin put it three years later: 'It is the relative independence of the parliamentary Labour Party, rooted in the almost automatic readoption of Labour MPs, which makes it easy for Labour governments to abandon Labour Party policies. The only way to undermine this independence and to make MPs more mindful of party decisions is to reduce their security of tenure.' *Campaign Newsletter*, 13 September 1978 (both quotations are in Seyd, *Rise and Fall*, p. 20).
16. Chris Mullin and Charlotte Atkins, *How to Select or Reselect Your MP*, Campaign for Labour Party Democracy and Institute for Workers' Control, IWC Pamphlet no. 77, 1981, pp. 3–5.
17. Ibid., p. 7.
18. Known as the Rushcliffe amendment, it was moved by Ken Coates. But Coates himself was not acting as part of the CLPD's campaign. Derer and Coates did not mix very well.
19. 'Before this change an unsuccessful candidate or MP could appeal to the Executive, on the grounds that were always subjective and generally insubstantial, against the heinous conduct of his Constituency Party in

choosing, instead of him, somebody else who, in his modest and objective judgement, was less worthy than he. Most often the Executive, on grounds that were always arbitrary and generally biased, would uphold the appeal, particularly if the national Agent could produce, out of those McCarthyite dossiers pioneered by Sara Barker, some smear against the selected candidate.' Ian Mikardo, *Backbencher*, p. 190.

20. 1974 *LPCR*, pp. 179–82.

21. 1974 *LPCR*, p. 173. The NEC's Organisation Committee denied the appeal by the deselected MP, Eddie Griffiths, on the grounds of there having been no procedural irregularities. In any case, the complaint by Griffiths that he was the victim of 'a well-planned coup by extremists' was, as Eric Shaw has put it, 'tendentious. He was removed for a whole series of reasons, including his poor record as a constituency MP, his unwillingness to consult with his local party as well as political differences between a right-wing MP and a CLP shifting to the left.' Shaw, *Discipline and Discord in the Labour Party*, p. 346, n.2.

22. Eddie Milne, who had been deselected by the Blythe CLP in November 1973, was very different from the other three by virtue of his having been 'on the left of the party, a firm supporter of state ownership and the planning of industry'. As Hilary Wainwright has noted, his deselection, led by local councillors and his own agent, was clearly related to his having played a major role in 'embarrassing the party machine' in north-east England. (Milne had helped expose the corruption scandals linking Labour local authorities to T. Dan Smith and John Poulson, and had especially crossed swords with the GMWU Regional Secretary, Andrew Cunningham, who was a member of the NEC until his own arrest for corruption in 1973.) It says a great deal about the *realpolitik* that defined the reaction to deselection at Westminster that whereas Taverne's and Prentice's deselection caused an uproar among Labour MPs, Milne's deselection was met with 'total silence – and probably a good deal of relief among the northern group of MPs who had effectively excommunicated Milne'. See Hilary Wainwright, *Labour: A Tale of Two Parties*, London 1987, p. 26.

23. Wainwright, *Labour*, p. 21.

24. Ibid, p. 17.

25. Seyd, *Rise and Fall*, p. 62.

26. See Shaw, *Discipline and Discord*, p. 188. For a very different view, which Shaw effectively refutes, see Paul McCormick, 'Prentice and the Newham North-East Constituency: The Making of Historical Myths', *Political Studies*, xxix, 1, pp. 73–99.

27. Shaw, *Discipline and Discord*, pp. 195–6.

28. See 'Mr Callaghan Swings Labour NEC on Safeguards for MPs', *The Times*, 25 March 1976.

29. Shaw, op. cit.

30. See Minkin, *The Contentious Alliance*, pp. 181–2.

31. Scanlon had earlier recalled his delegation and tried, but failed, to persuade them to change their vote. As Seyd notes, Scanlon's subsequent claim that he had been confused about the order in which various motions were taken

'seems difficult to accept when the Chairman had made quite clear on three occasions the procedure to be adopted'. *Rise and Fall*, p. 107.

32. Shaw, *Discipline and Discord*, p. 199.

33. Seyd and Minkin, 'The Labour Party and Its Members', p. 625. Cf. Bish, 'Working Relations Between Government and Party', in Ken Coates, ed., *What Went Wrong?*, pp. 163–206.

34. Minkin, *The Labour Party Conference*, p. 359.

35. Indeed, upon his election to the leadership, a profile in the *New Statesman* ('Lucky Jim', 9 April 1976, pp. 460–61) had likened Callaghan to Mayor Daley of Chicago. But very much unlike Daley, Callaghan at the same time affected the demeanour of the quintessential statesman. Mikardo amusingly captured Callaghan's shocked reaction in the 1960s to a proposal that the Select Committee on Nationalised Industries undertake an investigation of the Bank of England: 'The Chancellor of the Exchequer, Jim Callaghan, was rendered speechless with horror by this proposal: the idea of a group of questioning MPs crossing the sacred portals of the Bank caused him to react like a High Priest at the sight of the innermost sanctum, the Holy of Holies, being invaded by a group of malodorous swineherds.' *Backbencher*, pp. 178–9.

36. 1976 *LPCR*, pp. 193–4. Whatever suspicions the security apparatus had about Wilson, they knew that Callaghan, going all the way back to his being chief negotiator for the Police Federation in the 1950s, was very much on side. Within weeks of his taking the leadership Callaghan told Benn that he knew that three members of the NEC were in 'continual touch with Communists' and that 'everything that goes on in that Executive goes straight back to King Street. I have ways of knowing.' See Benn, *Against the Tide*, p. 561. Cf. pp. 557–66. Benn had been encouraged initially by the attention Callaghan gave to party matters. Although Callaghan had already played the crucial role in swinging the NEC against reselection in March, when Callaghan stayed for the whole day at the NEC's first consideration of Labour's programme in May, Benn felt that this showed 'what a proper sense of priorities he has, unlike Harold who would have dodged it'. In response to Callaghan's first warning that he might sack him for his criticisms of the Government's policies, Benn replied: 'I live in the naive hope that one day you will accept the policies I advocate.' Naive, indeed.

37 Stuart Hall et al., *Policing the Crisis*, London 1978, pp. 313–14. 'To put it simply, "the conspiracy" is the necessary and required form in which dissent, opposition or conflict has to be explained in a society which is, in fact, mesmerised by *consensus*. If society is defined as an entity in which all fundamental or structural class conflicts have been reconciled, and government is defined as the instrument of class reconciliation ... then, clearly conflict *must* arise because an evil minority of subversive and politically motivated men enter into a conspiracy to destroy by force what they cannot dismantle in any other way ...' pp. 309–10.

38. One right-wing trade union representative on the NEC, John Cartwright, later an SDP MP, called Bevan 'probably the most effective National Chairman of the Young Socialists there has been'. On the other hand, although the Proscribed List had been dropped by the NEC, the

practitioners of social democratic centralism were by no means gone from the party apparatus. Barrie Clarke (whose promotion to Political Education Officer had created the vacancy Bevan filled) had admitted that 'much of my job as National Youth Officer was "disorganising" as much as organising. I was acting like a fire brigade, going around the country saying "No, they can't do that."' Both quotations are in Michael Crick, *Militant*, London 1984, pp. 82, 93.

39. The NEC, explicitly rejecting 'a further descent into McCarthyism', narrowly endorsed Bevan's appointment at its December meeting, but in January it established a sub-committee composed of Heffer, Foot, two right-wing trade unionists and the General Secretary to look into the question of disciplinary action against Militant in light of Underhill's report. Although Foot had succumbed to pressure to cast his vote against Bevan, he joined with Heffer and Hayward to issue a report 'sufficiently anodyne to please almost all' but which nevertheless 'expressed opposition to the use of discipline as a method of settling political argument'. Shaw, *Discipline and Discord*, pp. 220-21. Cf. Peter Taffe, *The Rise of Militant*, London 1995, pp. 122-5, and Crick, *Militant*, pp. 90-93.

40. Quoted in Kogan and Kogan, *The Battle for the Labour Party*, p. 37.

41. The CLV was launched a few days after Shirley Williams issued a call to arms in a long article published in *The Guardian* (28 January 1977) on 'Trotskyism and Democracy'. In contrast to Benn's earlier eloquent essay calling for tolerance of Marxists in the party (*The Guardian*, 13 December 1977), Williams's discourse was not only ill-informed about Marxism but was exceedingly narrow in its parliamentarist definition of democracy.

42. Quoted in Kogan and Kogan, *The Battle for the Labour Party*, pp. 68-9.

43. One of the important ways in which the counter-insurgency was advanced in the unions was through linking the right-wing union leaders' traditional hostility to the left to their equally traditional concerns about what was done with the money they donated to the party. Callaghan had held the position of Treasurer of the Party from 1967 until he became leader in 1976. Because it was (until the changes of the 1980s) the only office elected from all sections of the Conference, Callaghan was more than ready 'to fairly claim I had the confidence of the whole party' (*Time and Change*, pp. 281-2). But when the left-wing MP Norman Atkinson (a close ally of Mikardo's) was elected to succeed Callaghan as Treasurer at the 1976 Conference, in a clear rebuke to the PLP over its choice of leader, this was used to fuel fears among the right-wing leaders that the money they donated to the party was no longer in safe hands. A key part in the counter-insurgency was initially played by Callaghan's close ally, Derek Gladwin, a member of the GMWU Executive who was also in the powerful position of chair of the party's Conference Arrangements Committee. Larry Whitty, the GMWU's research officer, later the party's General Secretary under Kinnock, became the TULV's first Secretary; and Reg Underhill, the party's National Agent and author of the leaked report on 'entryism', was designated to link the TULV with the party apparatus. For the most thorough account, only marred by sometimes tortured rationalisations for the role

played by Basnett and Whitty, see Minkin, *The Contentious Alliance* pp. 487ff.

44. Minkin, *The Contentious Alliance*, p. 194.

45. Thus in 1975 even the traditionally loyal General and Municipal Workers voted against platform four times on resolutions expressing criticism of the Government. And at the 1976 Conference, the NEC's attempts to protect the Government led to the platform being defeated seven times (three on housing, one on NHS, one on child benefit, and one on public expenditure cuts). Unions supporting the government were very reluctant to call for card votes, for this would show their activists how they voted. See esp. Minkin, *The Labour Party Conference*, p. 349.

46. Callaghan, *Time and Change*, p. 424.

47. Steve Jefferys, 'Striking into the Eighties', *International Socialism*, Series 2, no. 5, Summer 1979, pp. 33–5.

48. John Eaton, Michael Barratt Brown and Ken Coates, *An Alternative Economic Strategy for the Labour Movement*, *Spokesman* pamphlet no. 47, Nottingham 1975, p. 10.

49. *Against the Tide*, p. 441.

50. Benn, *Conflicts of Interest*, pp. 268–9. Cf. for his comments on Thatcher, *Against the Tide*, p. 311.

51. Gregor Murray, *Trade Unions and Incomes Policies, British Unions and the Social Contract in the 1970s*, PhD Thesis, University of Warwick 1985, p. 540.

52. Ibid, pp. 630–31.

53. See esp. R.H. Fryer, 'British Trade Unions and the Cuts', *Capital and Class*, 8, Summer 1979, pp. 95–112.

54. *Conflicts of Interest*, p. 359.

55. The fact that it was Mikardo they displaced, together with Kinnock's future trajectory, made this a rather pyrrhic victory – and indeed Skinner offered to stand down for Mikardo.

56. Andrew Ross, *Parliamentary Profiles*, 1984, pp. 295–6.

57. As Benn noted in his diary, Golding's threat was not only 'the talk of the day' among Labour MPs but was 'one of the most remarkable speeches I had ever heard in my twenty-eight years in Parliament'. It only convinced Benn all the more that 'it is indeed *because* you can pack one selection conference that reselection is necessary', but he admitted that Golding's and Cocks's cynicism left him feeling 'utterly sick'. Benn, *Conflicts of Interest*, pp. 286–7.

58. 'Williams Notices a Swing to Centre', *Financial Times*, 21 February 1979. The founders of the SDP who later complained most about the block vote had often been the ones who had most relied on the union leaders' abuse of it. Shirley Williams, for instance, held her seat on the National Executive thanks to the most undemocratic use of the block vote of all – that which gave the union leaders, without any accountability to their delegations, control over the elections to the women's section of the National Executive. Rarely was this hypocrisy confronted openly and honestly by the social democratic right of the party, as it was by David Marquand when he observed that 'parties belong to their members. It is because the Labour

right forgot that and tried to keep control of their party through clever backstairs manipulation, rather than through honest argument honestly put, that the Bennite left is now making the running at conference, in the National Executive, and in most constituencies.' *London Review of Books*, 1–14 October 1981, as quoted in Young, *The Reselection of MPs*, pp. 132–3.

59. Indeed, within the T&G, Jones's own encouragement of greater participation and decentralisation in his union had provided space for the especially active role that would be played by Walter Greendale, the T&G's lay Chairman and one of its representatives on the General Council, in support of Benn and the new left in the party. As Minkin has put it, 'the political legacy Jack Jones handed on [to his successor, Moss Evans] was very much that of his early phase rather than his accommodation with Labour leaders'. Minkin, *The Contentious Alliance*, p. 303.

60. David Hine, 'Leaders and Followers: Democracy and Manageability in the Social Democratic Parties of Western Europe', in William E. Patterson and Alastair H. Thomas, eds, *The Future of Social Democracy*, Oxford 1986, p. 279.

61. 'CLPD Priorities for 1979', p. 1.

62. Vladimir and Vera Derer, 'One Case for Positive Discrimination', Background Paper for CLPD Annual General Meeting, 1979.

63. Geoff Bish, 'Working Relations Between Government and Party', in Ken Coates, ed., *What Went Wrong?*, Nottingham 1979, pp. 164–5.

64. Andrew Gamble, *Britain in Decline: Economic Policy, Political Strategy and the British State*, 4th edn, London 1994, p. 185.

65. This work bore fruit in the publication of three important and influential books by the turn of the decade: the CSE London–Edinburgh Weekend Return Group's, *In and Against the State* in November 1979; the CSE State Apparatus and Expenditure Group's *Struggle Over the State: Cuts and Restructuring in Contemporary Britain* in December 1979; soon followed by the LCC and CSE's joint publication, *The Alternative Economic Strategy* (an elaboration of the London CSE Group's 'Crisis, the Labour Movement and the Alternative Economic Strategy', *Capital and Class* 8, Summer 1979).

66. Best exemplified perhaps from within the Labour Party by the publication in 1977 of Geoff Hodgson's *Socialism and Parliamentary Democracy* and, outside the party, by Sheila Rowbotham, Lynne Segal and Hilary Wainwright's *Beyond the Fragments* in 1979.

67. Interview, 10 October 1985. On Callaghan and the LCC, see Benn, *Conflicts of Interest*, pp. 469, 472.

68. Geoff Bish, 'Drafting the Manifesto', in Coates, ed., *What Went Wrong?*, p. 202. Cf. Bish, 'Working Relations', pp. 165–6.

69. See Minkin, *The Labour Party Conference*, p. 325.

70. Michael Rustin, 'The New Left and the Present Crisis', *New Left Review* 121, May/June 1980, p. 66. In a subsequent article, however, Rustin would show a more nuanced appreciation for what was involved in the Labour new left's constitutionalism. See his excellent essay, 'Different Conceptions of Party: Labour's Constitutional Debates', *New Left Review* 126, March/April 1981.

71. 'Secretary's Statement', CLPD Bulletin 11, January 1986, p. iii.

72. Perry Anderson, 'The Antinomies of Antonio Gramsci', *New Left Review* 100, November 1976/January 1977, pp. 28–9.

73. Ralph Miliband, 'Party Democracy and Parliamentary Government', *Political Studies*, vol. VI, 1958, pp. 170–74.

74. John Bochel and David Denver, 'Candidate Selection and the Labour Party: What the Selectors Seek', *British Journal of Political Science*, vol. 13, no. 1, 1983, p. 58; Cf. table 5, p. 53.

75. Ibid., p. 63.

76. See Alan Clarke, *The Rise and Fall of the Socialist Republic: A History of the South Yorkshire County Council*, Sheffield, 1986; D. Blunkett and G. Green, *Building from the Bottom: The Sheffield Experience*, Fabian tract 481, October 1983; Ken Livingstone, *If Voting Changed Anything, They'd Abolish It*, London 1987; M. Mackintosh and H. Wainwright, eds, *A Taste of Power*, London 1987; S. Lansley, S. Goss and C. Wolmar, *Councils in Conflict: The Rise and Fall of the Municipal Left*, London 1989; John Gyford, *The Politics of Local Socialism*, London 1985. Cf. Wainwright, *Labour*, ch. 3 and Seyd, *Rise and Fall*, ch. 6.

77. Maureen Mackintosh, 'Creating a Developmental State: Reflections on Policy as Process', in G. Albo, D. Langille and L. Panitch, eds, *A Different Kind of State? Popular Power and Democratic Administration*, Toronto 1993, p. 36.

78. See 1975 *LPCR*, pp. 274–5; and 1980 *LPCR*, pp. 48–9.

79. 'The Labour Party and the Geography of Inequality: A Puzzle', in Kavanagh, ed., *The Politics of the Labour Party*, pp. 150, 161.

80. A. Heath, R. Jowell and J. Curtice, *How Britain Votes*, London 1985, pp. 3–4.

81. See W. Mishler, M. Hoskin and R. Fitzgerald, 'British Parties in the Balance: A Time Series Analysis of Long-term Trends in Labour and Conservative Support', *British Journal of Political Science*, vol. 19, 1989, esp. pp. 225–7.

82. Although Labour Party identification among the middle classes and non-manual workers had actually continued to rise through the 1970s (standing at over 30 per cent among the latter by 1979), it had declined by the end of the decade to only 50 per cent of skilled and unskilled manual workers. See Ivor Crewe, 'On the Death and Resurrection of Class Voting: Some Comments on How Britain Votes', *Political Studies*, XXXIV, 1986, pp. 620–38; and Heath, Jowell and Curtice, 'Trendless Fluctuations: A Reply to Crewe', *Political Studies*, XXXV, 1987, pp. 256–77.

83. Patrick Seyd and Lewis Minkin, 'The Labour Party and Its Members', *New Society*, 20 September 1979, p. 615.

84. 'Thatcherism – a New Stage?', *Marxism Today*, February 1980, p. 27. Cf. Leo Panitch, 'Socialists and the Labour Party – a Reappraisal', *The Socialist Register 1979*.

8. The Crisis of Representation

1. These extracts are from John Soper's (the BBC's anchorman on party conference broadcasts) biography *Tony Blair: The Moderniser*, London

1995, pp. 50–51. Apart from the absurd characterisation of the activists who operated under CLPD's umbrella, the depths to which supposedly respectable journalism has sunk in the UK is indicated by the following sentence: 'Tony Benn had been part of the Cabinet throughout those years and had lived, apparently untroubled by the compromises and disarray that had marked the last years of the Labour Government' (p. 49).

2. Benn, *Conflicts of Interest*, p. 533.
3. See Richard Hefferman and Mike Marqusee, *Defeat from the Jaws of Victory: Inside Kinnock's Labour Party*, London 1992, pp. 166–8; see also Seyd, *Rise and Fall*, p. 86, and Kogan and Kogan, *The Battle for the Labour Party*, p. 52.
4. Shaw, *Discipline and Discord*, pp. 250–51.
5. See Greg Philo et al. (Glasgow University Media Group), *Really Bad News*, (London 1982) for the most thorough documentation of the media's tendency to cover the conflict in the party in 1980 and 1981 'almost exclusively from the point of view of the right wing of the Labour Party'.
6. Shaw, *Discipline and Discord*, p. 246.
7. The Rank and File Mobilising Committee, an alliance led by LCC and CLPD activists, also brought a number of other left organisations within the party under its umbrella in 1980–81, including Trotskyist ones like Militant and the Socialist Campaign for Labour Victory, although their actual role was minimal. It was entirely a campaigning organisation not a programmatic one, initially defining itself in terms of organising support for five specific constitutional demands; and subsequently constituting the main organising vehicle for Benn's campaign for the deputy leadership. Even in the context of the broad umbrella of the RFMC, activists (always including a handful of MPs) who associated themselves with the goals of the CLPD and LCC, still saw their differences with both the traditional Tribune left and with the Trotskyist groups inside and outside the party very much in the way Derer defined them at the beginning of the previous chapter.
8. Ken Livingstone, *If Voting Changed Anything, They'd Abolish It*, London 1987, pp. 91–2.
9. See the preface in Tony Benn, *Arguments for Democracy*, London 1981.
10. 'One of the great things about Tony Benn ... which makes him different from most other MPs, is that ... he does listen to what other people are saying and he acts upon it fairly often.' Nigel Stanley, quoted in Kogan and Kogan, *The Battle*, pp. 104–5. Stanley, later 'soft left', was at the time the Organising Secretary of the LCC, the organisation most often identified as 'Bennite' in contradistinction to the Trotskyist groups to which the LCC – and especially Stanley – were very hostile. Yet Stanley also reacted strongly against the label 'Bennite' because the Labour new left 'is not entirely structured around one person like the Bevanites were'.
11. 1979 *LPCR*, pp. 291–2.
12. Benn, *Arguments for Democracy*, pp. 10, 144–5.
13. They were encouraged in this respect by a wave of academic literature that pointed to Sweden or Austria as proof that full employment on these terms was possible, entirely oblivious to the capital mobility processes that were undermining even these social democratic regimes. The social democratic

governments through the 1980s, led by New Zealand and Australia, which were elected promising to emulate those models and quickly turned to neo-liberalism and competitive austerity, confirmed Benn's warning against the social democratic version of 'there is no alternative'.

14. Peter Hain, ed., *The Crisis and the Future of the Left: The Debate of the Decade*, London 1980, p. 45.

15. Benn, *Conflicts of Interest*, p. 508.

16. Benn, *Arguments for Democracy*, p. xii.

17. Francis Cripps, 'The British Crisis – Can the Left Win?', *New Left Review*, 128, July–August 1981, p. 94.

18. Benn, *Arguments for Democracy*, p. 221.

19. Cripps, p. 94.

20. Thus, Eric Shaw is incorrect in claiming that Labour new left 'exhibited curiously little interest in the profound changes that were reconstructing the political economy both at home and abroad and were undermining the feasibility of purely national-based alternative strategies', at least as regards the left's leading economic thinkers, and Benn himself. (Eric Shaw, *The Labour Party Since 1979*, London 1994, p. 200.) It was precisely their recognition of these profound changes that led them to advance the case for controls over capital movements and multinational corporations' investment plans. Whether such controls could be effective is a fair question to ask (Shaw, p. 14), but the fact is that it was the Labour leadership who were ignoring the profound structural changes in capitalism with their insistence that if Keynesianism was not viable in Britain it was only because they could not emulate the corporatist wage restraint of the Swedes and Austrians.

21. Benn, *Arguments for Democracy*, p. 11. Invited to address an International Monetary Conference in London in June 1979 attended by bankers from all over the world, Benn listened carefully to the chairman's 'arrogant but brilliant speech saying that, with the capacity to transmit information world-wide by electronics, all markets were now international, and this introduced a discipline greater than the gold standard. In effect, he was saying that all national governments were obsolete. The banking priest-hood's assumptions that politicians and Governments and hence democracy are entirely irrelevant to the world was breathtaking.' Benn, *Conflicts of Interest*, p. 511.

22. Cripps, pp. 96–7.

23. In addition to calling for 'the development of industrial democracy in the newspaper industry . . . while at the same time guaranteeing autonomy and freedom from interference in their day to day work of editorial and production workers', the resolution supported the creation of alternative newspapers 'of all kinds'; a National Printing Corporation, Producer Press Cooperatives, and a launch fund to assist new publications; an advertising revenue board to distribute revenues fairly between publications; and an independent Press Council with powers to initiate investigations and require equal space be given to corrections and omissions (1979 *LPCR*, pp. 383–9). For Benn's own ideas at this time, incorporating many of these proposals, but going beyond them to address broadcasting and especially the need for

'placing under the international control all companies using satellites' for commercial television, see his 'The Case for a Free Press' in *Arguments for Democracy*, esp. pp. 118–20.

24. Benn, *Arguments for Democracy*, pp. 170–71.

25. NEC Campaigns Committee, 'Campaign Strategy to 1983' Labour Party, RD:925A, June 1981, p. 7. And note further (pp. 8–9) 'We are already bringing together a wide range of economic policies under the rubric of the Alternative Economic Strategy. But we also have, or are developing, various policies related to people's rights *vis-à-vis* bureaucracies, and their opportunities for democratic control, in such areas as school governors, tenants' rights, nationalised industry and consumer representation, etc. These could be pulled together as a package – perhaps a "Labour Charter of Democratic Rights".'

26. Benn, *Conflicts of Interest*, p. 508.

27. Benn, *Arguments for Democracy*, preface.

28. Ibid.

29. See esp. Wainwright, *Labour: A Tale of Two Parties*, ch. 4.

30. Livingstone, *If Voting Changed Anything*, p. 91.

31. Benn, *Arguments for Democracy*, p. 168.

32. Ibid., p. 165.

33. *Minutes of the TUC–Labour Party Liaison Committee*, 24 November 1980.

34. *Arguments for Democracy*, pp. 166–8; and *Trade Unionism: A Strategy for the 1980s*, IWC Pamphlet no. 84, 1983, pp. 10–11.

35. See Benn, *Arguments for Democracy*, p. 167 and *Trade Unionism*, pp. 13–14.

36. Benn, *Arguments for Democracy*, p. 171.

37. 1979 *LPCR*, pp. 292–3.

38. Hain, ed., *The Crisis and the Future of the Left*, p. 50.

39. Ibid., pp. 47–8 (emphasis added).

40. 'Now I had a very clear idea in my mind that it would all be over within fifteen months, I didn't stand that year for the shadow cabinet because I thought it was dishonest to run a campaign for change from within the shadow cabinet. I assumed that what would happen would be that at the '79 conference, we'd lay the foundations; at the 1980 conference we would have changed the policy, got the two-thirds majority, got the Electoral College, got the reselection; and from '80 to '83, we'd have campaigned together on our policy.' Tony Benn, 'Britain: Lessons for the Left, an Interview with Leo Panitch', *Studies in Political Economy*, 13, Spring 1984, p. 11.

41. Benn, *Conflicts of Interest*, p. 538. This was not an isolated reflection. He repeated it to Willy Brandt in May 1980 (see p. 599) and even as he embarked on the deputy leadership campaign at the beginning of 1981, he saw the virulence of the backlash against the changes in the Labour Party as part of a larger 'nasty and unpleasant' change in the 'whole political atmosphere' (*The End of an Era*, p. 96). It was not just Reagan's election and the generally growing reaction among the European ruling classes that he had in mind, moreover, as may be seen in his remarkable diary entry for Friday, 13 March 1981 (p. 106) after he met with a group of unemployed

youth on job experience schemes under the Manpower Services Commission:

> It was one of the most depressing meetings I have ever been to. When I looked round, there were these kids of sixteen and seventeen, utterly hopeless and demoralised – punk rockers, a black boy with purple hair, guys in sort of Hell's Angels outfits with holes in their trousers. One guy with hair all over the place interrupted me all the time. The first thing he said was, 'What's the difference between nuclear weapons and machine guns? You're still killing people.' He went on and on about that. He might have been an anarchist or nihilist. They asked all sorts of questions – 'You're a millionaire anyway, aren't you?' 'There are millionaires in council houses, aren't there?' ... Then they expressed their hatred for the royal family – not the Queen, but all the hangers on.... They said there was nothing they could do. 'You just come here for our vote'.... It was a combination of hopelessness, defeatism and bitterness bred in our education system and encouraged by unemployment. But at the same time a really bitter critique, and at least they were arguing, which showed some confidence. But, by God, I could see them joining the National Front, and I thought the only people who might possibly make something of this crowd would be the Militant Tendency.... I felt for the first time the collective guilt of anyone who has held Cabinet office over the last fifteen years and who has allowed unemployment to rise, and allowed education to remain as it was, and allowed these people to be thrown into despair and apathy and hatred and confusion.'

42. Minkin, *The Contentious Alliance*, p. 196.
43. 7 July 1979.
44. See Callaghan, *Time and Change*, p. 565; Benn, *Conflicts of Interest*, p. 499.
45. See Chapter 3, p. 53.
46. Benn, *Conflicts of Interest*, pp. 496–7, 501, 514.
47. Minkin's *The Contentious Alliance* (Edinburgh 1991) is the definitive refutation of this shibboleth propagated by a good many academics as well as journalists and centre-right Labour and SDP politicians. For an earlier and less sympathetic (to the union leaders' role) argument, see also Leo Panitch, 'Socialist Renewal and the Problem of the Labour Party', *The Socialist Register 1988*.
48. Richard Evans and Christian Tyler, 'The Unions and the Labour Party', *Financial Times*, 26 September 1979.
49. John Cole, 'Year of Destiny for Denis and Roy', *The Observer*, 3 February 1980.
50. Benn, *Conflicts of Interest*, pp. 531. Cf. Peter Shore, *Leading the Left*, pp. 130, 132; Minkin, p. 197, n.17.
51. Minkin, *Contentious Alliance*, pp. 416–18.
52. This is the central theme of Minkin's treatment of the TULV in *The Contentious Alliance*. See esp. chs 7, 15 and 16.
53. Minkin, *Contentious Alliance*, p. 197.
54. Benn, *Conflicts of Interest*, p. 592.
55. Francis Prideaux, *CLPD Trade Union Sub-committee Secretary's Report*, Annual General Meeting, December 1979, p. 1. In pointing to this, the report was not at all romanticising the overall degree of support. Indeed it

was a very sober and cautious survey which also emphasised that the situation within the Engineering unions, where the right-wing executive 'gives enviable regular support to our campaign's political opponents ... [and takes] every opportunity to resist the reforms which we seek ... remains the central hinge of our eventual success or failure'.

56. Minkin, p. 198.
57. Richard Evans and Christian Tyler, 'The Unions and the Labour Party', *Financial Times*, 26 September 1979. For a fascinating account of the behaviour of Jim Murray, a key swing voter on the AUEW delegation at the time, see 'The Shoppie on the Scottswood Road', Chapter 3 of Andy McSmith's *Faces of Labour*, London 1996.
58. Francis Prideaux, *CLPD Trade Union Sub-committee Secretary's Report*, p. 2.
59. Minkin, *Contentious Alliance*, pp. 198–9.
60. *Report of the Labour Party Commission of Enquiry*, London 1980. For a detailed breakdown of the submissions, see Seyd, *The Rise and Fall*, pp. 124–6.
61. *Peace, Jobs, Freedom*, Statement by the National Executive Committee to the Special Conference, Wembley, 31 May 1981. For an excellent overview of economic policy-making after 1979 see Wickham-Jones, *Economic Strategy and the Labour Party*, pp. 167ff.
62. 1980 *LPCR*, p. 266. The quotations that follow in this paragraph may be found at pp. 130, 170 and 113 of the 1980 *LPCR*.
63. *The Times*, 31 August 1980.
64. Quoted in Shaw, *Discipline and Discord*, p. 251.
65. Quoted from the transcript of the BBC television documentary 'The Wilderness Years', Fine Arts Productions, 1995.
66. See Shaw, *Discipline and Discord*, p. 250.
67. Peter Jenkins, 'Labour Pushed a Step Nearer to Disintegration', *The Guardian*, 2 November 1980.
68. Raymond Williams, *Democracy & Parliament*, with an introduction by Peter Thatchell, a Socialist Society pamphlet, London 1982, pp. 12–13.
69. 1980 *LPCR*, p. 140.
70. Quoted from the transcript of the BBC television documentary 'The Wilderness Years', Fine Arts Productions, 1995.
71 1980 *LPCR*, pp. 143, 200.
72. Quoted from the transcript of the BBC television documentary 'The Wilderness Years', Fine Arts Productions, 1995.
73. Lewis Minkin, 'The 1980 Labour Party Conference: The Battle of Blackpool', *British Politics Group Newsletter*, no. 22, Autumn 1980, p. 2.
74. 1980 *LPCR*, p. 13.
75. Ibid, p. 31. In so far as Moss Evans had taken the same position on the control of the Manifesto, Benn did not spare him either: ' ... there is no point coming in with a big block vote ... and demanding policies, and then using the same block vote in such a way as to permit the policies you demand to be vetoed by Parliamentarians who are not accountable to this Conference'. In the event, Evans cast the TGWU vote in favour of the NEC as his delegation had been mandated to do, but the GMWU cast its vote

against, as it did on all three constitutional reforms on intra-party democracy.

76. 1980 *LCPR*, pp. 194–5.
77. See Kogan and Kogan, *The Battle*, p. 101. Benn only learned of this from Clive Jenkins on 13 April 1981, two weeks after he had declared his decision to contest the deputy leadership. He wrote in his diary that night: 'I had suspected there had been a general understanding but I had not realised exactly what had been agreed. It is scandalous that at the Conference in Wembley, when they were all arguing for a new franchise, they should have secretly agreed that the franchise would not be used, and now they are acutely embarrassed by what has happened.' *The End of an Era*, pp. 120–21.
78. Both these quotations are from the transcript of the BBC television documentary 'The Wilderness Years', Fine Arts Productions, 1995.
79. This was the phrase used by Benn in *A New Course for Labour*, Institute for Workers' Control, 1976, p. 10.
80. Peter Shore, *Leading the Left*, London 1993, p. 139.
81. Ibid, pp. 138–9; Clive Jenkins, *All Against the Collar*, London 1990, p. 188; and Ian Mikardo, *Backbencher*, London 1988, pp. 203–4.
82. This quotation is from the transcript of the BBC television documentary 'The Wilderness Years', Fine Arts Productions, 1995.
83. Heffer appears to have intended, immediately after the 1980 Conference, that Benn and he would run for leader and deputy leader respectively in a new electoral college. (See Benn, *The End of an Era*, pp. 36–7.) But once Foot was elected, Heffer apparently abandoned that idea, later explaining that he thought the left should enter a period of 'consolidation'. Unfortunately, Heffer's own subsequent account of these events is very thin, and even confuses the dates of the 1980 and 1981 Party Conferences. See his *Labour's Future: Socialist or SDP Mark II?*, London 1986, p. 28.
84. Benn, *The End of an Era*, p. 35.
85. *The End of an Era*, p. 43.

9. The Defeat of the Labour New Left

1. Hilary Wainwright describes how 'socialists with a few exceptions, everywhere (those over thirty, at least), inside the Labour Party and outside, felt some elation at the news of his election' (*Labour: A Tale of Two Parties*, p. 82). One of those exceptions was Ken Livingstone (still largely unknown until he burst on the stage with Labour's GLC election victory in May 1981), who took the view at the time that it would have been better if the PLP had elected Healey over Foot because that would have 'clarified matters' for the new left. In 1983, he adopted a similar position in preferring Hattersley to win over Kinnock (interview with Ken Livingstone, June 1987).
2. Michael Foot, 'The Labour Party and Parliamentary Democracy', *Guardian*, 10 September 1981.

3. Raymond Williams, 'An Alternative Politics', *The Socialist Register 1981*, p. 1.
4. For accounts of the labyrinthine complexity that governed the voting and the outcome at Wembley, see Kogan and Kogan, *The Battle*, pp. 94–7; Seyd, *Rise and Fall*, pp. 118–21; and Minkin, *Contentious Alliance*, pp. 200–202.
5. Quoted in Benn, *The End of an Era*, p. 83.
6. As was indicated by the fact that Militant candidates lost support in the constituency section votes for the National Executive at the 1980 Party Conference. See Minkin, 'The 1980 Labour Party Conference', p. 2.
7. 'Shore Rounds on the "Wreckers" of the Bennite Left', *The Times*, 24 March 1981; Cf. Kogan and Kogan, *The Battle*, pp. 102–3; and Panitch, 'Socialist Renewal', p. 361.
8. See 'Foot Under Pressure to Move Against Left', *Sunday Times*, 26 April 1981.
9. Benn, *The End of an Era*, p. 96.
10. Jon Lansman, *The Future of the Rank and File Mobilising Committee*, CLPD discussion paper, February 1981.
11. Ibid., emphasis in original.
12. Quoted in Kogan and Kogan, *The Battle*, p. 106.
13. Quoted in Benn, *The End of an Era*, p. 77.
14. Quoted in ibid., p. 16.
15. Ibid., p. 116; cf. p. 62.
16. *The End of an Era*, pp. 71–2.
17. See Jad Adams, *Tony Benn*, pp. 410–16; Benn, *End of An Era*, pp. 113, 121; Mikardo, *Backbencher*, p. 154; Heffer, *Labour's Future*, pp. 28–9; and John Silkin, *Changing Battlefields*, London 1987, p. 45.
18. *The End of an Era*, pp. 116, 118.
19. Healey, *The Time of My Life*, pp. 482–3.
20. Kogan and Kogan, *The Battle*, p. 110.
21. Interview, October 1986.
22. Quoted in Adams, *Tony Benn*, pp. 412–13.
23. Both quotations are from the transcript of the BBC television documentary 'The Wilderness Years', Fine Arts Productions, 1995.
24. Kogan and Kogan, *The Battle*, p. 113.
25. Benn, *End of an Era*, p. 138.
26. Ibid., p. 120.
27. See ibid., p. 139.
28. Even by 1985 only about 100 had been established (mostly in schools, colleges or local authority establishments) as both the party's national agents and the union leadership either actively discouraged them, or at best only responded passively to such initiatives from activists. This was partly because of the difficulty of fitting them easily into the existing party and union structures. But there was more to it than that. The unions had agreed to them only on the principle that they did not interfere with union work – and this had been embedded in the party's constitution. As Ken Coates plaintively asked at a Sunday-morning CLPD workshop on workplace branches before the 1983 Party Conference: 'How can workplace branches be effective if they don't bring political views to union questions?'
29. Minkin, *Contentious Alliance*, p. 328.

30. In addition to the sources cited in Chapter 7, n.76, see the outstanding study by Daniel Egan, *Relative Autonomy and Local Socialism: The Greater London Council's Local Economic Strategy*, PhD Dissertation, Department of Sociology, Boston College 1994.
31. Hilary Wainwright, *Labour: A Tale of Two Parties*, London 1987, pp. 97, 99.
32. *The Sunday Times*, 30 August 1981.
33. Ken Livingstone, *If Voting Changed Anything*, p. 177.
34. Manifesto Group letter to Ron Hayward, signed by Giles Radice (Chairman), George Robertson (Secretary) and Ken Weetch (Treasurer), 2 November 1981.
35. Peter Tatchell, *The Battle for Bermondsey*, London 1983, pp. 54–5.
36. *The End of an Era*, pp. 181–7.
37. See Robert Harris, *The Making of Neil Kinnock*, London 1984, pp. 69, 170–73.
38. See the detailed account in Shaw, *Discipline and Discord*, pp. 231–43.
39. *NEC Minutes*, 27 October 1982.
40. Shaw, *Discipline and Discord*, pp. 233–4.
41. *NEC Minutes*, 27 October 1982.
42. *New Statesman*, 26 November 1982. On Shore's strategy, see Mark Wickham-Jones, *Economic Strategy and the Labour Party*, London and New York 1996, pp. 108–11.
43. Although this anti-Benn campaign was undertaken in June 1982 under the banner of the TULV in the region, Minkin shows that this was led by a local GMWU official who had no such authority and was reprimanded for it by the national GMWU office. See *Contentious Alliance*, pp. 504–5. Retribution by the Bristol Labour new left was had when Cocks was deselected in 1984. Cocks sought his own retribution in his book, *Labour and the Benn Factor*, London 1989.
44. Tatchell, *The Battle for Bermondsey*, pp. 154–7.
45. The sharpest analysis remains Anthony Barnett's, *Iron Britannia*, London 1983.
46. W. Mishler, M. Hoskins and R. Fitzgerald, 'British Parties in the Balance: A Time-Series Analysis of Long-Term Trends in Labour and Conservative Support', *British Journal of Political Science*, vol. 19, 1989, p. 225.
47. W.L. Miller, 'There was No Alternative: The British General Election of 1983', *Parliamentary Affairs*, vol. 38, 1984, p. 373.
48. Ibid., p. 376.
49. Ibid., p. 383. This is essentially what Benn argued in his own post-mortem in *The Guardian*, 20 June 1983. Benn, characteristically, wanted to see a way forward. He thought it was significant that 8.5 million people still voted Labour given that Mrs Thatcher, with enormous support from the media, had insisted that the choice this 'historic election' offered was between 'two totally different ways of life', the prize being 'no less than the chance to banish from our land the dark, divisive clouds of Marxist Socialism'; and had done so despite the fact that Labour's leaders had not for their part made any positive case for socialism. That Labour nevertheless retained the loyalty of so many voters suggested to him that a 'democratic

socialist bridgehead' had been established over the course of the previous years, a base to build on if people could only get a chance to hear a socialist vision and strategy enthusiastically and creatively presented. What Benn forbore to say, in making this rather tortured case, was what he had admitted to himself the night before he voted for Foot as leader: that is, that no one with his political views was ever likely to lead the Labour Party. Meanwhile, Benn's personal sacrifice for the cause of the Labour new left had been immense: he had lost his seat on Labour's Front Bench, the Chairmanship of the NEC's Home Policy Committee and now even his seat in Parliament. Nothing could have shown more clearly than Benn's own fate that the Labour Party was not about to build on any 'socialist bridgeheads' – and that the party establishment didn't play games when confronted by a real threat. Foot's own post-mortem, meanwhile, was astonishingly charitable towards Callaghan's 'damaging' intervention ('an expression of view on the subject about which he felt most deeply'); his most critical remarks by far were still reserved for the new left orientation of the NEC in the 1979–81 period. Nor did he make any mention at all of Benn's or the Labour new left's remarkable discipline during the campaign. See Michael Foot, *Another Heart and Other Pulses*, London 1984, esp. pp. 87, 161.

50. Wickham-Jones, pp. 114–15.
51. Benn, *The End of an Era*, p. 296.
52. Hobsbawm's interventions in this period are collected in his *Politics for a Rational Left: Political Writing 1977–88*, London 1989.
53. Most notoriously expressed by Patrick Seyd in his 'Bennism without Benn', *New Socialist*, May 1985. Excellent accounts of this realignment are given in Heffernan and Marqusee, *Defeat from the Jaws of Victory*, esp. pp. 62ff.; and Eric Shaw, *The Labour Party Since 1979*, London 1994, pp. 160–66.
54. Labour Coordinating Committee, *Reconstruction: How the Labour Party – and the Left – Can Win*, March 1984.
55. Interview with Ken Livingstone, June 1987.
56. Donald Sassoon, *One Hundred Years of Socialism*, London 1996, p. 692.
57. Quoted in Benn, *The End of an Era*, p. 308.
58. Eric Shaw, *The Labour Party Since 1979*, London 1994, p. 163.
59. The number of individual CLPD members fell from 1,203 in 1982 to 668 in 1984 to 474 in 1986. Over the same period, CLP affiliations fell from 153 to 101 to 68; and trade union branch affiliations fell from 105 to 77 to 43. See Seyd, *The Rise and Fall*, Table 4.2, p. 87.

10. Disempowering Activism

1. Raymond Williams, 'Mining the Meaning: Key Words in the Miners' Strike', *New Socialist*, no. 5, 1985, p. 7, cited in Andrew J. Richards, *Miners on Strike: Class Solidarity and Division in Britain*, Oxford and New York 1996, p. 231.
2. Raphael Samuel, 'Introduction', in Samuel, Barbara Bloomfield and Guy

Boanas, eds, *The Enemy Within: Pit Villages and the Miners' Strike of 1984–5*, London 1986, pp. 6–10.

3. See esp. N. Dolby, *Norma Dolby's Diary: An Account of the Great Miners' Strike*, London 1987; and the testimony of Iris Preston and Barbara Bloomfield in Samuel et al., *The Enemy Within*.

4. Heffernan and Marqusee, *Defeat from the Jaws of Victory*, p. 49. See also Richards, *Miners on Strike*, pp. 140–44.

5. See Crick, *March of Militant*, pp. 261–2.

6. '[In the GLC] the Labour left considerably democratised the state policy process. Standing Orders which mandated a strict, hierarchical line of communication were changed to allow greater access for councillors to lower level officers and vice versa. Committee chairs were also given almost complete autonomy over the workings of their committees ... a number of committees created forums for labour and community organisations to criticise and advocate policies, thereby placing even more pressure on GLC officers (as well as Labour councillors themselves) to follow Labour's lead.' Daniel Egan, *Relative Autonomy and Local Socialism*, p. 216.

7. Ibid., p. 250. This support took a variety of forms: assistance to trade union support units to defend jobs and develop alternative production plans for firms facing layoffs or closure; centres for the unemployed; assistance for organisations working on women's and ethnic minorities employment issues, including domestic work; workplace childcare projects; workers' cooperatives; community technology networks – all integrated into one of the most remarkable political documents of the period, the *London Industrial Strategy* of 1985.

8. Andrew Richards's study of class consciousness in the miners' strike quotes several miners: 'I think why we didn't get a lot of support was ... people were frightened ... very frightened, because the Government had proved that they intended to win and never mind what it cost.' 'Why we didn't get that support ... is because ... there was people ... that were employed who knew that if they didn't play ball with the employers they would be pushed out.' 'I believe people were looking after their own jobs – they were threatened with "if you do support the miners with industrial action, you could close your own factory down".' *Miners on Strike*, p. 138.

9. Benn's warning, at the British left's 'Debate of the Decade' in 1980, not to take the use of revolutionary rhetoric too seriously, should be borne in mind in relation to a book like Martin Adeney's and John Lloyd's *The Miners' Strike*, London 1986, which is entirely premised on taking Scargill's designation of the strike as 'political' as proof that he had insurrectionary intentions. See Wainwright's excellent criticism of this interpretation in her *Labour: A Tale of Two Parties*, pp. 236ff.

10. Samuel et al., *The Enemy Within*, p. 33.

11. See Seumas Milne, *The Enemy Within: The MI5, Maxwell and the Scargill Affair*, London 1994.

12. *The Times*, 10 December 1985.

13. Neil Kinnock, 'Reforming the Labour Party', *Contemporary History Record*, vol. 8, no. 3, 1994, p. 537.

14. Lewis Minkin, *The Contentious Alliance*, Edinburgh 1991, p. 400.

15. House of Commons Public Information Office, personal communication.
16. Patrick Seyd and Paul Whiteley, 'Labour's Renewal Strategy', in Smith and Spear, p. 31.
17. Minkin, *The Contentious Alliance*, p. 409.
18. Kinnock confirms this in his account of the Policy Review following the 1987 election defeat: 'The Policy Review Process was also reinforced periodically by using the Shadow Communications Agency under Philip Gould to give presentations which emphasised Labour's strengths and weaknesses and assisted in the efforts to sustain the movement of the review in the desired direction. I would not impugn Philip Gould's integrity by saying that more emphasis was put on some things rather than others, but I saw to it that meetings were conducted in such a way as to make people remember the weaknesses far longer than they remembered the strengths.' 'Reforming the Labour Party', p. 544.
19. Quoted in Richard Heffernan and Mike Marqusee, *Defeat from the Jaws of Victory: Inside Kinnock's Labour Party*, London 1992, p. 211. According to Colin Hughes and Patrick Wintour in *Labour Rebuilt: The New Model Party*, London 1990 pp. 60–61, the crucial document of this kind was 'Labour and Britain in the 1990s', presented to the NEC and Shadow Cabinet in November 1987.
20. After 1989, therefore, Kinnock saw to it that 'responsibility for drafting the later Policy Review Reports ... was vested in smaller groups in which the influence of senior front-benchers and leadership aides was paramount'. Shaw, *The Labour Party Since 1979*, p. 111.
21. John Rentoul, *Tony Blair*, London 1995, pp. 344–5.
22. One of the points on which all commentators seem to agree is the uselessness of 'Labour Listens', however high-minded its original intentions. See for example, Hughes and Wintour in *Labour Rebuilt*, pp. 98–103, and Heffernan and Marqusee, *Defeat from the Jaws of Victory*, pp. 215–16.
23. Heffernan and Marqusee, *Defeat from the Jaws of Victory*, p. 115.
24. Typically, the whole affiliated membership of the union was counted as being in favour of the position taken at the conference by the majority of the union's conference delegates meeting beforehand. Normally the delegates would consider themselves bound by what they understood a majority of the membership to support, although there was often room for disagreement because the 'composite' motions voted on at the Party Conference would not necessarily match those voted on at the preceding conference of the union.
25. Larry Whitty, speech to the 1987 Labour Party Conference, quoted in Patrick Seyd and Paul Whiteley, *Labour's Grass Roots: The Politics of Party Membership*, Oxford 1992, p. 201.
26. Seyd and Whiteley, *Labour's Grass Roots*, p. 201.
27. The concession was the so-called 'levy plus' formula, according to which members of trade unions affiliated to the party by paying the political levy could have a special individual membership status on payment of a small additional subscription and on this basis, take part as individuals in ballots to select party candidates. This was later dropped under Blair's leadership, so that only ordinary individual members could vote.
28. The majority was 3.1 per cent of the total vote. As Rentoul points out, the

change would have been defeated by general opposition to OMOV among the large unions but for a split in the delegation of the Manufacturing, Science and Finance (MSF) union. The union conference had voted against OMOV but the delegation was persuaded to abstain, ostensibly because the resolution from the NEC proposing the change also covered the introduction of women-only shortlists in a number of safe Labour seats, to which some of the MSF delegation were strongly committed. See Rentoul, *Tony Blair*, pp. 337–9.

29. Andy McSmith, *John Smith*, London 1994, p. 220.
30. Ibid. One of them was Colin Byrne, the former deputy to Peter Mandelson in the Campaigns and Communications Directorate. He wrote a letter to *The Guardian* which clearly expressed the professional modernisers' frustration: '. . . what is his [Smith's] record, or that of a handful of centrally-placed right-wing Shadow Cabinet members and trade union leaders who are about to emerge as his campaign managers and backers, on the radical reforms Labour . . . must go on making if it is not to tread water, sink and die? What did the right ever do about Militant during the bitter years up to Neil Kinnock taking over? . . . What did they do about Europe? . . . What is Smith's view on trade union reform? What is his view on electoral reform? After years of intense debate in the party, ask yourself why we don't know these things . . .' (quoted in Andy McSmith, *John Smith*, pp. 221–2).
31. Ibid., p. 239.
32. Running against John Prescott and Margaret Beckett, Blair won with 60.5 per cent of the votes cast by 327 Labour MPs and MEPs; 58.2 per cent of the 172,356 votes cast by individual party members; and 52.3 per cent of the 779,426 votes cast by levy-paying members of trade unions and socialist societies. For comparison, in 1983, in pre-OMOV days, Kinnock won the leadership against Roy Hattersley, Eric Heffer and Peter Shore, with 49.3 per cent of the PLP vote, 68 per cent of the CLP vote, 72.6 per cent of the trade union vote; and in 1981 Tony Benn lost the deputy leadership in the run-off with Denis Healey with 34.1 per cent of the PLP vote, 60.8 per cent of the CLP vote, and 37.5 per cent of the trade union vote.
33. Henry M. Drucker, *Doctrine and Ethos in the Labour Party*, London 1979.
34. Part of the reason for this is that Blair joined the Labour Party in London in 1975 as it was entering into a period of bitter internal conflict, and when the labour movement was ceasing to be as representative of the whole working class as it had once felt and, in some respects, been. At the same time, in his early years in the party he seems to have been peculiarly cut off from what was still positive and morally compelling in the old party ethos; see Rentoul, *Tony Blair*, especially Chapters 3–4.
35. Seyd and Whitely, *Labour's Grass Roots*, pp. 54, 101.
36. Joy Johnson's departure as Director of Campaigns and Media was seen as being due to 'differences with key figures in the "moderniser" camp', and as aggravating 'tensions about centralisation of authority, as power has shifted from party headquarters at Walworth Road, south London . . . to Mr Blair's office and the new party media centre at Millbank Tower' (Seumas Milne and Rebecca Smithers in *The Guardian*, 22 January 1995).

Roland Wales, who resigned as Director of Policy in October 1995, subsequently wrote an article in the *New Statesman* criticising the leadership for downplaying the large expenditures that would in reality be entailed in dealing with the renewal of the country's infrastructure for which it was calling; he was then described by 'a senior Labour official' as having been 'left out of policy formation when he worked for the Labour Party and from what he said today you can see why ... His views were not taken seriously.' (*Guardian*, 2 February 1996).

37. Besides Mandelson and Hewitt the policy-making group included Roger Liddle (a former adviser to Bill Rodgers, one of the SDP's founding figures); Geoff Mulgan, the founder and director of Demos, a non-party think-tank; Derek Scott, a City-based economist and former adviser to Denis Healey as Chancellor of the Exchequer in the 1970s; and Sir Nicholas Monck, a former permanent secretary at the Department of Employment. As the press noted, none of Blair's Shadow Cabinet colleagues, nor the deputy leader, was included (Michael White, *Guardian*, 15 July 1995). A spokesman for Blair's office maintained that these were merely some individuals who had offered assistance on an ad hoc basis to 'write sections of speeches and background papers' (*Guardian*, 17 July 1995). Patricia Hewitt said their function was to help write speeches and 'bounce ideas' (interview, 2 August 1995).

38. *Guardian*, 8 August 1995. Sawyer added that he had also taken members of the National Executive Committee to the Cranfield Institute of Management to discuss the role of the committee, presaging proposals he would later make for changing its formal role to ensure that it served, rather than rivalled, a Labour government in office.

39. The figures are from an official Labour Party survey of a thousand new members in May 1955, reported by Anthea Davey in *Red Pepper*, February 1996, pp. 22–3. Ten per cent of the new members were in blue-collar jobs and 47 per cent in white-collar jobs; 9 per cent were unemployed, 9 per cent were students, and 25 per cent were retired.

40. Interview with Martin Kettle in *The Guardian*, 13 March 1995.

41. Using a less absolute conception of 'ownership' it could have been argued that 'on the basis of the common ownership of the means of production (etc.)' could mean leaving industry under private management but subject to much more rigorous regulation in the common interest. In early 1996 Labour's transport spokesperson, Clare Short, would argue on these lines when she refused to commit Labour to buying back privatised railway companies, while still maintaining that this was consistent with a commitment Blair had made at the 1995 Party Conference to a 'publicly owned and publicly accountable railway system'. *Guardian*, 28 May 1995.

42. In 1995 the unions' block vote was weighted at 70 per cent of the total vote cast. Only one union, the Communications Workers, balloted all its members on the issue. Ninety per cent voted for the change, while MORI polls found the same proportion of AEEU (Engineers union) members supporting change, and 85 per cent of trade union members generally, suggesting that in the unions, as in the constituencies, the rank and file were much more sympathetic to the modernisers than to the activists; the

modernisers' strategy had paid off. Constituency parties were not required to ballot their members, but under strong urging from party headquarters 501 did so. The 'turnout' or response rate in the first 133 constituency party ballots averaged 54 per cent; with seventy-nine CLPs still to report results on the eve of the special Conference, the percentage of individual members voting for the new Clause IV was 85.25; in only three of the constituencies that balloted their members was there a majority against change. The unions casting their conference vote against the change were the TGWU, UNISON, RMT, GPMU, NUM, FBU, EPIU, BFAWU, ASLEF and UCATT (data from *The Observer*, 23 April 1995 and *The Guardian*, 29 April 1995).

43. *Guardian*, 1 May 1995. The new Clause IV reads as follows (omitting as far as possible the rather numerous words and phrases that are surplus to its meaning):

> The Labour Party is a democratic socialist party. It believes that ... by ... common endeavour we achieve ... the means to create ... a community in which power, wealth and opportunity are in the hands of the many not the few ... To these ends we work for: a dynamic economy, serving the public interest, in which the enterprise of the market and the rigour of competition are joined with the forces of partnership and cooperation to produce the wealth the nation needs ... with a thriving private sector and high quality public services, where those undertakings essential to the common good are either owned by the public or accountable to them; a just society, which ... nurtures families, promotes equality of opportunity and delivers people from the tyranny of poverty, prejudice and the abuse of power; an open democracy, in which the government is held to account by the people; decisions are taken as far as practicable by the communities they affect; and where fundamental human rights are guaranteed; a healthy environment, which we protect, enhance and hold in trust for future generations.

The new clause did not commit the party to make women equal with men or blacks with whites.

44. Tony Blair announced this in a speech to the annual conference of the GMBU in June 1995 (*Guardian*, 8 June 1995).
45. Interview with Patrick Wintour and Michael White, *Guardian*, 1 May 1995.
46. For a summary of the history of the resistance, and the NEC's decision to impose women-only shortlists on nine constituencies that were refusing to comply with the policy, see *The Guardian*, 25 October 1995.
47. Two would-be male candidates brought a joint case before a tribunal in Leeds, which held that women-only shortlists discriminated against men who were seeking employment as MPs (*Independent*, 9 January 1996).
48. Liz Davies was the partner of Mike Marqusee, co-author of *Defeat from the Jaws of Victory*, a sustained critique of the modernisation of the party under Kinnock, and an editor of *Labour Briefing*, a magazine of the 'workerist' wing of the party's left activists. She was not, as Clare Short persistently insinuated on behalf of the NEC at the 1995 Conference, a Trotskyist or a member of the Militant Tendency. Liz Davies later success-fully sued three fellow borough councillors whose false allegations originally

formed part of the NEC's case against her (*Guardian*, 17 September 1996). A somewhat similar case, not involving women-only shortlists, attracted less publicity because it was dealt with at an earlier stage; in December 1995 the NEC's interview panel, which screens all potential candidates before shortlisting takes place, refused to approve the inclusion in the shortlist for Hemsworth constituency in West Yorkshire of Steve Kemp, a close ally of Arthur Scargill in the NUM, although he had far more nominations from ward parties than any other candidate (*Guardian*, 5 December 1995).

49. Andy McSmith, referring to the period after the Policy Review, in *John Smith*, p. 204.

50. *Guardian*, 8 June 1995.

51. Early in 1996 an internal report for the party's *Party into Power* review asked: 'how can we halt the current drift to constantly inquorate meetings [of NEC committees]?'

52. Dennis Potter, *Seeing the Blossom*, London 1994, p. 14.

53. *New Statesman and Society*, 11 August 1995.

54. The decision in early 1996 of Harriet Harman, a shadow minister, to send her son to an opted-out selective grammar school, gave particular offence, since the party had campaigned successfully throughout the country to stop most schools opting out from the comprehensive system. Resentment against Harman in the PLP threatened to lead to her removal from the Shadow Cabinet in the annual elections due in the autumn of 1996. These were brought forward to July and Harman was re-elected after much pressure had been brought to bear by the leadership. Public criticisms by several left-wing MPs about this pressure in turn led to disciplinary warnings from the Labour Chief Whip. Another issue was the leadership's decision in June, announced without prior consultation with the Scottish and Welsh MPs or the Scottish party executive, to submit plans for a Scottish Parliament and a Welsh Assembly to referenda, which led to the resignation of the party's Scottish affairs spokesman.

55. Roy Hattersley, 'Why Labour is Stumbling', *Independent*, 12 August 1995.

56. *Guardian*, 5 September 1995. In the same interview Blair was also quoted as saying that 'the party had no plans to reduce the trade unions' block vote to below 50 per cent', which the paper called 'a conciliatory gesture to the unions'. The trade unions might be forgiven for being irritated rather than conciliated by this statement, since it was not for the leader to say what plans 'the party' had on this matter (compare Blair's comments about changing the party's name, referred to above).

57. Labour's opinion poll lead over the Conservatives, adjusted for undecided voters, remained fairly steady at about 17 per cent down to the end of 1996, and was still about 13 per cent on the eve of the 1997 election; unlike in 1992, this figure was very close to the actual voting results.

58. Patrick Wintour and Larry Elliott in *The Guardian*, 28 March 1996.

59. Ballots were also sent to 2,600,000 affiliated trade union members, of whom 24 per cent responded, 90 per cent of them voting in favour (*Guardian*, 5 November 1996).

60. The first to be threatened with deselection on these grounds (for allegedly 'heckling at meetings and badgering Mr Blair as he attended a reception' at

the 1996 Party Conference) was the MEP Hugh Kerr, a veteran critic of 'New Labour'. The New Labour leader of the Labour MEPs said: 'He is being made an example of' (*Guardian*, 18 December 1996).

61. *Guardian*, 30 January 1997. Benn lost his seat on the NEC in 1993. Skinner himself was re-elected to it after having been defeated in 1992.

62. The forum is not mentioned in the party's rule book; its membership was listed in the NEC's 1994 (but not its 1995) annual report. In one of several symptomatically curious formulations *Labour into Power* envisaged that after two successive reviews by the Policy Forum policy documents would be published, in advance of the annual conference, by the 'NEC, including NEC members of the JPC' (p. 16).

63. *Labour into Power*, p. 14.

64. In this respect only it contrasted with a pamphlet published in 1996 by the now sedulously Blairite Labour Coordinating Committee, entitled *New Labour: A Stakeholder's Party*, which said that 'Labour should decide in principle that the party programme should only be voted on by a one member one vote ballot of party members and strip out the intermediary role of delegates voting on behalf of branches. The Conference should be used to showcase selected policy themes in Labour's programme ... the Conference should be made up of a mixture of plenary sessions and seminar groups. The plenary sessions will allow Tony Blair and other front-bench colleagues to present their policy themes and policy pronouncements and so shape the news agenda for that day ... Labour's National Executive should not be a policy-making body. Policy should be the preserve of individual members and Labour's Parliamentary Committee [the Shadow Cabinet]'.

65. So much so that pro-Blair commentators who saw themselves as liberals and democrats perceived the grounds of their support becoming uncomfortably narrow, and were spurred to new feats of *pseudo-mock* cynicism. See for example Hugo Young in *The Guardian*, 30 January 1997: on the one hand, 'To reduce [the Conference's] formal policy role is no more than realism, just as reconstructing the National Executive Committee, and redefining it as a cheerleader, is an act of democratic modernity.' On the other, the parties would soon resemble each other 'in becoming steadily more like a commodity; packaged on the basis of market research, sold by marketing methods, drained of dangerous ideological definition, and freed from alternative power-centres with the power to challenge the leadership'. It was 'the politics of the post-socialist millennium, centralist as well as centrist, preoccupied with power more than conviction . . .' (etc.).

66. Ironically, *Labour into Power* rationalised the removal of whatever power Conference delegates had once had to set policy and elect the members of the NEC as giving it, not to the leadership, but to more and different 'stakeholders' in the party, from the party's staff to 'voters and supporters'; it was ironic because by this time the idea of a 'stakeholding economy', after a brief appearance as a modernisers' keyword, had been abandoned.

67. See Chapter 7, pp. 145-6.

68. See Chapter 8, p. 178.

69. *Guardian*, 13 September 1996.

70. And 59 per cent of the public as a whole, according to an ICM poll (*The Observer*, 15 September 1996).
71. Andy McSmith and Peter Kellner, *Observer*, 15 September 1996.
72. David Hencke, *Guardian*, 7 September 1996.
73. In 1995 the sources of Labour Party income were: unions 54.2 per cent, fundraising 18.6 per cent, members 16.0 per cent and 'others' 11.0 per cent (*Guardian*, 7 September 1996). The separate 'Labour Leader's Office Fund', which came to light at the end of 1996, was an additional twist in the story of leadership autonomy. It was apparently in addition to the Leader's Office share (amounting to £324,000 in 1996) of the parliamentary funding (the 'Short' money) received by the opposition front bench, and to the £180,000 also given to the Leader's Office in 1996 by the unions. It was said to have been established in 1995 when 'a faction of the party' – on the National Executive? – objected to party funds being used to finance Blair's campaign to change Clause IV; in December 1996 pledges to it were said to have reached a total of £2 million, almost equal to donations to the party's election fund (*Sunday Times*, 1 December 1996). Business donors may thus have played a significant part in enabling Blair to overcome opposition to remaking the party in ways he – and presumably they – wanted.

11. Tony Blair: The Transition from Socialism to Capitalism

1. The Plant Report, named after its chairman Professor Raymond Plant. The Alternative Vote retains single member constituencies but requires winning candidates to have an absolute majority, through the distribution of the second and third preferences of voters whose first votes were for candidates who came lowest in the first-vote rankings. The Supplementary Vote differs in leaving it up to voters whether or not to indicate other preferences than their first preference.
2. It completed its report in July: see the Report of the Commission on Social Justice, *Social Justice: Strategies for National Survival*, London 1994.
3. John Rentoul, *Tony Blair* , London 1995, p. 247.
4. Seumas Milne, 'My Millbank', a review of Peter Mandelson and Roger Liddle, *The Blair Revolution*, in *London Review of Books*, 18 April 1996, p. 3.
5. The Labour Force Survey data for early 1997 showed unemployment at 2.2 million. Other official measures had lost credibility owing to over thirty Conservative Government redefinitions aimed at minimising the apparent unemployment levels.
6. *Guardian*, 20 March 1997. The evidence of newly-established independent medical testing and the results of appeal procedures against negative decisions showed that relatively few of those claiming sickness benefit were 'work-shy'.
7. *Guardian*, 19 March 1997.
8. The actual work was contracted out to firms of auditors (Peat Marwick etc.)

which expanded dramatically, hiring a wide variety of non-professional staff to do the work; see Michael Powers, *The Audit Explosion*, London 1995.

9. Peter Mandelson and Roger Liddle, *The Blair Revolution: Can New Labour Deliver?*, London 1996, p. 185. As Labour's unchallenged chief spin doctor Mandelson's views on this subject should carry weight.

10. The Borrie Report is actually a comprehensive programme of economic and social reform for national competitiveness.

11. For some of the leading work of Charter 88, see Stuart Weir and Wendy Hall, eds, *Ego Trip: Extra-governmental organisations in the United Kingdom and Their Accountability*, London: The Democratic Audit of the United Kingdom and Charter 88, 1994; and the same authors' *The Untouchables*, Scarman Trust and Human Rights Centre, University of Essex 1996. See also Anthony Barnett, *The Defining Moment*, London: Charter 88, 1995, setting out the constitutional issues at stake in the next general election.

12. From the statement, 'Why Demos?', in Demos's brochure.

13. Interview, 11 August 1995.

14. *The Guardian*'s political commentator Hugo Young claimed that the word 'new' occurred 137 times in Blair's speech to the 1996 Labour Party Conference.

15. I am grateful to Neal Lawson for the information on Nexus's origins and plans described here.

16. *The Need for Nexus*, published by Nexus, 'The *Renewal* Ideas Network', Summer 1996.

17. According to Heffernan and Marqusee, Mandelson once said it would be nice to abolish the Party Conference, but it was not worth the trouble (*Defeat from the Jaws of Victory*, p. 209); in private he made it clear that 'the unions were a nuisance and the sooner they were expelled from Labour headquarters the better' (ibid., p. 218).

18. *The Blair Revolution*, London 1996.

19. Ibid., p. 7.

20. Tony Blair, 'The Rights We Enjoy Reflect the Duties We Owe', The Spectator Lecture, 22 March 1995.

21. Speech to the Labour Party Conference issued by the Conference Media Office, 3 October 1995. The whole speech was a prose poem written in this format.

22. The term originated in debates about corporate governance and applied to the various parties such as employees and suppliers, as well as shareholders, who had an interest or 'stake' in company policy. Will Hutton, who was then *The Guardian*'s assistant editor and leading economic columnist, broadened the concept to one of 'stakeholder capitalism' in his best-selling book, *The State We're In*, first published in March 1995. It may be surmised that Blair's speech-writers, to whom Hutton had ample access, were not unaffected by his thinking; but Blair's Singapore speech used the narrower expression 'stakeholder economy', and in general New Labour conspicuously refrained from endorsing Hutton's general ideas, which argued for a British version of 'Rhineland' capitalism, with a radically re-regulated financial sector and far-reaching social and constitutional reforms.

23. Tony Blair, speech to the Singapore business community, 8 January 1996.

24. Ibid.

25. The Spectator Lecture, 22 March 1995.

26. It was noteworthy that in his last pre-election annual conference speech in October 1996, Blair made no reference to stakeholding, but only to being a united national 'team' in the global race. It is clear that whatever other influences are at work on New Labour as a whole, the most important source of Blair's politics is a relatively conservative version of Christian ethics.

27. Tony Blair, 'Faith in the City – Ten Years On', speech at Southwark Cathedral, 29 January 1996.

28. The retired MP Leo Abse, in his sometimes insightful, if excessively hostile and dogmatic, 'psycho-profile' of Blair, sees him as being unable to confront real social oppositions and traces this to a deep-seated pathology stemming from his relationship with his father (*The Man Behind the Smile: Tony Blair and the Politics of Perversion*, London 1996).

29. Henry Porter, 'Zealous Moderate', *Guardian*, 18 July 1995 (emphasis added).

30. Ibid. 'Quangos' are 'quasi non-governmental organisations', appointive and largely unaccountable bodies whose number and membership (consisting largely of Conservative supporters) increased dramatically under the Thatcher years, to the point where they had many more members than the total of the country's elected councillors, and were responsible for spending roughly as much money.

31. Andy McSmith, *Faces of Labour*, p. 295.

32. Tony Blair, 'The Flavour of Success', based on a speech made on 5 July 1995 to the Fabian Society, *Guardian*, 6 July 1995.

33. Gordon Brown, 'Labour's Macroeconomic Framework', speech 17 May 1995.

34. The third Maastricht criterion, that public debt should not be more than 60 per cent of GDP, Britain was well placed to meet. Mandelson emphasises the benefits of EMU, while acknowledging that without much bigger subsidies for poorer regions EMU 'could soon set up intolerable social and political strains that might undermine the legitimacy of both the single currency and the EU as a whole' (Mandelson and Liddle, *The Blair Revolution*, p. 179), and says the decision whether to join the EMU 'should be a pragmatic one. We should weigh the costs of staying out against the risks of participation . . .' (p. 170).

35. Colin Hay, 'That was Then, This is Now: The Revision of Policy in the "Modernisation" of the British Labour Party, 1992–96', paper presented to the Political Studies Association Conference, University of Ulster, 8–10 April 1997, pp. 14–15. See also Mark Wickham-Jones's careful study, 'The Ties that Bind: Blair's Search for Business Credibility', unpublished paper, Department of Politics, University of Bristol.

36. Tony Blair, speech to the British American Chamber of Commerce, New York, 11 April 1996.

37. Tony Blair, speech to the Annual Conference of the Federation of Small Businesses, 29 March 1996; and *Sunday Times*, 22 December 1996.

38. Gordon Brown, 'Labour's Tax Principles', speech 20 November 1995; at the 1996 Party Conference he reiterated the aim in terms which suggested it could be policy within the next parliament.

39. Tony Blair, speech to the CBI, *Guardian*, 14 November 1995; and *Sunday Times*, 22 December 1996.

40. Tony Blair, speech to the Scottish Labour Party Conference, 8 March 1996.

41. 'Senior sources confirmed ... that Brown saw the move both as a revenue-raiser and a powerful signal that a Blair government would "govern as New Labour from day one".' *The Sunday Times*, 9 March 1997.

42. Speech, 3 October 1995.

43. Brian Wilson MP, in a letter to all prospective investors in the privatised railways, 17 November 1995.

44. Clare Short, Labour's transport spokeswoman, referring to Railtrack, in a speech reported in *The Independent*, 30 March 1996. Other casualties included a delay in the promised abolition of the Assisted Places Scheme in private schools, the spending of local government balances from the sale of council housing (also subject to postponement), and 'green' plans for subsidising home insulation and other energy-saving schemes.

45. *The Blair Revolution*, p. 108.

46. Speech to the Scottish Labour Party, 8 March 1996.

47. Noel Thompson, 'Supply Side Socialism: The Political Economy of New Labour', *New Left Review*, no. 216, March–April 1996, pp. 53–4.

48. *The Observer*, 19 November 1995.

49. Cited by Naomi Klein in *The Toronto Star*, 7 April 1997; she went on to comment: 'Clearly, Labour is about "labor" the way ... Listermint mouthwash is about "letting your voice be heard". Blair's is not a labor party, but a labor-brand party, a sort of labor-scented party, with the appearance of egalitarian principles little more than a brand asset.'

50. *Guardian*, 11 November 1996. Labour would sign up to the existing provisions of the Social Chapter covering works councils and parental leave but would resist extending Qualified Majority Voting to any new policy area, including social security or worker representation on company boards of directors.

51. One of Leo Abse's shrewder observations is the way Blair's too frequent claims to feel 'passionately' about some policy issue betray a lack of passion (*The Man Behind the Smile*, p. 68). What he clearly did feel passionate about was getting out of opposition and into power; whenever he said this he struck no false notes.

52. Tony Blair, speech to the Singapore business community, 8 January 1996; and 'Faith in the City – Ten Years On', speech at Southwark Cathedral, 29 January 1996.

53. Labour Party estimates of the potential yield of such a tax were initially reported as £1 billion, but had risen to over £3 billion by late 1996.

54. Preview of speech to the National Association of Schoolmasters Union of Women Teachers at Glasgow, reported in *The Guardian*, 11 April 1996. It fell to the former Prime Minister Lord Callaghan to urge that whatever Gordon Brown might say before the election, he must be prepared to meet

'a big bill' to restore and improve state education (*Guardian*, 16 October 1996).

55. Labour's education proposals are contained in 'Diversity and Excellence', published in May 1995, and 'Excellence for Everyone', published in December 1995.

56. According to Labour's 1995 policy document, 'Renewing the NHS', the proportion of the NHS budget spent on administration had risen by over 100 per cent, and spending on managerial and administrative staff by £1 billion, as a result of the internal market introduced in 1990. Top managers alone now cost an additional £450 million a year, and £70 million a year was being spent on cars.

57. *Guardian*, 1 November 1996.

58. Both fundholders and hospital trust managers at their annual conferences treated Labour's shadow health ministers with striking hostility and contempt. Margaret Beckett stood up to them. When asked, after her rude treatment at the NHS Trust Federation's annual conference, to which she had been invited to outline Labour's plans, 'if Labour could work with health managers and directors who apparently disagreed so violently with the party's policy, [she] said: "That is a matter for them to do as they see fit"'(*Guardian*, 14 September 1995). Subsequent shadow health ministers were much less robust.

59. 'Renewing the NHS', p. 20. As the members of the boards were also to be drawn from 'people with experience in health and social care' and 'those with the expertise to oversee a large organisation', these bodies were not to become representative either.

60. Hay, 'That was Then, This is Now', p. 10.

61. Details of Labour's official proposals are contained in *Security in Retirement*, 1996; counter-proposals calling for raising the standard state pension, re-indexing it to average earnings, and restoring the State Earnings Related Pension Scheme (also emasculated by the Conservatives) are contained in Peter Townsend and Alan Walker, *New Directions for Pensions*, Nottingham: Spokesman/European Labour Forum, 1995.

62. Tony Blair, the John Smith Memorial Lecture, 7 February 1996. Blair repeatedly made clear his personal opposition to proportional representation, on the grounds that it gave too much power to small parties, although early in 1996, in what looked like a kite-flying exercise, he was reported (*Guardian*, 19 March), as having shifted to tentative support for the Alternative Vote.

63. Cf. Tony Travers, 'Hollowed Halls', *Guardian*, 5 March 1997.

64. What Blair said in his Smith Memorial Lecture was: 'The first right of a citizen in any mature democracy should be the right to information … Why, apart from obvious exceptions like national security, should people not know what is available on file about them? It is a great irony that in a democracy where people have increased information about almost everything else, they often cannot find out the simplest thing from government. If trust in the people means anything then there can be no argument against a Freedom of Information Act which will give people rights to public information.' What is the meaning of 'public' here? Robert Hazell, a former

civil servant and director of the independent research centre, the Constitution Unit, thought that experience elsewhere showed that without a 'ministerial champion', whom New Labour showed no intention of appointing, there would be no genuine Freedom of Information Act (*Guardian*, 21 October 1996).

65. In his Smith Memorial Lecture, 7 February 1996, Blair endorsed the idea that 'if [note: not when] there was a move to an elected second Chamber, provision for people of a particularly distinguished position or record could be made', adding that 'we are masters of our own rules and procedure'.

66. The agreement also covered two important procedural changes: first, that the committee stages of constitutional bills need no longer be taken in the full House of Commons, thus removing the threat that a Labour government would have to choose between the constitutional package and many other bills; and second, that unfinished legislative business need not fall but could be carried over from one Parliament to another.

67. Over 60 per cent of people polled said they supported PR in principle, but this figure fell to 50 per cent in exit polls at the 1992 election, suggesting that PR might well not carry the day without Labour's support; and Robin Cook, a supporter of PR, was careful to tell journalists that a bare majority for change in the referendum would not be enough to make a Labour government give it enough priority to become law.

68. Blair endorsed the American slogan of 'zero tolerance' for crime and let it be known that he did not encourage beggars by giving them anything. Straw wanted 'threatening' unemployed 'squeegee merchants' off the streets. David Blunkett and Tony Blair declared themselves in favour of restoring school uniforms to re-establish a 'sense of identity and discipline'.

69. The known views of prospective Conservative candidates for the 1997 election indicated that the parliamentary Conservative Party in defeat was likely to move still further to the right. See the *Economist*, 4 October 1996.

70. 'Opposition to the EU "government from Brussels" and German domination as it is characterised has ceased to be a crankish issue confined to the fringes ... a virulent nationalism ... looks increasingly like the Right's best weapon ...' Will Hutton, 'Drawing up New Terms of engagement', *Observer*, 28 April 1996.

71. On the analytic case for this option see Colin Hay, 'Anticipating Accommodations, Accommodating Anticipations: The Appeasement of Capital in the "Modernisation" of the British Labour Party', *Politics and Society*, vol. 25, no. 1, 1997.

12. Beyond Parliamentary Socialism

1. Karl Marx, 'The Class Struggles in France' (1850), in Karl Marx and Frederick Engels, *Selected Works*, London 1951, p. 129.
2. Norberto Bobbio, 'The Upturned Utopia', *New Left Review* 177, September/October 1989, p. 39.

3. Fritz W. Scharpf, *Crisis and Choice in European Social Democracy*, Ithaca 1991.

4. Donald Sassoon, in *One Hundred Years of Socialism*, London 1996, p. 702. Sassoon's judgement that the Labour new left's defeat was inevitable because of its 'profound conservatism' on both the constitution and on international issues is not a 'polemical exaggeration' but wrong – as Sassoon himself half recognises when he acknowledges that Benn (who, he accepts, was *the* leader of the Labour new left) was not a constitutional conservative but a radical democratiser (and, as it happens, a proponent of a written constitution, which Sassoon says the Labour new left opposed). Sassoon also appears in this passage to deride the Labour new left's opposition to the European Community, whose undemocratic, capitalist character he himself later criticises (p. 770), adding that 'to create [alternative, 'social-democratic'] European institutions and norms . . . will be a momentous enterprise whose outcome is uncertain'. In this light, and in contrast with Sassoon's silence with regard to how this momentous enterprise might be tackled, the position of the Labour new left in the 1970s looks quite clear-sighted and practical.

5. Ibid., p. 505.

6. In general, the onus is on left-inclined critics of the Labour new left to say what should be done about globalisation, as opposed to just being 'aware' of it. In a broadly approving commentary on New Labour's 'language' Sassoon says that it cannot rest content with 'the supine endorsement of the neo-liberal glorification of the market', and approvingly quotes Keynes as saying that 'capitalism is a beast to be tamed', but does not explore the problems involved in doing this (*Observer*, 24 November 1996). Another case in point is Eric Hobsbawm, a former critic of the Labour new left who makes globalisation a central theme of his remarkable survey, *Age of Extremes*, London 1995; he gives a pessimistic account of its impact on democratic politics (pp. 424–32 and 578–85) but declares that he has no solutions to offer (p. 568).

7. Among European socialists the Labour new left was particularly admired for its combativeness and political creativity. Even in 1984 the Swedish sociologist Goran Therborn could still call on Neil Kinnock to 'take care of this amazing socialist combativeness in the British Labour Party, so different from the demoralised gloom nearly everywhere else' (Goran Therborn, 'Britain Left Out', in James Curran, ed., *The Future of the Left*, London 1984, p. 7).

8. Lewis Minkin, *The Contentious Alliance*, Edinburgh 1991, p. 130.

9. For a vivid, but ultimately unresolved analysis of this problem, as presented by the 1988 Rover factory strike at Cowley, in Oxford, see David Harvey, 'Militant Particularism and Global Ambition: The Conceptual Politics of Place, Space and Environment in the Work of Raymond Williams', *Social Text*, no. 42, 1995, pp. 69–98.

10. For a survey of the practical problems involved see Hilary Wainwright's concluding chapter to Sheila Rowbotham, Lynne Segal and Hilary Wainwright, *Beyond the Fragments*, London 1979 – an analysis that stands up remarkably well twenty years later.

11. See Aram Eisenschitz and Jamie Gough, *The Politics of Local Economic Policy*, London 1993, pp. 75–6.

12. But for an example of how creatively some new left theorists were thinking about democracy see Raymond Williams, 'An Alternative Politics', in Ralph Miliband and John Saville, eds, *Socialist Register 1981*, London 1981, pp. 1–10.

13. The Labour new left's critics have not done any better in this respect. For example Eric Shaw, in his generally outstanding studies of the Labour Party, criticises reselection of MPs for having transferred so much power to local activists that the party became 'paralysed', since 'a party ... requires a degree of internal order and centralised direction' and a leadership able to respond flexibly to 'external challenges' (*The Labour Party Since 1979*, pp. 22–3). Leaving aside the question of whether the degree of power that reselection gave to local activists was really incompatible with these requirements, it is noteworthy that later in the book (p. 220) Shaw laments the loss of incentives for activism that the post-1983 reforms have entailed, because 'a core group of activists constitutes the driving force for recruiting, organising and motivating a wider involved membership'. Many of Labour's 'modernisers', of course, would not see any problem, as they want a wider membership but not an involved one.

14. The phrase is from Marx's epitaph for the Paris Commune of 1870: 'It was essentially a working-class government, the produce of the struggle of the producing against the appropriating class, the political form at last discovered under which to work out the economic emancipation of labour' (Karl Marx, *The Civil War in France*, in Marx and Engels, *Selected Works*, p. 473).

15. See e.g. Kevin Davey, 'The Impermanence of New Labour', in Mark Perryman, ed., *The Blair Agenda*, London 1996, pp. 76–99.

16. Sassoon, *One Hundred Years of Socialism*, pp. 58–9.

17. For a revealing review of these controversies see Pam Woodall, 'The World Economy', in the *Economist*, 28 September 1996.

18. Hilary Wainwright's comment on the Labour left's situation throughout its history is painfully apt: ' ... it has no independent access to the public. Its message comes out often only through the attacks made on it by the leadership – like sending prison letters through a revengeful censor', *Labour: A Tale of Two Parties*, London 1987, p. 58. Notably, it was when Tony Benn proposed a new media policy that the media, egged on by his bitterest opponents, turned the full weight of their resources against him. See Chapter 3, pp. 59–61 and 64–5.

19. Such a policy is less hard to define than the media proprietors would have us believe; significant elements of it already exist in the legislation and practice of many western countries. For valuable sketches of a democratic media regime see John Keane, *The Media and Democracy*, Cambridge 1991, Chapter 6; and *21st Century Media: Shaping the Democratic Vision*, the Media Manifesto of the Campaign for Press and Broadcasting Freedom, London 1996.

20. And by one kind of theorist against another; recall Edward Thompson's criticism of Anderson and Nairn's alleged 'teleology': 'History cannot be

compared to a tunnel through which an express races until it brings its freight of passengers out into sunlit plains. Or, if it can, then generation upon generation of passengers are born, live in the dark, and die while the train is still in the tunnel.' E.P. Thompson, 'The Peculiarities of the English', *The Socialist Register 1965*, London 1965, p. 358.

Epilogue: The Dénouement

1. Andrew Rawnsley, 'We Are a Nation Reborn', *The Observer*, 4 May 1997.
2. Tony Blair, *New Britain: My Vision of a Young Country*, London 1996, pp. xii–xiii.
3. Labour Party, *New Labour: Because Britain Deserves Better*, London 1997, *passim*.
4. Ibid., p. 3.
5. Noel Thompson, 'Supply Side Socialism: The Political Economy of New Labour', *New Left Review* 216, March/April 1996, p. 44.
6. Will Hutton, interviewed by David Coates on 20 October 1997 for the BBC/OU television programme *The 1997 Election: Traditions, Failures and Futures*.
7. Tony Blair, in a speech at the Annual Friends of Nieumspoort Dinner, The Hague, 20 January 1998.
8. The evidence seemed to support Blair's and Brown's contention that they had been ignorant of the gift when the policy change was made, but if it did not look corrupt, it looked naive.
9. See Tariq Ali, *Masters of the Universe? Nato's Balkan Crusade*, London 2000.
10. *The Guardian*, 4 September 2000; see also Peter Lawler, 'New Labour's Foreign Policy', in David Coates and Peter Lawler, eds, *New Labour in Power*, Manchester 2000, pp. 281–99.
11. DTI, *Our Competitive Future: Building the Knowledge Driven Economy*, Cm 4176, London 1998.
12. Tony Blair, *New Britain*, p. 92.
13. See David Coates, 'Labour Governments: Old Constraints and New Parameters', *New Left Review* 219, September/October 1996, pp. 62–78; and David Rubenstein, 'A New Look at New Labour', *Politics*, vol. 20, no. 3, 2000, pp. 161–8.
14. Larry Elliott, Charlotte Denny and Michael White, 'Poverty Gap Hits Labour's Boasts', *The Guardian*, 15 July 2000.
15. Tony Blair, presenting the Annual Report to the Commons, 13 July, 2000.
16. Anna Coote, 'The Helmsman and the Cattle Prod', in A. Gamble and T. Wright, eds, *The New Social Democracy*, Oxford 2000, pp. 129, 130.
17. See the excellent assessments by Tom Nairn, ('Ukania under Blair') and Anthony Barnett ('Corporate Populism and Partyless Democracy'), *New Left Review* 1 (January/February) and 3 (May/June) 2000.
18. To prevent Ken Livingstone from winning the Labour nomination, the leadership had to resort to persuading some of the unions involved to vote

against him without consulting their members. Livingstone then justified his decision to stand as an Independent in terms of this blatant failure to respect the 'one member one vote' democracy in terms of which Kinnock and Blair had campaigned to change the party's constitution.

19. *The Guardian*, 31 May 2000.

20. Colin Hay, *The Political Economy of New Labour: Labouring Under False Pretences?*, Manchester 1999, p. 168. Hay contrasts this record unfavourably with the function performed for Margaret Thatcher by the right-wing think-tanks. The nearest 'left' equivalent to what they offered, however – and one that is close to Hay's own position – was the set of ideas outlined in Will Hutton's best-seller *The State We're In*, published in 1996. The Labour 'modernisers' initially took up his 'stakeholder' theme, but soon distanced themselves from it when the degree of opposition to it from the City and business in general became clear.

21. Nick Cohen, *The Observer*, 28 November 1999.

22. The most famous of Gould's memos came to light through the bizarre activities of 'Benji the Binman': Benjamin Pell, a former trainee solicitor, collected documents from the rubbish bins of celebrities and sold them to the press via the agent Max Clifford. Blair's memo in response to Gould's, as well as others, seemed to have leaked more through a failure to heed the well-known dictum that e-mails are about as private as postcards (see *The Guardian* 26 July 2000).

23. See the evidence collected in Nick Cohen, *Cruel Britannia: Reports on the Sinister and the Preposterous*, London 1999, pp. 144–7, 149–57, 161–7. One of us has witnessed at first hand New Labour efforts to discredit and intimidate progressive academic critics of the Government's health care policies. People with policy interests interviewed during 1998–2000 constantly remarked on the fact that this was a novel development, unparalleled during the Thatcher–Major years.

24. *The Guardian*, 30 November 1997.

25. *The Guardian*, 2 July 1998.

26. Ewen MacAskill, 'Party Membership: Stuff that Envelope, Say the Activists', *The Guardian*, 23 June 1998.

27. Labour Party, *Building a Future for All: The Annual Report*, Conference 2000, p. 14.

28. According to the Labour Party, in the 1997 election the Conservatives had £43 million to spend, compared with Labour's £29 million (ibid.).

29. An exception was the maverick MP Dennis Skinner, who returned to the NEC by this route in 1999.

30. National Policy Forum, *Reports to Conference*, Conference 2000, p. 211.

31. Moreover, if such an alternative motion was moved within the NPF and failed to get 35 votes, no other resolution on that policy issue could be moved at the annual Conference.

32. Patrick Wintour, *The Guardian*, 31 May 2000. Wintour, who was sympathetic towards New Labour, said of the NPF's output: 'Rarely have so many platitudes been gathered together in one place. If this represents the combined insights of thousands of party members then Labour is either

ridiculously loyal or suffering from an excess of the culture of contentment.'.

33. *The Guardian*, 14 April 2000.
34. For instance, the Communication Workers Union annual conference refused a levy increase of 20 per cent on these grounds (*The Guardian*, 6 June 2000).
35. Kevin Maguire, *The Guardian*, 14 June 2000.
36. Upset but not surprised. Ann Black, a member of the NPF who was elected to the NEC in May 2000, had already experienced the process in the autumn of 1999, when the unions withdrew their support in the NPF for an alternative Conference resolution on pensions in return for another promise of a 'review' which never materialised (*The Guardian*, 31 May 2000).
37. Eighty-five per cent of the union vote (worth 50 per cent of the total) was cast for the resolution; 64 per cent of the constituency party vote (the other 50 per cent of the total) was cast against. This revealed an important shift in the balance between these forces compared with thirty years earlier; the CLPs were now predominantly supportive of the modernisers (*The Guardian*, 28 September 2000).
38. 'A welcome return to our principles': *The Guardian*, 2 October 2000.
39. A major exception was the movement for gay rights, which under New Labour achieved a reduction in the age of consent and other reforms, partly aided by the impact of the European Convention on Human Rights, which Labour also incorporated into UK law.
40. The use of this metaphor is not tendentious. Under New Labour the party's annual reports, like the Government's annual reports, were deliberately presented in the style of company reports.
41. Donald Sassoon: 'Socialism: Mission Accomplished or Mission Impossible?' *Dissent*, Winter 2000, pp. 56–61.
42. 'Business must lead this process of modernization by responding to the spur of competition and by exploiting market opportunities.' This formulation from 1998 White Paper, *Our Competitive Future: Building the Knowledge Driven Economy* (p. 6), reappears in the National Party Forum's Report to the 2000 Labour Party Conference (p. 7), identical in every respect except that 'should' replaces 'must' ('Business should lead . . .').
43. *Our Competitive Future*, p. 6.
44. From the *1949 TUC Report* as quoted in Leo Panitch, *Social Democracy and Industrial Militancy*, Cambridge 1976, p. 30.
45. See Peter Mair, 'Partyless Democracy', *New Left Review* 2, March/April 2000.
46. See Sam Gindin and Leo Panitch, 'Transcending Pessimism: Rekindling Socialist Imagination', in Leo Panitch and Colin Leys, eds, *Necessary and Unnecessary Utopias: Socialist Register 2000*, London 1999.
47. See the National Party Forum's Report to the 2000 Labour Party Conference, esp. pp. 7, 18–21.

Index